SMALL SHIPS
MANUAL

Photo: Werner Langer

SMALL SHIPS
MANUAL

12th Edition
Revised May 1996

Including Questions and Answers for examinations for Certificates of Competency

Published by

Queensland Department of Transport
G.P.O. Box 2595 Brisbane Queensland 4001

ACKNOWLEDGEMENTS

This manual was first produced in 1979 and is a tribute to the dedicated work of the late Captain Owen Bauer, Examiner for the Marine Board, Masters and Mates Certificates, who was the original editor and a major contributor of practical information on which this manual is based.

Acknowledgement is also extended to the late E.J. (Jack) Gilmore, Senior Engineer Surveyor of the Department of Harbours and Marine, who was responsible for the original engineering, electrical and refrigeration sections of the manual.

The Queensland Department of Transport is appreciative of the input provided by the following organisations:

Bureau of Meteorology
State Fire Services
Department of Transport and Communications
St Johns Ambulance Australia

SMALL SHIPS MANUAL

Published 1993

Queensland Department of Transport

ISBN 072425684 9

CONTENTS

LIST OF ILLUSTRATIONS

LIST OF ILLUSTRATIONS

LIST OF ILLUSTRATIONS

LIST OF ILLUSTRATIONS

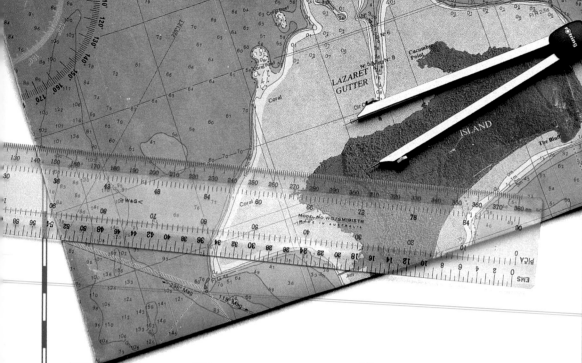

THE FIRST RULE OF
SAFE NAVIGATION.

As a boat owner you are required to carry the relevant chart when travelling in open waters.

Our Boating Safety Charts are brilliantly reproduced in full colour to make them easy to use. You should refer to an updated edition to enhance your boating safety and pleasure.

Choose the charts you'll need from the extensive range at selected Queensland Department of Transport customer service centres, Sunmap stockists, Land Service centres, or map/chart retailers.

BOATING SAFETY CHARTS

Moreton Bay Series:

MB1 Moreton Bay - Southport to Caloundra

MB2 Lower Brisbane River and Approaches

MB3 Upper Brisbane River

MB4 Pumicestone Passage

MB5 Point Danger to Gold Coast Bridge

MB6 Gold Coast Bridge to Jacobs Well

MB7 Jacobs Well to Coochiemudlo Island

MB8 Coochiemudlo Island to Wellington Point

MB9 Wellington Point to The Blue Hole

Sunshine Coast Series:

SC1 Caloundra to Double Island Point

SC2 Noosa River and Lakes

Great Sandy Strait Series:

GSS1 Double Island Point and Tin Can Bay to Boonlye Point

GSS2 Boonlye Point to Hervey Bay

Port Curtis Series:

PC1 Gladstone Harbour

PC2 The Narrows

Shute Harbour/Airlie Beach

Approaches and Guide to Moorings

Boat Harbour Series:

BH1 Manly Boat Harbour

BH2 Snapper Creek Boat Harbour

CHART A SAFER COURSE.

QUEENSLAND TRANSPORT

Chapter 1

INTERNATIONAL REGULATIONS
FOR
PREVENTING COLLISIONS
AT SEA

INTERNATIONAL CODE OF SIGNALS ALPHABETICAL FLAGS

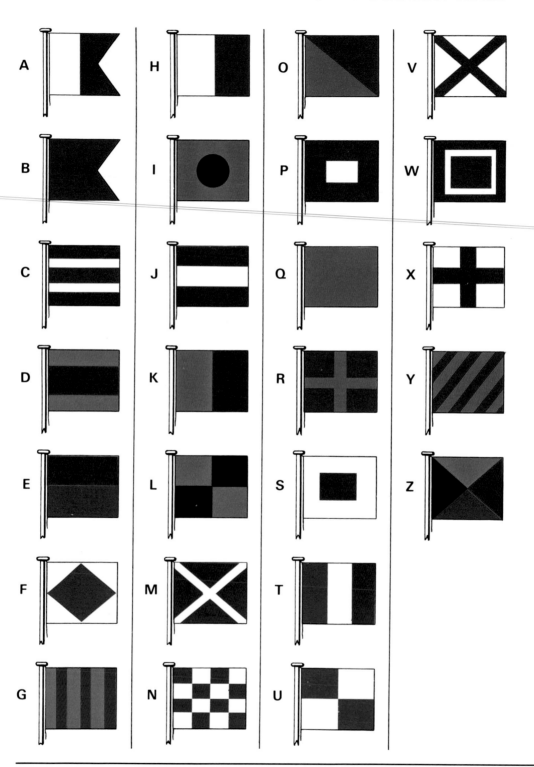

INTERNATIONAL CODE OF SIGNALS NUMERAL PENDANTS

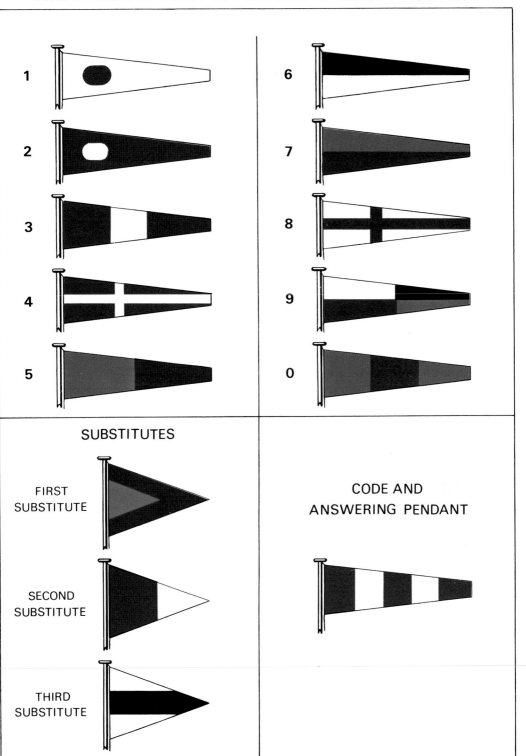

SUBSTITUTES

FIRST
SUBSTITUTE

SECOND
SUBSTITUTE

THIRD
SUBSTITUTE

CODE AND
ANSWERING PENDANT

SINGLE LETTER SIGNALS

**May be made by any method of signalling.
For those marked* see note (1) below**

A I have a diver down; keep well clear at slow speed.

*B I am taking in, or discharging, or carrying dangerous goods.

*C Yes (affirmative or "The significance of the previous group should be read in affirmative").

*D Keep clear of me; I am manoeuvring with difficulty.

*E I am altering my course to starboard.

F I am disabled; communicate with me.

*G I require a pilot. When made by fishing vessels operating in close proximity on the fishing grounds it means: "I am hauling nets".

*H I have a pilot on board.

*I I am altering my course to port.

J I am on fire and have dangerous cargo on board: keep well clear of me.

K I wish to communicate with you.

L You should stop your vessel instantly.

M My vessel is stopped and making no way through the water.

N No (negative or "The significance of the previous group should be read in the negative"). This signal may be given only visually or by sound. For voice or radio transmission the signal should be "NO".

O Man overboard.

P **In harbour.** All persons should report on board as the vessel is about to proceed to sea.
At sea. It may be used by fishing vessels to mean: "My nets have come fast upon an obstruction".

Q My vessel is 'healthy' and I request free pratique.

*S I am operating astern propulsion.

*T Keep clear of me; I am engaged in pair trawling.

U You are running into danger.

V I require assistance.

W I require medical assistance.

X Stop carrying out your intentions and watch for my signals.

Y I am dragging my anchor.

*Z I require a tug. When made by fishing vessels operating in close proximity on the fishing grounds it means: "I am shooting nets".

Notes:

1. Signals of letters marked* when made by sound may only be made in compliance with the requirements of the International Regulations for Preventing Collisions at Sea, Rules 34 and 35, accepting that sound signals "G" and "Z" may continue to be used by fishing vessels fishing in close proximity to other fishing vessels.

2. Signals "K" and"S" have special meanings as landing signals for small boats with crews or persons in distress. (International Convention for the Safety of Life at Sea, 1960, Chapter V, Regulation 16).

BEAUFORT WIND SCALE

Mean wave height in metres

BEAUFORT NUMBER....0

CALM 0-1 KTS
Sea like a mirror.

....1

LIGHT AIR 1-3 KTS. 0.1 WAVES
Ripples with appearance of scales; no foam crests

....2

LIGHT BREEZE 4-6 KTS. 0.2 WAVES
Small wavelets; crests of glassy appearance, not breaking.

....3

GENTLE BREEZE 7-10 KTS. 0.6 WAVES
Large wavelets; crests begin to break; scattered whitecaps.

....4

MODERATE BREEZE 11-16 KTS. 1.0 WAVES
Small waves, becoming longer; numerous whitecaps

....5

FRESH BREEZE 17-21 KTS. 2.0 WAVES
Moderate waves, taking longer form, many whitecaps; some spray.

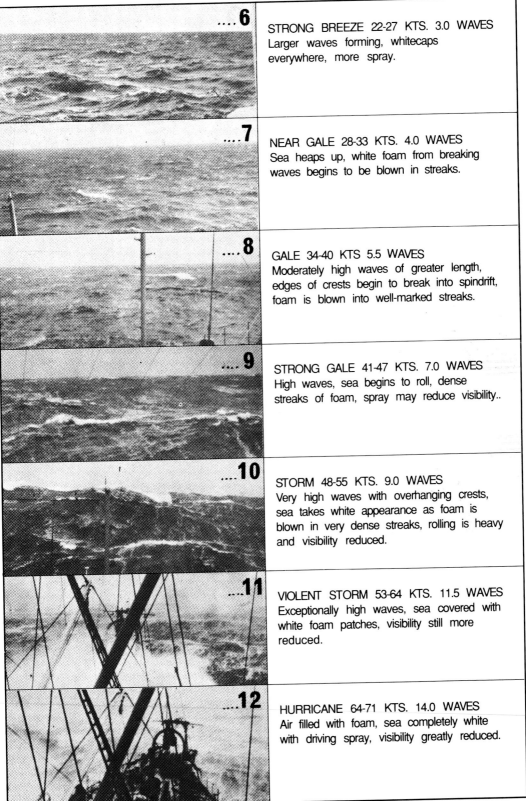

....6 STRONG BREEZE 22-27 KTS. 3.0 WAVES
Larger waves forming, whitecaps everywhere, more spray.

....7 NEAR GALE 28-33 KTS. 4.0 WAVES
Sea heaps up, white foam from breaking waves begins to be blown in streaks.

....8 GALE 34-40 KTS 5.5 WAVES
Moderately high waves of greater length, edges of crests begin to break into spindrift, foam is blown into well-marked streaks.

....9 STRONG GALE 41-47 KTS. 7.0 WAVES
High waves, sea begins to roll, dense streaks of foam, spray may reduce visibility..

....10 STORM 48-55 KTS. 9.0 WAVES
Very high waves with overhanging crests, sea takes white appearance as foam is blown in very dense streaks, rolling is heavy and visibility reduced.

....11 VIOLENT STORM 53-64 KTS. 11.5 WAVES
Exceptionally high waves, sea covered with white foam patches, visibility still more reduced.

....12 HURRICANE 64-71 KTS. 14.0 WAVES
Air filled with foam, sea completely white with driving spray, visibility greatly reduced.

INTERNATIONAL REGULATIONS

RULE 34

Manoeuvring and Warning Signals

○
meaning a
short blast

only to be sounded by vessels
IN SIGHT OF ONE ANOTHER

[ ]
meaning a
long blast

(a) "I am altering my course to starboard"

" I am altering my course to port"

"I am operating astern propulsion"

(b) Any vessel may supplement the whistle signals by light signals, repeated as appropriate, whilst the manoeuvre is being carried out:
one flash to mean "I am altering my course to starboard";
two flashes to mean "I am altering my course to port";
three flashes to mean "I am operating astern propulsion".

(c) When in sight of one another in a narrow channel or fairway.

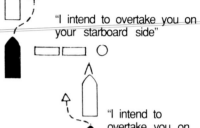

"I intend to overtake you on your starboard side"

"I intend to overtake you on your port side"

○○○○○

(d) When vessels in sight of one another are approaching each other and from any cause either vessel fails to understand the intentions or actions of the other, or is in doubt whether sufficient action is being taken by the other to avoid collision, the vessel in doubt shall immediately indicate such doubt by giving at least five short rapid blasts on the whistle. Such signal may be supplemented by a light signal of at least five short and rapid flashes.

A vessel indicating her agreement to being overtaken.

A vessel in doubt about signals, intentions or safety of the proposed manoeuvre of an overtaking vessel.

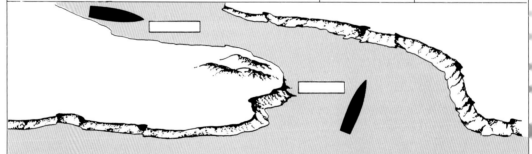

(e) A vessel nearing a bend or an area of a channel or fairway where other vessels may be obscured by an intervening obstruction shall sound one prolonged blast. Such signal shall be answered with a prolonged blast by any approaching vessel that may be within hearing around the bend or behind the intervening obstruction.

QUEENSLAND SPECIAL MANOEUVRING & WARNING SIGNALS

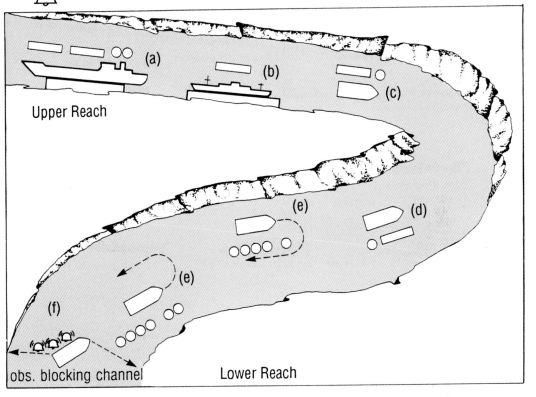

	A prolonged blast of from 4 to 6 seconds duration.
	A short blast of about 1 second duration.
	A short ring of the bell.

(a) A tanker which is not fitted with V.H.F. shall, not less than 30 minutes before scheduled to leave her berth in any Queensland Port sound two long blasts followed by two short blasts.

A tanker which is not fitted with V.H.F. shall when ready for tugs to be brought alongside during daylight hours exhibit the International Code flag "Z".

(b) Every steam or motor vessel of 40 metres or more in length shall immediately before casting off from any wharf or jetty in any river in Queensland give one prolonged blast of the whistle or siren.

(c) Every steam or motor vessel proceeding down any river in Queensland and approaching any bend shall sound one long blast followed by a short blast.

(d) Every steam or motor vessel proceeding up any river and approaching any bend shall sound one short blast followed by a long blast.

(e) When a steam or motor vessel underway in any river in Queensland is about to turn around the Master shall signify such purposes by four short blasts followed after a short interval if turning with her head to starboard by one short blast. And if her head to port by two short blasts.

(f) Any vessel with the channel blocked shall in or near areas of restricted visibility sound three short rings on the bell.

RULE 35   **Fog Signals**

TO BE SOUNDED IN OR NEAR AN AREA OF RESTRICTED VISIBILITY

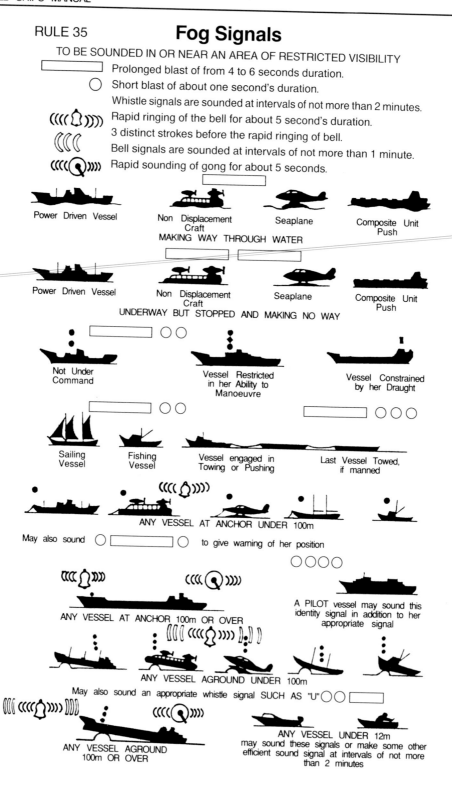

Prolonged blast of from 4 to 6 seconds duration.

Short blast of about one second's duration.

Whistle signals are sounded at intervals of not more than 2 minutes.

Rapid ringing of the bell for about 5 second's duration.

3 distinct strokes before the rapid ringing of bell.

Bell signals are sounded at intervals of not more than 1 minute.

Rapid sounding of gong for about 5 seconds.

Power Driven Vessel   Non Displacement Craft   Seaplane   Composite Unit Push

MAKING WAY THROUGH WATER

Power Driven Vessel   Non Displacement Craft   Seaplane   Composite Unit Push

UNDERWAY BUT STOPPED AND MAKING NO WAY

Not Under Command   Vessel Restricted in her Ability to Manoeuvre   Vessel Constrained by her Draught

Sailing Vessel   Fishing Vessel   Vessel engaged in Towing or Pushing   Last Vessel Towed, if manned

ANY VESSEL AT ANCHOR UNDER 100m

May also sound   to give warning of her position

ANY VESSEL AT ANCHOR 100m OR OVER

A PILOT vessel may sound this identity signal in addition to her appropriate signal

ANY VESSEL AGROUND UNDER 100m

May also sound an appropriate whistle signal SUCH AS "U"

ANY VESSEL AGROUND 100m OR OVER

ANY VESSEL UNDER 12m may sound these signals or make some other efficient sound signal at intervals of not more than 2 minutes

Day Shapes   ALL SHAPES ARE COLOURED BLACK

The vertical distance between shapes shall be at least 1.5 metres. In a vessel of less than 20 metres in length shapes of lesser dimensions but commensurate with the size of the vessel may be used and the distance apart may be correspondingly reduced.

A vessel when towing, when the length of the tow exceeds 200 metres

A vessel or object being towed, when the length of the tow exceeds 200 metres

A vessel proceeding under sail, when also being propelled by machinery

A vessel engaged in fishing

A vessel engaged in fishing of less than 20 metres in length

A vessel engaged in fishing, when there is outlying gear extending more than 150 metres horizontally from the vessel

A vessel engaged in fishing, when hauling nets

A vessel engaged in fishing, when shooting nets

A vessel engaged in fishing, when the net has come fast upon an obstruction

A vessel not under command

A vessel engaged in towing, unable to deviate from her course. Length of tow exceeds 200m

A vessel restricted in her ability to manoeuvre

A vessel restricted in her ability to manoeuvre, when at anchor

A vessel engaged in diving operations

A vessel engaged in minesweeping operations

A vessel constrained by her draught

A vessel at anchor

A vessel aground

Side of obstruction   Side to pass

A vessel engaged in dredging or underwater operations, when restricted in her ability to manoeuvre, and when an obstruction exists

Ball with diameter at least 0.6m
Cone: Base diameter at least 0.6m and height equal to diameter.
Cylinder: Diameter at least 0.6m and height twice diameter
Diamond shape is to be 2 cones with common base

Distress Signals

When a vessel is in distress and requires assistance she shall use or exhibit the signals prescribed.

1.  A gun or other explosive signal fired at intervals of about a minute.

2. 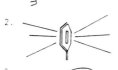 A continuous sounding with any fog-signalling apparatus

3.  Rockets or shells throwing red stars fired one at a time at short intervals

4.  A signal made by radio, telegraphy or by any other signalling method consisting of the group (SOS) in the morse code

5. 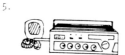 A signal sent by radio telephony consisting of the spoken word 'MAYDAY'

6. The international code signal of distress indicated by N.C.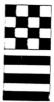

7. 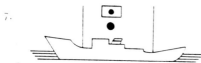 A signal consisting of a square flag having above or below it a ball or anything resembling a ball

8. 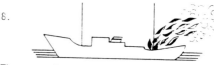 Flames on the vessel (as from a burning tar barrel, oil barrel etc.)

9. 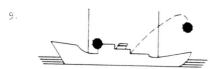 A rocket parachute flare or a hand flare showing a red light

10. 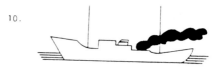 A smoke signal giving off orange-coloured smoke

11.  Slowly and repeatedly raising and lowering arms outstretched to each side

DISTRESS SIGNALS
Merchant Ship Search and Rescue Manual

Full regulations appear on page 65.

Definition of Lights

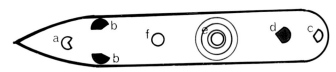

(a) "Masthead light" means a white light placed over the fore and aft centreline of the vessel showing an unbroken light over an arc of the horizon of 225 degrees and so fixed as to show the light from right ahead to 22.5 degrees abaft the beam on either side of the vessel.

(b) "Sidelights" means a green light on the starboard side and a red light on the port side each showing an unbroken light over an arc of the horizon of 112.5 degrees and so fixed as to show the light from right ahead to 22.5 degrees abaft the beam on its respective side. In a vessel of less than 20 metres in length the sidelights may be combined in one lantern carried on the fore and aft centreline of the vessel.

(c) "Sternlight" means a white light placed as nearly as practicable at the stern showing an unbroken light over an arc of the horizon of 135° and so fixed as to show the light 67.5° from right aft on each side of the vessel.

(d) "Towing light" means a yellow light placed in a vertical line above the stern light showing an unbroken light over an arc of 135 degrees and so fixed as to show the light 67.5 degrees from right aft on each side of the vessel. It is prescribed only for a vessel engaged in towing another vessel from the stern.

(e) "All-round light" means a light showing an unbroken light over an arc of the horizon of 360 degrees.

"Flashing light" means a light flashing at regular intervals at a frequency of 120 flashes or more per minute.

(f) "Manoeuvring light" means an all-round white light placed in the same fore and aft vertical plane as the masthead light or lights and, where practicable, at a minimum height of 2 metres vertically above the forward masthead light, provided that it shall be carried not less than 2 metres vertically above or below the after masthead light. On a vessel where only one masthead light is carried the manoeuvring light, if fitted, shall be carried where it can best be seen, not less than 2 metres vertically apart from the masthead light.

Rule 22 Page 41 refers.

Visibility of Lights

LIGHTS	Vessels of 50 metres or more in length	Vessels of 20 metres or more in length but less than 50 metres in length	Vessels of 12 metres or more in length but less than 20 metres in length	Vessels of less than 12 metres in length
	MILES	MILES	MILES	MILES
MASTHEAD	6	5	3	2
SIDE	3	2	2	1
ALL-ROUND	3	2	2	2
MANOEUVRING	5	5	5	5
TOWING	3	2	2	2
STERN	3	2	2	2

Definitions with respect to lights.
PRESCRIBED ARCS

Rule 21

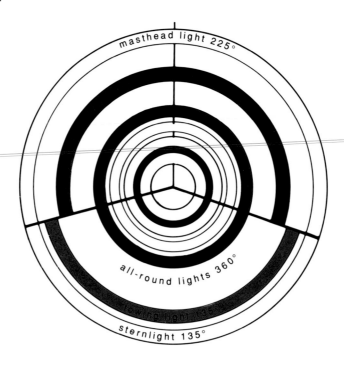

masthead light 225°

all-round lights 360°

towing light 135°

sternlight 135°

a   Not more than 5° for pratical cut off
b   Up to 5° 'I' may decrease by 50%
c   Minimum 'I' to this point
I   Means minimum required intensity
x   Prescribed limits

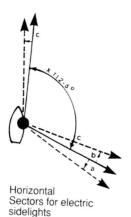

Horizontal
Sectors for electric
sidelights

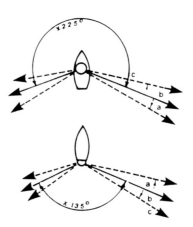

Horizontal Sectors for Electric
Masthead and Stern lights

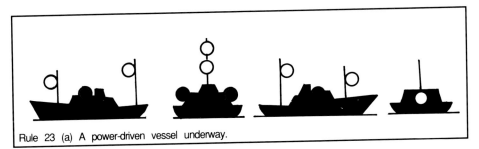

Rule 23 (a) A power-driven vessel underway.

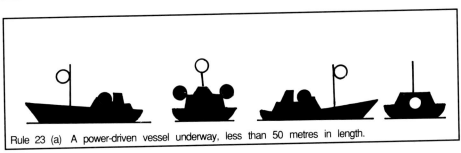

Rule 23 (a) A power-driven vessel underway, less than 50 metres in length.

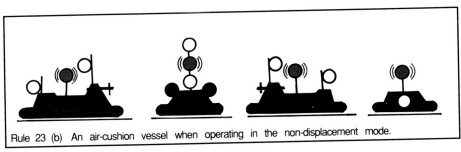

Rule 23 (b) An air-cushion vessel when operating in the non-displacement mode.

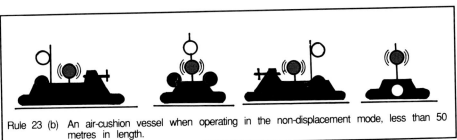

Rule 23 (b) An air-cushion vessel when operating in the non-displacement mode, less than 50 metres in length.

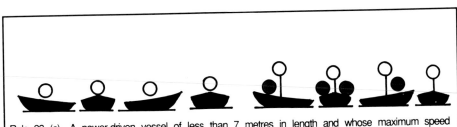

Rule 23 (c) A power-driven vessel of less than 7 metres in length and whose maximum speed does not exceed 7 knots.

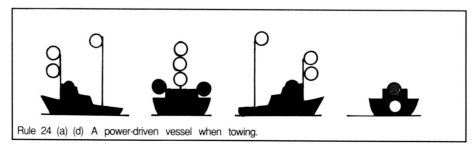

Rule 24 (a) (d) A power-driven vessel when towing.

Rule 24 (a) (d) A power-driven vessel of any size when towing and the length of the tow exceeds 200 metres

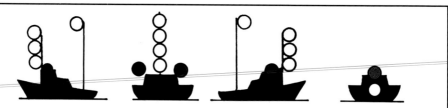

Rule 24 (a) A power-driven vessel of less than 50 metres in length when towing.

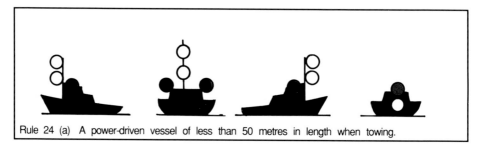

Rule 24 (a) A power-driven vessel of less than 50 metres in length when towing and the length of the tow exceeds 200 metres.

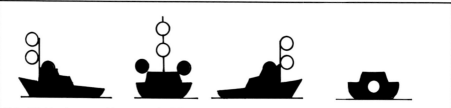

Rule 24 (c) A power-driven vessel of less than 50 metres in length when pushing ahead or towing alongside, except in the case of a composite unit.

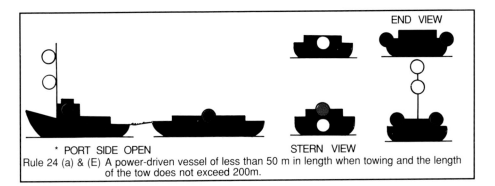

* PORT SIDE OPEN — END VIEW — STERN VIEW

Rule 24 (a) & (E) A power-driven vessel of less than 50 m in length when towing and the length of the tow does not exceed 200m.

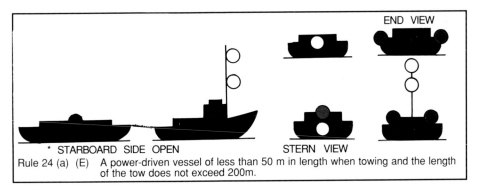

* STARBOARD SIDE OPEN — END VIEW — STERN VIEW

Rule 24 (a) (E) A power-driven vessel of less than 50 m in length when towing and the length of the tow does not exceed 200m.

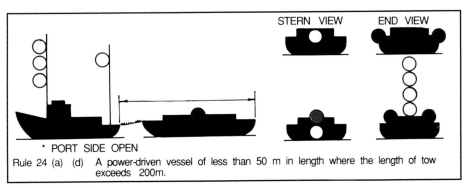

* PORT SIDE OPEN — STERN VIEW — END VIEW

Rule 24 (a) (d) A power-driven vessel of less than 50 m in length where the length of tow exceeds 200m.

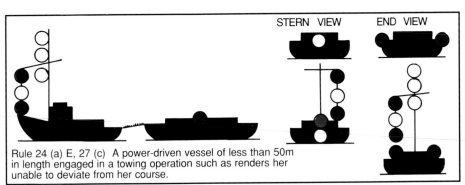

STERN VIEW — END VIEW

Rule 24 (a) E, 27 (c) A power-driven vessel of less than 50m in length engaged in a towing operation such as renders her unable to deviate from her course.

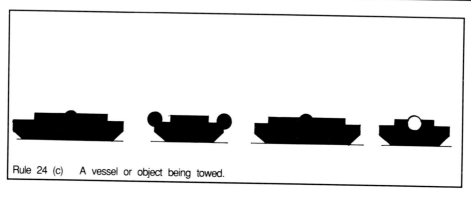

Rule 24 (c)   A vessel or object being towed.

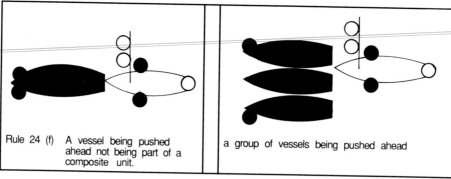

Rule 24 (f)   A vessel being pushed ahead not being part of a composite unit.

a group of vessels being pushed ahead

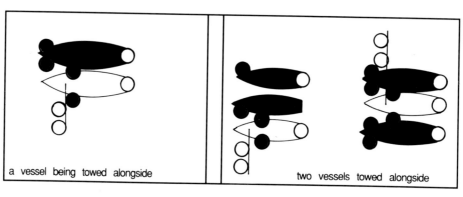

a vessel being towed alongside

two vessels towed alongside

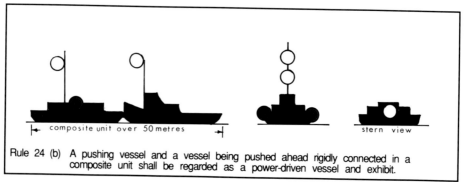

composite unit over 50 metres

stern view

Rule 24 (b)   A pushing vessel and a vessel being pushed ahead rigidly connected in a composite unit shall be regarded as a power-driven vessel and exhibit.

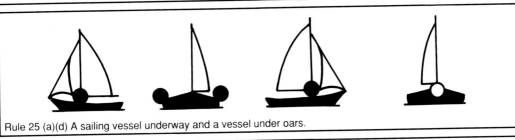

Rule 25 (a)(d) A sailing vessel underway and a vessel under oars.

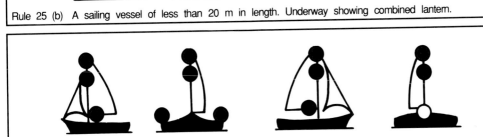

Stern View

Rule 25 (b) A sailing vessel of less than 20 m in length. Underway showing combined lantern.

Rule 25 (c)(d) A sailing vessel underway and a vessel under oars.

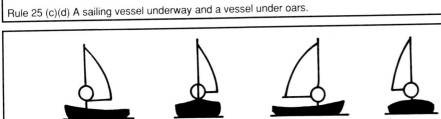

Rule 25 (d) A sailing vessel of less than 7 metres in length and a vessel under oars exhibited in sufficient time to prevent collision.

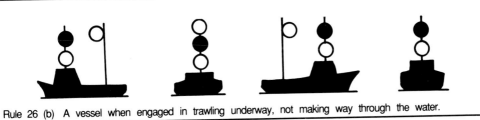

Rule 26 (b) A vessel when engaged in trawling underway, not making way through the water.

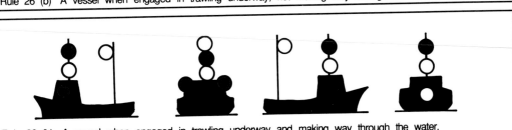

Rule 26 (b) A vessel when engaged in trawling underway and making way through the water.

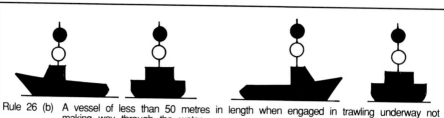

Rule 26 (b) A vessel of less than 50 metres in length when engaged in trawling underway not making way through the water.

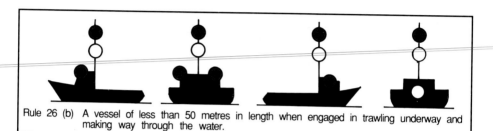

Rule 26 (b) A vessel of less than 50 metres in length when engaged in trawling underway and making way through the water.

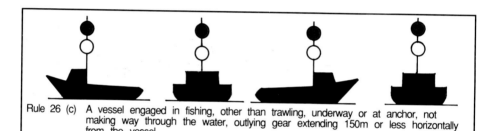

Rule 26 (c) A vessel engaged in fishing, other than trawling, underway or at anchor, not making way through the water, outlying gear extending 150m or less horizontally from the vessel.

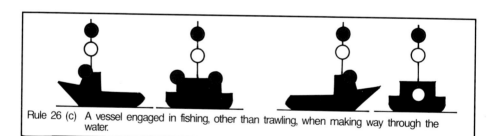

Rule 26 (c) A vessel engaged in fishing, other than trawling, when making way through the water.

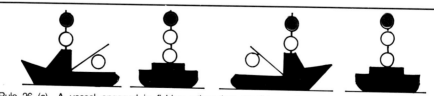

Rule 26 (c) A vessel engaged in fishing, other than trawling, underway or at anchor, not making way through the water, where there is no outlying gear extending more than 150m horizontally from the vessel.

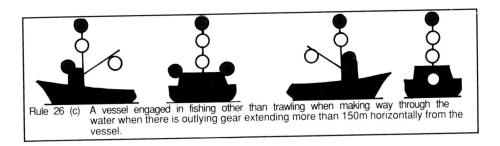

Rule 26 (c)   A vessel engaged in fishing other than trawling when making way through the water when there is outlying gear extending more than 150m horizontally from the vessel.

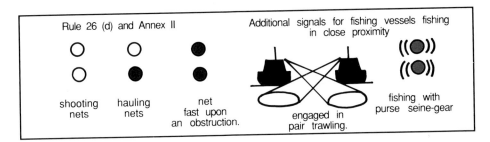

Rule 26 (d) and Annex II

Additional signals for fishing vessels fishing in close proximity

shooting nets

hauling nets

net fast upon an obstruction.

engaged in pair trawling.

fishing with purse seine-gear

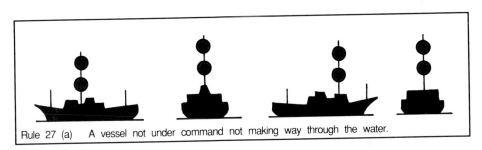

Rule 27 (a)   A vessel not under command not making way through the water.

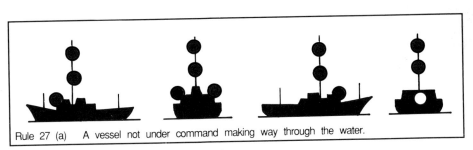

Rule 27 (a)   A vessel not under command making way through the water.

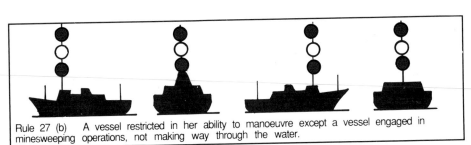

Rule 27 (b)   A vessel restricted in her ability to manoeuvre except a vessel engaged in minesweeping operations, not making way through the water.

Rule 27 (b) A vessel restricted in her ability to manoeuvre, except a vessel engaged in minesweeping operations when making way through the water.

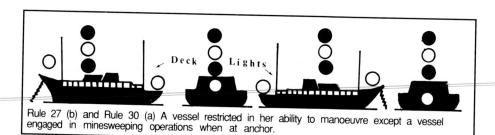

Deck Lights

Rule 27 (b) and Rule 30 (a) A vessel restricted in her ability to manoeuvre except a vessel engaged in minesweeping operations when at anchor.

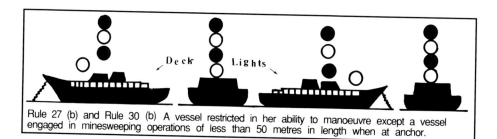

Deck Lights

Rule 27 (b) and Rule 30 (b) A vessel restricted in her ability to manoeuvre except a vessel engaged in minesweeping operations of less than 50 metres in length when at anchor.

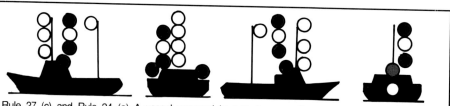

Rule 27 (c) and Rule 24 (a) A vessel engaged in a towing operation such as renders her unable to deviate from her course when the length of the tow exceeds 200 metres.

obs. obs obs. obs

Rule 27 (d) A vessel engaged in dredging or underwater operations when an obstruction exists when underway or at anchor but not making way through the water.

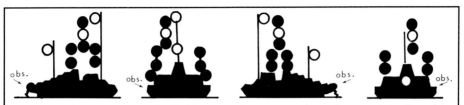

Rule 27 (d) A vessel engaged in dredging or underwater operations when an obstruction exists when making way through the water.

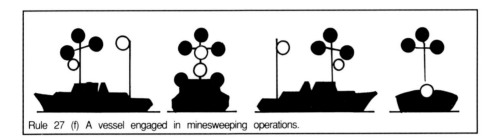

Rule 27 (f) A vessel engaged in minesweeping operations.

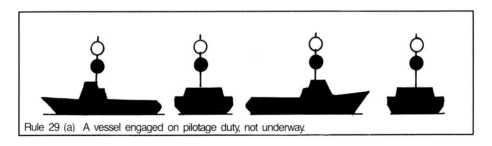

Rule 28 A vessel constrained by her draught.

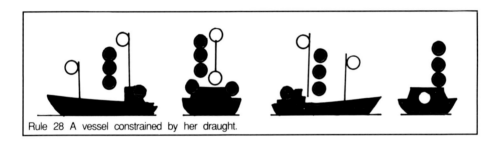

Rule 29 (a) A vessel engaged on pilotage duty, not underway.

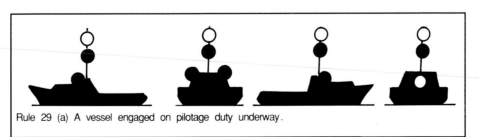

Rule 29 (a) A vessel engaged on pilotage duty underway.

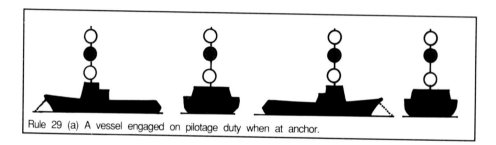

Rule 29 (a) A vessel engaged on pilotage duty when at anchor.

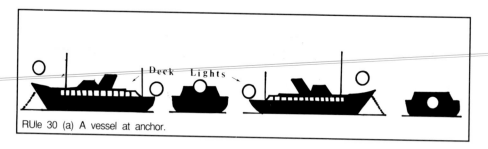

Deck Lights

RUle 30 (a) A vessel at anchor.

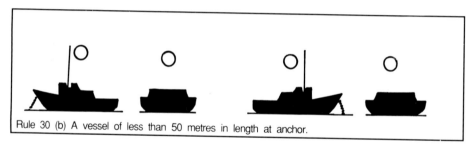

Rule 30 (b) A vessel of less than 50 metres in length at anchor.

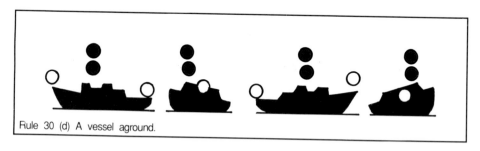

Rule 30 (d) A vessel aground.

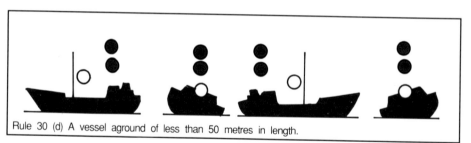

Rule 30 (d) A vessel aground of less than 50 metres in length.

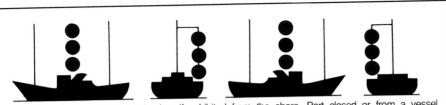

Rule 1 (b), (c) Queensland local rules, if exhibited from the shore, Port closed or from a vessel, channel blocked at night.

Rule 1 (b), (c) If exhibited from the shore, Port closed or from a vessel, channel blocked by day.

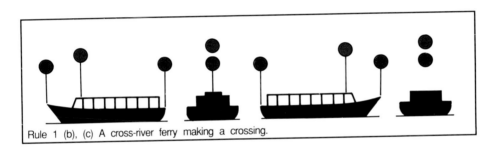

Rule 1 (b), (c) A cross-river ferry making a crossing.

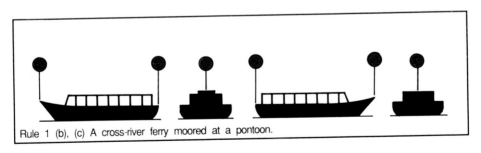

Rule 1 (b), (c) A cross-river ferry moored at a pontoon.

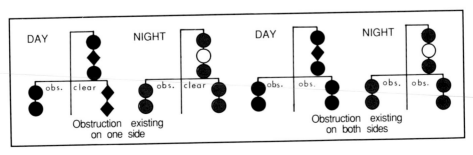

DAY · NIGHT · DAY · NIGHT

obs. · clear · obs. · clear · obs. · obs. · obs. · obs.

Obstruction existing on one side

Obstruction existing on both sides

INTERNATIONAL REGULATIONS FOR PREVENTING COLLISIONS AT SEA AND STEERING AND SAILING REGULATIONS

TERMS USED FOR BOATS AND SHIPS

STEERING DEVICES

It is probable that the first sailor was some primitive being who, while swimming across a river, climbed on a passing log and hand-paddled his way to his destination with much less effort.

Inevitably, improvements followed; such as hollow logs and then paddles and later skins were hoisted to take advantage of any favourable breeze, so as to further reduce the manual effort involved in such movement.

In time, the effect of a rudder became apparent; that is, a steering device which allowed the oarsmen to continually exert their greatest efforts while the craft was held on course instead of veering from side to side. When the rudder became a fixed device, it was secured to the right hand side in the canoe-shaped craft, because this allowed it to be operated by the right or stronger arm of the steersman, who, deciding the best course to pursue, naturally became the Master.

By way of interest, it is thought the right arm developed more strongly than the left because the left carried a shield to protect the body's left side in which the heart generally lies. It follows then, that the right arm would be much more exercised through sword play and spear throwing and that as the hand became more dextrous, writing or inscribing would be done with the right hand. The Chinese seem to have overcome any awkward left hand tendencies to write, by adopting a vertical method of writing and reading many centuries ago.

Illustrations of scenes from the Bayeaux Tapestry depict the Norman invasion of England, clearly showing the rudder invariably suspended from the rear of the right hand side. The effect of this is very apparent even in the present day.

So it is that many nautical terms have been handed down from the past, and this may be a good opportunity to explore the origin of some.

THE PARTS OF A VESSEL

Figure 2 shows a deck plan of a vessel with the various parts as they are named.

Fore and aft require no explanation, being obviously abbreviations of forward and after, and the same with quarter and bow. But starboard, port and abeam need to be discussed.

Up to the early part of this century, starboard and larboard (not port), were used to denote right and left. These terms, Scandinavian in origin, were used by the Norsemen as steerboard and leeboard, the steersman sitting in the right hand quarter with his steerboard, or rudder, hung over that side, while on the left side, a portable deep keel called a leeboard was lowered into the water to counteract leeway, or sideways drift caused by the wind. Leeboards can still be seen on some sailing barges in Europe.

This arrangement continued for centuries until progress and increasing sea-borne traffic demanded a change. Starboard and larboard could be too easily confused in helm orders with possibly disastrous results. As a consequence, a change had to be made, and since the rudder or steerboard became a fixed appendage reaching below keel level and protruding from the starboard quarter, it became customary, in order to avoid damage, to berth the vessel with the left side to the shore, (or when in port). When a right-handed propeller is put astern, the vessel's stern swings to the left and makes a port side to the wharf berthing much easier.

So the name of that side was changed from larboard to port, and as our ancient Steersman carried his effects in the starboard quarter, this is still the practice today, in that where only limited living space is available, we find the Master's accommodation always situated on the starboard side.

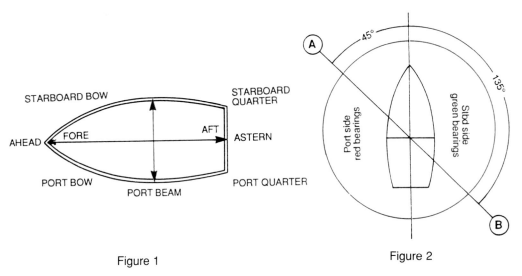

Figure 1

Figure 2

For example – in Figure 2, object A would be referred to as "4 points on the port bow" or "4 points for'd (forward) of the port beam". Similarly, object B would be referred to as being "4 points on the starboard quarter or 4 points abaft the starboard beam". (Note:– one point equals 11¹/₄° degrees). In figure 3 the same object A could be referred to as being "red 45 degrees" and object B as "Green 135 degrees.

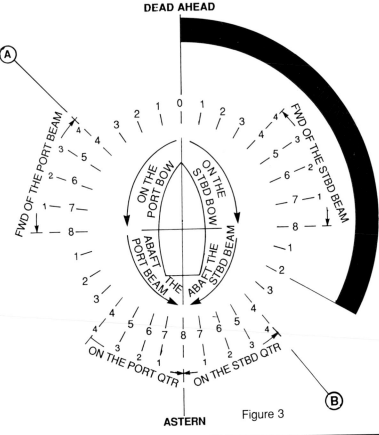

Figure 3

This convention is also followed with the superstructure of the present day aircraft carrier.

The advent of the overhanging or counter stern, (apart from providing reserve buoyancy) allowed the rudder post to be led up through an aperture above water level, and served also to protect this all important device which could now be placed in line with the keel and so operate more efficiently.

Incidentally, what used to be known as the helm is actually the tiller of today, and this also tended to complicate matters in the old days because when the Helmsman was ordered to "Starboard the Helm", the intention was to turn the vessel to port.

This practice persisted into the present century but has fallen into disuse and direct orders are now given to turn the vessel in the desired direction without mention of the word "helm".

Abeam

The decking of vessels is laid fore and aft on cross members or beams, (we have all heard of craft keeling over on to their beam ends), so the term beam or abeam indicates straight across, i.e., at right angles to the fore and aft line of the keel.

Direction from the vessel is usually referred to in points of the compass. The compass is a circle of 360° which is divided into 32 points each of $11\frac{1}{4}°$. To give a more precise direction of an object from the vessel, it is, for example, referred to as 2 points on the port bow or 3 points abaft the starboard beam. (See Figures 3(a) and 3(b) on previous page.)

Under the auspices of the Inter-Governmental Maritime Consultative Organisation (IMCO), a conference was held in October, 1972, at which the Convention on International Regulations for Preventing Collisions at Sea, 1972, was adopted. After being ratified by respective governments, these Regulations are now in force. They apply to all vessels upon the High Seas, and in all waters connected therewith, navigable by seagoing vessels.

However, special rules may also be made by Governments of States to cover roadsteads, harbours, rivers, lakes or inland waterways connected with the High Seas and navigable by seagoing vessels.

The importance of safety at sea can never be over-emphasized; and it is the duty and responsibility of anyone in charge of a vessel, big or small, to be able to correctly apply these rules in all circumstances, in a seamanlike manner and in the interests of their own safety and the safety of others using the seaways.

Much thought, backed by sound practical experience at sea, and international legal expertise, has been given to the construction of these regulations which, to be effective, have to be as clear and as simple as possible, and yet cover a variety of craft in different situations. No set of rules can adequately cover all situations at sea, without losing its effectiveness; therefore much has been left to the good sense of the seaman-like conduct of the mariner himself in taking prudent and timely actions to avert collisions within the framework of these international regulations. It is a prerequisite for the navigator that these regulations, and, in particular, the 'Steering and Sailing Rules' are learnt and understood thoroughly by him.

To provide a ready reference and to avoid ambiguity that could arise, the regulations are printed overleaf "ad verbatim". It is imperative that you study all of the rules until you have a good working knowledge of them.

One important point, is that since the adoption of the international system of units, the name 'Systems International d' Unites', with the abbreviation SI, from Systems International was adopted by the Eleventh General Conference on Weights and Measures in 1960. The range (distance) of visibility of navigation lights depends on the length in metres of vessels exhibiting them.

INTERNATIONAL REGULATIONS FOR PREVENTING COLLISIONS AT SEA, 1972 PART A

General: As amended to 18 April, 1991 —

RULE 1 - APPLICATION

(a) These Rules shall apply to all vessels upon the high seas and in all waters connected therewith navigable by seagoing vessels.

(b) Nothing in these Rules shall interfere with the operation of special rules made by an appropriate authority for roadsteads, harbours, rivers, lakes or inland waterways connected with the high seas and navigable by seagoing vessels. Such special rules shall conform as closely as possible to these rules.

(c) Nothing in these Rules shall interfere with the operation of any special rules made by the Government of any State with respect to additional station or signal lights, shapes or whistle signals for ships of war and vessels proceeding under convoy, or with respect to additional station or signal lights or shapes for fishing vessels engaged in fishing as a fleet. These additional station or signal lights, shapes or whistle signals shall, so far as possible, be such that they cannot be mistaken for any light, shape or signal authorised elsewhere under these Rules.

(d) Traffic separation schemes may be adopted by the Organisation for the purpose of these Rules.

(e) Whenever the Government concerned shall have determined that a vessel of special construction or purpose cannot comply fully with the provisions of any of these Rules with respect to the number, position, range or arc of visibility of lights or shapes, as well as to the disposition and characteristics of sound-signalling appliances, such vessel shall comply with such other provisions in regard to the number, position, range or arc of visibility of lights or shapes, as well as to the disposition and characteristics of sound-signalling appliances, as her Government shall have determined to be the closest possible compliance with these Rules in respect of that vessel.

RULE 2 - RESPONSIBILITY

(a) Nothing in these Rules shall exonerate any vessel, or the owner, master or crew thereof, from the consequences of any neglect to comply with these Rules or of the neglect of any precaution which may be required by the ordinary practice of seamen, or by the special circumstances of the case.

(b) In construing and complying with these rules, due regard shall be had to all dangers of navigation and collision and to any special circumstances, including the limitations of the vessels involved, which may make a departure from these Rules necessary to avoid immediate danger.

RULE 3 - GENERAL DEFINITIONS

For the purpose of these Rules, except where the context otherwise requires:

(a) The word "vessel" includes every description of water craft, including non-displacement craft and seaplanes, used or capable of being used as a means of transportation on water.

(b) The term "power-driven vessel" means any vessel propelled by machinery.

(c) The term "sailing vessel" means any vessel under sail provided that propelling machinery, if fitted, is not being used.

(d) The term "vessel engaged in fishing" means any vessel fishing with nets, lines, trawls, or other fishing apparatus which restrict manoeuvrability, but does not include a vessel fishing with trolling lines or other fishing apparatus which do not restrict manoeuvrability.

(e) The word "seaplane" includes any aircraft designed to manoeuvre on the water.

(f) The term "vessel not under command" means a vessel which through some exceptional circumstances is unable to manoeuvre as required by these Rules and is therefore unable to keep out of the way of another vessel.

(g) The term "vessel restricted in her ability to manoeuvre" means a vessel which from the nature of her work is restricted in her ability to manoeuvre as required by these Rules and is therefore unable to keep out of the way of another vessel.

DO NOT ASSUME THAT ALL OTHER CRAFT WILL KNOW AND OBEY THESE RULES. ALWAYS USE GREAT CAUTION IN A CLOSE QUARTERS SITUATION.

The term 'vessels restricted in their ability to manoeuvre' shall include but not be limited to:

(i) A vessel engaged in laying, servicing or picking up a navigation mark, submarine cable or pipeline.

(ii) A vessel engaged in dredging, surveying or underwater operations.

(iii) A vessel engaged in the launching or recovery of aircraft.

(iv) A vessel engaged in replenishment or transferring persons, provisions or cargo while underway.

(v) A vessel engaged in mine clearance operations.

(vi) A vessel engaged in a towing operation such as severely restricts the towing vessel and her tow in their ability to deviate from their course.

(h) The term "vessel constrained by her draught" means a power-driven vessel which, because of her draught in relation to the available depth and width of navigable water, is severely restricted in her ability to deviate from the course she is following.

(i) The word "underway" means that a vessel is not at anchor, or made fast to the shore, or aground.

(j) The words "length" or "breadth" of a vessel mean her length overall and greatest breadth.

(k) Vessels shall be deemed to be in sight of one another only when one can be observed visually from the other.

(l) The term "restricted visibility" means any condition in which visibility is restricted by fog, mist, falling snow, heavy rain-storms, sandstorms or any other similar causes.

PART B - STEERING AND SAILING RULES

Section I — Conduct of Vessels in any condition of visibility

RULE 4 - APPLICATION

Rules in this Section apply in any condition of visibility.

RULE 5 - LOOK-OUT

Every vessel shall at all times maintain a proper look-out by sight and hearing, as well as by all available means appropriate in the prevailing circumstances and conditions, so as to make a full appraisal of the situation and of the risk of collision.

RULE 6 - SAFE SPEED

Every vessel shall at all times proceed at a safe speed so that she can take proper and effective action to avoid collision and be stopped within a distance appropriate to the prevailing circumstances and conditions.

In determining a safe speed the following factors shall be among those taken into account:

(a) By all vessels:

(i) the state of visibility;

(ii) the traffic density including concentrations of fishing vessels or any other vessels;

(iii) the manoeuvrability of the vessel with special reference to stopping distance and turning ability in the prevailing conditions;

(iv) at night the presence of background light such as from shore lights or from back scatter of her own lights;

(v) the state of wind, sea and current, and the proximity of navigational hazards;

(vi) the draught in relation to the available depth of water.

(b) Additionally, by vessels with operational radar:

(i) the characteristics, efficiency and limitations of the radar equipment;

(ii) any constraints imposed by the radar range scale in use;

(iii) the effect on radar detection of the sea state, weather and other sources of interference;

(iv) the possibility that small vessels, ice and other floating objects may not be detected by radar at an adequate range;

(v) the number, locations and movement of vessels detected by radar;

(vi) the more exact assessment of the visibility that may be possible when radar is used to determine the range of vessels or other objects in the vicinity.

RULE 7 - RISK OF COLLISION

(a) Every vessel shall use all available means appropriate to the prevailing circumstances and conditions to determine if risk of collision exists. If there is any doubt such risk shall be deemed to exist.

(b) Proper use shall be made of radar equipment if fitted and operational, including long-range scanning to obtain early warning of risk of collision and radar plotting or equivalent systematic observation of detected objects.

(c) Assumptions shall not be made on the basis of scanty information, especially scanty radar information.

(d) In determining if risk of collision exists the following considerations shall be among those taken into account:

   (i) such risk shall be deemed to exist if the compass bearing of an approaching vessel does not appreciably change;

   (ii) such risk may sometimes exist even when an appreciable bearing change is evident, particularly when approaching a very large vessel or tow or when approaching a vessel at close range.

RULE 8 - ACTION TO AVOID COLLISION

(a) Any action taken to avoid collision shall, if the circumstances of the case admit, be positive, made in ample time and with due regard to the observance of good seamanship.

(b) Any alterations of course and/or speed to avoid collision shall, if the circumstances of the case admit, be large enough to be readily apparent to another vessel observing visually or by radar, a succession of small alterations of course and/or speed should be avoided.

(c) If there is sufficient sea room, alteration of course alone may be the most effective action to avoid a close-quarters situation provided that it is made in good time, is substantial and does not result in another close-quarters situation.

(d) Action taken to avoid collision with another vessel shall be such as to result in passing at a safe distance. The effectiveness of the action shall be carefully checked until the other vessel is finally past and clear.

(e) If necessary to avoid collision or allow more time to assess the situation, a vessel shall slacken speed or take all way off by stopping or reversing her means of propulsion.

(f) (i) A vessel which, by any of these Rules, is required not to impede the passage or safe passage of another vessel shall, when required by the circumstances of the case, take early action to allow sufficient sea room for the safe passage of the other vessel;

   (ii) A vessel required not to impede the passage or safe passage of another vessel is not relieved of this obligation if approaching the other vessel so as to involve risk of collision and shall, when taking action, have full regard to the action which may be required by the Rules of this part;

   (iii) A vessel the passage of which is not to be impeded remains fully obliged to comply with the Rules of this part when the two vessels are approaching one another so as to involve risk of collision.

RULE 9 – NARROW CHANNELS

(a) A vessel proceeding along the course of a narrow channel or fairway shall keep as near to the outer limit of the channel or fairway which lies on her starboard side as is safe and practicable.

(b) A vessel of less than 20 metres in length or a sailing vessel shall not impede the passage of a vessel which can safely navigate only within a narrow channel or fairway.

(c) A vessel engaged in fishing shall not impede the passage of any other vessel navigating within a narrow channel or fairway.

(d) A vessel shall not cross a narrow channel or fairway if such crossing impedes the passage of a vessel which can safely navigate only within such channel or fairway. The latter vessel may use the sound signal prescribed in Rule 34 (d) if in doubt as to the intention of the crossing vessel.

(e) (i) In a narrow channel or fairway when overtaking can take place only if the vessel to be overtaken has to take action to permit safe passing, the vessel intending to overtake shall indicate her intention by sounding the appropriate signal prescribed in

Rule 34(c)(i). The vessel to be overtaken shall, if in agreement, sound the appropriate signal prescribed in Rule (c)(ii) and take steps to permit safe passing. If in doubt she may sound the signals prescribed in Rule 34(d).

(ii) This Rule does not relieve the overtaking vessel of her obligation under Rule 13.

(f) A vessel nearing a bend or an area of narrow channel or fairway where other vessels may be obscured by an intervening obstruction shall navigate with particular alertness and caution and shall sound the appropriate signal prescribed in Rule 34(e).

(g) Any vessel shall, if the circumstances of the case admit, avoid anchoring in a narrow channel.

RULE 10 - TRAFFIC SEPARATION SCHEMES

(a) This Rule applies to traffic separation schemes adopted by the Organisation and does not relieve any vessel of her obligation under any other rule.

(i) proceed in the appropriate traffic lane in the general direction of traffic flow for that lane.

(ii) so far as practicable keep clear of a traffic separation line or separation zone.

(iii) normally join or leave a traffic lane at the termination of the lane, but when joining or leaving from either side shall do so at as small an angle to the general direction of traffic flow as practicable.

(b) A vessel shall, so far as practicable, avoid crossing traffic lanes but if obliged to do so shall cross on a heading as nearly as practicable at right angles to the general direction of traffic flow.

(c) A vessel shall not use an inshore traffic zone when she can safely use the appropriate traffic lane within the adjacent traffic separation scheme. However, vessels of less than 20 metres in length, sailing vessels and vessels engaged in fishing may use the inshore traffic zone.

(d) Notwithstanding paragraph (c), a vessel may use an inshore traffic zone when en route to and from a port, offshore installation or structure, pilot station or any other place situated within the inshore traffic zone, or to avoid immediate danger.

(e) A vessel other than a crossing vessel or a vessel joining or leaving a lane shall not normally enter a separation zone or cross a separation line except:

(i) in cases of emergency to avoid immediate danger

(ii) to engage in fishing within a separation zone.

(f) A vessel navigating in areas near the termination of traffic separation schemes shall do so with particular caution.

(g) A vessel shall so far as practicable avoid anchoring in a traffic separation scheme or in areas near its terminations.

(h) A vessel not using a traffic separation scheme shall avoid it by as wide a margin as is practicable.

(i) A vessel engaged in fishing shall not impede the passage of any vessel following a traffic lane.

(j) A vessel of less than 20 metres in length or a sailing vessel shall not impede the safe passage of a power-driven vessel following a traffic lane.

(k) A vessel restricted in her ability to manoeuvre when engaged in an operation for the maintenance of safety of navigation in a traffic separation scheme is exempted from complying with this Rule to the extent necessary to carry out the operation.

(l) A vessel restricted in her ability to manoeuvre when engaged in an operation for the laying, servicing or picking up of a submarine cable, within a traffic separation scheme, is exempted from complying with this Rule to the extent necessary to carry out the operation.

SECTION II – CONDUCT OF VESSELS IN SIGHT OF ONE ANOTHER

RULE 11 -

Rules in this Section apply to vessels in sight of one another.

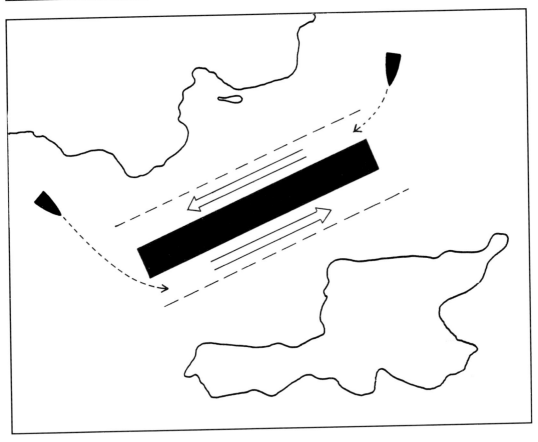

A vessel shall normally join or leave a traffic lane at its termination

Figure 4

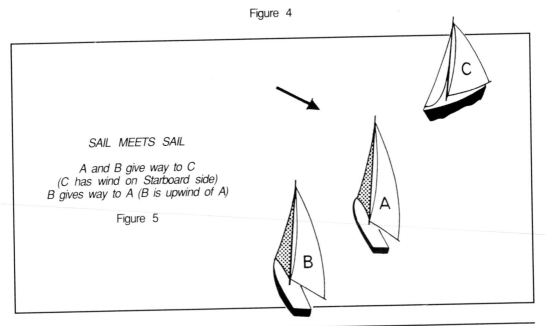

SAIL MEETS SAIL

A and B give way to C
(C has wind on Starboard side)
B gives way to A (B is upwind of A)

Figure 5

RULE 12 - SAILING VESSELS

(a) When two sailing vessels are approaching one another, so as to involve risk of collision, one of them shall keep out of the way of the other as follows:

   (i) when each has the wind on a different side, the vessel which has the wind on the port side shall keep out of the way of the other;

   (ii) when both have the wind on the same side, the vessel which is to windward shall keep out of the way of the vessel which is to leeward;

   (iii) if a vessel with the wind on the port side sees a vessel to windward and cannot determine with certainty whether the other vessel has the wind on the port or on the starboard side, she shall keep out of the way of the other.

(b) For the purposes of this Rule, the windward side shall be deemed to be the side opposite to that on which the mainsail is carried or, in the case of a square-rigged vessel, the side opposite to that on which the largest fore-and-aft sail is carried.

RULE 13 - OVERTAKING

(a) Notwithstanding anything contained in the Rules of Part B, Sections I and 11, any vessel overtaking any other shall keep out of the way of the vessel being overtaken.

(b) A vessel shall be deemed to be overtaking when coming up with another vessel from a direction more than 22.5 degrees abaft her abeam, that is, in such a position with reference to the vessel she is overtaking, that at night she would be able to see only the sternlight of that vessel but neither of her sidelights.

(c) When a vessel is in any doubt as to whether she is overtaking another, she shall assume that this is the case and act accordingly.

(d) Any subsequent alteration of the bearing between the two vessels shall not make the overtaking vessel a crossing vessel within the meaning of these Rules, or relieve her of the duty of keeping clear of the overtaken vessel, until she is finally past and clear.

RULE 14 - HEAD-ON SITUATION

(a) When two power-driven vessels are meeting on reciprocal or nearly reciprocal courses so as to involve risk of collision, each shall alter her course to starboard so that each shall pass on the port side of the other.

(b) Such a situation shall be deemed to exist when a vessel sees the other ahead or nearly ahead, and by night she could see the masthead lights of the other in a line or nearly in a line and/or both sidelights and by day she observes the corresponding aspect of the other vessel.

(c) When a vessel is in any doubt as to whether such a situation exists she shall assume that it does exist and act accordingly.

RULE 15 - CROSSING SITUATION

When two power-driven vessels are crossing so as to involve risk of collision, the vessel which has the other on her own starboard side shall keep out of the way and shall, if the circumstances of the case admit, avoid crossing ahead of the other vessel.

RULE 16 - ACTION BY GIVE-WAY VESSEL

Every vessel which is directed to keep out of the way of another vessel shall, so far as possible, take early and substantial action to keep well clear.

WHEN GIVING WAY:

Make your move in good time and make a fairly large movement so that your intentions are obvious. A change in course is more obvious than a change in speed when giving way to a boat crossing your path.

Avoid passing ahead of the boat you are giving way to.

Bear in mind that ships are unable to alter course or speed quickly. There is also a very big "Blind Spot" ahead of many ships. Avoid any close encounter with a ship.

RULE 17 - ACTION BY STAND-ON VESSEL

(a) (i) Where one of two vessels is to keep out of the way, the other shall keep her course and speed.

   (ii) The latter vessel may however take action to avoid collision by her manoeuvre alone, as soon as it

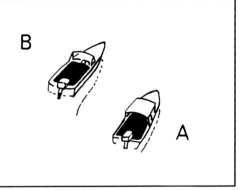

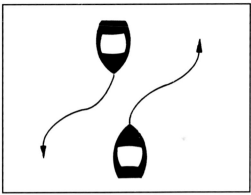

Overtaking: A keeps clear
Figure 6

Meeting Head-on:
Both alter course to Starboard
Figure 7

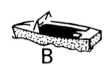

Crossing: A keeps clear
Figure 8

becomes apparent to her that the vessel required to keep out of the way is not taking appropriate action in compliance with these Rules.

b) When, from any cause, the vessel required to keep her course and speed finds herself so close that collision cannot be avoided by the action of the give-way vessel alone, she shall take such action as will best aid to avoid collision.

c) A power-driven vessel which takes action in a crossing situation in accordance with sub-paragraph (a)(ii) of this Rule to avoid collision with another power-driven vessel shall, if the circumstances of the case admit, not alter course to port for a vessel on her own port side.

d) This Rule does not relieve the give-way vessel of her obligation to keep out of the way.

RULE 18 - RESPONSIBILITIES BETWEEN VESSELS

Except where Rules 9, 10 and 13 otherwise require:

(a) A power-driven vessel underway shall keep out of the way of:
 (i) a vessel not under command
 (ii) a vessel restricted in her ability to manoeuvre
 (iii) a vessel engaged in fishing
 (iv) a sailing vessel.

(b) A sailing vessel underway shall keep out of the way of:
 (i) a vessel not under command
 (ii) a vessel restricted in her ability to manoeuvre
 (iii) a vessel engaged in fishing.

(c) A vessel engaged in fishing when underway shall, so far as possible, keep out of the way of:
 (i) a vessel not under command
 (ii) a vessel restricted in her ability to manoeuvre.

(d) (i) Any vessel other than a vessel not under command or a vessel restricted in her ability to manoeuvre shall, if the circumstances of the case admit, avoid impeding the safe passage of a vessel constrained by her draught, exhibiting the signals in Rule 28.

(ii) A vessel constrained by her draught shall navigate with particular caution having full regard to her special condition.

(e) A seaplane on the water shall, in general, keep well clear of all vessels and avoid impeding their navigation. In circumstances, however, where risk of collision exists, she shall comply with the Rules of this Part.

SECTION III – CONDUCT OF VESSELS IN RESTRICTED VISIBILITY

RULE 19 — CONDUCT OF VESSELS IN RESTRICTED VISIBILITY

(a) This Rule applies to vessels not in sight of one another when navigating in or near an area of restricted visibility.

(b) Every vessel shall proceed at a safe speed adapted to the prevailing circumstances and conditions of restricted visibility. A power-driven vessel shall have her engines ready for immediate manoeuvre.

(c) Every vessel shall have due regard to the prevailing circumstances and conditions of restricted visibility when complying with the Rules of Section 1 of this Part.

(d) A vessel which detects by radar alone the presence of another vessel shall determine if a close-quarters situation is developing and/or risk of collision exists. If so, she shall take avoiding action in ample time, provided that when such action consists of an alteration of course, so far as possible the following shall be avoided:

(i) an alteration of course to port for a vessel forward of the beam, other than a vessel being overtaken

(ii) an alteration of course towards a vessel abeam or abaft the beam.

(e) Except where it has been determined that a risk of collision does not exist, every vessel which hears apparently forward of her beam the fog signal of another vessel, or which cannot avoid close-quarters situation with another vessel forward of her beam, shall reduce her speed to the minimum at which she can be kept on her course. She shall necessary take all her way off and in any event navigate with extreme caution until danger of collision is over.

PART C LIGHTS AND SHAPES

RULE 20 – APPLICATION

(a) Rules in this Part shall be complied with in all weathers.

(b) The Rules concerning lights shall be complied with from sunset to sunrise, and during such times no other lights shall be exhibited, except such lights as cannot be mistaken for the lights specified in these Rules or do not impair their visibility or distinctive character, or interfere with the keeping of a proper look-out.

(c) The lights prescribed by these Rules shall, if carried, also be exhibited from sunrise to sunset in restricted visibility and may be exhibited in all other circumstances when it is deemed necessary.

(d) The Rules concerning shapes shall be complied with by day.

(e) The lights and shapes specified in these Rules shall comply with the provisions of Annex I to these Regulations.

RULE 21 - DEFINITIONS

(a) "Masthead light" means a white light placed over the fore and aft centreline of the vessel showing an unbroken light over an arc of the horizon of 225 degrees and so fixed as to show the light from right ahead to 22.5 degrees abaft the beam on either side of the vessel.

(b) "sidelights" means a green light on the starboard side and a red light on the port side each showing an unbroken light over an arc of the horizon of 112.5 degrees and so fixed as to show the light from right ahead to 22.5 degrees abaft the beam on its respective side. In a vessel of less than 20 metres in length the sidelights may be combined in one lantern carried on the fore and aft centre line of the vessel.

(c) "sternlight" means a white light placed as nearly as practicable at the stern showing an unbroken light over an arc of the horizon of 135 degrees and so fixed as to show the light 67.5 degrees from right aft on each side of the vessel.

(d) "Towing light" means a yellow light having the same characteristics as the "sternlight" defined in paragraph (c) of this Rule.

(e) "All-round light" means a light showing an unbroken light over an arc of the horizon of 360 degrees.

(f) "Flashing light" means a light flashing at regular intervals at a frequency of 120 flashes or more per minute.

RULE 22 - VISIBILITY OF LIGHTS

The lights prescribed in these Rules shall have an intensity as specified in Section 8 of Annex 1 to these Regulations; so as to be visible at the following minimum ranges:

(a) In vessels of 50 metres or more in length:
- a masthead light, 6 miles
- a sidelight, 3 miles
- a sternlight, 3 miles
- a towing light, 3 miles
- a white, red, green or yellow all–round light, 3 miles.

(b) In vessels of 12 metres or more in length but less than 50 metres in length:
- a masthead light, 5 miles; except that where the length of the vessel is less than 20 metres, 3 miles
- a sidelight, 2 miles
- a sternlight, 2 miles
- a towing light, 2 miles
- a white, red, green or yellow all–round light, 2 miles.

In commercial fishing vessels the stern light is usually placed, for convenience, at the rear of the wheelhouse to keep it clear of the working deck.

However, where practical, it should be placed right aft. (Rule 21(c)).

(c) In vessels of less than 12 metres in length:
- a masthead light, 2 miles
- a sidelight, 1 mile
- a sternlight, 2 miles
- a towing light, 2 miles
- a white, red, green or yellow all–round light, 2 miles.

(d) In inconspicuous, partly submerged vessels or objects being towed: - a white all-round light, 3 miles.

RULE 23 - POWER-DRIVEN VESSELS UNDERWAY

(a) A power-driven vessel underway shall exhibit:
(i) a masthead · light forward
(ii) a second masthead light abaft of and higher than the forward one; except that a vessel of less than 50 metres in length shall not be obliged to exhibit such light but may do so
(iii) sidelights
(iv) a sternlight.

(b) An air-cushion vessel when operating in the non-displacement mode shall, in addition to the lights prescribed in paragraph (a) of this Rule, exhibit an all-round flashing yellow light.

(c) (i) A power-driven vessel of less than 12 metres in length may in lieu of the lights prescribed in paragraph (a) of this Rule exhibit an all-round white light and sidelights.

(ii) A power-driven vessel of less than 7 metres in length whose maximum speed does not exceed 7 knots may in lieu of the lights prescribed in paragraph (a) of this Rule exhibit an all-round white light and shall, if practicable, also exhibit sidelights;

(iii) The masthead light or all-round white light on a power-driven vessel of less than 12 metres in length may be displaced from the fore and aft centreline of the vessel if centreline fitting is not practicable, provided that the sidelights are combined in one lantern which shall be carried on the fore and aft centreline of the vessel, or located as nearly as practicable in the same fore and aft line as the masthead light or the all-round white light.

RULE 24 - TOWING AND PUSHING

(a) A power-driven vessel when towing shall exhibit:
(i) instead of the light prescribed in Rule 23(a)(i) or (a)(ii), two masthead lights in a vertical line.

When the length of the tow, measuring from the stern of the towing vessel to the after end of the tow exceeds 200 metres, three such lights in a vertical line

(ii)   sidelights

(iii) a sternlight

(iv) a towing light in a vertical line above the sternlight

(v)   when the length of the tow exceeds 200 metres, a diamond shape where it can best be seen.

(b) When a pushing vessel and a vessel being pushed ahead are rigidly connected in a composite unit, they shall be regarded as a power-driven vessel and exhibit the lights prescribed in Rule 23.

(c) A power-driven vessel when pushing ahead or towing alongside, except in the case of a composite unit, shall exhibit:

(i)   instead of the light prescribed in Rule 23(a)(i) or (a)(ii), two masthead lights in a vertical line

(ii) sidelights

(iii) a sternlight.

(d) A power-driven vessel to which paragraph (a) or (c) of this Rule apply shall also comply with Rule 23(a)(ii)

(e) A vessel or object being towed, other than those mentioned in paragraph (g) of this Rule, shall exhibit:

(i)   sidelights

(ii) a sternlight

(iii) when the length of the tow exceeds 200 metres, a diamond shape where it can best be seen.

(f) Provided that any number of vessels being towed alongside or pushed in a group shall be lighted as one vessel.

(i)   a vessel being pushed ahead, not being part of a composite unit, shall exhibit at the forward end, sidelights

(ii) a vessel being towed alongside shall exhibit a sternlight and at the forward end, sidelights.

(g) An inconspicuous, partly submerged vessel or object, or combination of such vessels or objects being towed, shall exhibit:

(i)   if it is less than 25 metres in breadth, one all-round white light at or near the forward end and one at or near the after end, except that dracones need not exhibit a light at or near the forward end

(ii) if it is 25 metres or more in breadth, two additional all-round white lights at or near the extremities of its breadth

(iii) if it exceeds 100 metres in length, additional all-round white lights between the lights prescribed in sub-paragraphs (i) and (ii) so that the distance between the lights shall not exceed 100 metres

(iv) a diamond shape at or near the aftermost extremity of the last vessel or object being towed, and if the length of the tow exceeds 200 metres an additional diamond shape where it can best be seen and located as far forward as is practicable.

(h) Where from any sufficient cause it is impracticable for a vessel or object being towed to exhibit the lights or shapes prescribed in paragraph (e) or (g) of this Rule, all possible measures shall be taken to light the vessel or object towed or at least to indicate the presence of such vessel or object.

(i) Where from any sufficient cause it is impracticable for a vessel not normally engaged in towing operations to display the lights prescribed in paragraph (a) or (c) of this Rule, such vessel shall not be required to exhibit those lights when engaged in towing another vessel in distress or otherwise in need of assistance. All possible measures shall be taken to indicate the nature of the relationship between the towing vessel and the vessel being towed as authorized by Rule 36, in particular by illuminating the towline.

RULE 25 - SAILING VESSELS UNDERWAY AND VESSELS UNDER OARS

(a) A sailing vessel under way shall exhibit:

(i)   sidelights

(ii) a sternlight.

(b) In a sailing vessel of less than 20 metres

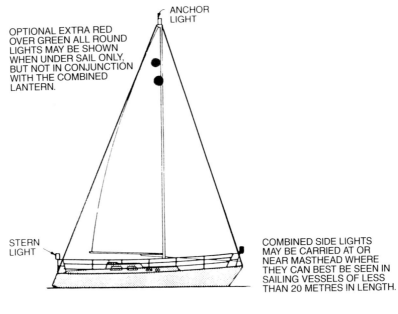

OPTIONAL EXTRA RED OVER GREEN ALL ROUND LIGHTS MAY BE SHOWN WHEN UNDER SAIL ONLY, BUT NOT IN CONJUNCTION WITH THE COMBINED LANTERN.

ANCHOR LIGHT

STERN LIGHT

COMBINED SIDE LIGHTS MAY BE CARRIED AT OR NEAR MASTHEAD WHERE THEY CAN BEST BE SEEN IN SAILING VESSELS OF LESS THAN 20 METRES IN LENGTH.

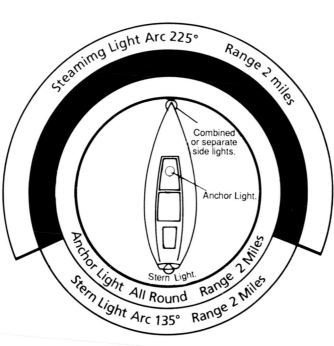

Steamimg Light Arc 225°   Range 2 miles

Combined or separate side lights.

Anchor Light.

Stern Light.

Anchor Light All Round   Range 2 Miles

Stern Light Arc 135°   Range 2 Miles

Lights exhibited by a Sailing Vessel of less than 20 metres in length.
Rule 25(a) and (b)

Figure 9

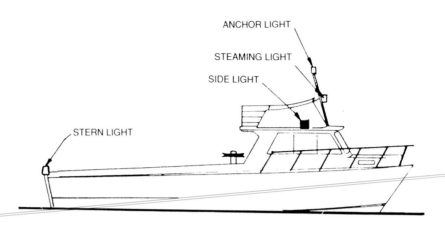

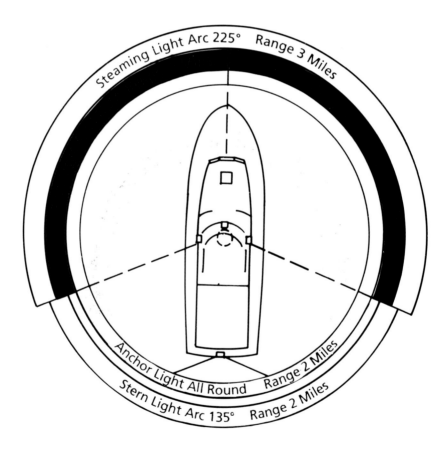

Light exhibited by a power-driven vessel of less than 20 metres in length.

Figure 10

TORCH
OR
LANTERN

Rule 25(d) (i)
A sailing vessel under 7 metres in length shall have ready at hand an electric torch or lighted lantern.

TORCH
OR
LANTERN

Rule 25(d) (ii)
A vessel under oars may show electric torch or lighted lantern.

Figure 11

in length, the lights prescribed in paragraph (a) of this Rule may be combined in one lantern carried at or near the top of the mast where it can best be seen.

(c) A sailing vessel underway may, in addition to the lights prescribed in paragraph (a) of this Rule, exhibit at or near the top of the mast, where they can best be seen, two all-round lights in a vertical line, the upper being red and the lower green, but these lights shall not be exhibited in conjunction with the combined lantern permitted by paragraph (b) of this Rule.

(d) (i) A sailing vessel of less than 7 metres in length shall, if practicable, exhibit the lights prescribed in paragraph (a) or (b) of this Rule, but if she does not, she shall have ready at hand an electric torch or lighted lantern showing a white light which shall be exhibited in sufficient time to prevent collision.

(ii) A vessel under oars may exhibit the lights prescribed in this Rule for sailing vessels, but if she does not, she shall have ready at hand an electric torch or lighted lantern showing a white light which shall be exhibited in sufficient time to prevent collision.

(e) A vessel proceeding under sail when also being propelled by machinery, shall exhibit forward, where it can best be seen, a conical shape apex downwards.

RULE 26 - FISHING VESSELS

(a) A vessel engaged in fishing, whether underway or at anchor, shall exhibit only the lights and shapes prescribed in this Rule.

(b) A vessel when engaged in trawling, by which is meant the dragging through the water of a dredge net or other apparatus used as a fishing appliance, shall exhibit:

(i) two all-round lights in a vertical line, the upper being green and the lower white, or a shape consisting of two cones with their apexes together in a vertical line one above the other; a vessel of less than 20 metres in length may instead of this shape exhibit a basket

(ii) a masthead light abaft of and higher than the all-round green light; a vessel of less than 50 metres in length shall not be obliged to exhibit such a light but may do so

(iii) when making way through the water, in addition to the lights prescribed in this paragraph, sidelights and a sternlight.

(c) A vessel engaged in fishing, other than trawling, shall exhibit:

(i) two all-round lights in a vertical line, the upper being red and the lower white, or a shape consisting of two cones with apexes together in a vertical line one above the other; a vessel of less than 20 metres in length may, instead of this shape, exhibit a basket

(ii) when there is outlying gear extending more than 150 metres horizontally from the vessel, an all-round white light or a cone apex upwards in the direction of the gear

(iii) when making way through the water, in addition to the lights prescribed in this paragraph, sidelights and a sternlight.

(d) a vessel engaged in fishing in close proximity to other vessels engaged in fishing may exhibit the additional signals described in Annex II to these Regulations.

(e) A vessel when not engaged in fishing shall not exhibit the lights or shapes prescribed in this Rule, but only those prescribed for a vessel of her length.

RULE 27 - VESSELS NOT UNDER COMMAND OR RESTRICTED IN THEIR ABILITY TO MANOEUVRE

(a) A vessel not under command shall exhibit:

(i) two all-round red lights in a vertical line where they can best be seen

(ii) two balls or similar shapes in a vertical line where they can best be seen

(iii) when making way through the water, in addition to the lights prescribed in this paragraph, sidelights and a sternlight.

(b) A vessel restricted in her ability to manoeuvre, except a vessel engaged in mineclearance operations, shall exhibit:

(i) three all-round lights in a vertical line where they can best be seen. The highest and lowest of these lights shall be red and the middle light shall be white

(ii) three shapes in a vertical line where they can best be seen. The highest and lowest of these shapes shall be balls and the middle one a diamond

(iii) when making way through the water, a masthead light or lights, sidelights and a sternlight, in addition to the lights prescribed in sub-paragraph (i)

(iv) when at anchor, in addition to the lights or shapes prescribed in sub-paragraphs (i) and (ii), the light, lights or shape prescribed in Rule 30.

(c) A power-driven vessel engaged in a towing operation such as severely restricts the towing vessel and the tow in their ability to deviate from their course shall, in addition to the lights or shapes prescribed in Rule 24(a), exhibit the lights or shapes prescribed in sub-paragraphs (b) (i) and (ii) of this Rule.

(d) A vessel engaged in dredging or underwater operations, when restricted in her ability to manoeuvre, shall exhibit the lights and shapes prescribed in sub-paragraphs (b)(i), (ii) and (iii) of this Rule and shall in addition, when an obstruction exists, exhibit:

(i) two all-round red lights or two balls in a vertical line to indicate the side on which the obstruction exists

(ii) two all-round green lights or two diamonds in a vertical line to indicate the side on which another vessel may pass

(iii) when at anchor, the lights or shapes prescribed in this paragraph instead of the lights or shape prescribed in Rule 30.

(e) Whenever the size of a vessel engaged in diving operations makes it impracticable to exhibit all lights and shapes prescribed in paragraph (d) of this Rule, the following shall be exhibited:

(i) three all-round lights in a vertical line where they can best be seen. The highest and lowest of these lights shall be red and the middle light shall be white

(ii) a rigid replica of the International Code flag "A" not less than 1 metre in height. Measures shall be taken to ensure its all-round visibility.

(f) A vessel engaged in mineclearance operations shall in addition to the lights prescribed for a power-driven vessel in Rule 23 or to the lights or shape prescribed for a vessel at anchor in Rule 30 as appropriate, exhibit three all-round green lights or three balls. One of these lights or shapes shall be exhibited near the foremast head and one at each end of the fore yard. These lights or shapes indicate that it is dangerous for another vessel to approach within I 000 metres of the mineclearance vessel.

(g) Vessels of less than 12 metres in length, except those engaged in diving operations, shall not be required to exhibit the lights and shapes prescribed in this Rule.

(h) The signals prescribed in this Rule are not signals of vessels in distress and requiring assistance. Such signals are contained in Annex IV to these Regulations.

RULE 28 - VESSELS CONSTRAINED BY THEIR DRAUGHT

A vessel constrained by her draught may, in addition to the lights prescribed for power-driven vessels in Rule 23, exhibit where they can best be seen three all-round red lights in a vertical line, or a cylinder.

(See Figure 15 on following page).

RULE 29 - PILOT VESSELS

(a) A vessel engaged on pilotage duty shall exhibit:

(i) at or near the masthead, two all-round lights in a vertical line, the upper being white and the lower red

(ii) when underway, in addition, sidelights and a sternlight

(iii) when at anchor, in addition to the lights prescribed in sub-paragraph

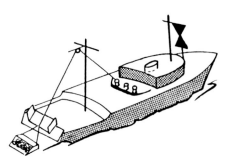

Scallop Dredger (classified as a trawler)
engaged in fishing
Rule 26 (b) (i)

Figure 12

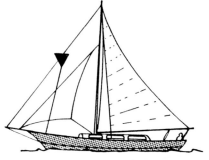

Vessel under sail and power
Rule 25 (e)

Figure 13

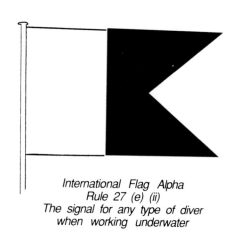

International Flag Alpha
Rule 27 (e) (ii)
The signal for any type of diver
when working underwater

Figure 14

(i), the light, lights or shape prescribed in Rule 30 for vessels at anchor

(b) A pilot vessel when not engaged on pilotage duty shall exhibit the lights or shapes prescribed for a similar vessel of her length.

RULE 30 - ANCHORED VESSELS AND VESSELS AGROUND

(a) A vessel at anchor shall exhibit where it can best be seen:

  (i)   in the fore part, an all-round white light or one ball

  (ii) at or near the stern and at a lower level than the light prescribed in

sub-paragraph (i), an all-round white light.

(b) A vessel of less than 50 metres in length may exhibit an all-round white light where it can best be seen, instead of the lights prescribed in paragraph (a) of this Rule.

(c) A vessel at anchor may, and a vessel of 100 metres and more in length shall, also use the available working or equivalent lights to illuminate her decks.

(d) A vessel aground shall exhibit the lights prescribed in paragraphs (a) or (b) of this Rule and in addition, where they can best be seen:

  (i)   two all-round red lights in a vertical line

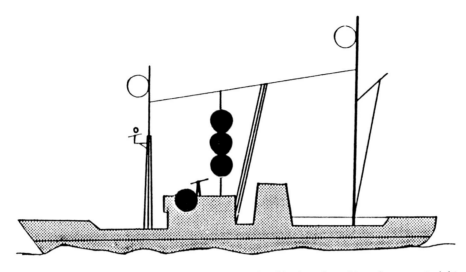

A power-driven vessel, over 50 metres, constrained by her draught under way at night
Rule 28 (Day Signal-Cylinder)

Figure 15

(ii)   three balls in a vertical line.

(e) A vessel of less than 7 metres in length, when at anchor, not in or near a narrow channel, fairway or anchorage, or where other vessels normally navigate, shall not be required to exhibit the lights of shape prescribed in paragraphs (a) and (b) of this Rule.

(f) A vessel of less than 12 metres in length, when aground, shall not be required to exhibit the lights or shapes prescribed in sub-paragraphs (d)(i) and (ii) of this Rule.

RULE 31 - SEAPLANES

Where it is impracticable for a seaplane to exhibit lights and shapes of the characteristics or in the positions prescribed in the Rules of this Part, she shall exhibit lights and shapes as closely similar in characteristics and position as is possible.

PART D SOUND AND LIGHT SIGNALS

RULE 32 - DEFINITIONS

(a) The word "whistle" means any sound signalling appliance capable of producing the prescribed blasts and which complies with the specifications in Annex III to these Regulations.

(b) The term "short blast" means a blast of about one second's duration.

(c) The term "prolonged blast" means a blast of from four to six seconds duration.

RULE 33 - EQUIPMENT FOR SOUND SIGNALS

(a) A vessel of 12 metres or more in length shall be provided with a whistle and a bell and a vessel of 100 metres or more in length shall, in addition, be provided with a gong, the tone and sound of which cannot be confused with that of the bell. The whistle, bell and gong shall comply with the specifications in Annex III to these Regulations. The bell or gong or both may be replaced by other equipment having the same respective sound characteristics, provided that manual sounding of the prescribed signals shall always be possible.

(b) A vessel less than 12 metres in length shall not be obliged to carry the sound signalling appliances prescribed in paragraph (a) of this Rule but if she does not, she shall be provided with some other means of making an efficient sound signal.

RULE 34 - MANOEUVRING AND WARNING SIGNALS

(a) When vessels are in sight of one another, a power-driven vessel underway, when manoeuvring as authorized or required by these Rules, shall indicate that manoeuvre by the following signals on her whistle:

- one short blast to mean "I am altering my course to starboard"

- two short blasts to mean "I am altering my course to port"

- three short blasts to mean "I am operating astern propulsion".

(b) Any vessel may supplement the whistle signals prescribed in paragraph (a) of this Rule by light signals, repeated as appropriate, whilst the manoeuvre is being carried out:

  (i) these light signals shall have the following significance:

- one flash to mean "I am altering my course to starboard"

- two flashes to mean "I am altering my course to port"

- three flashes to mean "I am operating astern propulsion".

  (ii) the duration of each flash shall be about one second, the interval between flashes shall be about one second, and the interval between successive signals shall be not less than ten seconds

  (iii) the light used for this signal shall, if fitted, be an all-round white light, visible at a minimum range of 5 miles, and shall comply with the provisions of Annex I to these Regulations.

(c) When in sight of one another in a narrow channel or fairway:

  (i) a vessel intending to overtake another shall in compliance with Rule 9(e)(i) indicate her intention by the following signals on her whistle

- two prolonged blasts followed by one short blast to mean "I intend to overtake you on your starboard side"

- two prolonged blasts followed by two short blasts to mean "I intend to overtake you on your port side"

  (ii) the vessel about to be overtaken when acting in accordance with Rule 9(e)(i) shall indicate her agreement by the following signal on her whistle:

- one prolonged, one short, one prolonged and one short blast in that order.

(d) When vessels in sight of one another are approaching each other and from any cause either vessel fails to understand the intentions or action of the other, or is in doubt whether sufficient action is being taken by the other to avoid collision, the vessel in doubt shall immediately indicate such doubt by giving at least five short and rapid blasts on the whistle. Such signal may be supplemented by a light signal of at least five short and rapid flashes.

(e) A vessel nearing a bend or an area of a channel or fairway where other vessels may be obscured by an intervening obstruction shall sound one prolonged blast. Such signal shall be answered with a prolonged blast by any approaching vessel that may be within hearing around the bend or behind the intervening obstruction.

(f) If whistles are fitted on a vessel at a distance apart of more than 100 metres, one whistle only shall be used for giving manoeuvring and warning signals.

RULE 35 - SOUND SIGNALS IN RESTRICTED VISIBILITY

In or near an area of restricted visibility, whether by day or night, the signals prescribed in this Rule shall be used as follows:

(a) A power-driven vessel making way through the water, shall sound at intervals of not more than 2 minutes, one prolonged blast.

(b) A power-driven vessel underway but stopped and making no way through the water, shall sound at intervals of not more than 2 minutes, two prolonged blasts in succession with an interval of about 2 seconds between them.

(c) A vessel not under command, a vessel restricted in her ability to manoeuvre, a vessel constrained by her draught, a sailing vessel, a vessel engaged in fishing and a vessel engaged in towing or pushing another vessel shall, instead of the signals prescribed in paragraphs (a) or (b) of this Rule, sound at intervals of not more than 2 minutes three blasts in succession, namely one prolonged followed by two short blasts.

(d) A vessel engaged in fishing, when at anchor, and a vessel restricted in her ability to manoeuvre when carrying out her work at anchor, shall instead of the signals prescribed in paragraph (g) of this Rule sound the signal prescribed in paragraph (c) of this Rule.

(e) A vessel towed or if more than one vessel is towed, the last vessel of the tow, if manned, shall at intervals of not more than 2 minutes sound four blasts in succession, namely one prolonged followed by three short blasts. When practicable, this signal shall be made immediately after the signal made by the towing vessel.

(f) When a pushing vessel and a vessel being pushed ahead are rigidly connected in a composite unit they shall be regarded as a power-driven vessel and shall give the signals prescribed in paragraphs (a) or (b) of this Rule.

(g) A vessel at anchor shall at intervals of not more than one minute ring the bell rapidly for about 5 seconds. In a vessel of 100 metres or more in length, the bell shall be sounded in the forepart of the vessel and immediately after the ringing of the bell the gong shall be sounded rapidly for about 5 seconds in the after part of the vessel. A vessel at anchor may in addition sound three blasts in succession, namely one short, one prolonged and one short blast, to give warning of her position and of the possibility of collision to an approaching vessel.

(h) A vessel aground shall give the bell signal and if required the gong signal prescribed in paragraph (g) of this Rule and shall, in addition, give three separate and distinct strokes on the bell immediately before and after the rapid ringing of the bell. A vessel aground may in addition sound an appropriate whistle signal.

(i) A vessel of less than 12 metres in length shall not be obliged to give the above mentioned signals but, if she does not, shall make some other efficient sound signal at intervals of not more than 2 minutes.

(j) A pilot vessel when engaged on pilotage duty may in addition to the signals prescribed in paragraphs (a), (b) or (g) of this Rule sound an identity signal consisting of four short blasts.

RULE 36 - SIGNALS TO ATTRACT ATTENTION

If necessary to attract the attention of another vessel, any vessel may make light or sound signals that cannot be mistaken for any signal authorized elsewhere in these Rules, or may direct the beam of her searchlight in the direction of the danger, in such a way as not to embarrass any vessel.

Any light to attract the attention of another vessel shall be such that it cannot be mistaken for any aid to navigation. For the purpose of this Rule the use of high intensity intermittent or revolving lights, such as strobe lights, shall be avoided.

RULE 37 - DISTRESS SIGNALS

When a vessel is in distress and requires assistance she shall use or exhibit the signals described in Annex IV to these Regulations.

PART E   EXEMPTIONS

RULE 38 - EXEMPTIONS

Any vessel (or class of vessels) provided that she complies with the requirements of the International Regulations for Preventing Collisions at Sea, 1960, the keel of which is laid or which is at a corresponding stage of construction before the entry into force of these Regulations may be exempted from compliance therewith as follows:

(a) The installation of lights with ranges prescribed in Rule 22, until four years after the date of entry into force of these Regulations.

(b) The installation of lights with colour specifications as prescribed in Section

7 of Annex 1 to these Regulations, until four years after the date of entry into force of these Regulations.

(c) The repositioning of lights as a result of conversion from Imperial to metric units and rounding off measurement figures, permanent exemption.

(d) (i) The repositioning of masthead lights on vessels of less than 150 metres in length, resulting from the prescriptions of Section 3(a) of Annex I to these Regulations, permanent exemption.

(ii) The repositioning of masthead lights on vessels of 150 metres or more in length, resulting from the prescription of Section 3(a) of Annex I to these Regulations, until nine years after the date of entry into force of these Regulations.

(e) The repositioning of masthead lights resulting from the prescriptions of Section 2(b) of Annex I to these Regulations until nine years after the date of entry into force of these Regulations.

(f) The repositioning of sidelights resulting from the prescriptions of Section 2(g) and 3(b) of Annex I to these Regulations, until nine years after the date of entry into force of these Regulations.

(g) The requirements for sound signal appliances prescribed in Annex III to these Regulations, until nine years after the date of entry into force of these Regulations.

(h) The repositioning of all-round lights resulting from the prescription of Section 9(b) of Annex I to these Regulations, permanent exemption.

ANNEX I

POSITIONING AND TECHNICAL DETAILS OF LIGHTS AND SHAPES

1. Definition

The term "height above the hull" means height above the uppermost continuous deck. This height shall be measured from the position vertically beneath the location of the light.

2. Vertical Positioning and Spacing of Lights

(a) On a power-driven vessel of 20 metres or more in length, the masthead lights shall be placed as follows:

(i) the forward masthead light, or if only one masthead light is carried, then that light, at a height above the hull of not less than 6 metres, and, if the breadth of the vessel exceeds 6 metres, then at a height above the hull not less than such breadth, so however that the light need not be placed at a greater height above the hull than 12 metres

(ii) when two masthead lights are carried, the after one shall be at least 4.5 metres vertically higher than the forward one.

(b) The vertical separation of masthead lights of power-driven vessels shall be such that in all normal conditions of trim, the after light will be seen over and separate from the forward light at a distance of 1 000 metres from the stem when viewed from sea level.

(c) The masthead light of a power-driven vessel of 12 metres but less than 20 metres in length shall be placed at a height above the gunwale of not less than 2.5 metres.

(d) A power-driven vessel of less than 12 metres in length may carry the uppermost light at a height of less than 2.5 metres above the gunwale. When, however, a masthead light is carried in addition to sidelights and a sternlight or the all-round light prescribed in rule 23 (c) (i) is carried in addition to sidelights, then such masthead light or all-round light shall be carried at least 1 metre higher than the sidelights.

(e) One of the two or three masthead lights prescribed for a power-driven vessel when engaged in towing or pushing another vessel, shall be placed in the same position as either the forward masthead light or the after masthead light; provided that, if carried on the aftermast, the lowest after masthead light shall be at least 4.5 metres vertically higher than the forward masthead light.

(f) (i) The masthead light or lights prescribed in Rule 23(a) shall be so placed as to be above and clear of all other lights and obstructions except as described in sub-paragraph (ii).

(ii)   When it is impracticable to carry the all-round lights prescribed by Rule 27(b)(i) or Rule 28 below the masthead lights, they may be carried above the after masthead light(s) or vertically in between the forward masthead light(s) and after masthead light(s), provided that in the latter case the requirement of Section 3(c) of this Annex shall be complied with.

(g)   The sidelights of a power-driven vessel shall be placed at a height above the hull not greater than three quarters of that of the forward masthead light. They shall not be so low as to be interfered with by deck lights.

(h)   The sidelights, if in a combined lantern and carried on a power-driven vessel of less than 20 metres in length, shall be placed not less than I metre below the masthead light.

(i)   When the Rules prescribe two or three lights to be carried in a vertical line, they shall be spaced as follows:

(i)   on a vessel of 20 metres in length or more, such lights shall be spaced not less than 2 metres apart, and the lowest of these lights shall, except where a towing light is required, be placed at a height of not less than 4 metres above the hull

(ii)   on a vessel of less than 20 metres in length such lights shall be spaced not less than 1 metre apart and the lowest of these lights shall, except where a towing light is required, be placed at a height of not less than 2 metres above the gunwale.

(iii)   when three lights are carried they shall be equally spaced.

(j)   The lower of the two all-round lights prescribed for a vessel when engaged in fishing shall be at a height above the sidelights not less than twice the distance between the two vertical lights.

(k)   The forward anchor light prescribed in Rule 30(a)(i), when two are carried, shall not be less than 4.5 metres above the after one. On a vessel of 50 metres or more in length this forward anchor light shall be placed at a height of not less than 6 metres above the hull.

3. *Horizontal Positioning and Spacing of Lights*

(a)   When two masthead lights are prescribed for a power-driven vessel, the horizontal distance between them shall not be less than one half of the length of the vessel but need not be more than 100 metres. The forward light shall be placed not more than one quarter of the length of the vessel from the stem.

(b)   on a power-driven vessel of 20 metres or more in length the sidelights shall not be placed in front of the forward masthead lights. They shall be placed at or near the side of the vessel.

(c)   When the lights prescribed in Rule 27(b)(i) or Rule 28 are placed vertically between the forward masthead light(s) and the after masthead light(s) these all-round lights shall be placed at a horizontal distance of not less than 2 metres from the fore and aft centreline of the vessel in the athwartship direction.

4. *Details of Location of Direction-Indicating Lights for Fishing Vessels, Dredgers and vessels Engaged in Underwater operations*

(a)   The light indicating the direction of the outlying gear from a vessel engaged in fishing as prescribed in Rule 26(c)(ii) shall be placed at a horizontal distance of not less than 2 metres and not more than 6 metres away from the two all-round red and white lights. This light shall be placed not higher than the all-round white light prescribed in Rule 26(c)(i) and not lower than the sidelights.

(b)   The lights and shapes on a vessel engaged in dredging or underwater operations to indicate the obstructed side and/or the side on which it is safe to pass, as prescribed in Rule 27(d)(i) and (ii), shall be placed at the maximum practical horizontal distance, but in no case less than 2 metres, from the lights or shapes prescribed in Rule 27(b)(i) and (ii). In no case shall the upper of these lights or shapes be at a greater height than the lower of the three lights or shapes prescribed in Rule 27(b)(i) and (ii).

5. Screens for Sidelights

The sidelights of vessels of 20 metres or more in length shall be fitted with inboard screens painted matt black, and meeting the requirements of Section 9 of this Annex. On vessels of less than 20 metres in length the sidelights, if necessary to meet the requirements of Section 9 of this Annex, shall be fitted with inboard matt black screens. With a combined lantern, using a single, vertical filament and a very narrow division between the green and red sections, external screens need not be fitted.

6. Shapes

(a) Shapes shall be black and of the following sizes:

    (i)   a ball shall have a diameter of not less than 0.6 metre

    (ii)   a cone shall have the base diameter of not less than 0.6 metre and a height equal to its diameter

    (iii)   a cylinder shall have a diameter of at least 0.6 metre and a height of twice its diameter

    (iv)   a diamond shape shall consist of two cones as defined in (ii) above having a common base.

(b) The vertical distance between shapes shall be at least 1.5 metres.

(c) In a vessel of less than 20 metres in length, shapes of lesser dimensions but commensurate with the size of the vessel may be used, and the distance apart may be correspondingly reduced.

7. Colour Specification of Lights

The chromaticity of all navigation lights shall conform to the following standards, which lie within the boundaries of the area of the diagram specified for each colour by the International Commission of Illumination (CIE). The boundaries of the area for each colour are given by indicating the corner co-ordinates, which are as follows:

(i) White

    x 0.525 0.525 0.452 0.310 0.310 0.443
    y 0.382 0.440 0.440 0.348 0.283 0.382

(ii) Green

    x 0.028 0.009 0.300 0.203
    y 0.385 0.723 0.511 0.356

(iii) Red

    x 0.680 0.660 0.735 0.721
    y 0.320 0.320 0.265 0.259

(iv) Yellow

    x 0.612 0.618 0.575 0.575
    y 0.382 0.382 0.425 0.406

8. Intensity of Lights

(a) The minimum luminous intensity of lights shall be calculated by using the formula —

$$I = 3.43 \times 10^6 \times T \times D^2 \times K^D$$

where I is luminous intensity in candelas under service conditions.

T is threshold factor 2×10^{-7} lux

D is range of visibility (luminous range) of the light in nautical miles,

K is atmospheric transmissivity.

For prescribed lights the value of K shall be 0.8, corresponding to a meteorological visibility of approximately 13 nautical miles.

(b) A selection of figures derived from the formula is given in the following table:

Range of visibility (luminous range) of light in nautical miles	Luminous intensity of light in candelas for K = 0.8
D	I
1	0.9
2	4.3
3	12
4	27
5	52
6	94

NOTE: The maximum luminous intensity of navigation lights should be limited to avoid undue glare. This shall not be achieved by a variable control of the luminous intensity.

4. Horizontal sectors

(a) (i)   in the forward direction, sidelights as fitted on the vessel shall show the minimum required intensities. The intensities shall decrease to reach practical cut-off between 1 degree and 3 degrees outside the prescribed sector.

    (ii)   For sternlights and masthead lights and at 22.5 degrees abaft the beam for sidelights, the minimum required intensities shall be maintained over the arc of the horizon up to 5 degrees within the limits of the sectors prescribed in Rule 21. From 5 degrees within the prescribed sectors the intensity may decrease by 50 per cent up to the prescribed limits; it shall decrease steadily to reach practical cut-off at not more than 5 degrees outside the prescribed sectors.

(b) All-round lights shall be so located as not to be obscured by masts, topmasts or structures within angular sectors of more than 6 degrees, except anchor lights prescribed in Rule 30, which need not be placed at an impracticable height above the hull.

10. *Vertical Sectors*

(a) The vertical sectors of electric lights as fitted, with the exception of lights on sailing vessel underway shall ensure that:

   (i) at least the required minimum intensity is maintained at all angles from 5 degrees above to 5 degrees below the horizontal

   (ii) at least 50 per cent of the required minimum intensity is maintained from 7.5 degrees above to 7.5 degrees below the horizontal.

(b) In the case of sailing vessels underway, the vertical sectors of electric lights as fitted shall ensure that:

   (i) at least the required minimum intensity is maintained at all angles from 5 degrees above to 5 degrees below the horizontal

   (ii) at least 50 per cent of the required minimum intensity is maintained from 25 degrees above to 25 degrees below the horizontal.

(c) In the case of lights other than electric these specifications shall be met as closely as possible.

11. *Intensity of non-electric Lights*

Non-electric lights shall so far as practicable comply with the minimum intensities, as specified in Table 2 given in Section 8 of this Annex.

12. *Manoeuvring Light*

Notwithstanding the provisions of paragraph 2(f) of this Annex the manoeuvring light described in Rule 34(b) shall be placed in the same fore and aft vertical plane as the masthead light or lights and, where practicable, at a minimum height of 2 metres vertically above the forward masthead light, provided that it shall be carried not less than 2 metres vertically above or below the after masthead light. On a vessel where only one masthead light is carried the manoeuvring light, if fitted, shall be carried where it can best be seen, not less than 2 metres vertically apart from the masthead light.

13. *Approval*

The construction of lights and shapes and the installation of lights on board the vessel shall be to the satisfaction of the appropriate authority of the State whose flag the vessel is entitled to fly.

ANNEX II
ADDITIONAL SIGNALS FOR FISHING VESSELS FISHING IN CLOSE PROXIMITY

1. *General*

The lights mentioned herein shall, if exhibited in pursuance of Rule 26 (d), be placed where they can best be seen. They shall be at least 0.9 metre apart but at a lower level than lights prescribed in Rule 26(b)(i) and (c)(i). The lights shall be visible all round the horizon at a distance of at least 1 mile but at a lesser distance than the lights prescribed by these Rules for fishing vessels.

2. *Signals for Trawlers*

(a) Vessels when engaged in trawling, whether using demersal or pelagic gear, may exhibit:

   (i) when shooting their nets:

   two white lights in a vertical line;

   (ii) when hauling their nets:

   one white light over one red light in a vertical line;

   (iii) when the net has come fast upon an obstruction:

   two red lights in a vertical line.

(b) Each vessel engaged in pair trawling may exhibit:

   (i) by night, a searchlight directed forward and in the direction of the other vessel of the pair;

   (ii) when shooting or hauling their nets or when their nets have come fast upon an obstruction, the lights prescribed in 2(a) above.

3. *Signals for Purse Seiners*

Vessels engaged in fishing with purse seine gear may exhibit two yellow lights in a vertical line. These lights shall flash alternately every second and with equal light and occultation duration. These lights may be exhibited only when the vessel is hampered by its fishing gear.

ANNEX III

TECHNICAL DETAILS OF SOUND SIGNAL APPLIANCES

1. Whistles

(a) Frequencies and Range of Audibility

The fundamental frequency of the signal shall lie within the range 70-700 Hz.

The range of audibility of the signal from a whistle shall be determined by those frequencies, which may include the fundamental and/or one or more higher frequencies, which lie within the range 180-700 Hz (+/- 1 per cent) and which provide the sound pressure levels specified in paragraph I(c) below.

(b) Limits of Fundamental frequencies

To ensure a wide variety of whistle characteristics, the fundamental frequency of a whistle shall be between the following limits:

   (i)   70-200 Hz, for a vessel 200 metres or more in length

   (ii) 130-350 Hz, for a vessel 75 metres but less than 200 metres in length

   (iii) 250-700 Hz, for a vessel less than 75 metres in length.

(c) Sound Signal Intensity and Range of Audibility

A whistle fitted in a vessel shall provide, in the direction of maximum intensity of the whistle and at a distance of 1 metre from it, a sound pressure level in at least one 1/3rd octave band within the range of frequencies 180–700 Hz ($\pm$/- 1 per cent) of not less than the appropriate figure given in the table below.

Length of vessel in metres	$\frac{1}{3}$ rd octave band level at 1 metre in dB referred to 2×10^{5} N/m^2	Audibility range in nautical miles
200 or more	143	2
75 but less than 200	138	1.5
20 but less than 75	130	1
less than 20	120	0.5

The range of audibility in the table above is for information and is approximately the range at which a whistle may be heard on its forward axis with 90 per cent probability in conditions of still air on board a vessel having average background noise level at the listening posts (taken to be 68 dB in the octave band centred on 250 Hz and 63 dB in the octave band centred on 500 Hz).

In practice the range at which a whistle may be heard is extremely variable and depends critically on weather conditions; the values given can be regarded as typical but under conditions of strong wind or high ambient noise level at the listening post, the range may be much reduced.

(d) Directional Properties

The sound pressure level of a directional whistle shall not be more than 4 dB below the prescribed sound pressure level on the axis at any direction in the horizontal plane within +/- 45 degrees of the axis. The sound pressure level at any other direction in the horizontal plane shall be not more than 10 dB below the prescribed sound pressure level on the axis, so that the range in any direction will be at least half the range on the forward axis. The sound pressure level shall be measured in that prescribed 1/3rd octave band which determines the audibility range.

(e) Positioning of whistles

When a directional whistle is to be used as the only whistle on a vessel, it shall be installed with its maximum intensity directed straight ahead.

A whistle shall be placed as high as practicable on a vessel, in order to reduce interception of the emitted sound by obstructions and also to minimise hearing damage risk to personnel. The sound pressure level of the vessel's own signal at listening posts shall not exceed 110 dB (A) and so far as practicable should not exceed 100 dB (A)

5. Fitting of More Than One Whistle

If whistles are fitted at a distance apart of more than 100 metres, it shall be so arranged that they are not sounded simultaneously.

(g) Combined Whistle System

If, due to the presence of obstructions, the sound field of a single whistle or of one of the whistles referred to in paragraph I(f) above is likely to have a zone of greatly reduced signal level, it is recommended that a combined whistle system be fitted so as to overcome this reduction. For the purpose of the Rules a combined whistle system is to be regarded as a single whistle. The whistles of a combined system shall be located at a distance apart of not more than 100 metres and arranged to be sounded simultaneously. The frequency of any one whistle shall differ from those of the others by at least 10 Hz.

2. Bell or Gong

(a) Intensity of Signal

A bell or gong, or other device having similar sound characteristics shall produce a sound pressure level of not less that 110 dB at a distance of 1 metre from it.

(b) Construction

Bells and gongs shall be made of corrosion-resistant material and designed to give a clear tone. The diameter of the mouth of the bell shall be not less than 300 mm for vessels of 20 metres or more in length, and shall be not less than 200 mm for vessels of 12 metres or more but of less than 20 metres in length. Where practicable, a power-driven bell striker is recommended to ensure constant force but manual operation shall be possible. The mass of the striker shall be not less than 3 per cent of the mass of the bell.

3. Approval

The construction of sound signal appliances, their performance and their installation on board the vessel shall be to the satisfaction of the appropriate authority of the State whose flag the vessel is entitled to fly.

ANNEX IV

1. DISTRESS SIGNALS

1. The following signals, used or exhibited either together or separately, indicate distress and need of assistance:

(a) a gun or other explosive signal fired at intervals of about a minute

(b) a continuous sounding with any fog-signalling apparatus

(c) rockets or shells, throwing red stars fired one at a time at short intervals

(d) a signal made by radiotelegraphy or by any other signalling method consisting of the group . . . . - - - . . . (SOS) in the Morse Code

(e) a signal sent by radiotelephony consisting of the spoken word "Mayday"

(f) the international Code Signal of distress indicated by N.C.

(g) a signal consisting of a square flag having above or below it a ball or anything resembling a ball

(h) flames on the vessel (as from a burning tar barrel, oil barrel, etc.)

(i) a rocket parachute flare or a hand flare showing a red light

(j) a smoke signal giving off orange-coloured smoke

(k) slowly and repeatedly raising and lowering arms outstretched to each side

(l) the radiotelegraph alarm signal

(m) the radiotelephone alarm signal

(n) signals transmitted by emergency position-indicating radio beacons;

(o) approved signals transmitted by radio-communication systems.

2. The use or exhibition of any of the foregoing signals except for the purpose of indicating distress and need of assistance and the use of other signals which may be confused with any of the above signals is prohibited.

3. Attention is drawn to the relevant sections of the International Code of Signals, the Merchant Ship Search and Rescue Manual and the following signals:

(a) a piece of orange-coloured canvas with either a black square and circle or other appropriate symbol (for identification from the air)

(b) a dye marker.

2. DISTRESS PROCEDURES

(a) Distress by Radio

By Wireless Telegraph on 500 Hz (600 m)

Distress Call

SOS SOS SOS de GSWR (made three times).

(from Callsign)

By Radio Telephone on 2182 KHz

Distress Call - Mayday Mayday Mayday this is Seacat (callsign or name) (repeated 3 times)

The frequencies shown are the International Distress Frequencies in the Marine M/F bands but the initial distress call and message, when time is an essential factor, can be made first on whatever working frequency is used. You then switch to the International distress frequency.

A distress call must always be followed by a full distress message giving your call sign and position. The nature of distress is to be added if time is available.

All vessels hearing a distress call being made must stop transmitting on that frequency to listen out.

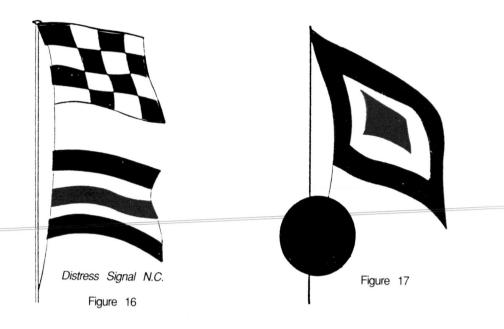

Distress Signal N.C.

Figure 16

Figure 17

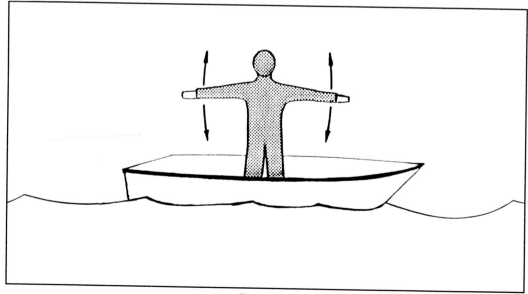

Figure 18

A distress call and message may be sent only on the authority of the master or a person responsible for the safety of a vessel.

(b) SOS or XXX

MAYDAY or PAN-PAN

DISTRESS OR URGENCY

(Reproduced with permission from the "Australian Coastal Surveillance Centre", Canberra).

A question often asked is what is the difference between MAYDAY and PAN-PAN, under what circumstances should one or other be used. Well we will try and answer this one briefly. In both cases we will assume that a risk to life exists, but the key to the answer is whether the ship is in serious and imminent danger.

If it is now then make a mayday call; if it is later then make it a pan-pan call. Perhaps a couple of examples will assist:

(a) You are drifting helplessly in bad weather a couple of miles off a rocky lee shore .... MAYDAY.

(b) You are drifting helplessly in bad weather about 20 miles off a rocky lee shore......... PAN-PAN.

In other words are you going to be dashed on the rocks within the hour or in about ten hours time? NOW or LATER

In many cases brought to our attention the circumstances did not warrant the use of either mayday or pan-pan; a routine call would have been sufficient. For example, the skipper of a craft which has broken down in good weather in a sheltered area should seriously consider making a routine call for assistance and anchoring if necessary, and not immediately start calling mayday. Don't forget that a mayday call indicates that you are threatened by grave and imminent danger and the scenario above hardly meets this criteria.

QUESTIONS AND ANSWERS ON THE INTERNATIONAL REGULATIONS FOR PREVENTING COLLISIONS AT SEA

General Definitions from Rule 3

Define the following terms.

Vessel	A vessel includes every description of water craft, including non-displacement craft and seaplanes, used or capable of being used as a means of transportation on water.
Power driven	Means any vessel propelled by machinery.
Engaged in fishing	Means any vessel fishing with nets, lines, trawls or other fishing apparatus which restrict manoeuvrability, but does not include a vessel fishing with trolling lines or other fishing apparatus which do not restrict manoeuvrability.
Vessel not under command	Means a vessel which through some exceptional circumstance is unable to manoeuvre as required by these Rules and is therefore unable to keep out of the way of another vessel.
Vessel restricted in her ability to manoeuvre	Means a vessel which from the nature of her work is restricted in her ability to manoeuvre as required by these Rules and is therefore unable to keep out of the way of another vessel.
Vessel constrained by her draught	Means a power-driven vessel which because of her draught in relation to the available depth of water is severely restricted in her ability to deviate from the course she is following.
Underway	Means that a vessel is not at anchor, or made fast to the shore, or aground.
Length, and breadth of a vessel	Means her length over all and greatest breadth.
In sight of one another	Vessels shall be deemed to be in sight of one another only when one can be observed visually from the other.
Restricted visibility	Means any condition in which visibility is restricted by fog, mist, falling snow, heavy rainstorms, sandstorms or any other similar causes.

Definitions from Rule 21 - Lights

Masthead light	Means a white light placed over the fore and aft centreline of the vessel showing an unbroken light over an arc of the horizon of 225 degrees and so fixed as to show the light from right ahead to 22.5 degrees abaft the beam on either side of the vessel.
Sidelights	Means a green light on the starboard side and a red light on the port side each showing an unbroken light over an arc of the horizon of 112.5 degrees and so fixed as to show the light from right ahead to 22.5 degrees abaft the beam on its respective side. In a vessel of less than 20 metres in length the sidelights may be combined in one lantern carried on the fore and aft centreline of the vessel.
Sternlight	Means a white light placed as nearly as practicable at the stern showing an unbroken light over an arc of the horizon of 135 degrees and so fixed as to show the light 67.5 degrees from right aft on each side of the vessel.
Towing light	Means a yellow light placed in a vertical line above the stern light showing an unbroken light over an arc of 135 degrees and so fixed

as to show the light 67.5 degrees from right aft on each side of the vessel. It is prescribed only for a vessel engaged in towing another vessel from the stern.

All round light	Means a light showing an unbroken light over an arc of the horizon of 360 degrees.
Flashing light	Means a light flashing at regular intervals at a frequency of 120 flashes or more per minute.
Manoeuvring light	Means an all round white light placed in the same fore and aft vertical plane as the masthead light or lights and where practicable at a minimum height of 2 metres vertically above the forward masthead light, provided that it shall be carried not less than 2 metres vertically above or below the after masthead light. On a vessel where only one masthead light is carried the manoeuvring light, if fitted, shall be carried where it can best be seen, not less than 2 metres vertically apart from the masthead light.

Definitions from Rule 32 – Sound Signals

Whistle	Means any sound signalling appliance capable of producing the prescribed blasts and which complies with the specifications in that the fundamental frequency of the signal shall lie within the range 70–700 Hz, giving an audibility range of 0.5 to 2 nautical miles.
Short blast	Means a blast of about one second's duration.
Prolonged blast	Means a blast of from four to six second's duration.

Responsibility from Rule 2

Nothing in these Rules shall exonerate any vessel, or the owner, master or crew, thereof, from the consequences of any neglect to comply with these Rules or of the neglect of any ordinary practice of seamen, or by the special circumstances of the case.

Look-out

Q.1 What is the obligation of every vessel underway maintaining a lookout?

A. from Rule 5

Every vessel shall at all times maintain a proper lookout by sight and hearing, as well as by all available means appropriate in the prevailing circumstances and conditions, so as to make a full appraisal of the situation and of the risk of collision.

Safe Speed

Q.2 What due regard must a vessel have with reference to speed?

A. from Rule 6

Every vessel shall at all times proceed at a safe speed so that she can take proper and effective action to avoid collision and be stopped within a distance appropriate to the prevailing circumstances and conditions.

Risk of Collision

Q.3 In determining risk of collision what considerations shall be among those taken into account?

A. from Rule 7

(a) Such risk shall be deemed to exist if the compass bearing of an approaching vessel does not appreciably change.

(b) Such risk may sometimes exist even when an appreciable bearing change is evident, particularly when approaching a very large vessel, or a tow, or when approaching a vessel at close range.

Action to Avoid Collision

Q.4 What considerations should be considered in the action to avoid collision?

A. from Rule 8

Any action taken to avoid collision shall
— be positive; made in ample time with due regard to good seamanship.

Be large enough, in course alteration, to be apparent visually or by radar.

Be effective enough to prevent a close quarters situation until the other vessel is finally passed and clear.

Allow more time to assess the situation by slackening her speed, stopping or reversing.

Take early action to allow sufficient sea room for the safe passage of the other vessel.

Narrow Channels

Q.5 What is the rule for proceeding along the course of a narrow channel or fairway?

A. from Rule 9

The vessel shall keep as near to the outer limit of the channel or fairway which lies on her starboard side as is safe and practicable.

Q.6 What vessels shall not impede the passage of a vessel which can navigate only within a narrow channel or fairway safely?

A.   (a) A vessel of less than 20 metres (65 feet) in length.

(b) A sailing vessel.

(c) A vessel engaged in fishing.

(d) A vessel crossing the channel or fairway.

Traffic Separation Schemes

Q.7 What is the rule for a vessel using a traffic separation scheme?

A. from Rule 10

The vessel shall-

(a) Proceed in the appropriate traffic lane in the general direction of traffic flow for that lane.

(b) So far as practicable keep clear of a traffic separation line or separation zone.

(c) Normally join or leave a traffic lane at the termination of the lane, but when joining or leaving from the side shall do so at as small an angle to the general direction of traffic flow as practicable.

Sailing Vessels

Q.8 Study diagram of four sailing vessels A,B,C & D.

What action should vessel "A" take?

A. from Rule 12

Vessel A should keep clear of vessels B,C & D.

Q.9 Study diagram of four sailing vessels A,B,C & D. What action should vessel B take?

A. from Rule 12

Vessel B should keep clear of vessel C and stand on for vessels A & D.

Q.10 Study diagram of four sailing vessels A,B,C & D. What action should vessel C take?

A. from Rule 12

Vessel C stands on for A,B & D.

Q.11 Study diagram of four sailing vessels A,B,C & D. What action should vessel D take?

A. from Rule 12

Vessel D keeps clear of B & C and stands on for A.

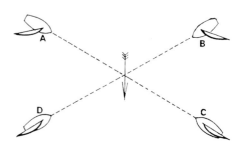

Figure 19 – *Sailing vessels in a crossing*

Overtaking

Q.12 What is the rule for overtaking vessels?

A. from Rule 13

Notwithstanding anything contained in the Rules of the conduct of vessels in sight of one another, any vessel overtaking any other shall keep out of the way of the vessel being overtaken.

Q.13 When is a vessel deemed to be overtaking another?

A.   A vessel shall be deemed to be overtaking when coming up with another vessel from a direction more than 22.5 degrees abaft her beam, that is, in such a position with reference to the vessel she is overtaking, that at night she would be able to see only the sternlight of that vessel but neither of her sidelights.

Q.14 Should a vessel be in doubt as to whether she is an overtaking vessel, how should she act?

A. She shall assume she is an overtaking vessel and act accordingly.

Head-on Situation

Q.15 What is the rule to be observed when two vessels are meeting head-on?

A. from Rule 14

When two power driven vessels are meeting on reciprocal courses so as to involve risk of collision each shall alter her course to starboard so that each shall pass on the port side of the other.

Crossing Situation

Q.16 When shall a situation of vessels meeting head-on deem to exist?

A. from Rule 15

When a vessel sees the other ahead or nearly ahead-and by night she could see the masthead lights of the other in a line or nearly in a line and/or both sidelights and by day she observes the corresponding aspect of the other vessel.

Q.17 What is the rule for a crossing situation?

A. When two power driven vessels are crossing so as to involve risk of collision, the vessel which has the other on her own starboard side shall keep out of the way and shall, if the circumstances of the case admit, avoid crossing ahead of the other vessel.

Action by Give-way Vessel

Q.18 What action shall be taken by a vessel giving-way

A. from Rule 16

Every vessel which is directed by these Rules to keep out of the way of another vessel shall, so far as possible, take early and substantial action to keep well clear.

Action by Stand-on Vessel

Q 19 What action shall be taken by a vessel standing-on?

A. from Rule 17

(a) Where by any of these Rules one of two vessels is to keep out of the way the other shall keep her course and speed.

(b) The latter vessel may however take action to avoid collision by her manoeuvre alone, as soon as it becomes apparent to her that the vessel required to keep out of the way is not taking appropriate action in compliance with these Rules.

Q.20 What should a power driven vessel, which takes action in a crossing situation, have due regard for?

A. If the circumstances of the case admit, she should not alter course to port for a vessel on her own port side.

Responsibilities between Vessels

Q.21 From what vessels shall a power driven vessel underway clear?

A. from Rule 18

(a) A vessel not under command.

(b) A vessel restricted in her ability to manoeuvre.

(c) A vessel engaged in fishing.

(d) A sailing vessel.

Q.22 From what vessels shall a sailing vessel underway keep clear?

A. (a) A vessel not under command.

(b) A vessel restricted in her ability to manoeuvre.

(c) A vessel engaged in fishing.

Q.23 From what vessels shall a vessel engaged in fishing when underway keep clear?

A. (a) A vessel not under command.

(b) A vessel restricted in her ability to manoeuvre.

Q.24 What vessels, if the circumstances of the case admit, should avoid impeding the safe passage of a vessel constrained by her draught, exhibiting by night three all round red lights in a vertical line or a black cylinder by day.

A. Any vessel other than a vessel not under command or a vessel restricted in her ability to manoeuvre.

Conduct of Vessels in Restricted Visibility

Q.25 What are the rules for the conduct of vessels in restricted visibility?

A. from Rule 19

(a) Every vessel shall proceed at a safe speed adapted to the prevailing circumstances and conditions of restricted visibility.

(b) A power driven vessel shall have her engines ready for immediate manoeuvre.

(c) A vessel which detects by radar alone the presence of another vessel shall determine if a close-quarters situation is developing and/ or risk of collision exists.

(d) She shall take avoiding action in ample time.

(e) An alteration of course to port for a vessel forward of the beam, other than for a vessel being overtaken, shall be avoided.

(f) An alteration of course towards a vessel abeam or abaft the beam shall be avoided.

(g) Every vessel which hears apparently forward of her beam the fog signal of another vessel shall reduce her speed to the minimum at which she can be kept on her course.

(h) Every vessel shall if necessary take all her way off and in any event navigate with extreme caution until danger of collision is over.

Application

Q.26 When do the rules concerning lights apply?

A. from Rule 20

The rules concerning lights as specified shall be complied with from sunset to sunrise in all weathers, restricted visibility and may be exhibited in all other circumstances when it is deemed necessary. During such times no other lights shall be exhibited, except such lights as cannot be mistaken for the lights specified in these rules or do not impair their visibility or distinctive character, or interfere with the keeping of a proper lookout.

Q.27 When do the rules concerning shapes apply?

A. The rules concerning shapes as specified shall be complied with by day.

Q.28 What are the minimum ranges for lights to be visible in the following vessels?

A. In vessels of 50 metres (164 feet) or more in length.

A masthead light, 6 miles.
A sidelight, 3 miles.
A sternlight, 3 miles.
A towing light, 3 miles.
A white, red, green or yellow all-round light, 3 miles.

In vessels of 20 metres (66 feet) or more in length but less than 50 metres (164 feet) in length.

A masthead light, 5 miles.
A sidelight, 2 miles.
A sternlight, 2 miles.
A towing light, 2 miles.
A white, red, green or yellow all-round light, 2 miles.

In vessels of 12 metres (40 feet) or more in length but less than 20 metres (66 feet) in length.

A masthead light, 3 miles.
A sidelight, 2 miles.
A sternlight, 2 miles.
A towing light, 2 miles.
A white, red, green or yellow all-round light, 2 miles.

In vessels of less than 12 metres (40 feet) in length.

A masthead light, 2 miles.
A sidelight, 1 mile.
A sternlight, 2 miles.
A towing light, 2 miles.
A white, red, green or yellow all-round light, 2 miles.

Power-driven vessels underway

Q.29 What lights shall a power-driven vessel underway exhibit?

A. from Rule 23

(a) A masthead light forward.

(b) A second masthead light abaft of and higher than the forward one; except that a vessel of less than 50 metres (164 feet) in length shall not be obliged to exhibit such light but may do so.

(c) Sidelights (Vessels under 20m may exhibit a combined lantern).

(d) A sternlight.

Q.30 What lights shall an air cushion vessel when operating in the non-displacement mode exhibit?

A. (a) A masthead light forward.
    (b) A second masthead light abaft of and higher than the forward one; except that a vessel of less than 50 metres (164 feet) in length shall not be obliged to exhibit such light but may do so.
    (c) Sidelights.
    (d) A sternlight.
    (e) An all-round flashing yellow light.

Q.31 What lights shall a power-driven vessel of less than 7 metres (23 feet) in length and whose maximum speed does not exceed 7 knots exhibit?

A. In lieu of the normal navigation lights she may exhibit an all-round white light, and if practicable, sidelights.

Towing and Pushing

Q.32 What lights shall a power-driven vessel when towing from the stern exhibit?

A from Rule 24
    (a) Two masthead lights forward in a vertical line.
    (b) Sidelights.
    (c) A sternlight.
    (d) A towing light in a vertical line above the sternlight.

Note: Three masthead lights forward in a vertical line when the length of tow, measuring from the stern of the towing vessel to the after end of the tow, exceeds 200 metres (600 feet), and a diamond shape where it can best be seen.

Q.33 What lights shall a pushing vessel and a vessel being pushed ahead when rigidly connected in a composite unit exhibit?

A. (a) A masthead light forward.
    (b) Sidelights.
    (c) A sternlight.

Note: If the composite unit is more than 50 metres (164 feet) in length a second masthead light abaft of and higher than the forward one must be exhibited.

Q.34 What lights shall a power-driven vessel when pushing ahead or towing alongside, except in the case of a composite unit, exhibit?

A. (a) Two masthead lights forward in a vertical line.
    (b) Sidelights.
    (c) A sternlight.

Note: If the power-driven vessel is more than 50 metres (164 feet) in length a second masthead light abaft of and higher than the forward one must be exhibited.

Q.35 What lights shall a vessel or object being towed exhibit?

A. (a) Sidelights.
    (b) A sternlight.
    (c) When the length of the tow exceeds 200 metres (600 feet), a diamond shape where it can best be seen.

Q.36 What lights shall a vessel being towed alongside exhibit?

A. (a) A sternlight.
    (b) At the forward end, sidelights.

Note: When two or more vessels are towed on the one side of the power-driven vessel the outer one shall carry the sternlight.

Q.37 What lights shall a vessel pushed ahead, not being part of a composite unit, exhibit?

A. At the forward end, sidelights.

Sailing Vessels underway and Vessels under Oars

Q.38 What lights shall a sailing vessel underway exhibit?

A. from Rule 25
    (a) Sidelights.
    (b) Sternlights.

Q.39 What lights may a sailing vessel of less than 20 metres exhibit?

A. The lights prescribed for a sailing vessel may be combined in one lantern carried at or near the top of the mast, where it can best be seen.

Q.40 What lights may a sailing vessel when underway, in addition to the prescribed lights, exhibit?

A. At or near the top of the mast, where they can best be seen, two all-round lights in a vertical line, the upper being red and the lower green, but these lights shall not be exhibited in conjunction with the combined lantern.

Q.41 What lights shall a sailing vessel less than 7 metres (23 feet) exhibit?

A. If practicable, exhibit the lights prescribed for a sailing vessel, but if she does not she shall have ready at hand an electric torch or lighted lantern showing a white light which shall be exhibited in sufficient time to prevent collision.

Q.42 What lights shall a vessel under oars exhibit?

A. She may exhibit the lights prescribed for sailing vessels, but if she does not she shall have ready at hand an electric torch or lighted lantern showing a white light which shall be exhibited in sufficient time to prevent collision.

Q.43 What signal shall a vessel when proceeding under sail exhibit to indicate that she is also being propelled by machinery.

A. A conical shape, apex downwards, where it can best be seen.

Fishing Vessels

Q.44 What signals are exhibited by a vessel when engaged in trawling?

A. from Rule 26

A vessel when engaged in trawling, by which is meant the dragging through the water of a dredge net or other apparatus used as a fishing appliance, shall exhibit:-

(a) Two all-round lights in a vertical line, the upper being green and the lower white, or a shape consisting of two cones with their apexes together in a vertical line one above the other; a vessel of less than 20 metres (66 feet) in length may instead of this shape exhibit a basket.

(b) A masthead light abaft of and higher than the all-round green light; a vessel of less than 50 metres (164 feet) in length shall not be obliged to exhibit such a light but may do so.

(c) When making way through the water, in addition to the lights prescribed in this paragraph, sidelights and a sternlight.

Q.45 What signals are exhibited by a vessel engaged in fishing, other than trawling?

A. (a) Two all-round lights in a vertical line, the upper being red and the lower white, (but no masthead light) or a shape consisting of two cones with apexes together in a vertical line one above the other.

Note: A vessel of less than 20 metres (66 feet) in length may in lieu of the two cones with apexes together exhibit a fishing basket.

(b) When there is outlying gear extending more than 150 metres (500 feet) horizontally from the vessel, an all-round white light or a cone apex upwards in the direction of the gear.

(c) When making way through the water, in addition to the lights prescribed in this paragraph, exhibit sidelights and a sternlight.

Note: The following are signals for fishing vessels fishing in close proximity and are additional to the navigation requirement. They shall be at least 0.9 metres apart but at a lower level than the prescribed lights. The light shall be all-round lights visible for at least 1 mile but less than the prescribed lights.

Q.46 What signals would a trawler exhibit in addition to her characteristic lights to indicate she was shooting her nets?

A. By day: The international code flag signal 'Z'

By night: Two all-round white lights in a vertical line.

By sound: The letter 'Z' in morse code, i.e. two prolonged blasts, followed by two short blasts.

Q.47 What signals would a trawler exhibit in addition to her characteristic lights to indicate she was hauling her nets?

A. By day: The international code flag signal 'G'.

By night: An all-round white over an all-round red light in a vertical line.

By sound: The letter 'G' in morse code, i.e. two Prolonged blasts, followed by one short blast.

Q.48 What signals would a trawler exhibit in addition to her characteristic light, to indicate her nets had become fast upon an obstruction?

A. By day: The international code flag signal 'P'.

By night: Two all-round red lights in a vertical line.

By sound: The letter 'P' in morse code, i.e. one short blast, followed by two prolonged blasts, followed by one short blast.

Q.49 What signal may each vessel exhibit when engaged in pair trawling?

A. By day:The international code flag signal 'T'

By night: A searchlight directed forward and in the direction of the other vessel of the pair.

Note:When shooting or hauling their nets or when their nets have come fast upon an obstruction, the lights prescribed for these signals may be exhibited.

Q.50 What signal may be exhibited for vessels when engaged in fishing with purse seine gear?

A. She may exhibit two yellow lights in a vertical line. These lights shall flash alternately every second and with equal light and occultation duration.

Note: These lights may be exhibited only when the vessel is hampered by its fishing gear.

Vessels not under Command or Restricted in their Ability to Manoeuvre

Q.51 What signals would a vessel not under command exhibit?

A. from Rule 27

By day: Two balls or similar shapes in a vertical line where they can best be seen.

By night: Two all-round red lights in a vertical line where they can best be seen.

Note: When making way through the water, in addition to the lights prescribed in this paragraph, exhibit sidelights and a sternlight.

Q.52 What signals would a vessel restricted in her ability to manoeuvre, except a vessel engaged in minesweeping operations, exhibit?

A. By day: Three shapes in a vertical line where they can best be seen. The highest and lowest of these shapes shall be balls and the middle one a diamond.

By night: Three all-round lights in a vertical line where they can best be

seen. The highest and lowest of these lights shall be red and the middle light shall be white.

Note: When making way through the water, masthead lights, sidelights and a sternlight, in addition shall be exhibited.

When at anchor, the anchor signals applicable for the vessel, in addition shall be exhibited.

Q.53 What signals would a vessel engaged in a towing operation, such as renders her unable to deviate from her course, exhibit?

A. In addition to the lights or shapes prescribed for a vessel restricted in her ability to manoeuvre, the lights and shapes applicable to the vessel's towing operation.

Q.54 What signals would a vessel engaged in dredging or underwater operations, when restricted in her ability to manoeuvre, exhibit?

A. By day: Three shapes in a vertical line where they can best be seen. The highest and lowest of these shapes shall be balls and the middle one a diamond. In addition when an obstruction exists two balls in a vertical line to indicate the side on which the obstruction exists, and two diamonds in a vertical line to indicate the side on which another vessel may pass.

By night: Three all-round lights in a vertical line where they can best be seen. The highest and lowest of these lights shall be red and the middle light shall be white. In addition when an obstruction exists two all- round red lights in a vertical line to indicate the side on which the obstruction exists, and two all-round green lights in a vertical line to indicate the side on which another vessel may pass.

Note: When making way through the water, in addition to the lights prescribed, masthead lights, sidelights and a sternlight, in addition shall be exhibited.

When at anchor she shall exhibit the lights or shapes prescribed for an obstruction, instead of those for at anchor.

Q.55 What signal would be made by a vessel engaged in diving operations where size makes it impracticable to

exhibit the lights or shapes prescribed for the operation?

A. A rigid replica of the international code flag 'A' not less than 1 metre in height, shall be exhibited. Measures shall be taken to ensure all-round visibility.

Q.56 What signal would a vessel engaged in minesweeping exhibit?

A. In addition to the navigation lights, i.e. masthead lights, sidelights and a sternlight, three all-round green lights or three balls. One of these lights or shapes shall be exhibited at or near the foremast head and one at each end of the fore yard. These lights or shapes indicate that it is dangerous for another vessel to approach closer than 1,000 metres astern or 500 metres on either side of the minesweeper.

Q.57 What vessels are exempt from exhibiting the lights prescribed for minesweeping vessels not under command or restricted in their ability to manoeuvre?

A. Vessels of less than 7 metres in length.

Vessels constrained by their Draught

Q.58 What signals would a vessel constrained by her draught exhibit?

A. from Rule 28

A vessel constrained by her draught may, in addition to the masthead lights, sidelights and sternlight, exhibit where they can best be seen three all-round red lights in a vertical line, or a cylinder.

Pilot Vessels

Q.59 What signals would a pilot vessel on duty exhibit?

A. from Rule 29

At or near the masthead, two all-round lights in a vertical line, the upper being white and the lower red.

Note: When underway, in addition, she shall exhibit sidelights and a sternlight. When at anchor, in addition, she shall exhibit the anchor light, lights or shape.

Anchored Vessels and Vessels aground

Q.60 What signals would a vessel at anchor exhibit?

A. from Rule 30

By day: In the fore part, one ball where it can best be seen.

By night: In the fore part, an all-round white light where it can best be seen and, in addition, at or near the stern at a lower level an all-round white light.

Note: A vessel of less than 50 metres in length may exhibit an all-round white light where it can best be seen, instead of the lights prescribed.

A vessel at anchor may, but a vessel of 100 metres and more in length shall, also use the available working or equivalent lights to illuminate her decks.

Q.61 What signals would a vessel aground exhibit?

A. By day: Three balls in a vertical line.

By night: In addition to the prescribed anchor lights two all-round red lights in a vertical line.

Equipment for Sound Signals

Q.62 What equipment for sound signals are vessels required to carry?

A. from Rule 33

Vessels less than 12 metres in length shall be provided with some means of making an efficient sound signal.

A vessel of 12 metres or more in length shall be provided with a whistle and a bell.

A vessel of 100 metres or more in length shall be provided with a whistle, a bell and a gong, the tone and sound of which cannot be confused with that of the bell.

Note: The bell or gong or both may be replaced by other equipment having the same respective sound characteristics, provided that manual sounding of the required signals shall always be possible.

Manoeuvring and Warning Signals

Q.63 Describe the manoeuvring signals for vessels in sight of one another and underway.

A. from Rule 34

One short blast to mean 'I am altering my course to starboard'.

Two short blasts to mean 'I am altering my course to port'.

Three short blasts to mean 'I am operating astern propulsion'.

Two prolonged blasts followed by one short blast to mean 'I intend to overtake you on your starboard side'.

Two prolonged blasts followed by two short blasts to mean 'I intend to overtake you on your port side'.

One prolonged, one short, one prolonged and one short blast, in that order, to mean 'I agree to be overtaken'.

At least five short and rapid blasts to mean 'I am in doubt whether sufficient action is being taken to avoid collision'.

One prolonged blast to mean that 'a vessel is nearing a bend or an area of a channel, or fairway where other vessels may be obscured by an intervening obstruction'. Also to be an answer by any approaching vessel that may be within hearing, around the bend or behind the intervening obstruction.

Sound Signals in restricted Visibility

Q.64 Describe the sound signals in restricted visibility.

A. from Rule 35

In or near an area of restricted visibility, whether by day or night, the signals prescribed in this Rule shall be used as follows:-

(a) A power-driven vessel making way through the water shall sound at intervals of not more than 2 minutes one prolonged blast.

(b) A power driven vessel underway, but stopped and making no way through the water, shall sound at intervals of not more than 2 minutes two prolonged blasts in succession with an interval of about 2 seconds between them.

(c) A vessel not under command, restricted in her ability to manoeuvre, constrained by her draught, engaged in fishing, engaged in towing or pushing another vessel, or a sailing vessel shall sound at intervals of not more than 2 minutes three blasts in succession, namely one prolonged followed by two short blasts.

(d) A vessel towed or if more than one vessel is towed the last vessel of the tow, if manned, shall at intervals of not more than 2 minutes sound four blasts in succession, namely one prolonged followed by three short blasts.

Note: When practicable, this signal shall be made immediately after the signal made by the towing vessel.

When a pushing vessel and a vessel being pushed ahead are rigidly connected in a composite unit they shall be regarded as a power-driven vessel.

(e) A vessel at anchor shall at intervals of not more than one minute ring the bell rapidly for about 5 seconds. In a vessel of 100 metres or more in length the bell shall be sounded in the forepart of the vessel and immediately after the ringing of the bell the gong shall be sounded rapidly for about 5 seconds in the after part of the vessel. A vessel at anchor may in addition sound three blasts in succession, namely one short, one prolonged and one short blast, to give warning of her position and of the possibility of collision to an approaching vessel.

(f) A vessel aground shall give the bell signal and if required the gong signal. In addition give three separate and distinct strokes on the bell immediately before and after the rapid ringing of the bell. A vessel aground may in addition sound an appropriate whistle signal. An example of such a signal would be the letter 'U' one short blast, followed by one short blast, followed by one prolonged blast. The meaning of this signal is 'you are standing into danger'. Any such appropriate signal may be given, as long as it cannot be confused with those of the Regulation.

Q.65 What signals would a vessel of less than 12 metres in length sound if in restricted visibility?

A. The vessel shall not be obliged to give the appropriate signals but, if she does not, shall make some other efficient sound signal at intervals of not more than 2 minutes.

Q.66 What signal distinguishes a pilot vessel on duty by way of sound in restricted visibility?

A. A pilot vessel on duty may in addition to the signals prescribed sound an identity signal consisting of four short blasts.

Signals to attract Attention

Q.67 What signals are used to attract attention?

A. from Rule 36

If necessary to attract the attention of another vessel any vessel may make light or sound signals that cannot be mistaken for any signal authorised elsewhere in these Rules, or may direct the beam of her searchlight in the direction of the danger, in such a way as not to embarrass any vessel.

Q.68 Define the term 'height above the hull'.

A. The term 'height above the hull' means height above the uppermost continuous deck.

Q.69 How are screens for sidelights fitted?

A. The sidelights shall be fitted with inboard screens painted matt black. Sidelights as fitted on the vessel must show the minimum required intensities in the forward direction. The intensities must decrease to reach practical cut-off between 1 degree and 3 degrees outside the prescribed sectors.

Q.70 Where should a whistle be positioned on a vessel?

A. A whistle shall be placed as high as practicable with its maximum intensity directed straight ahead.

Distress Signals

Q.71 Describe the distress signals?

A. from Rule 37

(a) A gun or other explosive signal fired at intervals of about a minute.

(b) A continuous sounding with any fog signalling apparatus.

(c) Rockets or shells, throwing red stars fired one at a time at short intervals.

(d) A signal made by radiotelegraphy or by any other signalling method consisting of the group . . . . - - . . . (SOS) in the morse code.

(e) A signal sent by radiotelephony consisting of the spoken word "Mayday".

(f) The international Code Signal of distress indicated by N.C.

(g) A signal consisting of a square flag having above or below it a ball or anything resembling a ball.

(h) Flames on the vessel (as from a burning tar barrel, oil barrel, etc)

(i) A rocket parachute flare or a hand flare showing a red light.

(j) A smoke signal giving off orange coloured smoke.

(k) Slowly and repeatedly raising and lowering arms outstretched to each side.

(l) The radiotelegraph alarm signal.

(m) The radiotelephone alarm signal.

(n) Signals transmitted by emergency position indicating radio beacons.

(o) Approved signals transmitted by radiocommunication systems.

Positioning and Technical Details of Lights and Shapes

Q.72 Describe the positioning of a masthead light of a vessel under 12 metres in length?

A. from Annex I

The vessel may carry the uppermost light at a height of less than 2.5 metres above the gunwale. When however a masthead light is carried in addition to sidelights and a sternlight, then such masthead light shall be carried at least 1 metre higher than the sidelights.

Q.73 Describe the positioning of a masthead light of a vessel 12 metres but less than 20 metres in length.

A. The masthead light shall be placed at a height above the gunwale of not less than 2.5 metres.

Q.74 Describe the positioning of a masthead light on a power-driven vessel of 20 metres or more in length.

A. (a) The forward masthead light, or if only one masthead light is carried, then that light, at a height above the hull of not less than 6 metres, and, if the breadth of the vessel exceeds 6 metres, then at a height above the hull not less than such breadth, so however that the light need not be placed at a greater height above the hull than 12 metres.

(b) When two masthead lights are carried the after one shall be at least

4.5 metres vertically higher than the forward one.

Q.75 Describe the positioning of the masthead lights for a power-driven vessel when engaged in towing.

A. One of the two or three masthead lights shall be placed of a height above the hull of not less than 6 metres, and, if the breadth of the vessel exceeds 6 metres, then at a height above the hull not less than such breadth, so however that the light need not be placed at a greater height above the hull than 12 metres.

Q.76 What care should be exercised in the positioning of all masthead lights?

A. They shall be so placed as to be above and clear of all other lights and obstructions.

Q.77 Describe the positioning of sidelights on a power driven vessel.

A. They shall be placed at a height above the hull not greater than three quarters of that of the forward masthead light. They shall not be so low as to be interfered with by deck lights.

Q.78 Should the sidelights be in a combined lantern and carried on a power-driven vessel less than 20 metres in length, what is the vertical distance below the masthead light at which they should be placed?

A. One metre.

Q.79 When the Rule prescribes two or three lights to be carried in a vertical line, how shall they be spaced?

A. (a) On a vessel of 20 metres in length or more such lights shall be spaced not less than two metres apart, and the lowest of these lights shall, except where a towing light is required, not be less than four metres above the hull.

(b) On a vessel of less than 20 metres in length such lights shall be spaced not less than one metre apart and the lowest of these lights shall, except where a towing light is required, not be less than two metres above the gunwale.

Note: When three lights are carried they shall be equally spaced.

Q.80 At what height should the lower of the two all-round lights prescribed for a fishing vessel when engaged in fishing be carried above the sidelights?

A. Not less than twice the distance between the two vertical lights

Q.81 At what height should the forward anchor light be carried above the after one?

A. 4.5 metres.

Q.82 At what height above the hull should a vessel of 50 metre or more in length carry the forward anchor light?

A. Not less than 6 metres.

Q.83 What is the diameter of a ball?

A. Not less than 0.6 metres.

Q.84 Describe the horizontal positioning and spacing of lights.

A. (a) When two masthead lights are prescribed for a power-driven vessel, the horizontal distance between them shall not be less than one half of the length of the vessel but need not be more than 100 metres. The forward light shall be placed not more than one quarter of the length of the vessel from the stem.

(b) On a vessel of 20 metres or more in length the sidelights shall not be placed in front of the forward masthead lights. They shall be placed at or near the side of the vessel.

Q.85 Describe the details of location of direction indicating lights for fishing vessels.

A. The light indicating the direction of the outlying gear from a vessel engaged in fishing shall be placed at a horizontal distance of not less than 2 metres and not more than 6 metres away from the two all-round red and white lights. This light shall be placed not higher than the all-round white light and not lower than the sidelights.

Q.86 Describe the details of location of direction-indicating lights for dredgers and vessels engaged in underwater operations.

A. The lights and shapes on a vessel engaged in dredging or underwater operations to indicate the obstructed side and/or the side on which it is safe to pass shall be placed at the maximum practical horizontal distance, but in no case less than two metres, from the lights or shapes indicating a vessel not under command or restricted in her ability to manoeuvre. In no case shall the upper of these lights or shapes be at a greater height than the lower of the three lights or shapes.

Q.87 What is the colour of all shapes?

A. Black.

Q.88 What is the size of a cone?

A. A cone shall have a base diameter of not less than 0.6 metre and a height equal to its diameter.

Q.89 What is the size of a cylinder?

A. A cylinder shall have a diameter of at least 0.6 metre and a height of twice its diameter.

Q.90 What is the size of a diamond shape?

A. A diamond shape shall consist of two cones having a common base.

The horizontal spacing of the diamond points to be 0.6 metres and the vertical spacing between points to be 1.2 metres.

Q.91 What is the vertical distance between shapes?

A. At least 1.5 metres.

Q.92 What allowance is made in the size of shapes for vessels of less than 20 metres in length?

A. Shapes of less dimensions but commensurate with the size of the vessel may be used and the distance apart may be correspondingly reduced.

Q.93 Describe the positioning and spacing of a manoeuvring light?

A. It shall be placed in the same fore and aft vertical plane as the masthead light or lights and, where practicable, at a minimum height of two metres vertically above the forward masthead light, provided that it shall be carried not less than two metres vertically above or below the after masthead light. On a vessel where only one masthead light is carried the manoeuvring light, if fitted, shall be carried where it can best be seen, not less than two metres vertically apart from the masthead light.

DEFINITIONS

"**Board**" – The Marine Board of Queensland continued by or constituted under this Act.

"**Shipping Inspector**" – Any person for the time being to be appointed as shipping Inspector under and for the purposes of this Act; The term includes any person for the time being appointed to act in that capacity or to perform any of the duties of a shipping Inspector.

"**Surveyor**" – Any person for the time being appointed or deemed to be appointed, or recognised, to be a marine surveyor under the purposes of this Act: The term includes any person for the time being appointed to act in any such capacity or to perform any of the duties of any such person.

"**Master**" – In relation to any ship, any person (except a pilot) having command or charge for the time being of that ship.

"**Owner**" – In relation to any ship, includes the owner or part owner of the ship and any and every person for the time being responsible for the navigation and management of the ship; and, in all cases where the owner is a body corporate, includes both the manager and the secretary of the body corporate.

"**The jurisdiction**" – Queensland, including the territorial waters of Queensland and the Inland navigable waters of the State.

"**Vessel**" – Includes any ship, boat, and any other description of vessel used or designed for use for any purpose on the sea or in navigation: Without limiting the generality of the aforegoing, the term includes any dinghy, lighter, barge, punt, hulk, raft, houseboat, pontoon, seaplane, air cushion vehicle, or like vessel.

"**Commercial Vessel**" – A vessel which is not used solely for pleasure or recreation and the use of which is made, allowed or authorised in the course of any business or in connection with any commercial transaction and subject to any State legislation includes any Government vessel other than one under the control of the Minister for Reference.

"**Fishing Vessel**" – Any vessel equipped for or employed or intended to be employed in taking aquatic organisms for a commercial purpose: The term does not include a vessel employed primarily in transporting such organisms taken from another vessel or in processing such organisms or a vessel that is employed at any time in trade.

"**Boat**" — Every vessel not a ship as herein defined, which is used in navigation.

"**Equipment**" — Includes boats, tackle, pumps, apparel, furniture, life saving appliances of every description, spars, masts, rigging and sails, fog signals, lights, and signals of distress, medicines and medical and surgical stores and appliances, and every thing or article belonging to or to be used in connection with or necessary for the navigation and safety of the vessel, including apparatus for preventing or extinguishing fires, buckets, compasses, charts, axes, lanterns, and loading and discharging gear and apparatus of all kinds, and such other things as may be prescribed.

"**Go to sea**" or "**proceed to sea**" — Includes plying seaward beyond the limits of any port in the jurisdiction, and the getting under way or attempting to get under way for the purpose of going to sea: "sea-going" and "take to sea" and "send to sea" have corresponding meanings.

"**Machinery**" – Includes boilers, engines, and everything connected therewith employed in propelling any ship having mechanical means of propulsion, and every description of machinery used on a vessel for the purpose of the vessel or her cargo and all other apparatus or things attached to or connected therewith or used with reference to any engine or under the care of an engineer.

"**Casualty**" – Includes the loss, abandonment, collision, or grounding of, and any mishap, accident, injury, or damage, whether by fire or otherwise howsoever, to any ship.

"**Incompetent**" – Unable, from any cause whatever, to perform efficiently the duty of the person in relation to whom the term is used.

"**Misconduct**" – Includes reckless or careless navigation, drunkenness, tyranny, any failure of duty or want of skill, or any improper conduct.

"**Lighter**" – Includes any barge, hulk, or other vessel of a like nature possessing no independent motive power or means of propelling itself.

"**Passenger coaster**" – Any coaster that carries onboard or is certificated to carry on board more than six passengers.

"**Coaster**" – A sea-going ship employed in trading in the jurisdiction or going between ports in the jurisidiction: The term includes a sea-going ship employed in carrying passengers to sea and returning to the port of departure, or employed for charter or letting out for hire or reward.

"**Ship**" – Every vessel used in navigation not ordinarily propelled by oars only.

"**Speedboat**" – Means any motor boat or motor vessel powered by propulsion machinery of not less than 4.5kW brake power or 6 horse power and capable of a speed in excess of 10 knots and with a hull which is designed to be a planing or non-displacement hull.

MARITIME BUOYAGE SYSTEM "A"

INTRODUCTION

The introduction of Maritime Buoyage System "A" began in 1977 and its use has now spread throughout Europe, Australia, New Zealand, Africa, the Gulf and some Asian countries.

All states in Australia have agreed to adopt Maritime Buoyage System "A" and implementation of it is now virtually complete in this country. Changes to buoyage to comply with System "A" are notified in Notices to Mariners.

I.A.L.A. MARITIME BUOYAGE SYSTEM "A"

Q.1 What do the letters I.A.L.A. stand for.

A. International Association of Lighthouse, Authorities. The International Association of Lighthouse Authorities (IALA) is a non-governmental body which brings together representatives from the aids to navigation services of signatory countries in order to exchange information and recommend improvements to aids to navigation based on the latest technology.

(Note) IALA has decided that a single world-wide system of buoyage cannot be achieved at present, but considers that the use of only two alternative systems is practicable. The two systems are termed:

System "A" – Combined Cardinal and Lateral System (Red to Port)

System "B" – Lateral System only

(Red to Starboard)

While System "B" is still being studied, the rules of System "A" have been completed and have the support of the Inter-governmental Maritime Organisation (IMO).

Q.2 Describe the Scope of System "A"

A. System "A" applies to all fixed and floating marks, other than lighthouses, sector lights, leading lights and marks, lightships and "lighthouse buoys", and serves to indicate:

The sides and centrelines of navigable channels; natural dangers and other obstructions such as wrecks (which are described as "New Dangers" when newly discovered); Areas in which navigation may be subject to regulation or other features of importance to the manner.

Q.3 Are fixed marks included in System "A"?

A. It should be understood that most lighted and unlighted beacons, other than leading marks, are included in the system. In general, beacon topmarks will have the same shape and colours as those used on buoys.

Q.4 How many types of marks may be used in combination under this System?

A. Five Types - namely

1. Lateral marks indicate the port and starboard hand sides of channels.

2. Cardinal marks used in conjunction with the compass, indicating that navigable water lies to the named side of the mark.

3. Isolated Danger marks erected on, or moored directly on or over dangers of limited extent.

4. Safe Water marks, such as mid-channel buoys.

5. Special marks, the purpose of which is apparent from reference to the chart of other nautical documents.

Q.5 Broadly give the characteristics of the marks

A. By day - Colour, shape and topmark.

By night – Light colour and rhythm.

Q.6 Give the Colours of Marks used in System "A"

A. Red and green (without stripes or bands) are reserved, respectively for port and starboard Lateral marks, and yellow for Special marks. The other types of marks have horizontal bands or vertical stripes, as described later.

Q.7 Name the five basic buoy shapes used in System "A"

A. 1. Can – pass on the port hand when approaching from seaward.

2. Conical – pass on the starboard hand when approaching from seaward.

3. Spherical – to be passed on either side.

4. Pillar - is used to describe any buoy which is smaller than a "lighthouse buoy" and which has a tall central structure on a broad base; it includes beacon buoys, high focal plane buoys and others (except spar buoys) whose body shape does not indicate the correct side to pass.

5. Spar – the shape has no special significance.

Q.8 Outline the topmarks used under System "A"

A. 1. Can – pass on the port hand when approaching from seaward.

2. Conical – pass on the starboard hand when approaching from seaward.

3. Spherical – Isolated Danger Marks or Safe Water Marks.

4. X-Shaped Topmarks – Special Purpose Marks.

Q.9 What colour lights are used under System "A"?

A. Red – reserved for port lateral marks.

Green – reserved for starboard marks.

Yellow – reserved for Special Purpose Marks.

White – reserved for other types distinguished from one another by rhythm.

Q.10 Give the rhythm of lights used under System "A"

A. Red — may have any rhythm. The colour shows on which side to pass.

Green — may have any rhythm. The colour shows on which side to pass.

Yellow — reserved for special marks. May have any rhythm not reserved for white lights of the system.

White — have clearly specified rhythms:

— various quick flashing rhythms for Cardinal marks.

— group flashing (2) for Isolated Danger marks.

— relatively long periods of light for Safe Water marks.

Q.11 How is the direction of buoys defined under System "A"?

A. Lateral Marks – This direction is defined in one of two ways:

a Local direction of buoyage – The direction taken by the mariner when approaching a harbour, river estuary or other waterway from seaward.

b. General direction of buoyage – In other areas, a direction determined by the buoyage authorities, following a clockwise direction around continental land masses, given in Sailing Directions, and, if necessary, indicated on charts by a symbol.

Cardinal Marks – used in conjunction with the compass to indicate where the mariner may find the best navigable water. It is placed in one of the four quadrants (North, East, South and West), bounded by the true bearings NW-NE, NE-SE, SE-SW, SW-NW, taken from the point of interest. A Cardinal Mark takes its name from the quadrant in which it is placed.

(Note) The mariner is safe if he passes N of a North mark, E of an East mark, S of a South mark and W of a West mark.

Q.12 Give the characteristics of Lateral Marks

A. A. A port hand mark is coloured red and its basic shape is can, for either buoy body or topmark, or both and by night is lit by a red light. (any rhythm may be used) i.e. flashing Occ. iso. etc.

B. A starboard hand mark is normally coloured green and its basic shape is conical, for either buoy body or topmark (point up) or both and by night is lit by a green light (any rhythm may be used).

(Note) Lateral colours of red or green will frequently be used for minor shore lights, such as those marking pierheads and the extremities of jetties.

Q.13 Outline any variations to the lateral marks

A. Variations on the simple system will occur in particular instances: Starboard hand marks may exceptionally be coloured black instead of green.

In some places, particularly straits (being open at both ends), the local direction of buoyage may be overridden by the general direction.

Special marks, with can and conical shapes but painted yellow, may be used in conjunction with the standard Lateral marks for special types of channel marking.

Q.14 Name the uses Cardinal Marks may be installed for

A. A. Indicate that the deepest water in an area is on the named side of the mark; i.e. if a North Mark best water is to be found in the quadrant NW to NE of the Point of interest.

B. Indicate the safe side on which to pass a danger.

C. Draw attention to a feature in a channel such as a bend, junction, bifurcation, or end of a shoal.

Q.15 Outline the topmarks used for Cardinal Marks

A. Black double-cone topmarks are the most important feature, by day, of Cardinal marks: the arrangement of the cones must be memorised.

North both cones pointing upwards (Points up)

South both cones pointing downwards (Points down)

East top cone pointing upwards and the bottom cone downwards (Points outward)

West bottom cone pointing upwards and the top cone pointing downwards (Points inward)

Q.16 Outline the colours to identify Cardinal Marks

A. Black and yellow horizontal bands are used to colour a Cardinal mark. The position of the black band, or bands, is related to the points of the black topmarks, thus:

North – Points up: Black band above yellow band

South – Points down: Black band below yellow band

West – Points inward: Black band with yellow bands above and below

East – Points outward: Black bands above and below yellow band

Q.17 Outline the shape of Cardinal Marks

A. The shape of a Cardinal mark is not significant, but in the case of a buoy will be pillar or spar.

Q.18 How are Cardinal Marks lighted?

A. When lighted a cardinal mark exhibits a white light, its characteristics are based on a group of quick or very quick flashes which distinguish it as a Cardinal Mark and indicate its quadrant.

The distinguishing quick or very quick flashes are:

North -- Uninterrupted

East – 3 flashes in a group

South – 6 flashes in a group followed by a long flash

West – 9 flashes in a group.

Q.19 Describe for what use an Isolated danger mark is erected

A. An Isolated Danger mark is erected on, or moored on or above, an isolated danger of limited extent which has navigable water all round it. The extent of the surrounding navigable water is immaterial: such a mark can, for example, indicate either a shoal which is well offshore, or an islet separated by a narrow channel from the coast.

Q.20 How is the position of an Isolated Danger mark registered on a chart?

A. On a chart, the position of a danger is the centre of the base line indicated by a small circle.

Q.21 Describe the topmark used to indicate an Isolated Danger mark

A. A black double-sphere topmark is by day, the most important feature of an Isolated Danger mark, and whenever practicable, this topmark will be carried, with the spheres as large as possible, disposed vertically, and clearly separated.

Q.22 Describe the colour used to indicate an Isolated Danger mark

A. Black with one or more red horizontal bands are the colours used for Isolated Danger marks.

Q.23 Describe the shape used to indicate an Isolated Danger mark

A. The shape of an Isolated Danger mark is not significant, but in the case of a buoy will be pillar or spar.

Q.24 When an Isolated Danger Mark is lighted what type of light would it exhibit?

A   When lighted, a white flashing light showing a group of two flashes is used to denote an Isolated Danger mark. The association of two flashes and two spheres in the topmark may be a help in remembering these characteristics.

Q.25 Describe for what use a Safe Water Mark is erected

A.   A Safe Water mark is used to indicate that there is navigable water all round the mark. Such a mark may be used as a centreline, mid channel or landfall buoy.

Q.26 Describe the colour used to indicate a Safe Water Mark

A.   Red and white vertical stripes are used for Safe Water marks, and distinguish them from the black-banded danger-marking marks.

Q.27 Describe the shape used to indicate a Safe Water Mark

A.   Spherical, pillar or spar buoys may be used as Safe Water marks.

Q.28 Describe the topmark used to indicate a Safe Water Mark

A.   A single red sphere topmark will be carried whenever practicable, by a pillar or spar buoy used as a Safe Water mark.

Q.29 When a Safe Water Mark is lighted what type of light would it exhibit?

A.   When lighted, Safe Water marks exhibit a white light, occulting, or isophase, or showing a single long flash or Morse Letter 'A'. If a long flash (i.e. a flash of not less than 2 seconds) is used, the period of the light will be 10 seconds.

The association of a single flash and a single sphere in the topmark may be a held   in   remembering   these characteristics.

Q.30 Describe for what use a Special Mark is erected

A.   A Special mark may be used to indicate to the mariner a special area or feature, the nature of which is apparent from reference to a chart, sailing directions or notices to mariners.

A Special mark may be used to define a channel within a channel. For example, a channel for deep draught vessels in a wide estuary, where the limits of the channel for normal navigation are marked by red and green Lateral buoys, may have the boundaries of the deep channel Indicated by yellow buoys of the appropriate Lateral shapes, or its centre line marked by yellow spherical buoys.

Examples of usage:

1. Ocean Data Acquisition Systems (ODAS), i.e. buoys carrying oceanographic or meteorological sensors;
2. Traffic separation marks;
3. Spoil ground marks;
4. Military exercise zone marks;
5. Cable or pipeline marks, including outfall pipes;
6. Recreation zone marks.

Q.31 Describe the colour used to indicate a Special Mark

A.   Yellow is the colour used for Special marks.

Q.32 Describe the shape used to indicate a Special Mark.

A.   The shape of a "Special Mark" is optional but must not conflict with that used for a Lateral or a Safe Water mark. For example, an outfall buoy on the port hand side of a channel could be can-shaped but not conical.

Q.33 Describe the topmark used to indicate a Special Mark

A.   When a topmark is carried it takes the form of a single yellow X.

Q.34 When a Special Mark is lighted what type of light would it exhibit?

A.   When a light Is exhibited It is yellow; the rhythm may be any, other than those used for the white lights of Cardinal, Isolated Danger and Safe Water marks i.e.

Cardinal marks–

North Mark – Quick (or very quick) flashing

East Mark —   VQ (3) every 5 secs
or Q (3) every 10 secs.

South Mark – Quick (or very quick) flashing (6) and long flash 15 seconds (or 10 seconds)

West Mark – Quick (or very quick) flashing (9) 15 seconds (or 10 seconds)

Isolated Danger Mark – Group flashing (2)

Safe Water Mark – Occulting, Isophase, Long flash 10 seconds or Morse "A"

Q.35 Define what is meant by New Dangers under Maritime Buoyage System "A".

A. A newly discovered hazard to navigation not yet indicated in nautical documents or sufficiently promulgated by notices to mariners, is termed a New Danger. The term covers naturally occurring obstructions such as sandbanks or rocks, or man-made dangers such as wrecks.

Q.36 Describe the marks used to indicate New Dangers

A New Danger is marked by one or more Cardinal or Lateral Marks in accordance with the System "A" rules. If the danger is especially grave, at least one of the marks will be duplicated as soon as practicable by an identical mark until the danger has been sufficiently notified to mariners.

Q.37 What lights are exhibited on New Danger Marks?

A. If a lighted mark is used for a New Danger, it must exhibit a quick flashing or very quick flashing light: if it is a Cardinal Mark, it must exhibit a whitelight: if a Lateral Mark, a red or green light.

Q.38 Should a New Danger be fitted with a Racon what code and signal length would be used?

A. The duplicate mark may carry a racon, coded D showing a signal length of one nautical mile on a radar display.

LIGHTS

Cautionary notes to be considered concerning lights.

(a) lights placed at a great elevation are more frequently obscured by cloud than those near sea level.

(b) The distance of an observer from a light cannot be estimated from its apparent brightness.

(c) The distance at which lights are sighted varies greatly with atmospheric refraction.

(d) The distance at which lights are sighted is reduced by fog, haze, dust, smoke or rain.

(e) A light of low intensity is easily obscured by any of the above conditions.

(f) The limits of sectors should not be relied upon, they should be checked by compass bearing.

(g) The limits of the arc of visibility are rarely clear cut, especially at a short distance.

(h) At the boundary of sectors of different colour there is usually a small arc in which the light may be either obscured, indeterminate in colour, or white.

(i) In cold weather the glass and screens are often covered with moisture. This increases the width of the sector of uncertainty. Bird life also have a tendency to perch close to the light for warmth partially obscuring the light.

White lights may have a reddish hue under some atmospheric conditions.

Definitions

Period of a light is the time taken to exhibit one complete sequence.

Phase is each element of the sequence (e.g. a flash, an eclipse).

Elevation is the vertical distance between the focal plane of the light and the level of mean high water springs or mean higher high water, whichever is given in Admiralty Tide Tables.

Loom is the diffused glow observed from a light below the horizon or hidden by an obstacle, due to atmospheric scattering.

Sector light is a light presenting different appearances, either of colour or character, over various parts of the horizon of interest to maritime navigation.

Leading lights are two or more lights associated so as to form a leading line to be followed.

Lights described as " Lts in line" are particular cases, and are intended to mark limits of areas, alignments of cables, alignments for anchoring. etc; they do not mark a direction to be followed.

Direction light is a light showing over a very narrow sector forming a single leading light. This sector may be flanked by sectors of greatly reduced intensity, or by sectors of different colours or character.

Direction lights are also used to mark the limits of areas, etc, in the same way as "Lts in line".

Range - Luminous range is the maximum distance at which a light can be seen at a given time, as determined by the intensity of the light and the meteorological visibility prevailing at that time; it takes no account of elevation, observer's height of eye or the curvature of the earth.

Nominal range is the luminous range when the meteorological visibility is 10 nautical miles.

Geographical range is the maximum distance at which light from a light can theoretically reach an observer, as limited only by the curvature of the earth and the refraction of the atmosphere, and by the elevation of the light and the height of eye of the observer.

Aeromarine lights are marine-type lights in which a part of the beam is deflected to an angle of $10°$-$15°$ above the horizon for the use of aircraft.

Note: When a light is cut off by sloping land the bearing on which the light will disappear will vary with its distance and the observer's height of eye; the arc of visibility will increase in width with any increase in either of these factors.

Lights

Light Characteristics

For an explanation of lights on
IALA System A see L70

Fathoms and Metric Charts

CLASS OF LIGHT		International abbreviations	Older form (where different)	Illustration Period shown _____
21	Fixed *(steady light)*	F		
22	Occulting *(total duration of light more than dark)*			
22	Single-occulting	Oc	Occ	
27	Group-occulting *e.g.*	Oc(2)	Gp Occ(2)	
(Ka)	Composite group-occulting *e.g.*	(Oc(2 + 3)	Gp Occ (2 + 3)	
23a	Isophase *(light and dark equal)*	Iso		
23	Flashing *(total duration of light less than dark)*			
23	Single-flashing	Fl		
(kb)	Long-flashing *(flash 2s or longer)*	LFl		
28	Group-flashing *e.g*	Fl(3)	GpFl(3)	
(Kc)	Composite group-flashing *e.g*	Fl(2 + 1)	GpFl(2 + 1)	
24	Quick *(50 to 79 - usually either 50 or 60 - flashes per minute)*			
24	Continous quick	Q	QkFl	
(Kd)	Group quick *e.g*	Q(3)	QkFl(3)	
25	Interrupted quick	IQ	IntQkFl	
(Ke)	Very Quick *(80 to 159 - usually either 100 or 120 - flashes per minute)*			
(Ke)	Continous very quick	VQ	VQkFl	
(Kf)	Group very quick *e.g.*	VQ(3)	VQFl(3)	
(Kg)	Interrupted very quick	IVQ	InVQkFl	
(Kh)	Ultra Quick *(160 or more - usually 240 to 300 - flashes per minute)*			
(Kh)	Continous ultra quick	UQ		
(Ki)	Interrupted ultra quick	IUQ		
30a	Morse Code *e.g.*	Mo(K)		
29	Fixed and Flashing	FFl		
26	Alternating *e.g.*	Al.WR	Alt.WR	

COLOUR		International Abbreviations	Older form (where different)	RANGE in sea miles	International abbreviations	Older form
67	White	W (may be omitted)		Single range e.g.	15M	
66	Red	R				
64	Green	G		2 ranges e.g.	14/12M	14,12M
(Kj)	Yellow	Y				
65	Orange	Y	Or	3 or more ranges e.g.	22.18M	22,20,18M
63	Blue	Bu	Bl			
61	Violet	Vi				
ELEVATION is given in metres (m) or feet (Ft)				PERIOD in seconds e.g.	5s	5 sec

Q. 1 How are light houses distinguished from one another at night?

A. Light houses are distinguishable from one another by the character, colour and period of their light arc.

Q. 2 Describe the term "arc of visibility".

A The arc of visibility of a light means the sector over which the light can be seen.

Note: Arc of visibility bearings are taken as from seaward.

Q.3 Describe the term "range of visibility".

A. The range of visibility of a light is the distance from which the light may be seen. When reference is made to this term nominal range is specified. The standard for assessing the nominal range of a light is the luminous distance at which it may be seen in atmospheric conditions where the meteorological visibility is ten (10) sea miles.

Q. 4 From what level are the heights of lights and hills measured ?

A. Mean high water spring tide.

Q.5 Is it permitted to anchor on or near lines of leading lights and beacons?

A. No. Under regulations it is an offence to do so. There is risk of collision and of a vessel's lighting being confused with the navigational aids.

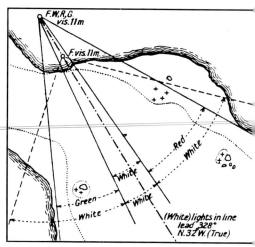

Figure 20 – *Sectored Leading Lights*

Chapter 2

TIDES AND
TIDAL STREAMS

TIDES AND TIDAL STREAMS

The periodic rise and fall of the level of the sea constitute what is known as tides. The rise or fall does not occur simultaneously over the surface of an ocean or sea, but appears to radiate outwards from some central area in that ocean or sea. The periodic rises and falls of tides are fairly regular, and therefore the height of the tide at any particular time and place can be predicted with a reasonable degree of accuracy.

It is most important that 'tides' should not be confused with 'tidal streams', although loose terminology has undoubtedly come to use the word 'tide' for both. Tides affect the depth of water at a place; tidal streams affect the course to be steered. Corrections to counteract such influences result in the course made good. See Chapter 4 for further details.

CURRENTS AND STREAMS

Q.1 What are tidal streams?

A.   **Tidal streams** are periodic horizontal movements of the water that result from the tides.

Q.2 What is the difference between tidal streams and currents?

A.   **Tidal streams** flood and ebb, that is they flow in one direction while flooding and in most cases, though not necessarily, the opposite while ebbing. A **current** is seasonal and flows in the same direction for the season. The rate may change with the season.

Q.3 Are currents influenced by winds?

A.   Yes. A local current setting in the direction of the wind may be produced in the surface water of an area over which strong winds are blowing.

Strong winds may influence the rate of the current. An example is the South East Trade in the Papuan Gulf. The rate of the current increases as the wind blows harder. Strong South Easterly winds will back water up in the Gulf. Should they cease or back to easterly, the heaped up water in the Gulf will cause the current to reverse and flow strongly in the opposite direction along the coast.

Q.4 Where would you get the information regarding the direction and rate of tidal streams?

A.   This information is available from the following:

(a) The chart pertaining to the area.

(b) The Australia Pilot Book of Sailing Directions.

Note: A special tabulation for the Prince of Wales Channel, Torres Strait, may be found in the Tide and Boating Guide.

TIDES

Q.5 What are tides?

A.   **Tides** are the periodic rise and fall of the sea surface at any given point.

Q.6 What is a spring tide?

A.   In consequence of the solar cycle and the occurrence of new or full moon at a place, the highest high waters and the lowest low waters occur. These highest and lowest tides are called spring tides.

Q.7 What is a neap tide?

A.   Seven and a quarter days after full or new moon with first and last quarters of the moon, the lowest high waters and the highest low waters will occur. These are called neap tides.

Q.8 In what way do spring tides differ from neap tides?

A.   Spring tides are the highest of high waters and the lowest of low waters whereas neap tides are the lowest of high waters and the highest of low waters. It then follows that tidal streams flow at a faster rate during spring tides than neap tides.

Q.9 How is the duration of the tide ascertained?

A.   The duration of the tide is related to the rise and fall of the tide. The duration of rise is the time the tide takes to rise from the low to the high water level. The duration of fall is the time the tide takes to fall from the high to the low water level. The duration of rise and fall are not usually of the same period as is illustrated by the figure 22 showing the graph of the tidal oscillation.

Q.10 How many high waters (HW) and low

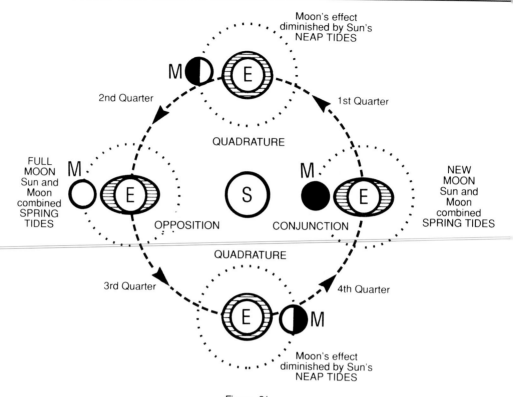

Figure 21

The influence of the Solar Cycle on Tides

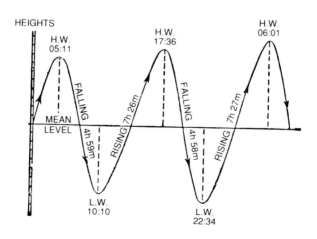

Figure 22

Graph of Tidal Oscillation

waters (LW) are usually experienced each day?

A. There are usually two high waters and two low waters in each day. The approximate time interval between high waters is 12 hours 25 minutes. This is because tides are related to the position of the moon and that a lunar day consists of approximately 24 hours 50 minutes. Theoretically, low water succeeds high water after an interval of 6 hours 13 minutes.

Q.11 What is a standard port as referred to in the Tide Tables?

A. A standard port is a port for which the time and heights of high and low water are tabulated for every day of the year. The zone time used for the predicted time is the standard time for the area and is given at the head of each page. Care should be taken to ensure that this is the same as the time being used. e.g. Daylight Saving Time. NB: This example may not be politically acceptable in Queensland. The predicted time should be adjusted if necessary.

Q.12 Where may details of the occurrence of high and low water be found for standard ports?

A. In the Tide and Boating Guide where the times and height of high and low waters are tabulated for each day of the year.

Q.13 What is a secondary place as referred to in the Tide and Boating Guide?

A. Secondary places are those at which the time and height of high and low water are obtained by applying the corrections based on the standard port. These are tabulated in the Tide and Boating Guide (Table 2).

Q.14 Is the greatest depth of water to be found, at spring low water or at neap low water?

A. The greatest depth of water will be found at neap low water.

Q.15 How would you ascertain the depth of water for a specific position on the chart at any given time?

A. Calculate the height of the tide at that position and add the result to the soundings marked on the chart.

Note: Along the Queensland Coast in the winter months, the highest tides occur at night and the lowest tides during the day. In summer this is reversed.

Q.16 Describe the method of finding the time and height of tide for a secondary place by the Rise Ratio and time difference method.

A. (i) **Time** Add or subtract the time correction as given by Columns 1 and 2 respectively (for required Secondary Place) to the predicted time for high and low tide for the Standard Port.

    (ii) **Height** Multiply the height of high/low water for the Standard Port by the ratio given in Column 9 (for the required Secondary Place). To the result add or subtract (as given by the sign) the datum adjustment from Column 10 (for the required Secondary Place). The sum is the height of high/low water at the Secondary Port.

Refer to Tables 3 and 4 Queensland Transport Tide and Boating Guide for further details of the method.

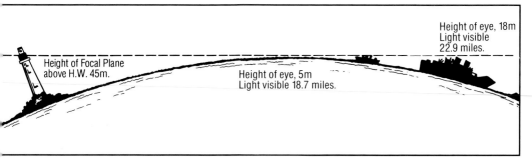

Height of eye, 18m
Light visible 22.9 miles.

Height of Focal Plane above H.W. 45m.

Height of eye, 5m
Light visible 18.7 miles.

Figure 23 – Illustrating the range of light due to the earth's curvature

METEOROLOGICAL INFLUENCES

Q.17 How are tides affected by wind?

A. The effect of wind on sea level – and therefore on tidal heights and times – is variable, depending on the topography of the area in question. In general, it can be said the wind will raise sea level in the direction towards which it is blowing. Strong winds blowing straight onshore will pile up the water and cause high waters to be higher than predicted. Winds blowing off the land will have the reverse effect.

Q.18 What effect has atmospheric pressure on tides?

A. When the aneroid barometer is reading

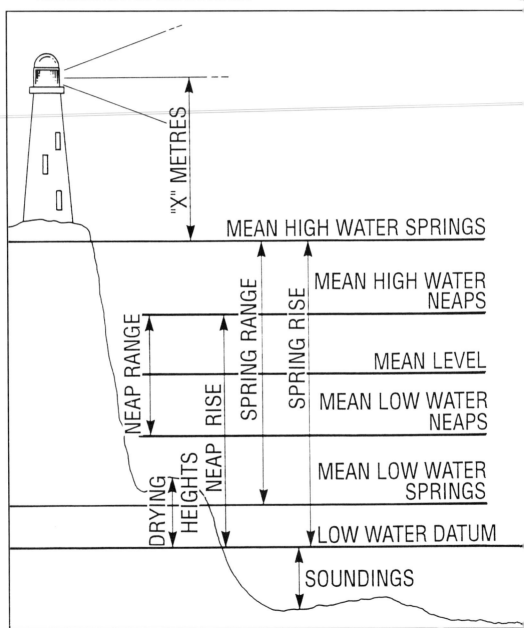

Figure 24 – *Illustrating the Phases of the Tide*

high the height of the tide can be affected by the greater atmospheric pressure exerted on the surface of the water. In this instance the tide may not reach the predicted height.

RANGE OF LIGHTS

Q.19 What influence has the rise and fall of the tides on the "light's" range of visibility from a "light house"?

A. At low tide the light's range of visibility from a light house is increased when seen from a vessel. The light to an observer on a vessel is elevated to the difference in height between high and low tide. Due to the curvature of the earth the distance of an observer's horizon will be greater as the height increases. See Figure 23 (Page 95).

DEFINITIONS

Q.20 What is datum for tidal predictions?

A. The datum for tidal predictions must be the same as the chart datum for soundings since the total depth of water is found by the addition of the charted depth of the height of tide.

Q.21 What is chart datum?

A. Chart datum is the reference height for soundings on the chart. All soundings are measured below chart datum; tidal heights and drying heights are measured above it. See figure 24. Details of the standard port datum levels may be found in Table 1 of the Tide and Boating Guide. Chart datum is set at a height that the tides rarely fall below.

Note: For practical purposes it can be taken that chart datum or zero level is the lowest low water springs.

Q.22 What are H.A.T. and L.A.T.?

A. **H.A.T. (Highest Astronomical Tide) L.A.T. (Lowest Astronomical Tide)** – These are the highest and lowest levels which can be predicted to occur under average meteorological conditions and any combination of astronomical conditions. These levels will not be reached every year. H.A.T. and L.A.T. are not the extreme levels which can be reached, as storm surges may cause considerably higher and lower levels to occur.

Q.23 What is the "height of tide"?

A. The **height** of the tide is the vertical distance at any moment between the water level and the chart datum.

Q.24 What is the rise of the tide?

A. The **rise** of the tide is the height of high water above chart datum.

Q.25 What is the range of the tide?

A. The **range** of the tide is the difference between the height of "high water" and the next succeeding or last preceding "low water".

Q.26 What is the mean range?

A. **Mean range** is the difference between mean high water and mean low water.

Q.27 What is mean spring rise and mean neap rise?

A. **Mean spring rise** and **mean neap rise** are the heights of mean high water springs and mean high water neaps respectively.

Q.28 What does M.H.W.S. stand for and indicate?

A. **Mean High Water Springs**. Long term average of the heights of two successive high waters during those periods of 24 hours (approximately once a fortnight) when the range of tide is greatest, at full and new moon.

Q.29 What does M.H.W.N. stand for and indicate?

A. **Mean High Water Neaps**. The average throughout a year of the heights of two successive high waters when the range of tide is the least, at the time of first and last quarter of the Moon..

Q.30 What does M.H.W. and M.L.W. stand for and indicate?

A. **Mean High Water, Mean Low Water** and are the average heights of high and low waters over a long period.

Q.31 What does M.S.L. stand for and indicate?

A. **Mean** (or half) **Sea Level** and is the mean between the levels of mean high water and mean low water.

Q.32 What do M.S.R. and M.N.R. stand for and Indicate?

A. **Mean Spring Range** and **Mean Neap Range** – the difference between mean high water springs and mean low water springs and mean high water neaps and mean low water neaps respectively.

Q.33 What is meant by standard time?

A. **Standard time** Is the legal time adopted by a country for its time zone time e.g. A.E.S.T. (Australian Eastern Standard Time) is taken from "-10 hour zone", and is the legal time for Queensland, New South Wales and Victoria. Zone time is named minus, from Greenwich eastward to 180° E. and plus, westward to 180° W. Fifteen degrees (15°) of longitude is equivalent to one hour of time in either direction.

The range of tides on the Queensland Coast

Between Cape Moreton and Sandy Cape, the range averages 1.5 metres to 1.8 metres. North of Sandy Cape, the range increases reaching a maximum of about 7.6 metres at Wavely Creek, Broadsound. It then gradually decreases to 3.6 metres at the Whitsunday Passage. From there northward the range lies between 2.4 metres and 3.6 metres.

Torres Strait is the meeting place for the Arafura and Coral Seas. The tides in this area are peculiar in behaviour as on occasions it can be high water at Booby Island when almost simultaneously it may be low water at Ince Point on Wednesday Island. While there is only a distance of 30 nautical miles between the two points, there is about one week"s difference in the age of the tide. This means that when it is spring tide at one place it is neap tide at the other. Special tide tables are now produced for this area giving predictions for both vertical and horizontal movements for the significant places throughout the length of the Prince of Wales Channel. The highest rise of tide in Torres Strait is 3.6 metres and the maximum velocity of 7 knots at Hammond Rock.

Conversion Scale – Metres to Feet

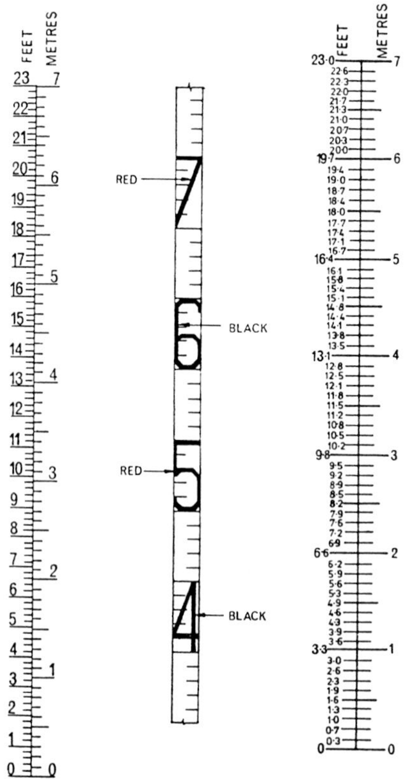

Figure 25 – *The Markings of a Tide Board. Note: All heights are calculated in metres*

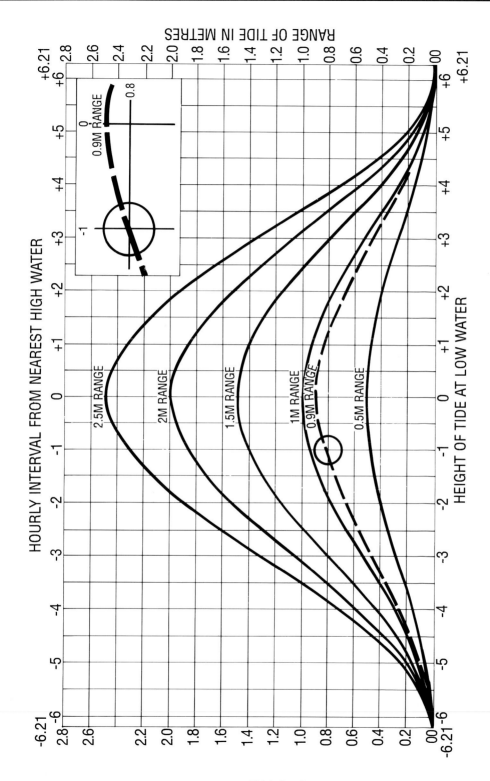

Figure 26 – *Tidal Graph*

Chapter 3
COMPASS

COMPASS

Deprived of visual indications, man loses all sense of direction. The most important navigational instrument in a vessel is the Compass. There is an old saying that rings true, "The Compass is the heart, and the anchor is the hand of the ship".

Every Mariner is advised to have the Compass in his vessel adjusted and then to trust in it. It is more common to encounter disaster through one's disbelief than the contrary. The Compass does have errors but they can be determined very accurately, and it will guide him to safety provided he exercises care. He should not permit any magnetic substance to be placed near it to cause an unknown error.

Q.1 Name the two main classifications of Compass.

A. Magnetic and Gyro.

Q.2. In what direction does the Magnetic Compass point?

A. Magnetic North.

Q.3 In what direction does the Gyro Compass point?

A. True North.

Note: Caution. The same procedure should be adopted with a Gyro as with a Magnetic Compass in checking for accuracy.

Q.4 Why are liquid Magnetic Compasses sometimes preferable to dry Card Compasses?

A. The liquid in the Compass bowl has a dampening effect on the Card, steadying it in movement thus making it easier to read.

Q.5 What is a dead beat Compass?

A. A Compass in which the Card has been sufficiently dampened to make the Card steady when the vessel is rolling heavily.

Q.6 Why is a mixture of alcohol and water used for the liquid in a Compass?

A. To prevent freezing.

Q.7 How is the expansion of the liquid overcome in a Compass?

A. (1) In an old pattern Compass two small expansion chambers were fitted on the sides of the bowl.

(2) In a modern Compass, the base consists of an expansion chamber.

Q.8 How are bubbles removed?

A. Bubbles should only be removed by a qualified Compass Technician.

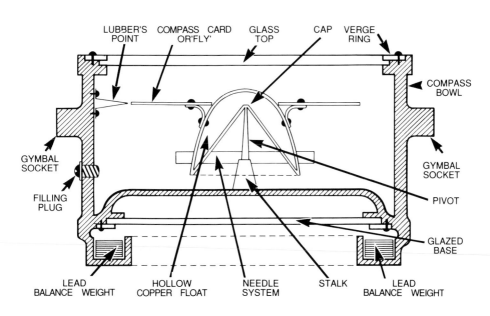

Figure 27 – *Section of a Liquid Compass*

Q.9 What is the lubber line?

A. A mark or projection on the Compass bowl. It is in line with the vessel's keel so that the direction in which the vessel is heading may be read from the Card. It may be a line marked on the inside of the Compass bowl or a fine pointed wire, level with the Card, projecting inwards.

Q.10 What is a Shadow Pin?

A. A vertical wire which is fitted in the centre of the Compass bowl for taking bearings.

Q.11 What is the Flinders Bar?

A. A vertical bar of soft iron, named after Captain Matthew Flinders. The bar is inside a brass cylindrical case, which is secured to the foreside of the binnacle.

Q.12 What is the purpose of the Flinders Bar?

A. The Flinders Bar is used to counteract the effect of the ship's vertical iron on the Compass, e.g. mast, derricks, funnels, etc.

Q.13 How does the Compass bowl remain level at sea?

A. The Compass bowl is suspended in gimbals so that it remains horizontal in a seaway. It is desirable to have the fore-and-aft axis of the gimballing on the outer arc. Otherwise, in heavy rolling and pitching, the lubber line may move slightly with respect to the fore-and-aft line of the ship, thus reducing, to a small extent, the accuracy of the instrument.

Q.14 How is a north seeking end of a Magnet identified?

A. The north seeking end of a Magnet is termed the north, red, or marked end to distinguish it from the south, blue or unmarked end. An aid to memorise the difference is by use of the three R's and three U's, as illustrated.

| noRth | Red | maRked |
| soUth | blUe | Unmarked |

Q.15 For what purpose are the Iron Spheres on each side of the Standard Compass?

A. The Iron Spheres on each side of the Standard Compass are constructed of soft iron. Their purpose is to correct the quadrantal deviation caused by the horizontal steel in the vessel. The centres of the Spheres are on the same horizontal plane as the Compass needle.

Q.16 What objects are positioned and locked inside the binnacle ?

A. Inside these lockers, bar magnets are placed fore-and-aft and athwartship, to compensate deviation when the Compass was adjusted.

Q.17 What is an Azimuth mirror used for?

A. For taking a bearing of the sun. stars or any object. (Fig. 29).

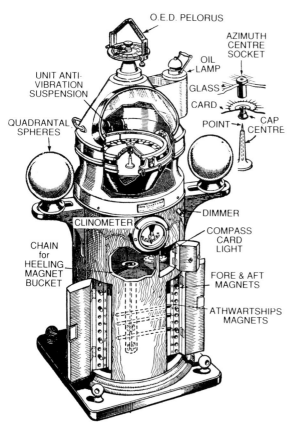

Figure 28 - *Section of a Standard Compass*

Q.18 There are two positions for taking bearings with an Azimuth mirror. How are they described?

A. Reference is made to the positions as "arrow up" or arrow down". "Arrow up" is used when observing heavenly bodies. "Arrow down" is used to take bearings of objects on the horizon.

Q.19 Where would you find the arrow?

A. Engraved on the milled wheel used to turn the prism.

Q.20 How may the error of an Azimuth mirror be detected and adjusted?

A. An error in the Azimuth mirror may be detected by taking a bearing of a distant object with the arrow up, and again with the arrow down. The two bearings should agree. If they do not, the prism must be adjusted by means of its retaining screws until they do.

What is a "Pelorus" and what is it used for?

A. The Pelorus may be described as a dumb Compass Card engraved on metal. The dumb Card is mounted on a central axis so that it can be rotated freely or clamped in any position. Sight vanes that may be rotated are fitted to read off a bearing from the Card. The Pelorus is used where a Standard Compass is not fitted. Its purpose is to take bearings which are not visible from the steering Compass.

Q.22 How many Compasses are carried on a well fitted vessel?

A. Two, the Standard and the Steering.

Q.23 Why is the Standard Compass so named?

A. Because it is the principal direction-finder In the vessel, from which bearings are taken and courses set.

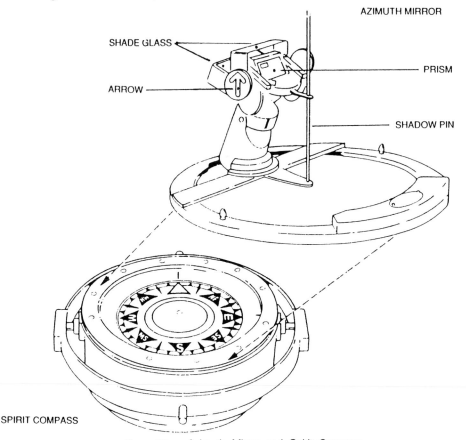

Figure 29 – *Azimuth Mirror and Spirit Compass*

Figure 30 – *Pelorus with sight vanes extended*

Q.24 Where is the Standard Compass Installed?

A. In the centre line of the vessel, high up, giving the observer an unobstructed view.

Q.25 What consideration should be given to the siting of all Compasses?

A. The site should be free from iron, magnetic and electrical wiring influences.

Q.26 What is meant by the "compass bearing" of an object ?

A. The bearing of an object is the point where the shadow pin cuts the Compass Card, when the eye, shadow pin and object are in line.

Q.27 Define the term "Variation".

A. "Variation" is the angle between True and Magnetic North.

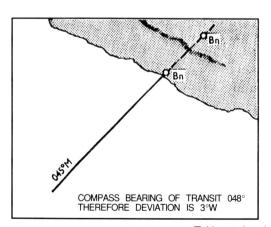

COMPASS BEARING OF TRANSIT 048°
THEREFORE DEVIATION IS 3°W

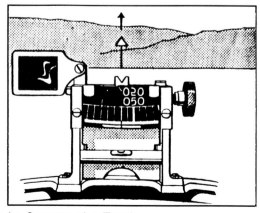

Figure 31 – *Taking a bearing by Compass of a Transit*

Q.28 Define the term "Deviation".

A. "Deviation" is the angle between Magnetic and Compass North.

Q.29 Define the term "Error".

A. "Error" is the sum of Variation and Deviation.

Q.30 What is the cause of Variation? Where is its value recorded and why is it different at different places ?

A. The Earth's magnetic field has its north pole situated in Hudson Bay. It is not stationary. The angular difference between the terrestrial pole and the magnetic pole is termed variation. Its value is recorded on the Compass rose printed on the charts. It differs in various places because the relative positions of the poles alter. It may be easterly or westerly.

Q.31 What magnetic variation is found along the Queensland coast?

A. From 5° East in Torres Strait to about 11° East at Point Danger.

Q.32 What causes deviation to change in name and amount?

A. The change in direction of the vessel's head alters the angle of the magnetic field within the vessel to that of the Earth. When these fields are acting at right angles to each other, maximum deflection of the Compass magnetic needles occur. The magnetic field within the vessel may be influenced by cargo such as steel drums etc.

Q.33 When is deviation named East and when West?

A. When viewing from the centre of the Compass and looking directly at magnetic north, deviation is named according to whether the Compass north lies to the right or left.

Easterly if to the right.

Westerly if to the left.

Q.34 Name the jingles commonly used as a guide in applying error to a Compass course in order to get the True course, or to the True course in order to get the Compass course.

A. The jingles for applying error to convert a Compass to a True course or vice versa are made up of the letters C.E.R.T. or T.E.L.C. respectively.

Interpreted means:

C.E.R.T. Compass to true easterly right.

T.E.L.C. True to compass easterly left.

In modern chartwork using circular notation (000° to 359°), the following rhyme is used.

Compass least error East.

Compass best error West.

"CADET" which means Compass to true add eastly.

"C" — meaning compass
"AD" — meaning add
"E" — meaning eastly
"T" — meaning true

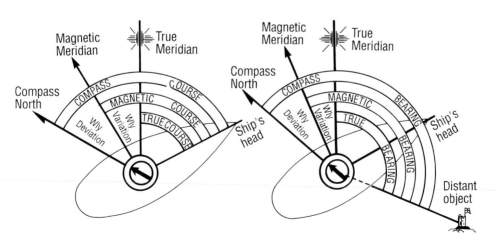

Figure 32 – *Courses and Bearings*

Q.35 Draw a figure illustrating "compass course", "magnetic course" and "true course", designating the angles by name.

A.   See Fig. 32 on previous page.

Q.36 How far from the Magnetic Compass, should a transceiver or portable transistor radio be kept?

A.   At least 4 metres (13 feet).

Q.37 Is a Magnetic Compass affected by a transistor radio, which is turned off?

A.   It may have some effect, as it is usual to have a permanent magnet in the loudspeaker. Some sets have metal cases which could affect the Compass.

Note: Iron or steel objects must not be placed within 2 metres of the Compass bowl. Care should be taken not to place tools, knives etc, near the Compass.

Q.38 What precautions should be taken before swinging a vessel for a deviation check?

A.   (a) Check that the Compass Card is sensitive:

To do this hold a screw driver or a magnet near the Compass to deflect the needle. Remove the screw driver or magnet and the needle should return to its previous position. The lubber line will indicate the same course as it did previously. Should it not do so, the point of the pivot or the cap is worn.

(b) Check that the lubber line is in the fore-and-aft position of the vessel. It must be parallel to the vessel's keel.

(c) Electrical wiring near the Compass should be twin wire. Single wire with an earth return should be tested by switching on to see if there is a deflection of the Compass needle.

Q.39 Name three methods of Swinging a vessel's Compass

A.   (1) By mooring a vessel in line with two conspicuous objects using two anchors. The anchors are placed one either side and at right angles to the alignment of the bearings. The anchor chains are then adjusted to align the vessel with the

two objects. The vessel is then swung and bearings of the objects compared with the Compass as the vessel's head is pointed in the direction of the major eight points of the Compass. (Figure 33)

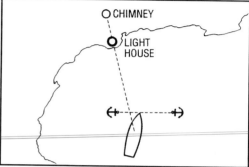

Figure 33 – *Moored in position to swing Compass for a deviation check*

This method may also be adopted by the vessel under way, crossing and recrossing the line of transit on different courses, taking a bearing each time the objects come in line. (Figure 34)

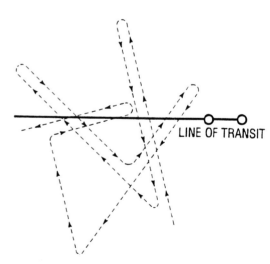

Figure 34 – *The course to steer for a deviation check using a transit*

A table is drawn up, the Compass bearings recorded and compared with the magnetic bearing. The difference is the deviation for that heading.

| Ship's head by Compass | Hamilton Reach Brisbane River Upstream Leads | | Deviation |
	Comp. Bearing	Mag. Bearing	
N ..	280° ..	278°	.. 2°W.
NE..	282° ..	"	.. 4°W.
E ..	281° ..	"	.. 3°W.
SE..	279° ..	"	.. 1°W.
S ..	276° ..	"	.. 2°W.
SW..	274° ..	"	.. 4°W.
W ..	275° ..	"	.. 3°W.
NW..	278° ..	"	.. NIL.

A deviation curve may be constructed on graph paper from the above table allowing all easterly deviations to the right of a centre line and all westerly to the left. (Figure 35)

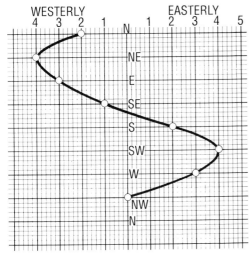

Figure 35 – *Deviation curve set out on graph paper*

(2) By selecting a distinct object at least eight miles away. The vessel is steamed around in a small circle and the object's bearing is recorded each time the vessel's direction coincides with a major point on the Compass. The magnetic bearing of the object cannot be read from the chart as the vessel's position is not definite. All bearings observed are added together and divided by the number of bearings recorded in order to obtain the average. A table is then constructed as in "No. 1"

method, using this average as the magnetic bearing of the object.

(3) By comparing a Compass bearing of the sun rising or setting with a true bearing of the sun extracted from the amplitude tables.

Care should be exercised when using the tables that you:-

(a) Do not measure the angle from north to south.

An amplitude is the angle between the true east point and the bearing of the sun when rising, or between the true west point and the bearing of the sun when setting.

(b) Always observe the bearing of the sun when the body is half its own height above the horizon.

Note: Amplitude tables are listed in Appendices.

The arguments required for observing an Amplitude are:-

(1) Latitude of the vessel (obtained from position on the chart).

(2) Declination of the sun (obtained from Nautical Almanac).

(3) Bearing of the sun (obtained when the body is half of its height above the horizon).

Order of Work:

Observe the bearing of the sun noting vessel's head and time.

Enter the current Almanac with time converted to Greenwich Mean Time (from Queensland local time subtract 10 hours).

Take out the declination of the sun.

Obtain the D.R. latitude of the vessel.

Enter the Amplitude tables with the vessel's latitude and the declination of the sun.

Take out the figure.

To name the bearing, precede the figure with east if the sun is rising, west if the sun is setting, then follow with the name of the declination either north or south (the bearing is true). Subtract the figure from 90 if east and north. Add if east and south. Subtract the figure from 270 if west and south. Add if west and north.

Compare the bearings for error.

Allow for variation.

The result is the deviation for the vessel's heading at the time.

Example: The bearing of the morning sun on the horizon was observed to be 064° by the standard Compass. If the D.R. of the vessel was latitude 18° south and the sun's declination was 19° north, what was the deviation for the vessel's heading at the time?

With latitude 18° S., and declination 19°N, enter the Amplitude table; figure reads 20. 1.

20. 1.

Disregard the decimal point.

Name East and North as the sun is rising and the declination is north. Therefore the bearing is East 20° North.

Subtract from	090°
	20°
Sun's true bearing	070°
Compass bearing	064°
Error	6°E.
Variation 10° E.	
Deviation	4°W.

TABLE OF DEVIATIONS OF THE STANDARD COMPASS

DEVIATION CARD NO. 5

Ship's Compass	Head by Magnetic	Deviation	Ship's Compass	Head by Magnetic	Deviation
000°	000°	NIL	180°	190°	10°E
010°	015°	5°E	190°	205°	15°E
020°	030°	10°	200°	220°	20°E
030°	045°	15°	210°	225°	15°E
040°	060°	20°	220°	230°	10°E
050°	065°	15°E	230°	235°	5°E
060°	070°	10°E	240°	240°	NIL
070°	075°	5°E	250°	245°	5°W
080°	080°	NIL	260°	250°	10°W
090°	085°	5°W	270°	255°	15°W
100°	090°	10°W	280°	260°	20°W
110°	095°	15°W	290°	275°	15°W
120°	100°	20°W	300°	290°	10°W
130°	115°	15°W	310°	305°	5°W
140°	130°	10°W	320°	320°	NIL
150°	145°	5°W	330°	335°	5°E
160°	160°	NIL	340°	350°	10°E
170°	175°	5°E	350°	355°	5°E

DEVIATION CARD NO. 1

Ship's Head by Standard Compass		Deviation	Ship's Head by Standard Compass		Deviation
000°	North	2°W	180°	South	2°E
010°	N10°E	2½°W	190°	S10°W	2½°E
020°	N20°E	3°W	200°	S20°W	3°E
030°	N30°E	3½°W	210°	S30°W	3½°E
040°	N40°E	4°W	220°	S40°W	4°E
050°	N50°E	4°W	230°	S50°W	4°E
060°	N60°E	4°W	240°	S60°W	3½°E
070°	N70°E	3½°W	250°	S70°W	3½°E
080°	N80°E	3°W	260°	S80°W	3°E
090°	East	3°W	270°	West	3°E
100°	S80°E	2°W	280°	N80°W	2½°E
110°	S70°E	1°W	290°	N70°W	2°E
120°	S60°E	NIL	300°	N60°W	1°E
130°	S50°E	1°E	310°	N50°W	NIL
140°	S40°E	1°E	320°	N40°W	½°W
150°	S30°E	1½°E	330°	N30°W	½°W
160°	S20°E	1½°E	340°	N20°W	1°W
170°	S10°E	1½°E	350°	N10°W	1½°W

For explanation of the use of Deviation Card No. 5 see Appendix G

Chapter 4

CHARTWORK

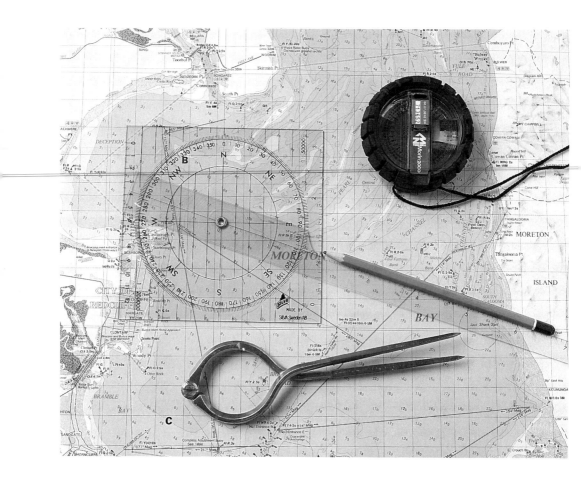

CHARTWORK

Navigation is the art of taking ships from one place to another.

The chart is a map of an area of the sea showing the position of channels, shoals, reefs and the depth of water relative to the land, the main features of which are also indicated where possible. All information of use to the navigator in the area is conveyed mainly by conventional symbols and abbreviations.

Hints to remember when using charts.

(a) Always use the largest scale chart, because:

    (i) Any errors are reduced to a minimum.

    (ii) If the chart is distorted, these errors will have the least effect.

    (iii) More detail is shown.

    (iv) The plate from which it is made is corrected before the plates of small scale charts.

(b) Transfer positions from one chart to another by bearing and distance from a point, common to both charts and check by latitude and longitude. This is most necessary because the graduations on the two charts may differ.

(c) Always check the vessel's position as soon as possible after her position has been transferred from one chart to another.

(d) Always use the nearest compass rose because:-

    (i) There will be less effect of distortion and the correct variation will be used.

    (ii) An error will be avoided if the chart used is drawn on the gnomonic projection.

(e) Remember the change of variation printed on each compass rose.

Q.1 Name the basic equipment required for chart work.

A.
Parallel ruler	Compass protractor
Dividers	Australia Pilot
Compass	Tide Tables
Soft rubber	Deviation table
Soft leaded	Admiralty List of Lights
pencils (2B)	Pencil sharpener

Q.2 What type of projection is used on charts for marine navigation ?

A. Mercator projection. Since the world is actually a sphere, some distortion is necessary before it can be represented as a flat surface. This "distortion" has to be carried out in a strictly proportionate manner, in order that the shape of the land, compass bearings and distances will remain relatively correct.

Q.3 How do you distinguish a well surveyed chart?

A. By the following points:-

    (a) The survey must be reasonably modern.

    (b) Soundings are shown close together and regular, with no blank spaces.

    (c) Fathom and contour lines must be shown.

    (d) There should be plenty of detail.

    (e) All the coastline must be drawn in distinctly with no dotted line indicating lack of information.

Q.4 Where is the information given on the chart to indicate whether the soundings are in metres or fathoms?

A. All information concerning the chart is tabulated in the title.

Q.5 What are soundings and how are they identified on a chart?

A. Soundings are identified by numerical figures indicating the depth of water at certain positions on the chart. They represent fathoms and feet (on the old charts), metres and tenths of a metre (on the new).

Q.6 To what level are the soundings on charts reduced?

A. Chart datum.

Lights

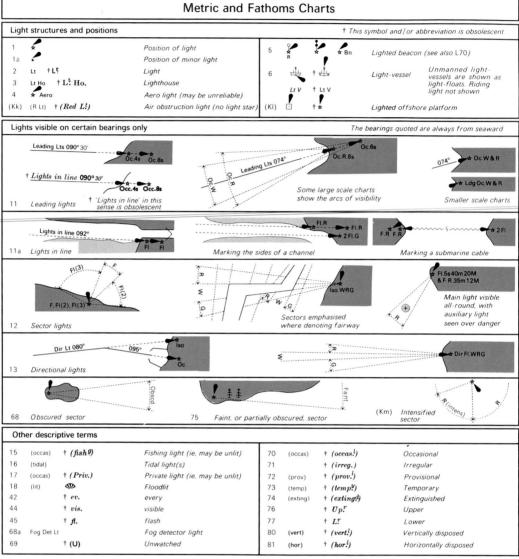

Metric and Fathoms Charts

Light structures and positions

† This symbol and/or abbreviation is obsolescent

1		Position of light
1a		Position of minor light
2	Lt †Lt	Light
3	Lt Ho †Lt Ho.	Lighthouse
4	★ Aero	Aero light (may be unreliable)
(Kk)	(R Lt) †(Red Lt)	Air obstruction light (no light star)

5	R ★ ★ ★ Bn	Lighted beacon (see also L70.)
6	Lt V †Lt V	Light-vessel — Unmanned light-vessels are shown as light-floats. Riding light not shown
(Kl)	□ †★	Lighted offshore platform

Lights visible on certain bearings only

The bearings quoted are always from seaward

Leading Lts 090° 30'
Oc.4s   Oc.8s

† *Lights in line 090° 30'*
Occ.4s   Occ.8s

11   Leading lights   † 'Lights in line' in this sense is obsolescent

Leading Lts 074°
Oc.R.6s   Oc.6s
Oc.W   Oc.R
Some large scale charts show the arcs of visibility

074°   ★ Oc.W & R
★ Ldg Oc.W & R
Smaller scale charts

Lights in line 092°
Fl   Fl

11a   Lights in line

Fl.R   ★ Fl.R
★ 2Fl.G
Marking the sides of a channel

F.R F.R   ★ 2Fl
Marking a submarine cable

Fl(3)   F
Fl(2)
F, Fl(2), Fl(3)

12   Sector lights

R
W
G
Sectors emphasised where denoting fairway

Iso.WRG

★ Fl.5s40m20M & F.R.35m12M
Main light visible all-round, with auxiliary light seen over danger

Dir Lt 080°   095°
Iso
Oc

13   Directional lights

R
G

★ Dir Fl.WRG

Obscd

68   Obscured sector

Faint

75   Faint, or partially obscured, sector

(Km)   Intensified sector
R (intens)   R

Other descriptive terms

15	(occas)	†(fish g)	Fishing light (ie, may be unlit)
16	(tidal)		Tidal light(s)
17	(occas)	†(Priv.)	Private light (ie, may be unlit)
18	(lit)	☀	Floodlit
42		†ev.	every
44		†vis.	visible
45		†fl.	flash
68a	Fog Det Lt		Fog detector light
69		†(U)	Unwatched

70	(occas)	†(occas!)	Occasional
71		†(irreg.)	Irregular
72	(prov)	†(prov!)	Provisional
73	(temp)	†(temp y)	Temporary
74	(exting)	†(exting d)	Extinguished
76		†Up r.	Upper
77		†L r.	Lower
80	(vert)	†(vert!)	Vertically disposed
81	(hor)	†(hor!)	Horizontally disposed

Example of a light description on a **metric** chart, using international abbreviations: ★ Fl(3)WRG.15s13m7-5M

Fl(3) Class, or character, of light: in this example a group flashing light, regularly repeating a group of three flashes.

WRG Colours of light: white, red and green, exhibiting the different colours in defined sectors.

15s Period of light in seconds, ie, the time taken to exhibit one full sequence of 3 flashes and eclipses: 15 seconds.

13m Elevation of focal plane above MHWS or MHHW or, where there is no tide, above MSL: 13 metres.

7-5M Luminous range in sea miles: the distance at which a light of a particular intensity can be seen in 'clear' visibility, taking no account of earth curvature. In countries such as Gt. Britain where 'clear' is defined as a meteorological visibility of 10 sea miles, the range may be termed 'nominal'. In this example the luminous ranges of the colours are: white 7 miles, green 5 miles, red between 7 and 5 miles.

Example of a light description on a **fathoms** chart, using international abbreviations: ★ Al.Fl.WR.30s110ft23/22M

Al.Fl. Class, or character, of light: in this example exhibiting single flashes of differing colours alternately.

WR. Colours of light shown alternately: white and red all-round (ie, not a sector light).

30s Period of light in seconds, ie, the time taken to exhibit the sequence of two flashes and two eclipses: 30 seconds.

110ft Elevation of focal plane above MHWS or MHHW or, where there is no tide, above MSL: 110 feet.

23/22M Range in sea miles. Until 1971 the lesser of **geographical** range (based on a height of eye of 15 feet) and luminous range was charted. Now, when charts are corrected, luminous (or nominal) range is given. In this example the luminous ranges of the colours are: white 23 miles, red 22 miles. The geographical range can be found from the table in the Admiralty List of Lights (for the elevation of 110 feet, it would be 16 miles).

Figure 36

Dangers

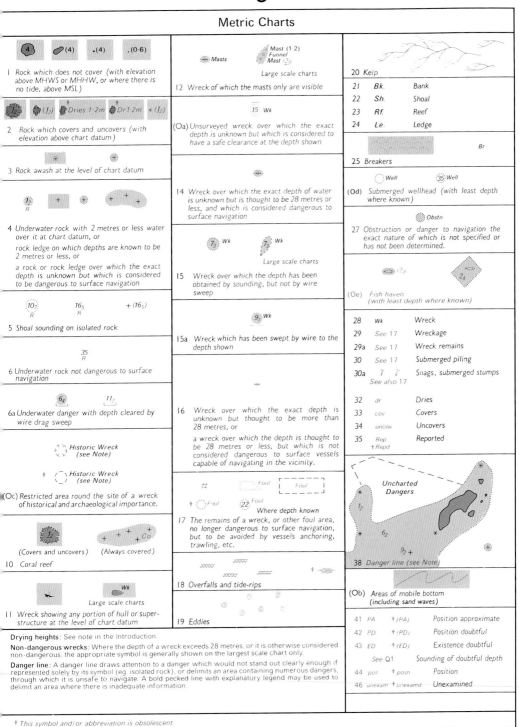

Metric Charts

1 Rock which does not cover (with elevation above MHWS or MHHW, or where there is no tide, above MSL)

2 Rock which covers and uncovers (with elevation above chart datum)

3 Rock awash at the level of chart datum

4 Underwater rock with 2 metres or less water over it at chart datum, or
rock ledge on which depths are known to be 2 metres or less, or
a rock or rock ledge over which the exact depth is unknown but which is considered to be dangerous to surface navigation

5 Shoal sounding on isolated rock

6 Underwater rock not dangerous to surface navigation

6a Underwater danger with depth cleared by wire drag sweep

Historic Wreck (see Note)

Historic Wreck (see Note)

(Oc) Restricted area round the site of a wreck of historical and archaeological importance.

(Covers and uncovers)   (Always covered)

10 Coral reef

11 Wreck showing any portion of hull or super-structure at the level of chart datum

Masts

Mast (1·2)
Funnel
Mast (2·1)
Large scale charts

12 Wreck of which the masts only are visible

15 Wk

(Oa) Unsurveyed wreck over which the exact depth is unknown but which is considered to have a safe clearance at the depth shown

14 Wreck over which the exact depth of water is unknown but is thought to be 28 metres or less, and which is considered dangerous to surface navigation

Wk   Wk
Large scale charts

15 Wreck over which the depth has been obtained by sounding, but not by wire sweep

Wk

15a Wreck which has been swept by wire to the depth shown

16 Wreck over which the exact depth is unknown but thought to be more than 28 metres, or
a wreck over which the depth is thought to be 28 metres or less, but which is not considered dangerous to surface vessels capable of navigating in the vicinity.

Foul   Foul

Foul   Foul
Where depth known

17 The remains of a wreck, or other foul area, no longer dangerous to surface navigation, but to be avoided by vessels anchoring, trawling, etc.

18 Overfalls and tide-rips

19 Eddies

20 Kelp

21 Bk.   Bank
22 Sh.   Shoal
23 Rf.   Reef
24 Le.   Ledge

Br

25 Breakers

Well   Well
(Od) Submerged wellhead (with least depth where known)

Obstn
27 Obstruction or danger to navigation the exact nature of which is not specified or has not been determined.

(Oe) Fish haven (with least depth where known)

28 Wk   Wreck
29 See 17   Wreckage
29a See 17   Wreck remains
30 See 17   Submerged piling
30a   Snags, submerged stumps
    See also 17
32 dr   Dries
33 cov   Covers
34 uncov   Uncovers
35 Rep   Reported
    †Repd

Uncharted Dangers

38 Danger line (see Note)

(Ob) Areas of mobile bottom (including sand waves)

41 PA   †(PA)   Position approximate
42 PD   †(PD)   Position doubtful
43 ED   †(ED)   Existence doubtful
    See Q1   Sounding of doubtful depth
44 pos   †posn   Position
46 unexam †unexamd Unexamined

Drying heights: See note in the Introduction.

Non-dangerous wrecks: Where the depth of a wreck exceeds 28 metres, or it is otherwise considered non-dangerous, the appropriate symbol is generally shown on the largest scale chart only.

Danger line: A danger line draws attention to a danger which would not stand out clearly enough if represented solely by its symbol (eg isolated rock), or delimits an area containing numerous dangers, through which it is unsafe to navigate. A bold pecked line with explanatory legend may be used to delimit an area where there is inadequate information.

† This symbol and/or abbreviation is obsolescent

Figure 37

Ports and Harbours

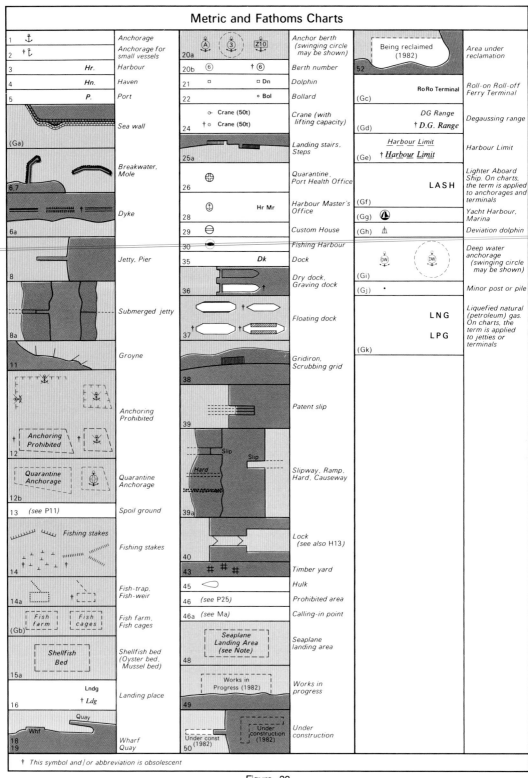

Metric and Fathoms Charts

1 ⚓	Anchorage	
2 † ⚓	Anchorage for small vessels	
3 **Hr.**	Harbour	
4 **Hn.**	Haven	
5 **P.**	Port	
(Ga)	Sea wall	
6,7	Breakwater, Mole	
6a	Dyke	
8	Jetty, Pier	
8a	Submerged jetty	
11	Groyne	
12 Anchoring Prohibited	Anchoring Prohibited	
12b Quarantine Anchorage	Quarantine Anchorage	
13 (see P11)	Spoil ground	
14 Fishing stakes	Fishing stakes	
14a	Fish-trap, Fish-weir	
(Gb) Fish farm / Fish cages	Fish farm, Fish cages	
15a Shellfish Bed	Shellfish bed (Oyster bed, Mussel bed)	
16 Lndg † Ldg	Landing place	
18 Whf / Quay / 19	Wharf Quay	

20a Ⓐ ③ Z10	Anchor berth (swinging circle may be shown)	
20b ⑥ † ⑥	Berth number	
21 ▫ ▫ Dn	Dolphin	
22 ◦ Bol	Bollard	
24 ⊶ Crane (50t) † ◦ Crane (50t)	Crane (with lifting capacity)	
25a	Landing stairs, Steps	
26 ⊕	Quarantine, Port Health Office	
28 ⊕ Hr Mr	Harbour Master's Office	
29 ⊖	Custom House	
30	Fishing Harbour	
35 **Dk**	Dock	
36	Dry dock, Graving dock	
37 † †	Floating dock	
38	Gridiron, Scrubbing grid	
39	Patent slip	
39a Hard / Slip Slip	Slipway, Ramp, Hard, Causeway	
40	Lock (see also H13)	
43 # # #	Timber yard	
45	Hulk	
46 (see P25)	Prohibited area	
46a (see Ma)	Calling-in point	
48 Seaplane Landing Area (see Note)	Seaplane landing area	
49 Works in Progress (1982)	Works in progress	
50 Under const (1982) / Under construction (1982)	Under construction	

52 Being reclaimed (1982)	Area under reclamation
(Gc) RoRo Terminal	Roll-on Roll-off Ferry Terminal
(Gd) DG Range † D.G. Range	Degaussing range
(Ge) Harbour Limit † Harbour Limit	Harbour Limit
(Gf) **LASH**	Lighter Aboard Ship. On charts, the term is applied to anchorages and terminals
(Gg) ⚓	Yacht Harbour, Marina
(Gh) ⚓	Deviation dolphin
(Gi) (DW) (DW)	Deep water anchorage (swinging circle may be shown)
(Gj) •	Minor post or pile
(Gk) **LNG** **LPG**	Liquefied natural (petroleum) gas. On charts, the term is applied to jetties or terminals

† *This symbol and/or abbreviation is obsolescent*

Figure 38

Topography: Artificial Features

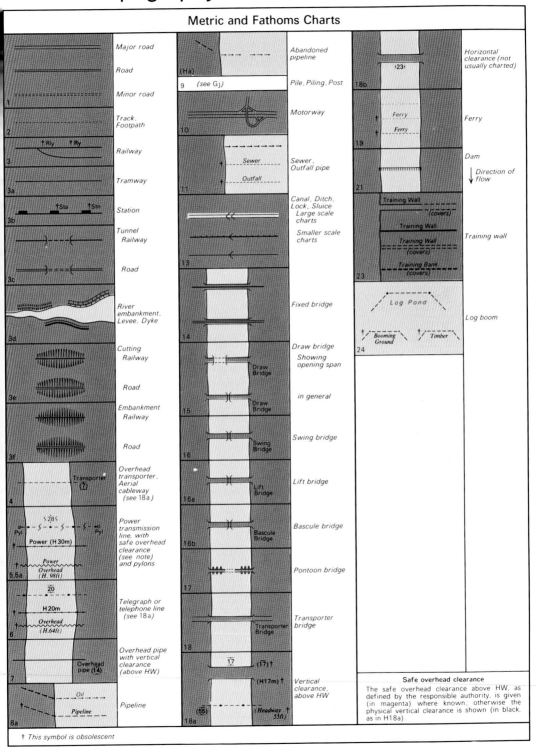

Metric and Fathoms Charts

1 Major road / Road / Minor road	**9** (Ha) *(see Gj)* Abandoned pipeline
2 Track, Footpath	**10** Pile, Piling, Post / Motorway
3 †Rly †Ry Railway	**11** Sewer / Outfall Sewer, Outfall pipe
3a Tramway	**13** Canal, Ditch, Lock, Sluice / Large scale charts / Smaller scale charts
3b †Sta †Stn Station	**14** Fixed bridge
3c Tunnel Railway / Road	**15** Draw bridge / Showing opening span / Draw Bridge / in general / Draw Bridge
3d River embankment, Levee, Dyke	**16** Swing Bridge Swing bridge
3e Cutting Railway / Road	**16a** Lift Bridge Lift bridge
3f Embankment Railway / Road	**16b** Bascule Bridge Bascule bridge
4 Transporter (7) Overhead transporter, Aerial cableway (see 18a)	**17** Pontoon bridge
5,5a Pyl Power (H 30m) Pyl / Power Overhead (H. 98ft) Power transmission line, with safe overhead clearance (see note) and pylons	**18** Transporter Bridge Transporter bridge
6 H 20m / Overhead (H.64ft) Telegraph or telephone line (see 18a)	**18a** (17)† / (H17m)† Vertical clearance, above HW / (55) (Headway 55ft)†
7 Overhead pipe (14) Overhead pipe with vertical clearance (above HW)	**18b** ‡23‡ Horizontal clearance (not usually charted)
8a Oil / Pipeline Pipeline	**19** Ferry / Ferry Ferry
	21 Dam / Direction of flow
	23 Training Wall / (covers) / Training Wall / Training Wall (covers) / Training Bank (covers) Training wall
	24 Log Pond / †Booming Ground / †Timber Log boom

Safe overhead clearance

The safe overhead clearance above HW, as defined by the responsible authority, is given (in magenta) where known; otherwise the physical vertical clearance is shown (in black, as in H18a).

† This symbol is obsolescent

Figure 39

Buildings

Miscellaneous Stations

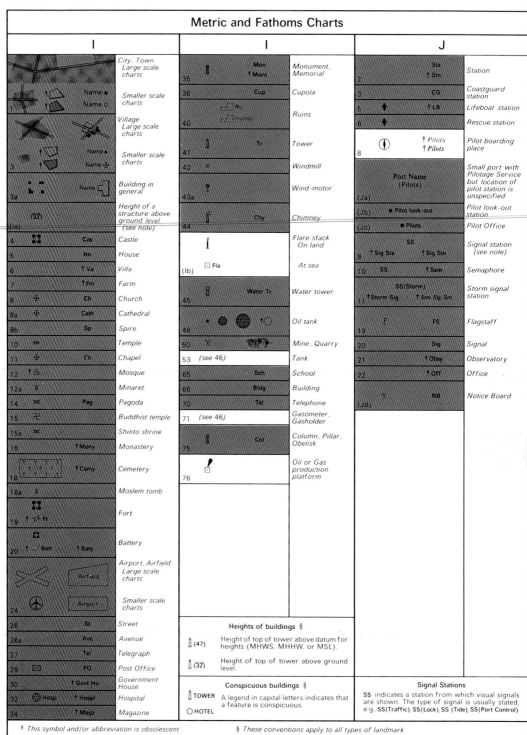

Metric and Fathoms Charts							
I		**I**		**J**			
City, Town Large scale charts	1	Mon † Mont	35	Monument, Memorial	2	Sta † Stn	Station
Name ■ Name o	1	Smaller scale charts	Cup	36	Cupola	3	CG	Coastguard station
Village Large scale charts	Ru (ruins)	40	Ruins	5	✦	† LB	Lifeboat station
Name ■ Name ⊕	3	Smaller scale charts	Tr	41	Tower	6	✦	Rescue station
Name	3a	Building in general	42	Windmill	8	† Pilots † Pilots	Pilot boarding place
(32)	(1a)	Height of a structure above ground level (see note)	43a	Wind-motor	(Ja)	Port Name (Pilots)	Small port with Pilotage Service but location of pilot station is unspecified
Cas	4	Castle	Chy	44	Chimney	(Jb)	■ Pilot look-out	Pilot look-out station
Ho	5	House	Fla	(1b)	Flare stack On land	(Jc)	■ Pilots	Pilot Office
† Va	6	Villa			At sea	9	SS † Sig Sta † Sig Stn	Signal station (see note)
† Fm	7	Farm	Water Tr	45	Water tower	10	SS † Sem	Semaphore
Ch	8	Church		46	Oil tank	11	SS(Storm) †Storm Sig † Stm.Sig.Stn.	Storm signal station
Cath	8a	Cathedral				19	FS	Flagstaff
Sp	8b	Spire				20	Sig	Signal
Temple	10			Mine, Quarry	53	(see 46)	Tank	21	† Obsy	Observatory
Ch	11	Chapel	Sch	65	School	22	† Off	Office
†	12	Mosque	Bldg	66	Building	(Jd)	NB	Notice Board
12a	Minaret	Tel	70	Telephone			
Pag	14	Pagoda	71	(see 46)	Gasometer, Gasholder			
15	Buddhist temple	Col	75	Column, Pillar, Obelisk			
15a	Shinto shrine	76	Oil or Gas production platform			
† Mony	16	Monastery						
† Cemy	18	Cemetery						
18a	Moslem tomb						
† Ft	19	Fort						
† ⌣ Batt † Baty	20	Battery						
Airfield	Airport, Airfield Large scale charts						
Airport	24	Smaller scale charts						
St	26	Street						
Ave	26a	Avenue						
Tel	27	Telegraph						
PO	29	Post Office						
† Govt Ho	30	Government House						
Hosp † Hospl	32	Hospital						
† Magz	34	Magazine						

Heights of buildings §

(47) — Height of top of tower above datum for heights (MHWS, MHHW, or MSL).

(32) — Height of top of tower above ground level.

Conspicuous buildings §

TOWER — A legend in capital letters indicates that a feature is conspicuous.

○ HOTEL

Signal Stations

SS indicates a station from which visual signals are shown. The type of signal is usually stated, e.g. SS(Traffic), SS(Lock), SS (Tide), SS(Port Control).

† This symbol and/or abbreviation is obsolescent   § These conventions apply to all types of landmark

Figure 40

Q.7 Interpret the following symbols and abbreviations:-

Cy	answer	clay	s	answer	sand
Co	"	coral	Bn	"	beacon
Sh	"	shell	(P.D.)	"	position doubtful
M	"	mud			
Oz	"	ooze	(E.D.)	"	existence doubtful
St	"	stone			

Q.8 What is a "clearing" line and how, is it shown on a chart?

A. A clearing line may be two objects in line, a bearing of an object, or arc of light, that shows navigable water one side, and danger to navigation on the other. It is commonly indicated by a red sector of light. (Fig. 41)

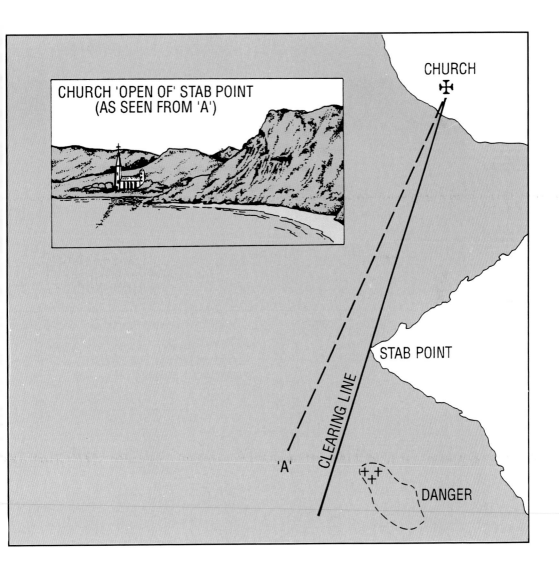

CHURCH 'OPEN OF' STAB POINT
(AS SEEN FROM 'A')

CHURCH

STAB POINT

CLEARING LINE

'A'

DANGER

Figure 41 – *Clearing Marks and Clearing Line*

Q.9 What is a "leading" line and how is it shown on a chart?

A. A leading line consists of two beacons or lights or objects in line which will lead a vessel over a bar in the best water into a harbour. They appear on a chart as "Lights or Beacons or Objects" in line.

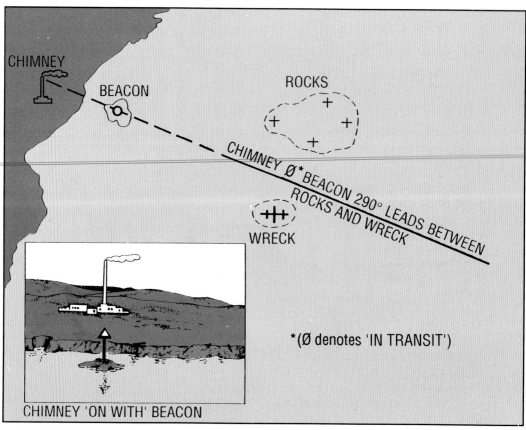

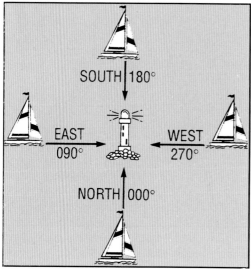

CHIMNEY 'ON WITH' BEACON

*(Ø denotes 'IN TRANSIT')

Figure 42 – *Leading marks and leading line*

Note: The bearing marked on either clearing or leading line is given as a true bearing from seaward. (Fig. 43)

Figure 43 – *Bearings true from seaward*

Q.10 What is latitude?

A The latitude of a place is its angular distance from the equator and is measured in degrees and minutes north and south of the equator.

Parallels of latitude are "small circles" parallel to the equator. All places on the same parallel are in the same latitude.

Q.11 How is the latitude of a place on the chart found?

A. Parallel rulers or dividers may be used. (Fig. 44)

First method: (Using dividers)

  (a) Open out the dividers and place the point of one leg exactly on the named position.

  (b) Adjust the divider span until the point of the other leg just touches the nearest parallel of latitude at a point vertically above or below the named position.

  (c) Transfer this divider distance to the latitude scale in the chart margin, opposite to the position.

  (d) Place one divider leg on the parallel of latitude used, and the other on the latitude scale.

  (e) Read off the latitude indicated by the position.

Second Method: (Using parallel ruler)

  (a) Put the long edge of the ruler along a parallel of latitude conveniently close to the named point, but so that one end just overlaps the graduated latitude scale at the margin of the chart.

  (b) Move the ruler horizontally up (or down) the chart until a long edge passes exactly through the position the latitude of which is sought.

  (c) Read off the latitude shown on the latitude scale on the same edge of the ruler.

Q.12 What is longitude?

A. The longitude of a place is the angular distance along the equator between the meridian through Greenwich, and the meridian through the place. It is measured east or west of the Greenwich meridian in degrees and minutes from 0° to 180°.

Q.13 How is the longitude of a place on the chart found?

A. Parallel rulers or dividers may be used. (Fig. 45)

First Method: (If dividers are used)

  (a) Measure the exact horizontal distance between the place and the nearest vertical meridian.

  (b) Transfer this measurement to the longitude scale at the top or bottom of the chart.

  (c) Put one leg of the dividers on the meridian already used and the other leg in the direction of the place along the scale.

  (d) Read off the longitude indicated by the position.

Second Method: (If a parallel ruler is used)

  (a) Put the long edge of the ruler along the nearest meridian, so that one end overlaps the marginal longitude scale.

  (b) Move the ruler across the chart until one long edge cuts the position given.

  (c) Read off the longitude at the scale from the same edge.

Q.14 Describe meridian of longitude?

A. Meridians are great circles passing through the poles. The Prime Meridian is that one passing through Greenwich Observatory from which longitude is measured east and west. All places on the same meridian are in the same longitude.

Note: The equator and meridians of longitude are all considered the same size circles, known as "great circles", parallels of latitude decrease in circumference towards the poles and are known as "small circles".

All meridians of longitude are great circles but all great circles on the surface of the earth are not meridians. You may have great circles on the earth's surface in any direction. The arc of a great circle is the shortest distance between any given points.

Q.15 How should a position be marked off on the chart – given latitude and longitude?

A. (a) With the dividers measure up, or down, from a convenient parallel at the latitude scale.

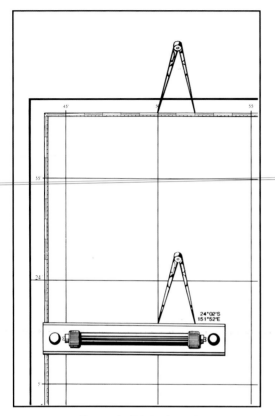

Figure 44 – *To read off latitude or longitude on the chart by parallel rule or dividers*

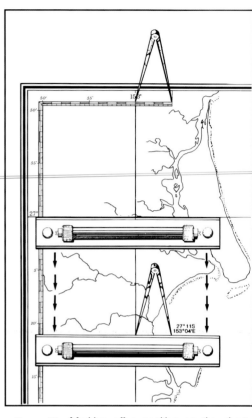

Figure 45– *Marking off a position on the chart*

(b) Transfer this divider distance upwards or downwards from the same parallel to a meridian conveniently near that of the given longitude.

(c) Put the parallel ruler edge accurately to one of the engraved parallels of latitude. Move it up the chart until its leading edge cuts exactly the latitude thus marked by the dividers.

(d) With the dividers again, and from the meridian already used, measure off on the longitude scale, the exact given longitude.

(e) Transfer this distance with one divider leg from the same meridian and spread along the leading edge of the parallel ruler.

(f) The position of the point of the other leg will be the exact position required. (Refer Fig. 45)

Q.16 Define the term "direction" ?

A.   Direction is determined by the point on the horizon towards which a vessel is heading, or the point on the horizon to which a person is looking.

Q.17 Given the position of one place and the true bearing or direction of another, how would you lay-off the time bearing or direction ?

A. (a) First locate the given position.

(b) Put the long edge of a parallel ruler across the face of the compass rose nearest to the reference point.

(c) Then slew it so that the edge cuts the centre of the rose and also the graduation on the outer true ring which represents the bearing.

(d) As an extra check on the accuracy of the rulers angle the same edge should not only pass through the centre of the rose and the desired bearing, but also on the other side of the centre through the reciprocal bearing.

(e) Now move the ruler across the chart, carefully preserving its inclination to the meridian, until one of its long edges passes exactly through the centre of the reference point .

(f) Draw a light line along this edge of the ruler, taking care that the line is drawn in the direction indicated by the compass rose angle, and not in the reverse direction.

Note: When measuring angles of direction such as the vessel's course, the compass rose nearest to the point of reference on the chart should always be used.

Never do rough marking or calculation on the chart. Use scribblers for this purpose.

Q.18 Why doesn't the true north of the compass rose usually coincide with the magnetic north?

A. Magnetic north's geographical position varies from that of the North Pole. The angular difference is called variation; hence true north of the compass rose does not usually coincide with magnetic north.

Q.19 Explain the term "error" with reference to the compass.

A. Compass error is the sum of variation and deviation.

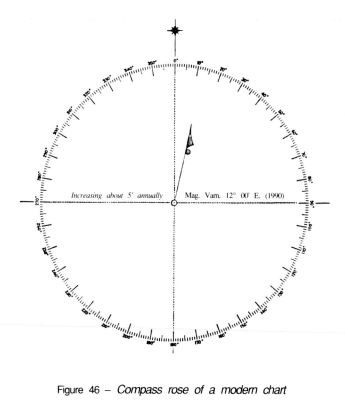

Increasing about 5' annually   Mag. Varn. 12° 00' E. (1990)

Figure 46 – *Compass rose of a modern chart*

Q.20 Where on the chart would you find the variation to apply to the compass?

A. Marked on the compass rose nearest the vessel's position.

Q.21 The variation given on a chart is 10°20'E. (1964) increasing 3' annually, what will the variation be for 1974 ?

A. 10°50'East. (note - for practical purposes 11°E)

Q.22 Where is the deviation table for the correction of the compass to be found?

A. A table of deviations is compiled for the application to compass headings and kept on the bridge. On larger vessels error checks of the standard compass are taken frequently and the data entered in the compass error book.

Q.23 How may the deviation be found from the bearing of shore objects?

A. The deviation may be found by taking a bearing of shore objects in transit. The true bearing of the object, or transit is taken from the chart.

Variation is applied converting it to a magnetic bearing. The two bearings are then compared and the difference is the deviation for the direction of the vessel's head at the time. (Fig. 31)

Q.24 A distant object is known to bear 045° magnetic. It bears 048° by the standard compass and 050° by the steering compass. Explain why there is a difference.

A. The difference between the magnetic bearing and vessel's compass is due to deviation for that particular heading of the ship. The difference between the bearing by the standard compass and the steering compass is due to the positions in which they are located in the vessel. The standard compass is mounted as clear as possible of all magnetic and electrical influences within the vessel. On the other hand the steering compass is mounted in a convenient position from which to steer resulting in it being subjected to more deflection by the magnetism within the ship than the standard compass. (Fig. 31)

Q.25 Interpret the following symbols:-

(a) F., Fl., Oc., Al., Iso.

(b) F.Fl., (3) 20s, 40 m, 15M.

(c) Oc. W.R. 15s, 10M. (U).

A. (a) Fixed: Flashing: Occulting: Alternating: Isophase,

(b) Fixed Group Flash: three every twenty seconds: forty metres high: visibility fifteen nautical miles.

(c) Occulting white and red in sectors of those colours every fifteen seconds: Visibility ten miles: Unattended.

Q.26 Define the term "set"?

A. Set Is the direction in which a current or tidal stream is flowing.

Q.27 Define the term "drift"?

A. Drift is the distance at which a vessel deviates from Its course due to wind, current, or tidal Influences.

Note: To name the wind, take the direction from which It blows.

To name the set, take the direction to which it flows.

Q.28 How are tidal streams marked on charts?

A. Tidal streams are marked by arrows pointing In the direction of the set with the rate of the set marked on the shaft. Flood tide is distinguished by an arrow having feathers on one side of the tail and ebb tide by no feathers at all.

Q.29 How Is a current marked on the chart?

A. A current is marked with an arrow pointing in the direction of the set. The arrow has a wriggle in the shaft and no feathers. The rate of the set is marked on the shaft.

Q.30 How are mountain peaks marked on the charts?

A. Mountain peaks are marked by a small dot with the height in feet or metres alongside of it.

Note: Heights are measured from above mean high water spring tides where as soundings are taken from below mean low water spring tides.

Q.31 How is the position of the vessel fixed when within sight of land?

A. By taking compass bearings of two or more prominent objects marked on the chart.

Q.32 When out of sight of land, how is the position of a vessel fixed?

A. (a) By observation of heavenly bodies with a sextant.

(b) Modern systems have been devised, incorporating radio signals, satellite systems etc, to plot positions accurately and conveniently for ocean going vessels.

Q.33 How would you establish on a chart the direction between two points?

A. The position of the two points of reference must first be identified on the chart.

To ascertain the direction from one to the other such as in charting a course:-

(a) Put the long edge of the parallel ruler directly between both places so that the centre of each is touching the edge.

(b) Lightly draw a pencil line connecting them.

(c) Move the ruler over the chart - carefully preserving its direction - until a long edge exactly cuts the centre of the nearest compass rose.

(d) Then read off the direction angle - on the outer ring of the compass rose.

(e) The direction bearing is true.

(Refer Fig. 47)

Q.34 How would you establish a course on a chart if your parallel rulers were damaged?

A. By using a length of straight round bar, or anything that could be used as a roller. In the same manner as outlined for a roller parallel ruler. (Fig. 47)

Q.35 What other equipment may be used?

A. Two Set Squares or Douglas Protractor

Q.36 If the compass were damaged could a chart be used for navigation ?

1. Yes to a limited degree. Navigate from the soundings on the chart with the assistance of the echo sounder, allowing for tidal rise calculated from the tide tables.

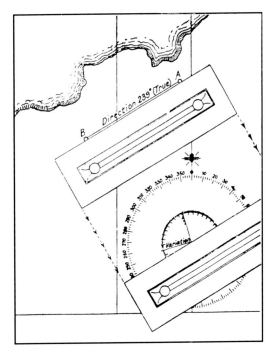

Figure 47 – *Laying off direction on the chart – charting a course*

2. By horizontal sextant angles.

3. By using prominent points and islands etc, for transit bearings (bridge navigation).

Q.37 How might the distance between two places on a chart be measured?

A. (a) If the chart is of large scale and the distance is short:-

(i) Identify the exact positions on the chart of the two places.

(ii) Open out dividers until the point of each leg rests upon one of the places.

(iii) Transfer this divider distance to the distance scale (latitude scale) on the right or left hand margins of the chart.

(iv) Be sure that the centre of the distance comes approximately at the mean latitude of the interval being measured.

(v) Read off the graduations of the latitude scale between the divider points.

(vi) Measure every degree of latitude as 60 nautical miles and every minute as one nautical mile.

(b) If the distance to be measured is long, or almost in the direction of a parallel, the best way to measure it accurately is:-

   (i) Draw a pencil line connecting the two points.

   (ii) Set the dividers to a convenient distance (say 10 miles) on the distance scale abreast this line.

   (iii) Measure the length of the whole line in steps of 10 miles.

   (iv) Measure off separately any portion which does not coincide with the ten mile step.

Q.38 How is a position plotted by means of its direction (or bearing) and distance from a known reference point ?

A.   (a) Identify the known reference point. (Fig. 48)

   (b) Through its exact centre, draw the appropriate line of direction at the proper angle with the meridian.

   (c) Along this line, from the point of reference, measure off the distance given.

   (d) Mark with a small circle the required position. Note: If necessary, the latitude and longitude of this point, could now be read off the marginal scales.

Q.39 When taking bearings by compass, which would be taken first?

A.   The bearings of the objects nearest the bow or stern firstly and then those abeam. The latter change more rapidly than those towards the bow or stern.

Q.40 On taking three bearings of distant objects, it is found when laying the corrected bearings on the chart that they do not meet at the same point and so form a triangle. What is this triangle called?

A.   A cocked hat. (Fig. 49)

Q.41 In the cocked hat where may the position of the vessel be assumed?

A.   If the area of the cocked hat is very small it can be assumed the vessel's position to be the centre of the triangle. Should the area be large the position is best assumed to be the angle of the triangle nearest the danger.

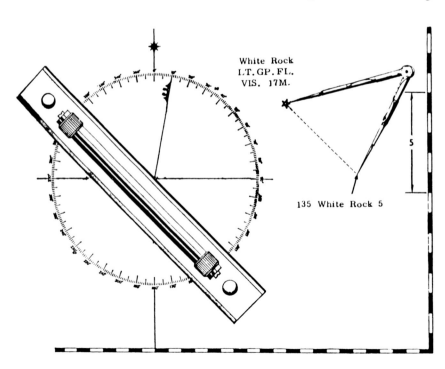

White Rock
L.T. GP. FL.
VIS. 17M.

135 White Rock 5

Figure 48 – Plotting a position by bearing and distance

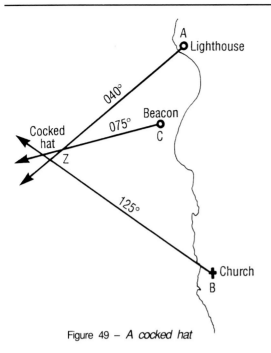

Figure 49 – *A cocked hat*

Note: If cocked hats are excessively large the bearings should be taken again.

Q.42 What is the first check to be made should the bearings keep giving cocked hats?

A. See that there are no objects near the compass such as screw drivers, hammers, transistor radios, etc to affect its performance.

Q.43 What is the second check to be made?

A. Check the deviation. Make sure the deviation being applied to the bearing is the deviation for the vessel's heading at the time of taking the bearings.

Q.44 Name other causes that could produce a cocked hat?

A. (a) Local magnetic anomaly (e.g. iron ore in the sea bed).

(b) Gyration of the compass card. (Inaccurate reading due to a swinging card).

(c) Lubber line not parallel to the vessel's keel.

(d) Incorrect reading of the compass card figures when inverted by the azimuth mirror.

(e) Error in the azimuth (prism not adjusted correctly).

Q.45 What is the best method of transferring a vessel's position from one chart to another?

A. The safest method when transferring the vessel's plotted position from one chart to another is to take a fixed land point common to both charts. Then

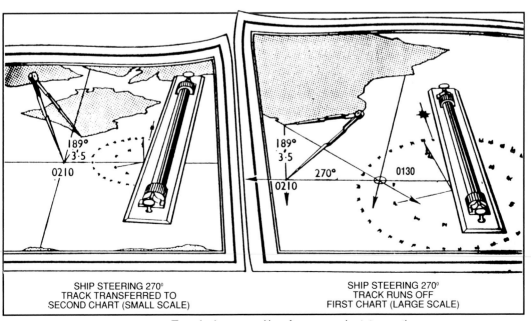

Figure 50 – *Transferring a position from one chart to another*

finding out the vessel's bearing and distance from the land point on the one chart, transfer it as a bearing and distance to the other.

Q.46 Why should care be exercised in transferring a vessel's position from one chart to another?

A. Charts may distort in the printing process. A chart may shrink evenly but it does not follow the distortion of another will be the same.

Note: On charts that have been compiled from two separate surveys one of the outlying islands and another of the mainland's foreshores, it is wise to select bearings from one or the other (those nearest the vessel) and not try to combine the two when fixing the vessel's position, otherwise the bearings may not coincide. A good example of such charts are those on the northern coast of New Guinea towards the West Irian border.

Q.47 Chart a course so that a vessel will pass a determined distance off an object.

A. Draw a circle whose radius is the required distance off the object using the position of the object as the centre. Then draw the course line so that it just touches the outer edge of the circle as in Fig. 51.

Q.48 Explain briefly the method of finding the course to steer from A to B to counteract a given current.

(a) Mark off positions A and B and join by a straight line (vessel's true course).

(b) Hourly rate of set is 3 knots 344°T. Vessel's speed 8 knots.

(c) From C lay off CD 344°T three miles which is the set of the tide in one hour. With centre D and radius 8 nautical miles (the vessel's speed

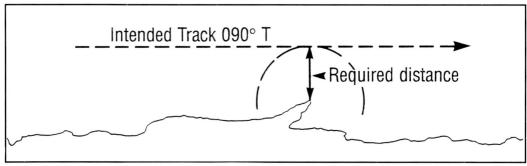

Figure 51 – *Laying a course to pass a determined distance off an object*

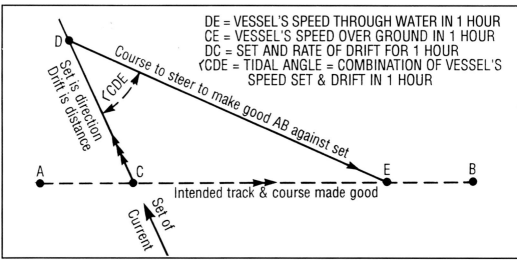

Figure 52 – *To counteract a given current*

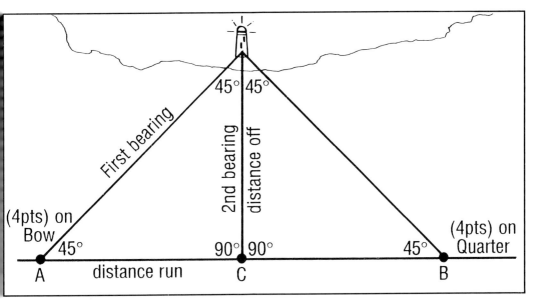

First bearing

2nd bearing

distance off

(4pts) on Bow

45°

90° 90°

45°

(4pts) on Quarter

A

distance run

C

B

Figure 53 – *Four point bearing*

in one hour) make an arc cutting the track at E join DE. Then DE is the direction the vessel must head to counteract the effect of the tide. CE should be the course made good and speed over the ground in one hour. (Fig. 52)

Four Point Bearing or Doubling the Angle on the Bow.

Q.49 Explain and illustrate with sketches what is meant by a four point bearing or doubling the angle on the bow. (Fig. 53)

A. The log reading is noted when an object is 45° on the bow and again when it is 90° on the bow. The distance run over the ground between these points is the distance from the object when it is abeam.

If a current is setting directly with or against the vessel its effect on the speed as indicated by the log must be allowed for. If the vessel is steaming obliquely through a tide it is better to plot the bearings, the course and the current on the chart as for an ordinary running fix with current. Note: The best results are obtained when the angles on the bow are as broad as possible. This is the reason why the four point

bearing is used in determining the beam distance when passing a light or headland.

Q.50 Outline the main disadvantage of a four point bearing.

A. A disadvantage in the four point bearing is that the object is abeam before the distance off can be found. It is sometimes desirable to know in advance how far off the object will be when it comes abeam in order to clear some outlying danger to seaward of the object, such as a sunken wreck.

Combination of Angles on the Bow.

Q.51 How might the distance a vessel will lie off an object when abeam, be determined in advance?

A. This might be accomplished by noting the time when the angle of an object is 35° on the bow, and later, when the angle is 67° on the bow. The distance sailed between bearings should be the distance the vessel will pass off the object when abeam. In the figure, angle A = 35°. angle B = 67° The distance run between A and B is the distance off the object when abeam. (Fig. 54)

Note: Other combinations of angles that may be used are 26½° and 45°, 32° and 59°, 37° and 72°

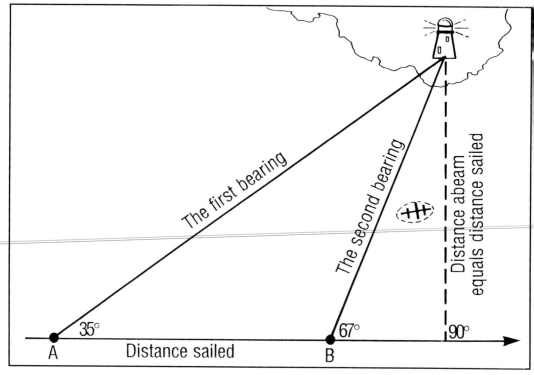

Figure 54 – *To predetermine the distance off when abeam*

A Running Fix.

Q.52 Plot a vessel's position by the procedure of a running fix.

A. A running fix may be used to establish the vessel's position with a fair degree of accuracy when there is only a single point of land or lighthouse in sight. The method of work is as follows:-

In figure 55 the vessel is supposed to be steaming along the course line from A to B.

Observe a bearing of point C by compass and note the time.

Convert to a true bearing by applying compass error the sum of the deviation for the vessel's head and the variation).

Lay off the true bearing on the chart represented in figure 55 by the line CQ.

It is now known that the vessel is somewhere on the line CQ heading in the direction of AB.

For convenience let the vessel's position be assumed to be at D.

Should that not be the correct position any error must be in the same direction as CQ since the vessel is somewhere on that line.

Allow the vessel to steam at her speed (say 5 knots) for two hours then observe a second bearing of the point C.

Convert to a true bearing and lay off on the chart represented in figure 55 by the line CE.

The vessel is now somewhere on the second line of bearing.

From point D measure ten miles (distance steamed in two hours) along the course line AB and mark point F.

If point D had been the vessel's position at the time of observing the first bearing, point F would coincide with point E on the line of bearing CE.

If point F does not coincide, an error has been made in assuming the first position of the vessel to be D.

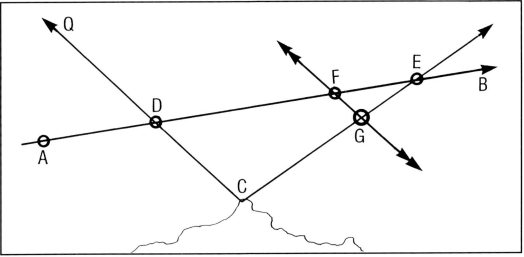

Figure 55 – *A running fix*

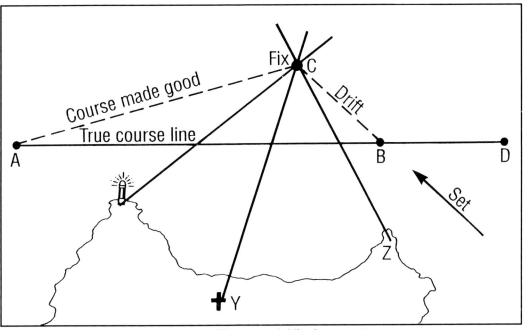

Figure 56 – *The set and drift of a current*

The error as revealed in the figure 55 lies in the direction of the first bearing CQ.

A line parallel to CQ is therefore drawn through position F cutting the line of the second bearing CE at G which is the vessel's position at that time, providing there is no current.

Note: Where the set and drift of a current is known allowance must be made accordingly.

Set and Drift of a Current.

Q.53 Find the set and drift of a current.
The vessel reached Position C (resolved by cross bearings) after steaming for one hour at ten knots from known position A. (Fig. 56)

A. Vessel departs position A along her course line for D.

Mark off run of one hour (10 miles) along her course line at B - vessel's expected position at time of bearings, also known as the Dead Reckoning (D.R.) position.

Resolve bearings observed as in figure 55 and mark vessel's actual position at C.

The current has set the vessel from her expected (or D.R.) position at B to her actual position at C.

The direction from B to C expressed as a true direction is the set of the current experienced.

Lay the parallel rulers along the line BC, move them over the nearest compass rose and read off set.

The reading from the compass rose must always be taken in the direction from the expected (D.R.) to the actual position.

The drift of the current is the distance in miles from B to C measured on the latitude scale.

Leeway

Q.54 What is Leeway?

A. Leeway is the amount which a vessel drifts or makes to leeward of her course by compass, when she is steaming with the wind on her side. It is another factor to take into consideration when trying to determine the actual course a vessel is making good. These days Leeway is expressed in degrees and is basically a matter for judgement by the navigator.

Q.55 What factors influence the navigators estimate of the leeway being made by a vessel?

A. (a) strength of the wind.

(b) draught of the vessel. i.e. a barge type has little grip, in the water.

(c) Design of the vessel. i.e. High super structure has a much larger surface exposed.

(d) Direction of the wind with relation to the vessels heading i.e. the wind on the beam of the vessel will cause maximum leeway. As the angle of the direction of the wind decreases towards the bow or stern so does the leeway.

(e) Speed of the vessel. i.e. when two vessels are on parallel courses the slower will make the greater angle of leeway. The faster vessel has the influence on the apparent wind causing it to draw more from ahead than in the slower vessel, thus causing less side thrust. Faced with the above factors, it is clearly seen why leeway is always approximate and depends a lot on the judgement and experience of the navigator. After a little practice it may be estimated by looking astern and noting the angle of the vessel to the log line or wake.

Q.56 How is leeway applied?

A. To compensate for leeway, the amount when estimated should always be applied to the true course. This is the golden rule whether converting a course from true to compass or compass to true. The reason for this is that while variation is relatively consistent in a locality, the deviation more especially in a vessel where the compass hasn't been adjusted or corrected could vary greatly with the difference in direction of the vessel's heading.

For example (1) True to Compass, given the true course required to be made good or intended track to the 106° a wind blowing from the N.E. strength 6 giving a leeway of 5°. Variation for the locality 10°E. Deviation Card supplied No. 5, work out the compass course to steer to make good the Intended track.

Method of Working:-

True course to make good	106°
Apply Leeway for wind from N.E. blowing on Port Side	5°
Gives the True Course to steer	101°
Apply Variation for locality	10°E
Gives Magnetic Course to steer	091°
Enter Deviation Card No. 5 supplied, take out deviation for ship's heading	091°
Magnetic Deviation	11°W
Gives Compass Course to steer	102°
Total Compass Error	1°W

Chapter 5

RADAR

RADAR

Q.1 What are the main controls on a radar set?

A. General group consists of:

(1) Brilliance;

(2) Rain Clutter;

(3) Gain;

(4) Tuning;

(5) Sea Clutter;

Those affecting accuracy of bearings are:

(6) Horizontal and vertical shift;

(7) Alignment of heading marker;

Other controls used during operation are:

(8) Range switch;

(9) Stand by switch;

(10) Remove heading marker switch

(11) Rain switch;

Q.2 What attention should be given to the position of controls before switching on for proper adjustment and to avoid damaging the set?

A. Turn the Brilliance and Gain controls right down to minimum and the sea clutter to give maximum clutter.

Q.3 Give the correct procedure in the operation of the Radar Controls to get the best results from the set.

A. (1) See that the scanner is clear of all obstructions.

(2) Turn the Brilliance, Gain (Sensitivity) and Sea-clutter off.

(3) Set the pulse length switch to 'Long', if possible.

(4) Set the rain switch to 'Normal' if so marked.

(5) Set the 'Stand-by/Transmit' Switch to 'Transmit'.

(6) Select a long or medium range on the relative unstabilized display.

(7) Switch on and wait about three minutes for the transmission to start.

(8) Turn up the brilliance control until the rotating trace is just visible.

(9) Switch on the range rings and adjust the focus control by slowly rocking it across the point of minimum thickness of the rings, gradually reducing the movement until the thinnest lines possible are obtained.

(10) Turn off the range rings and adjust the brilliance so that the trace just disappears.

(11) Check that the centre spot is directly under the centre of the bearing cursor. This can be done by switching on the electronic bearing Marker and setting it at 90° from the heading marker, then seeing that the mechanical bearing cursor will lie directly over them both in turn. where the electronic marker is not fitted, the heading marker may be used on both 000° and 090°.

(12) Reset the heading marker to 000°

(13) Turn up the Sensitivity (Gain) so that a faint speckled background extends to the edge of the display.

(14) Turn to the 3-mile range and switch on the performance monitor and adjust the manual tuning control (where fitted) for maximum length of plume. If a performance monitor is not fitted, then tune for maximum sea clutter. Some sets have a neon light or meter to facilitate tuning.

(15) Switch off the performance monitor and adjust the anti-clutter control so that sea echoes are just painting on the screen (using the short pulse length).

Note: The Sea-clutter control is very critical. If too much is used, targets as well as sea echoes may be removed and, if too little is used, then target echoes will not be seen against the bright background of the sea-clutter. It must be emphasized, however, that the anti-clutter control does not possess any magical powers and any targets which return weaker echoes than the sea surrounding them cannot be made to appear.

(16) Check for correct number of range rings and that they are evenly spaced.

Q.4 Could bad tuning of the operational controls affect the performance of a radar set?

A.   Yes, it is most important that the radar be correctly tuned to gain maximum benefit from it as a navigational aid. If it is badly adjusted the radar picture may-

(a) Obscure important targets.

(b) Not show a number of short and long range targets.

(c) Not give the correct range and bearing information of important targets.

(d) Reduce the life of the radar display tube.

Q.5 How is a bearing taken of a target on the radar screen?

A.   The bearing is taken by moving a radial line (on a transparent disc covering the screen) so that the line lies over the centre of the target. The outer end of the line will then point to the relative bearing on a scale of degrees round the edge of the screen. For accurate bearings, the inner end of the line must coincide with the centre of the picture, and the heading target with zero on the scale. This is adjusted by the horizontal and vertical shift controls and the heading marker.

Q.6 How would the range of a target on the radar screen be measured?

A.   The range may be measured in two different ways (on most sets).

(1) Fixed range rings superimposed on the radar picture at regular intervals (e.g. 2,4,6,8, miles on the 10 mile range). It is necessary to estimate just where the target is between the rings.

(2) Variable range marker, which is a single ring which may be moved in and out by turning a knob. The position of the ring is indicated on a dial. The inside of the ring should be made to coincide with the nearest part of the target, and the range of the target is read from the dial. This unit is liable to be slightly less accurate than the fixed rings.

Q.7 Name the three factors affecting the reflecting properties of targets?

A.   (1) Size.

(2) Shape and aspect.

(3) Composition.

(1) SIZE

The bigger the target is, the stronger the echo it returns.

(2) SHAPE AND ASPECT

Just like a ray of light striking a reflecting surface, the strongest echo or reflection will take place when the reflecting surface is flat, and at right angles to the line of transmission. If the surface is curved or flat but at an angle to the line of transmission (aspect), a large amount of the energy may be deflected in another direction, and only a small amount returned in the echo.

(3) COMPOSITION

The ability of the target to reflect or re-transmit radar energy will depend on its electrical qualities, good conductors of electricity being normally the best reflectors.

NOTE

In assessing the reflecting properties of a target, these three should generally be considered in order of importance, except when shape — aspect and/or composition are so poor that the target will return only a weak echo (if any) in spite of possible very large size. For example, a flat sandy beach or mud flat gives a very poor aspect, an iceberg very poor composition.

Factors affecting the production of radar echoes may be arranged thus:-

R	ange	E	nvironment
A	rea	C	omposition
D	uration of pulse	H	eight
A	spect	O	bstruction
R	efraction	E	fficiency
		S	urface

Q.8 Name the factors affecting recognition of sub-standard performances of all information from radar?

A.   (1) Performance monitor

(2) Non standard refraction

(3) Rain or other precipitation

(4) Sea clutter

(5) Spurious Echoes

(6) Interference from other radars

Q.9 Roughly describe a performance monitor?

A. Some means of checking whether the equipment is operating properly. A switch on the display unit causes either a disc or a feather shaped gleam of light to appear on the screen. The radius of the disc or length of the plume is measured using range rings or a marker and compared to that specified in the manual supplied with the radar. Any appreciable reduction indicates a reduction in the performance, which may be sufficient to delete echoes which would otherwise appear.

Q.10 Give an example of non standard refraction.

A. As radar waves travel over the earth's surface, they experience refraction which causes them to tend to follow the earth's curvature, and this increases the range of the radar. If, however, lapse rate of the atmosphere (decreases temperature and pressure with increase in height) is above or below average this will increase or decrease the amount of refraction, and in extreme cases may cause a very marked increase or decrease of the detection range of the target.

Q.11 Give the effects of rain or other precipitation.

A. Rain has a two fold affect on the performance of radar. Firstly, an echo from a target within or beyond the rain will appear weaker than usual, and secondly, an echo from a target within the rain area may be masked by the rain echoes themselves which appear as a smudge on the radar screen.

Q.12 Describe the effect of sea clutter?

A. Sea clutter is caused by echoes returning from wave crests around the vessel, and the correct adjustment of the sea clutter control is extremely critical. Too much sea clutter masks the target echo, and the removal of all sea clutter from the screen, also removes the target echo.

Q.13 In what forms do we find spurious echoes?

A. Spurious or unwanted echoes take a number of forms.

(1) Second trace echoes caused by abnormal atmospheric conditions, which can return echoes from targets (usually higher land) at distances far in excess of the normal radar range.

(2) Multiple echoes caused by repeated reflection back and forth of the radar signal between the hulls of two ships close to each other, which shows a line of equally spaced echoes on the correct bearing. The nearest is the true echo.

(3) Indirect echo caused by reflection of radar signal from mast or funnel of your own vessel.

(4) Side lobe echoes caused by small amounts of energy being transmitted at oblique angles on either side of the main lobe of transmission, which shows an arc of weak echoes at the correct range spreading on either side of the true echo.

(5) Rain and sea return mentioned before.

(6) Interference from other vessel's radar may appear on the screen, usually as a series of curved dotted lines radiating from the centre.

WARNING

A reduction of these false echoes may be made by reducing gain, but this should be done with extreme caution, if at all, in case wanted echoes are lost.

Q.14 What care should be taken in the installation of radar equipment?

A. (1) Technical advice should always be followed and installation should be carried out by a competent technician.

(2) The scanner should be as high as possible and should be clear of all objects in order to minimise all shadow sectors, blind arcs and false echoes.

(3) The scanner position should be on the starboard side if there is a choice

of two sides on the top of the wheelhouse. This prevents any problems associated with confusing information about targets coming down on your starboard side to whom you are obliged to give way.

(4) P.P.I. Displays should not be placed where direct sunlight falls on the tube face (since this makes it very difficult to see during daylight). It should be shielded in some manner to avoid this difficulty.

(5) The radar should be calibrated and the heading line accuracy checked on installation. Further checking may be subsequently carried out by noticing any variations in the ranges of the same target on different range scales. If any difference occurs they should be adjusted immediately so that your range and heading are accurate.

Q.15 State in order of preference the methods of position fixing by radar.

A.   (a) Radar range and visual bearing of a prominent isolated object.

     (b) Radar ranges of several radar-conspicuous objects plotted in position circles.

     (c) Radar range and radar bearing of a radar conspicuous object.

     (d) Radar bearings of several radar conspicuous objects.

NOTE Radar ranges combined with radar bearings should be used with caution although errors will be minimised by using small isolated objects.

Bearing accuracy is improved by reducing the gain to obtain a fine echo of the target, thereby reducing the 1/2 beam width distortion.

Q.16 In restricted visibility and from radar information alone, what factors should be considered before making an alteration of course in a close quarters situation?

A.   (1) There must be sufficient sea room.

     (2) The alteration is made in good time.

     (3) The alteration must be substantial. A succession of small alterations of course should be avoided.

     (4) The alteration does not result in a close quarters situation with the other vessel.

     5. The following should be avoided:

       (i) An alteration of course to port for a vessel forward of the beam, other than for a vessel being overtaken.

       (ii) An alteration of course towards a vessel abeam or abaft the beam.

Q.17 Why should all radar operators be required to carry out a simple plotting exercise?

A.   (a) To project whether a dangerous or close quarters situation is developing.

     (b) To determine the true course and speed of the target vessel in order that the correct avoiding action may be taken if deemed necessary.

Q.18 What plotting method is most commonly used?

A.   The plotting method most commonly used is referred to as the Relative Motion Plot (Plotting method - Ship's Head UP).

NOTE Relative motion refers to the movement of the target relative to the vessel which is considered to be a fixed point, even though both vessels have their own speeds and courses of travel.

Q.19 How are relative bearings indicated?

A.   Relative bearings are indicated G (green or starboard) or R (red or port). An example would be that if a bearing were given as G26° this would mean that it would be a bearing 26° to starboard of the ships head. Can also be expressed as bearing 035° Relative 268° Relative. Examples only.

Q.20 Describe the method of constructing a relative motion plot.

A.   (1) Select a radar plotting sheet. Mark your vessel's position in the centre as a capital letter C. Show the vessel's course on the centre line as CH. Refer fig. 58.

     (2) Plot the first position of the target and name it O - note the time, alongside of the letter O.

     (3) Plot the subsequent echoes at equal noted time intervals and name the position of the last echo A (suggest six minute intervals).

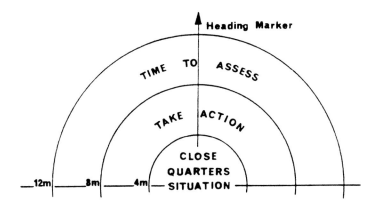

Figure 57 – *Taking avoiding action in ample time. (For a vessel travelling at less than 16 knots)*

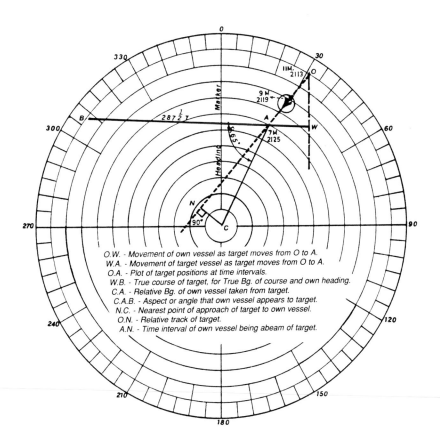

O.W. - Movement of own vessel as target moves from O to A.
W.A. - Movement of target vessel as target moves from O to A.
O.A. - Plot of target positions at time intervals.
W.B. - True course of target, for True Bg. of course and own heading.
C.A. - Relative Bg. of own vessel taken from target.
C.A.B. - Aspect or angle that own vessel appears to target.
N.C. - Nearest point of approach of target to own vessel.
O.N. - Relative track of target.
A.N. - Time interval of own vessel being abeam of target.

Figure 58 – *Typical relative motion plot*

(4) Join OA with a line and indicate with circled arrow (<). This is the relative track of the target vessel.

(5) From O, draw a line parallel to own track but in opposite direction. Mark off from O the distance your vessel would have travelled during the time interval the target travelled from O to A, and call that position W (OW then will equal the distance your own vessel travels in the time interval of OA).

(6) Join WA which represents the course of the target and whose length represents the distance travelled by the target vessel in the time interval of OA.

(7) Continue line any distance past A and terminate, calling the termination B.

(8) Continue the relative track line OA so as to continue the line beyond C.

(9) From the centre of the P.P.I. (C) draw a line to intersect the continued relative track line OA at right angles. Call the intersection N.

(10) CN will then represent the distance off your vessel will be when the target is closest to your own vessel.

(11) AN represents the relative distance to nearest point of approach based on the time taken to cover the distance from O to A.

(12) Join C with a line to A making the angle BAC. The angle BAC is referred to as the ASPECT of the target vessel.

NOTE The movement of the target on the radar screen (O.A.) is caused by two things. The apparent movement of the target caused by and opposite to the movement of your own ship (O.W.), and the actual movement (course and speed) of the target (W.A.).

Given that own vessels' course and speed is 015°T and 16 knots and that at 2113 hours echo of target vessel bears G.31° – 11 miles, and at 2119 hours echo bears G.29° – 9 miles and at 2125 hours echo bears G.26° – 7 miles.

Find:–

(a) Time and distance of nearest point of approach of Target vessel.

(b) Targets' course, speed and aspect.

Hints for operators of radar

(1) P.P.I. Display means Plan Position Indicator that is the ordinary viewing area of the radar screen.

(2) The maximum range a fixed target will be seen on marine radar under normal conditions is the visual horizon plus 6%. Under abnormal meteorological conditions it may be increased or decreased.

(3) The P.P.I. Picture is normally built up at the rate of one rotation of the sweep every three seconds and is a relief map of the area immediately around the ship which becomes a valuable navigational aid at night and in conditions of restricted visibility.

(4) The radar horizon under normal conditions may be given by the formula $2.21\sqrt{h}$ where h equals the scanner height in metres and the result is in nautical miles.

For example, with a scanner height of 9 metres the radar horizon would be $2.21\sqrt{9} = 2.21 \times 3 = 6.63$ nautical miles.

To obtain the detection range from this vessel of a peak of land 81 metres high we would add $2.21\sqrt{81} = 19.89$ miles giving 6.63 + 19.89 miles – 26.52 nautical miles.

NOTE The formula must be applied to the height of the scanner as well as the height of the peak separately and the results added to give the distance. The correct distance cannot be obtained by adding the height of the scanner and peak respectively first and then applying the formula to the total of the heights:.

Two important parameters of any radar system are range and bearing discrimination which in simple terms mean how close do two targets come together in range or bearing before they are displayed as one echo?

Bearing discrimination is governed by the horizontal beam width of the scanner which depends to a great extent on its physical size. Range discrimination depends on pulse length; shorter pulse lengths which may be repeated at a faster rate (higher pulse repetition frequency) on short ranges will give good range discrimination at those ranges.

Sea clutter gives greatest response to windward. This is because the steep wave fronts provide stronger echoes than smooth ones.

(7) Ships turning circles may be measured by simply turning the clutter control to an appropriate level and as the ship turns a dark circle within the clutter pattern indicates the vessel's wake.

(8) Radar reflectors when displayed from yachts, fishing vessels or other smaller vessels should always site their reflector from an angle of 45° and not perpendicular. This gives a far better target on the P.P.I.

SHAPE	RELATIVE ECHO POWER
Sphere	1
Plane	1200
Cones	100
Cylinder	300
Corner Reflector	12

(9) It is necessary, to adjust controls on radar displays whenever the vessel's course is changed, more especially after a long period on one particular heading.

(10) Range errors will increase as the range decreases.

(11) The shift controls are adjusted to bring the trace origin beneath the crossed lines of the perspex bearing cursor.

(12) It should be noted that the range rings permanently on the P.P.I. are more accurate than the variable range marker.

(13) When taking bearings site spot in the centre, be careful of parallax error. Position yourself directly above the bearing so that you get a correct reading. If the circle spot in the centre is too large the set needs readjusting.

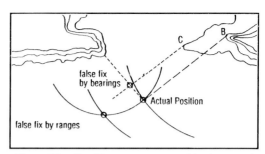

Figure 59 – *Position errors caused by incorrect interpretation of target echoes*

TABLE OF RADAR HORIZON RANGES

HEIGHT of SCANNER		APPROXIMATE RADAR HORIZON DISTANCE	HEIGHT of SCANNER		APPROXIMATE RADAR HORIZON DISTANCE
ft.	m	nautical miles	ft.	m.	nautical miles
6	2	3	215	66	18
12	4	4	240	73	19
18	5	5	265	81	20
24	7	6	320	98	22
32	10	7	380	116	24
42	13	8	445	136	26
54	16	9	520	159	28
66	20	10	595	181	30
80	24	11	680	207	32
95	29	12	770	235	34
111	34	13	860	262	36
130	40	14	960	293	38
150	46	15	1060	323	40
170	52	16	1130	344	41
190	58	17	1190	363	42

MINUTES	KNOTS 5	6	7	8	9	MINUTES
1	.1	.1	.1	.1	.2	1
2	.2	.2	.2	.3	.3	2
3	.3	.3	.4	.4	.5	3
4	.3	.4	.5	.5	.6	4
5	.4	.5	.6	.7	.8	5
6	.5	.6	.7	.8	.9	6
7	.6	.7	.8	.9	1.1	7
8	.7	.8	.9	1.1	1.2	8
9	.8	.9	1.1	1.2	1.4	9
10	.8	1.0	1.2	1.3	1.5	10
11	.9	1.1	1.3	1.5	1.7	11
12	1.0	1.2	1.4	1.6	1.8	12
13	1.1	1.3	1.5	1.7	2.0	13
14	1.2	1.4	1.6	1.9	2.1	14
15	1.3	1.5	1.8	2.0	2.3	15
16	1.3	1.6	1.9	2.1	2.4	16
17	1.4	1.7	2.0	2.3	2.6	17
18	1.5	1.8	2.1	2.4	2.7	18
19	1.6	1.9	2.2	2.5	2.9	19
20	1.7	2.0	2.3	2.7	3.0	20
21	1.8	2.1	2.5	2.8	3.2	21
22	1.8	2.2	2.6	2.9	3.3	22
23	1.9	2.3	2.7	3.1	3.5	23
24	2.0	2.4	2.8	3.2	3.6	24
25	2.1	2.5	2.9	3.3	3.8	25
26	2.2	2.6	3.0	3.5	3.9	26
27	2.3	2.7	3.2	3.6	4.1	27
28	2.3	2.8	3.3	3.7	4.2	28
29	2.4	2.9	3.4	3.9	4.4	29
30	2.5	3.0	3.5	4.0	4.5	30
31	2.6	3.1	3.6	4.1	4.7	31
32	2.7	3.2	3.7	4.3	4.8	32
33	2.8	3.3	3.9	4.4	5.0	33
34	2.8	3.4	4.0	4.5	5.1	34
35	2.9	3.5	4.1	4.7	5.3	35
36	3.0	3.6	4.2	4.8	5.4	36
37	3.1	3.7	4.3	4.9	5.6	37
38	3.2	3.8	4.4	5.1	5.7	38
39	3.3	3.9	4.6	5.2	5.9	39
40	3.3	4.0	4.7	5.3	6.0	40
41	3.4	4.1	4.8	5.5	6.2	41
42	3.5	4.2	4.9	5.6	6.3	42
43	3.6	4.3	5.0	5.7	6.5	43
44	3.7	4.4	5.1	5.9	6.6	44
45	3.8	4.5	5.3	6.0	6.8	45
46	3.8	4.6	5.4	6.1	6.9	46
47	3.9	4.7	5.5	6.3	7.1	47
48	4.0	4.8	5.6	6.4	7.2	48
49	4.1	4.9	5.7	6.5	7.4	49
50	4.2	5.0	5.8	6.7	7.5	50
51	4.3	5.1	6.0	6.8	7.7	51
52	4.3	5.2	6.1	6.9	7.8	52
52	4.4	5.3	6.2	7.1	8.0	52
54	4.5	5.4	6.3	7.2	8.1	54
55	4.6	5.5	6.4	7.3	8.3	55
56	4.7	5.6	6.5	7.5	8.4	56
57	4.8	5.7	6.7	7.6	8.6	57
58	4.8	5.8	6.8	7.7	8.7	58
59	4.9	5.9	6.9	7.9	8.9	59
60	5.0	6.0	7.0	8.0	9.0	60

MINUTES	KNOTS 10	11	12	13	14	MINUTES
1	.2	.2	.2	.2	.2	1
2	.3	.4	.4	.4	.5	2
3	.5	.6	.6	.7	.7	3
4	.7	.7	.8	.9	.9	4
5	.8	.9	1.0	1.1	1.2	5
6	1.0	1.1	1.2	1.3	1.4	6
7	1.2	1.3	1.4	1.5	1.6	7
8	1.3	1.5	1.6	1.7	1.9	8
9	1.5	1.7	1.8	2.0	2.1	9
10	1.7	1.8	2.0	2.2	2.3	10
11	1.8	2.0	2.2	2.4	2.6	11
12	2.0	2.2	2.4	2.6	2.8	12
13	2.2	2.4	2.6	2.8	3.0	13
14	2.3	2.6	2.8	3.0	3.3	14
15	2.5	2.8	3.0	3.3	3.5	15
16	2.7	2.9	3.2	3.5	3.7	16
17	2.8	3.1	3.4	3.7	4.0	17
18	3.0	3.3	3.6	3.9	4.2	18
19	3.2	3.5	3.8	4.1	4.4	19
20	3.3	3.7	4.0	4.3	4.7	20
21	3.5	3.9	4.2	4.6	4.9	21
22	3.7	4.0	4.4	4.8	5.1	22
23	3.8	4.2	4.6	5.0	5.4	23
24	4.0	4.4	4.8	5.2	5.6	24
25	4.2	4.6	5.0	5.4	5.8	25
26	4.3	4.8	5.2	5.6	6.1	26
27	4.5	5.0	5.4	5.9	6.3	27
28	4.7	5.1	5.6	6.1	6.5	28
29	4.8	5.3	5.8	6.3	6.8	29
30	5.0	5.5	6.0	6.5	7.0	30
31	5.2	5.7	6.2	6.7	7.2	31
32	5.3	5.9	6.4	6.9	7.5	32
33	5.5	6.1	6.6	7.2	7.7	33
34	5.7	6.2	6.8	7.4	7.9	34
35	5.8	6.4	7.0	7.6	8.2	35
36	6.0	6.6	7.2	7.8	8.4	36
37	6.2	6.8	7.4	8.0	8.6	37
38	6.3	7.0	7.6	8.2	8.9	38
39	6.5	7.2	7.8	8.5	9.1	39
40	6.7	7.3	8.0	8.7	9.3	40
41	6.8	7.5	8.2	8.9	9.6	41
42	7.0	7.7	8.4	9.1	9.8	42
43	7.2	7.9	8.6	9.3	10.0	43
44	7.3	8.1	8.8	9.5	10.3	44
45	7.5	8.3	9.0	9.8	10.5	45
46	7.7	8.4	9.2	10.0	10.7	46
47	7.8	8.6	9.4	10.2	11.0	47
48	8.0	8.8	9.6	10.4	11.2	48
49	8.2	9.0	9.8	10.6	11.4	49
50	8.3	9.2	10.0	10.8	11.7	50
51	8.5	9.4	10.2	11.1	11.9	51
52	8.7	9.5	10.4	11.3	12.1	52
53	8.8	9.7	10.6	11.5	12.4	53
54	9.0	9.9	10.8	11.7	12.6	54
55	9.2	10.1	11.0	11.9	12.8	55
56	9.3	10.3	11.2	12.1	13.1	56
57	9.5	10.5	11.4	12.4	13.3	57
58	9.7	10.6	11.6	12.6	13.5	58
59	9.8	10.8	11.8	12.8	13.8	59
60	10.0	11.0	12.0	13.0	14.0	60

MINUTES	KNOTS 15	16	17	18	19	MINUTES
1	.3	.3	.3	.3	.3	1
2	.5	.5	.6	.6	.6	2
3	.8	.8	.9	.9	1.0	3
4	1.0	1.1	1.1	1.2	1.3	4
5	1.3	1.3	1.4	1.5	1.6	5
6	1.5	1.6	1.7	1.8	1.9	6
7	1.8	1.9	2.0	2.1	2.2	7
8	2.0	2.1	2.3	2.4	2.5	8
9	2.3	2.4	2.6	2.7	2.9	9
10	2.5	2.7	2.8	3.0	3.2	10
11	2.8	2.9	3.1	3.3	3.5	11
12	3.0	3.2	3.4	3.6	3.8	12
13	3.3	3.5	3.7	3.9	4.1	13
14	3.5	3.7	4.0	4.2	4.4	14
15	3.8	4.0	4.3	4.5	4.8	15
16	4.0	4.3	4.5	4.8	5.1	16
17	4.3	4.5	4.8	5.1	5.4	17
18	4.5	4.8	5.1	5.4	5.7	18
19	4.8	5.1	5.4	5.7	6.0	19
20	5.0	5.3	5.7	6.0	6.3	20
21	5.3	5.6	6.0	6.3	6.7	21
22	5.5	5.9	6.2	6.6	7.0	22
23	5.8	6.1	6.5	6.9	7.3	23
24	6.0	6.4	6.8	7.2	7.6	24
25	6.3	6.7	7.1	7.5	7.9	25
26	6.5	6.9	7.4	7.8	8.2	26
27	6.8	7.2	7.7	8.1	8.6	27
28	7.0	7.5	7.9	8.4	8.9	28
29	7.3	7.7	8.2	8.7	9.2	29
30	7.5	8.0	8.5	9.0	9.5	30
31	7.8	8.3	8.8	9.3	9.8	31
32	8.0	8.5	9.1	9.6	10.2	32
33	8.3	8.8	9.4	9.9	10.5	33
34	8.5	9.1	9.6	10.2	10.8	34
35	8.8	9.3	9.9	10.5	11.1	35
36	9.0	9.6	10.2	10.8	11.4	36
37	9.3	9.9	10.5	11.1	11.7	37
38	9.5	10.1	10.8	11.4	12.0	38
39	9.8	10.4	11.0	11.7	12.4	39
40	10.0	10.7	11.3	12.0	12.7	40
41	10.3	10.9	11.6	12.3	13.0	41
42	10.5	11.2	11.9	12.6	13.3	42
43	10.8	11.5	12.2	12.9	13.6	43
44	11.0	11.7	12.5	13.2	13.9	44
45	11.3	12.0	12.8	13.5	14.3	45
46	11.5	12.3	13.0	13.8	14.6	46
47	11.8	12.5	13.3	14.1	14.9	47
48	12.0	12.8	13.6	14.4	15.2	48.
49	12.3	13.1	13.9	14.7	15.5	49
50	12.5	13.3	14.2	15.0	15.8	50
51	12.8	13.6	14.5	15.3	16.2	51
52	13.0	13.9	14.7	15.6	16.5	52
53	13.3	14.1	15.0	15.9	16.8	53
54	13.5	14.4	15.3	16.2	17.1	54
55	13.8	14.7	15.6	16.5	17.4	55
56	14.0	14.9	15.9	16.8	17.7	56
57	14.3	15.2	16.2	17.1	18.1	57
58	14.5	15.5	16.4	17.4	18.4	58
59	14.8	15.7	16.7	17.7	18.7	59
60	15.0	16.0	17.0	18.0	19.0	60

SPEED, TIME AND DISTANCE TABLES
For intervals up to 60 minutes
Figure 60

The information following is for vessels in <u>Radar contact only and not visible to each other.</u>
Assuming all vessels abide by these rules of conduct and plot efficiently, collisions in or near areas of restricted visibility between single vessels are a near impossiblity. NOTE: <u>Vessels in Radar contact only and not visible to each other.</u>

(a) Relative Plot

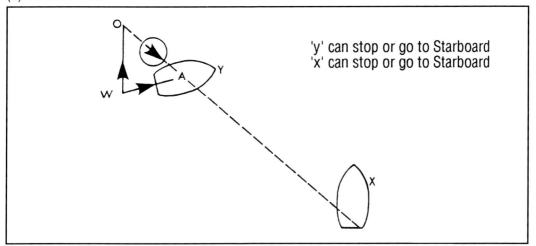

'y' can stop or go to Starboard
'x' can stop or go to Starboard

(b) Relative Plot

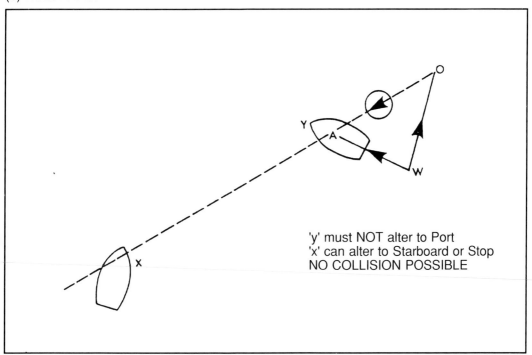

'y' must NOT alter to Port
'x' can alter to Starboard or Stop
NO COLLISION POSSIBLE

(c) Relative Plot

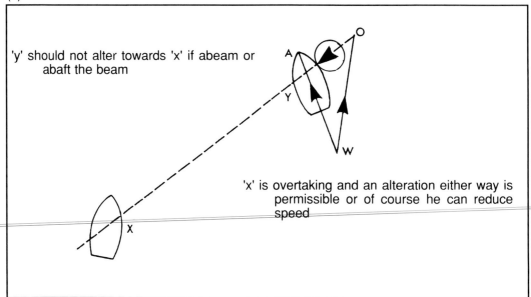

'y' should not alter towards 'x' if abeam or abaft the beam

'x' is overtaking and an alteration either way is permissible or of course he can reduce speed

(d) Relative Plot

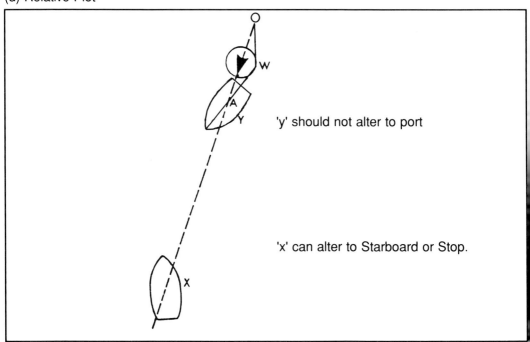

'y' should not alter to port

'x' can alter to Starboard or Stop.

(e) Relative Plot

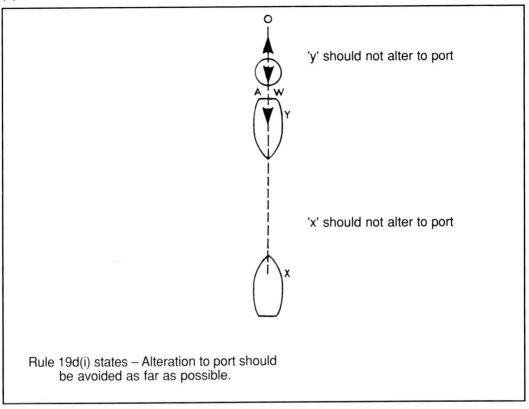

'y' should not alter to port

'x' should not alter to port

Rule 19d(i) states – Alteration to port should
be avoided as far as possible.

(f) Relative Plot

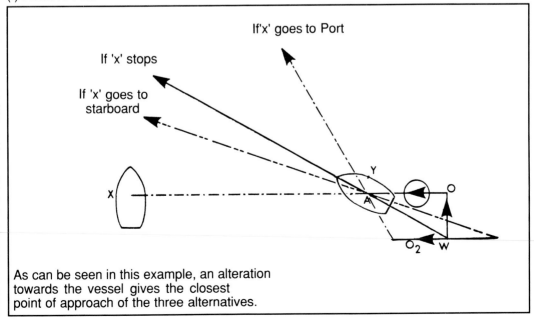

If 'x' goes to Port

If 'x' stops

If 'x' goes to
starboard

As can be seen in this example, an alteration
towards the vessel gives the closest
point of approach of the three alternatives.

(g) Relative Plot

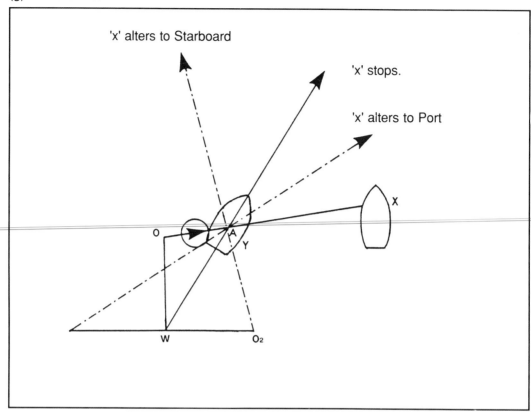

'x' alters to Starboard

'x' stops.

'x' alters to Port

(h) Relative Plot

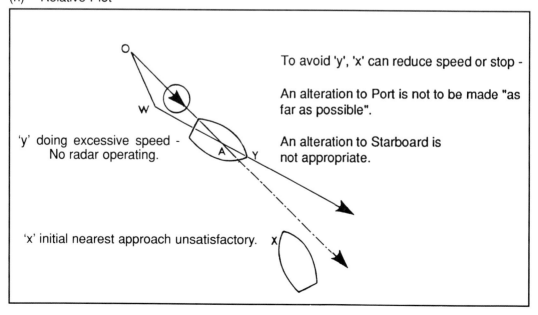

To avoid 'y', 'x' can reduce speed or stop -

An alteration to Port is not to be made "as far as possible".

An alteration to Starboard is not appropriate.

'y' doing excessive speed - No radar operating.

'x' initial nearest approach unsatisfactory.

(i)   Relative Plot

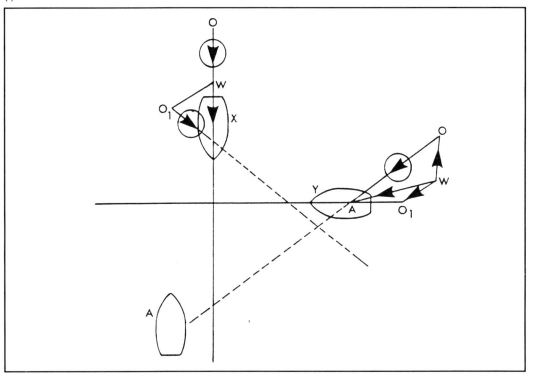

'A' can alter across 'x's track and avoid 'y' by an alteration to Starboard;

'A' can stop... small nearest approach with 'x' is unaltered;

'A' could go to port 120° and have a good nearest approach with both vessels.

As has been shown, sometimes a Port alteration is preferable; when we are faced by a vessel–

(a) doing an excessive speed and

(b) in certain situations where navigational hazards exist or multi-ship situations are being dealt with.

If your vessel is obeying the rules in all respects and the other vessel is doing likewise, only incorrect Plotting can cause accidents.

However, it is also possible that the vessels in the area may not be obeying the rules implicitly and a departure under the heading of 'as far as possible' may be essential.

(j) Relative Plot

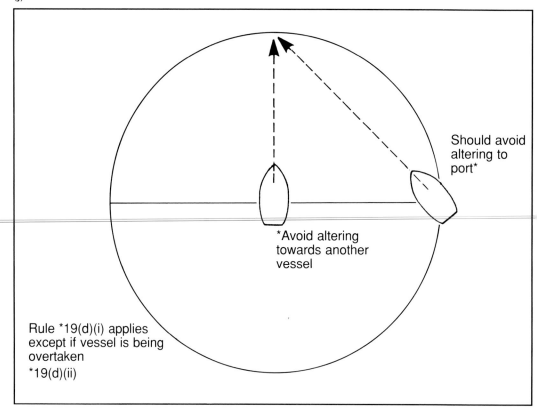

Should avoid altering to port*

*Avoid altering towards another vessel

Rule *19(d)(i) applies except if vessel is being overtaken
*19(d)(ii)

Chapter 6

REGULATIONS

REGULATIONS
NOTES RELATING TO THE REGULATION – EXTRACTS FROM TRANSPORT OPERATIONS (MARINE SAFETY) ACT 1994 AND TRANSPORT OPERATIONS (MARINE SAFETY) REGULATIONS AND STANDARDS 1995.

Q.1 **What is the duty of the master in the case of collision?**

A.   **Part 11 Section 124** of the Act.

124.(1) This section applies to a marine incident involving 2 or more ships.

(2) The master of each ship involved in the marine incident must, to the extent that the master can do so without danger to the master's ship or persons on board the master's ship –

(a) give to each other ship involved in the incident, its master and persons on board the ship the help necessary to save them from danger caused by the marine incident;

(b) stay by the other ship until the other ship does not need further help; and

(c) give to the master of the other ship reasonable particulars adequate to identify the ship and its owner.

Maximum penalty –

(a) for contravention of paragraph (a) or (b) – 500 penalty units or imprisonment for 1 year;

(b) for contravention of paragraph (c) – 40 penalty units.

(3) However, if the contravention of subsection 2(a) or (b) causes the death of, or grievous bodily harm to, a person, the master commits an indictable offence and is liable to a maximum penalty of 5 000 penalty units or imprisonment for 2 years.

Q.2 **What is the duty of the master in the case of accident or damage?**

A.   **Part 11 Section 125** of the Act.

125.(1) If a marine incident causing or involving the loss or presumed loss or abandonment of a ship happens, the owner of the ship must report the marine incident to a shipping inspector at the earliest opportunity, but within 48 hours after the owner becomes aware of the incident, unless the owner has a reasonable excuse for not complying with this subsection.

(2) If –

(a) a ship is involved in another type of marine incident; or

(b) a ship's master has reason to believe that the ship has been involved in another type of marine incident.

The master of the ship must report the marine incident to a shipping inspector within 48 hours after the incident happens, unless the master has a reasonable excuse for not complying with this subsection.

(3) If the report under subsection (1) or (2) is not made to the shipping inspector in the approved form, the owner or master must make a further report about the marine incident to a shipping inspector in the approved form at the earliest opportunity.

Maximum penalty – 40 penalty units.

Q.3 **When two power-driven vessels are approaching one another in opposite directions so as to be likely to meet in a restricted channel, which vessel must give way?**

A.   The master of the vessel going against the tide shall reduce speed and allow the other vessel to pass through the restricted channel first.

Q.4 **When vessels are approaching each other in opposite directions and are likely to meet in a narrow channel, which vessel gives way?**

A.   The vessel coming with the tide is to be allowed to pass through first.

Q.5 **What must vessels observe when passing another vessel aground?**

A.   Vessels on nearing any vessels aground are to slacken their speed until safely past.

Note: The master of a vessel shall not in any port navigate the vessel at a speed which is likely to cause damage to –

(a) any moored vessel or its moorings;

(b) any vessel engaged in dredging;

(c) any vessel engaged in tending any buoy or beacon;

(d) any vessel aground;

(e) any bank of a river; or

(f) any buoy, beacon, navigation channel, wharf or other harbour work, and, notwithstanding that the vessel is being navigated at the relevant time at a speed within the speed limit prescribed by the Regulations.

Q.6 What signal is exhibited should a doctor be required?

A. The international code flag signal 'W' is displayed.

Q.7 How would a signal that a diver was engaged in underwater activities from a vessel be exhibited?

A. The master or person in charge of any vessel from which diving operations are being conducted within the limits of a port shall exhibit on the vessel where it can best be seen from other vessels Flag "A" of the International Code of Signals (Maritime) as the signal denoting "I have a diver down, keep well clear at slow speed".

Q.8 What signal is exhibited for a vessel on fire?

A. The signal C.B.6 displayed by international code flags and or continuous short blasts on the vessel's whistle or siren.

Q.9 Describe the International Code Flag A.

A. Flag "A" of the International Code of Signals is a burgee or two tailed flag, vertically divided in a white section and a royal blue section, with blue to the fly.

Q.10 Describe the size, Flag "A" shall be exhibited by vessels of less than 12 metres.

A. When flown from a vessel less than 12 metres in length the flag shall be not less than 0.75 metre in length and 0.6 metre in breadth.

Q.11 Describe the size, Flag "A" shall be exhibited by vessels over 12 metres.

A. When flown from a vessel 12 metres or more in length the flag shall be not less than 1 metre in length and 0.8 metre in breadth.

Q.12 Describe where a person engaged in diving operations away from the immediate vicinity of a vessel towing a float, the size Flag "A" he shall exhibit?

A. He shall exhibit therefrom Flag of "A" of a size not less than 0.25 metre in length and 0.2 metre in breadth.

Q.13 What are the obligations of a master when sighting Flag "A" being flown from a vessel.

A. The master or person in charge of any vessel, on sighting Flag "A" being flown, shall keep as far away as practicable from the vessel exhibiting the flag, and shall proceed as slowly, as safe navigation permits until finally past and clear, meanwhile keeping a good look out.

Q.14 What signal is exhibited for taking in or discharging dangerous goods?

A. The international code flag signal 'B' in daylight and an all round red light at night.

Q.15 For which signal should skippers be alert when entering the Port of Townsville?

A. That the "Closed port signal" is not exhibited from the port control tower.

Q.16 How are these signals distinguished by day and night?

A. By day: The answering pennant.
By night: A red light occuring every 22 seconds.

Q.17 When repairing machinery or handling other materials of a greasy or oily nature on deck, why should the skipper exercise great care with the operations?

A. There are very severe penalties for offences against the Transport Operation (Marine Pollution) Act 1995. When washing down after repairs, measures must be taken to prevent oil and grease finding its way over the side.

Q.18 What must the master of a cross-river ferry observe before departing from the wharf or pontoon?

A. He must ensure the crossing may be attempted with safety.

Q.19 What else is he to have due regard to?

A. (a) The proximity and speed of any approaching vessel.

(b) Whether any approaching vessel can be only navigated inside a narrow channel.

(c) Any other special circumstance or condition likely to cause a danger of collision.

Dredger and Channel Blocked Signals

Q.20 What are the signals for a dredger when it is blocking the channel?

A. (1) In addition to the lights, shapes and sound signals prescribed by the Collision Regulations for a vessel engaged in dredging or underwater operations, when a channel in any port is closed or blocked the master of the dredger or other vessel causing such closure or blockage shall cause the following signals to be exhibited:-

By day:- Three black shapes in a vertical line where they can best be seen. The highest and lowest of these shapes shall be balls and the middle one a cone apex, upwards.

By night:- Three all round lights in a vertical line where they can best be seen. The highest and lowest of these lights shall be red and the middle light shall be green.

(2) In or near an area of restricted visibility the master of a vessel closing or blocking a channel shall cause a sound signal to be given by the vessel, consisting of three short rings on the bell every minute (letter "S").

Q.21 What other lights are required to be carried by an air cushion vehicle?

A. In addition to the lights prescribed by the said Collision Regulations, the owner of an air cushion vehicle shall cause to be carried thereon, in a position so as to be visible all round the horizon and distinguishable from other prescribed lights, a yellow light capable of flashing at a rate of 120 times per minute with an apparent intensity of fifty-four candelas.

Fishing Vessels

Q.22 What flags are required to be carried by fishing vessels?

A. Two, the international code flags 'N' and 'C'.

Q.23 For what use is it deemed necessary to carry these flags?

A. To exhibit as a signal if in distress, and requiring immediate assistance.

Q.24 How should the signal be displayed?

A. Flag 'N' is flown over 'C' on the main hoist or where the signal can best be seen.

Q.25 For the calculation of tonnage for fishing vessels what tonnage is used?

A. Gross tonnage.

Q.26 What is a non sea going fishing vessel?

A. A non sea going fishing vessel is one which does not proceed beyond the limits of any port or operate within partially smooth limits.

Q.27 How often must fishing vessels be re-registered?

A. Every twelve calendar months.

Q.28 Where is the Certificate of Registration to be kept?

A. On board the vessel and available for inspection at any time.

Q.29 What constitutes a seaworthy fishing vessel with reference to crewing?

A. No fishing vessel would be deemed seaworthy unless crewed as prescribed in the Transport Operations (Marine Safety) Regulations and Standards 1995.

Q.30 When changing ownership of fishing vessels, what are the requirements?

A. Notification in writing of any change in ownership shall be made within fourteen days giving:-
(a) The date of change in ownership.

(b) The name and address of the person to whom the vessel has been sold or otherwise disposed.

Q.31 In the case of wreck, collision, grounding, etc, what is the first requirement of the Regulations?

A. A full report to be forwarded within 48 hours of the incident by the master or owner, or where it is impossible to do so, as soon thereafter.

Information on Regulations with reference to inflatable life-rafts:

Q.32 What are the endurance requirements for a coastal inflated life-raft?

A. It must be capable of withstanding exposure for 30 days afloat in all sea conditions. Refer to Appendix J of The Uniform Shipping Laws Code.

Q.33 What range of temperatures are inflatable coastal life rafts designed to operate?

A. The life-raft shall be capable of operating in any temperature ranging between the temperatures minus 18°C and 66°C.

Q.34 What is the maximum weight permissible for a life-raft?

A. The life-raft and its valise or other container shall not exceed a total mass of 180 kg, including equipment.

Q.35 Describe the construction test for a coastal life-raft?

A. The life-raft shall be so constructed that, if it is dropped into the water from its stowed position, or from a height of 6 metres, whichever is the greater, neither the life-raft nor its equipment will be damaged.

Q.36 How are life-rafts inflated?

A. The buoyancy compartments of a life-raft shall be inflated by a gas which, if it escapes, is not injurious to persons in the life-raft.

Q.37 How is inflation pressure maintained in a life-raft?

A. Provision is made for maintaining pressure with a topping up pump or bellows.

Q.38 Describe the cover of a life-raft?

A. The life-raft shall be fitted with a cover of a highly visible colour which shall be automatically erected on the inflation of the life-raft and shall be capable of protecting the occupants against injury from exposure with provision to enable the collection of rain water precipitated on the cover, and the top and the inside of the cover shall be fitted with a lamp which derives its power from a sea-activated cell.

Q.39 Can a life-raft be turned upright if floating upside down?

A. Yes. The life-raft shall be capable of being readily righted by one person if it inflates in an inverted position.

Q.40 How is a life-raft designed with reference to buoyancy?

A. The buoyancy of the life-raft shall be divided into an even number of compartments so arranged that either half of the total number of compartments is capable of supporting out of the water the number of persons included in the carrying capacity of the life-raft.

Q.41 What provisions are made to regulate the temperature of survivors in a life-raft?

A. The floor of the life-raft shall be waterproofed.

Q.42 What provision is made for towing and for life lines?

A. The life-raft shall be fitted with means enabling it to be towed readily, and shall be fitted with a painter and shall have a line securely becketed around the outside and a life line fitted around the inside.

Q.43 How are life-rafts marked?

A. Each inflatable life-raft shall be clearly and permanently marked with a serial number, the manufacturer's name, the carrying capacity on the life-raft and on the valise or other container in which the life-raft is contained.

Q.44 How is a life-raft stowed?

A. A life-raft shall be stowed so that, as far as it is practicable the life-raft is capable of being launched down the straight side of the vessel. Means shall be provided for illuminating the stowage position of a life-raft.

Q.45 How is a dinghy stowed?

A.   A dinghy shall be stowed so that the dinghy will not impede the rapid handling of any lifeboat, life-raft, buoyant apparatus or other dinghy. It shall be carried in such a manner that the dinghy can be put into the water, even when the trim of the vessel is 10° and the vessel is listed 15° either way.

Means shall be provided for illuminating the stowage position.

Q.46 How are lifejackets stowed?

A.   Lifejackets shall be so stowed as to be easily located by, and readily accessible to the persons for whose use they are intended and such stowage clearly marked as necessary.

Q.47 How are lifebuoys stowed?

A.   Lifebuoys shall be stowed:–

(a) In such a manner that they are not permanently secured in any way;

(b) So as to be readily accessible to all persons on board; and

(c) So as to be rapidly cast loose.

Where practicable, two lifebuoys with self-igniting lights and smoke signals attached shall be stowed so as to be capable of quick release from the navigation bridge.

Q.48 Describe a "V" sheet.

The sheet is rectangular, of suitable material, is orange and bearing the letter 'V' in black.

It shall be not less than 1.2 metres x 1.8 metres in size, the 'V' not less than 0.8 metres in height, and the strokes forming the 'V' not less than 130 mm in breadth.

USE OF THE SHEET

The sheet shall have lanyards attached to the four corners, and is to be exhibited in a manner so as to best attract the attention of searching aircraft, surface craft, or persons in the vicinity.

NOT LESS THAN 1.8M   N.B. RATIO 2:3

NOT LESS THAN 1.2M

Chapter 7

CARE AND
USE OF ANCHORS

CARE AND USE OF ANCHORS

A vessel's anchors, cables and associated gear must be efficient and able to withstand the strains imposed by foul weather and strong tidal streams, otherwise her crew will suffer from lack of rest and her engines would be overworked in order to ensure the vessel's safety.

Terms

How are the following terms used in anchor work?

Q.1 Cat Davit
A. A davit fitted in older vessels for use in stowing anchors on deck.

Q.2 Bitts
A. Deck fixtures which are used for securing the cable when at anchor.

Q.3 Hawse Pipes
A. Cast steel pipes near the bow of a ship, between upper deck or forecastle and the ship's side through which a cable passes.

Q.4 Spurling Pipes
A. Steel pipes in the decks through which die chain cable passes from chain lockers to cable deck, also known as the 'navel pipes'.

Q.5 Veer
A. To use power in paying-out the cable and not to let it run free.

Q.6 Surge
A. To let the cable run out without using power.

Q.7. Snub
A. To brake sharply.

Q.8 Scope
A. The ratio of the cable out to the depth of water when vessel rides at anchor.

Q.9 Clear Anchor
A. When the anchor is unencumbered and has not picked up its own cable, chain, wire, etc. Otherwise, the anchor is foul.

Q.10 Brought up
A. When the cable is taut between ship and anchor.

Q.11 Rode
A. The anchor line or cable between the attachment on the vessel and the anchor.

Q.12 Catenary
A. The curve formed by a uniform chain hanging freely from two points not in one vertical line.

Q.13 Clear Hawse
A. When using two anchors, the cables are clear of one another.

Q.14 Foul Hawse
A. The hawse is foul when the cables have a cross, an elbow or a round turn, depending on the number of times the vessel has swung around in the one direction.

Q.15 Anchor Dragging
A. When it is not holding on the bottom.

Q.16 Anchor Coming Home
A. When weighing anchor, if the anchor is dragged towards the ship instead of the ship being hove up to it.

Q.17 Grow
A. The direction in which the cable leads outside the hawse pipe. When the cable grows vertically downwards from the hawse pipe it is said to be 'Up-and-Down'.

Q.18 Weigh Anchor
A. To heave in cable until the anchor is broken out of the ground and clear of the water. The anchor is aweigh immediately it is broken out of the ground.

Q.19 Short or Long Stay.
A. The cable is at short stay if it leads steeply downwards from the hawse pipe and at long stay if it leads well away and less Steeply.

Q.20 Hove in Sight
A. As soon as the anchor can be seen when weighing.

Q.21 Weather Tide
A. Tide against the wind.

Q.22 Lee Tide
A. Tide with the wind.

Q.23 Bull Rope
A. A hawser led through a block on a spar to keep a mooring buoy clear of the stem.

Q.24 Spring
A. (a) A hawser led in a 'fore and aft' direction from the ship to wharf to

prevent the ship moving ahead or astern.

(b) A hawser led from aft and made fast to the anchor cable to point the ship in a required direction.

Q.25 Kedging

A. Moving a vessel by means of small anchors and hawsers.

The princpal parts of an anchor are shank, crown, arms, flukes or palms, bills or peas, stock, ring or shackle.

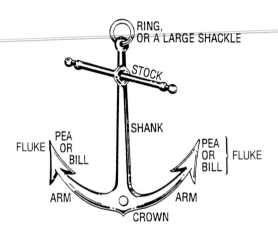

Figure 61 – *Principal parts of the anchor*

Types of Anchors

Anchors vary in design and performance as well as in size.

The holding power of a modern anchor is strictly dependent upon its design, and is proportional to the area of the flukes and the depth to which they are buried in the bottom. The weight of the anchor is only one factor.

All anchors, rigid or pivoted, rely on the principle of the ploughshare. A flat or curved piece of metal (the fluke) catches obliquely in the bottom. When anchors reach the bottom they may slip or slide for a period of time dependent on the type of anchor, its weight, its angle of incidence, its proportions, etc.

There are two principal forces which affect the anchor after it reaches the bottom, viz.

(a) A horizontal pull against the drift of

the vessel, which is called a retentive force.

(b) A vertical, downward force, which is called a penetrative force.

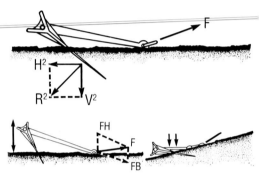

Figure 62 – *Retentive & Penetrative force as applied to anchors.*

Q.26 Describe an Admiralty Pattern Anchor.

A. In spite of its name, this anchor is much older than the Admiralty itself. Over the years it has been considered by many seamen to have the greatest holding power, weight for weight for all types of bottoms. However some of the modern anchors are superior in this respect. When the anchor is let go the stock comes to rest horizontally on the bottom, and as the flukes are set at right angles to the stock the lower fluke digs into the bottom and holds. The weight of the stock must be equal to one-fourth the specified weight of the anchor.

Q.27 What are some disadvantages of an Admiralty Pattern Anchor?

A. Disadvantages are-

(a) Because the upper fluke sticks up from the bottom, the anchor may well be dislodged through being fouled by the bight of its own cable as the vessel swings to wind and tidal stream.

(b) If the anchor is let go in shallow water, a vessel may impale herself on the upper fluke when the tide falls.

(c) It cannot be stowed in a hawse pipe, and so it must be stowed on deck. It is therefore difficult to let go in an emergency.

(d) A large anchor of this type may be awkward to handle.

Q.28 Describe a Standard Stockless Anchor.

A. As its name implies, this anchor has no stock and can therefore be hove right home in the hawse pipe, where it is easily secured and quickly made ready for letting go. The maximum holding pull is less than that of the Admiralty Pattern. It is often used for the anchors of steel trawlers and larger vessels. The flukes pivot about a pin which passes through the crown. As the anchor is dragged along the bottom the weight of the flukes and the design of the tripping palm tilt both flukes downward so that they dig into the bottom. The angle through which the flukes can tilt is limited by stops forged in the crown. It is so constructed that the head will turn on its axis and the arms will open out to an angle of 45° with the shank, but no further. The head must weigh not less than three-fifths of the total weight

Q.29 Describe a C.Q.R.

A. This anchor has a better holding power than the older type of anchor and the holding power to weight ratio increases as the size decreases. It has a bent shank with a plough-shaped fitting hinged to the end. It is generally used only for small craft, because it is difficult to stow in a hawse pipe. The sharp point of the fluke increases the risk of damage to the hull plating when weighing.

Q.30 Describe a Danforth Anchor.

A. This anchor is of comparatively new design, giving a better holding power for a given weight than the older small-ship anchors. The ratio of the holding power to the weight of the anchor increases as the size decreases. It can therefore be used as a general purpose anchor in small vessels such as coastal and inshore fishing vessels. It resembles a lightly built stockless anchor, both in appearance and method of operation, but it has a small stock passing through the crown to prevent the anchor from rolling when its flukes dig into the bottom. It fits snugly into the hawse pipe and can be secured as efficiently as a stockless anchor, but, as with all other anchors, it loses holding power considerably when at short stay.

The Danforth lightweight type anchor is a good example of balanced components. Any variation in the balance drastically reduces the holding power. The use of heat-treated alloy steel makes it possible to have thin flukes with sharpened edges without sacrificing strength. The penetrating potential and hence holding power of the gear is thereby increased.

Q.31 Describe the Reef Anchor or Grapnel.

A. A common reef anchor is constructed of a two to three foot length of G.I. pipe through which two lengths of 3/4" to 1" round iron bent in halves is inserted. The bights of the round steel protrude at one end of the pipe. At the opposite end the round steel is bent in the shape of the ribs of an umbrella. The anchor line used with a reef anchor is usually of synthetic rope joined to a length of chain which is shackled to the anchor. The purpose of the length of chain is to prevent possible chafing of the rope on a foul bottom and to assist in exerting a horizontal pull on the anchor. A steel ball or similar weight may be attached where the rope joins the chain in order to increase the horizontal pull and to lessen the effect of the surge of the vessel.

When dropped on the reef this anchor will foul but with extreme vertical pull at short stay, the round steel rods tend to straighten releasing the hold.

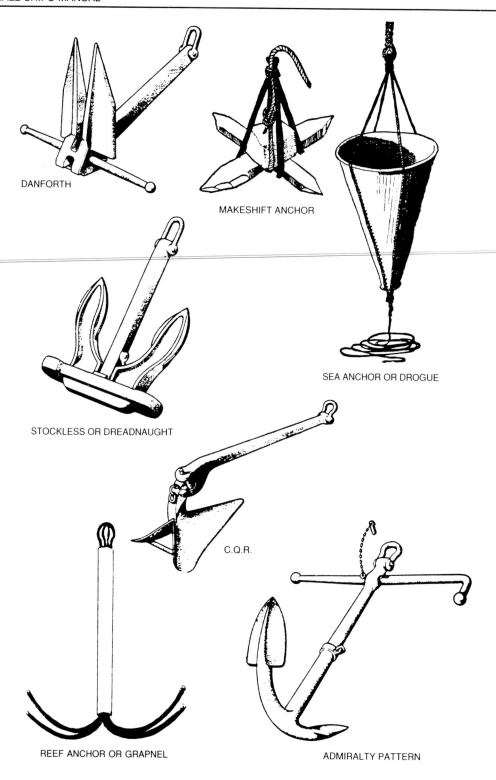

DANFORTH

MAKESHIFT ANCHOR

SEA ANCHOR OR DROGUE

STOCKLESS OR DREADNAUGHT

C.Q.R.

REEF ANCHOR OR GRAPNEL

ADMIRALTY PATTERN

Figure 63 – *Types of Anchors*

Note:A vessel should never be left unattended with a reef anchor in use. At night fall it is prudent to seek a better anchorage when a more conventional type anchor may be used.

Q.32 Describe a Floating Anchor.

A.   While the Floating Anchor or 'sea anchor' by no means fulfils the traditional function of an anchor, that of keeping a vessel firmly attached to a selected point on the sea bed, its own function is of importance. That function is, briefly, to provide a point of hold and resistance in the water when it is not possible to obtain such a point on the bottom. It is a sort of elastic mooring in particular circumstances – far out at sea, lying-to in heavy weather, adrift, out of reach of the bottom, etc. Its usefulness is sometimes a matter of controversy, depending on the type of vessel, the state of the sea, and possibly the personal opinion of the mariner. Fishing vessels may readily substitute a standard sea anchor by streaming their nets or otter boards. Another effective measure to control the drift of the vessel in most areas along the Queensland shelf is to unshackle the anchor and stream the anchor chain, allowing it to drag on the bottom.

Q.33 What action might be taken if another anchor was required in an emergency ?

A.   Should this be necessary to construct an anchor in an emergency, select two pieces of 100mm X 100mm hardwood approximately 1 metre long. Sharpen rough points on each of the ends, then nail them together to form a cross. Select an oblong stone or suitable weight and lash it in the centre of the cross. The lashing is passed around the arms of the cross and tied at the top over the stone to form a bridle. Fasten mooring lines to it and it is ready for use.

The nature of the bottom upon which anchors are dropped may affect the efficiency of their respective holding qualities. Bottoms may vary from thick soft mud to hard rock and from sand to cavernous reef.

The anchor line itself is a major controlling factor in an anchoring system. Sufficient 'scope' (the ratio of the length of the line to the depth of the water) helps to keep the anchor from dragging. A long rode (the anchor line between the vessel and the anchor), tends to exert a horizontal pull and helps the anchor dig in. For optimum performance the line should lead away from the anchor at an angle of not more than 8° to the bottom.

The most important thing about scope is how it acts in a blow when wind and seas build up a strain on the rode. Under these conditions the catenary (sagging curve) in the line cushions the load on the anchor and absorbs shocks that would be transmitted directly to the ground tackle if there were a straight line pull on the rode.

This catenary effect is so important that it is common practice to weight the anchor line (half way down) to create a shock absorbing curve. Properly anchored and given freedom to move with the waves, a vessel puts relatively little stress on her rode and anchor.

Q.34 Name three factors that determine the load a vessel places on ground tackle.

A.   (a) Wind drag
     (b) Current
     (c) Wave action

Wind drag.

Wind blowing against the cross sectional area of the vessel causes wind drag which increases with the square of the velocity of the wind. If the velocity triples – say from 20 to 60 knots – wind force on the vessel is increased nine times.

Current.

The drag of the current adds to the load on the anchor line, but it is a vital factor only in areas of exceptional river currents or extreme tidal changes.

Wave action.

Wave action load is set up by the pitching, yawing and heaving motions of the vessel. If there is sufficient length and catenary in the rode, and the vessel can move freely, the load on the line will be comparatively

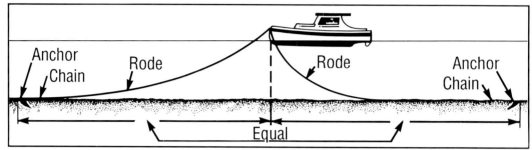

Figure 64 – *Parts of an anchoring system*

slight. Under normal conditions a 35' – 40' vessel exerts a load of about 200lb. Putting it another way, if a vessel has enough line to 'ride' the seas without being pulled up short, she won't bury and surge. Therefore, if the scope is right, the weight of the vessel is a less significant factor in the load on the anchor.

Wave action may cause resonance, a phonomenon that develops a critical load on the anchoring system. This occurs when the vessel and the sea get on the same wave length. Every vessel has a normal pitching period and when this coincides with the frequency of wave motion, the vessel will pitch violently even in moderate seas. This puts a shock load on the rode and will tend to break out the anchor.

Q.35 What length of line should be run out on a sea anchor ?

A.   When the waves are tending to break, it is of the first importance that the anchor should not be turned back on itself at the exact moment when the boat is going to be caught up by a wave. When the sea is 'regular', that is to say when the distances between wave crests are approximately equal, then the length of hawser should be half the distance between crests multiplied by at least five. Care must be taken that the multiplier is an odd number, so that the sea anchor and the vessel will not be on a wave crest at the same time.

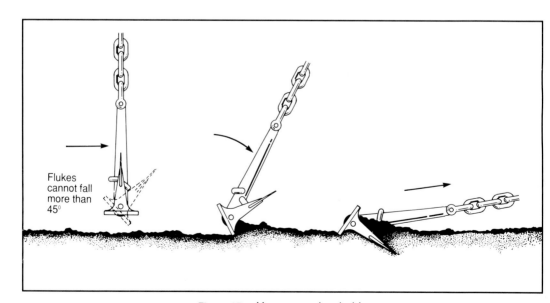

Flukes cannot fall more than 45°

Figure 65 – *How an anchor holds*

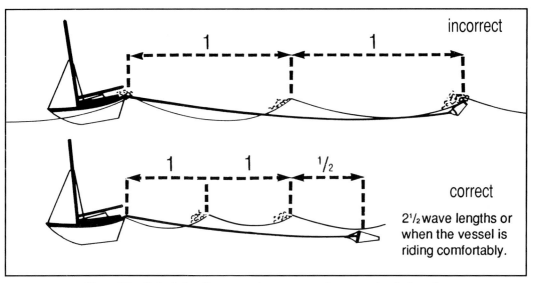

incorrect

correct

2¹/₂ wave lengths or when the vessel is riding comfortably.

Figure 66 – *Calculating the scope for a sea anchor - running before the sea.*

Q.36 What scope should be allowed when coming to anchor?

A. Formulae for this vary. Five to one – the length of cable five times the depth of water – is considered to be a useful guide. In water 6 to 9 metres (20 to 30 feet) deep use seven to one. In deeper water less scope may be used because of catenary effect by the system.

Note: Light rode with plenty of stretch to it is more efficient than inflexible line three times its size.

Q.37 What conditions should be considered before anchoring?

A. The depth of water at the place and its approaches. Rise and fall of the tide.

Nature of the bottom.

Direction and strength of tide or current.

The direction and probable strength of the prevailing wind.

Any other obstacles in the vicinity.

Q.38 What particulars should be noted on coming to anchor?

A. Depth of water.

Which anchor dropped.

Length of cable.

Bearing of position.

Time of anchoring.

Q.39 What are some common anchoring troubles ?

A. Anchoring troubles may be listed as follows:–

Entanglement of fluke.

Jamming under rocks.

Failure to regrip after slipping.

Breakage of the gear itself.

Too short a cable.

Kinks and twists in cables.

Q.40 When anchoring in reef waters how is it advisable to rig the anchor?

A. Shackle or fasten the chain to the anchor crown, then run the chain along the shank and seize it to the anchor ring with rope yarn. Should the anchor foul, on weighing, the surging will part the rope yarn under vertical strain and the anchor will be heaved out crown first.

Q.41 Describe the method of using anchors in tandem.

A. Under stormy conditions and where the swinging room is not limited it is often advisable to anchor with anchors in tandem in preference to using two separate anchors and chains. The leading anchor is the working anchor and is shackled onto the crown of the storm anchor using only one chain with as long a scope as possible to the vessel.

Figure 67 – *Anchor prepared for use in foul ground*

Q.42 To what end do you fasten the inboard end of the chain or rope?

A.　For fishing vessels a ring is welded to the keel or stem bar of the vessel. The chain is then connected by a dog, so that in an emergency it can readily be slipped. On wooden vessels it is usually fastened to the foot of the sampson post or breast hook.

Q.43 What fittings are necessary to prevent chafing of the vessel or anchor line?

A.　Fixed fairleads or roller fairleads. A roller farilead on the stem post gives additional strength without imposing additional strains. It also offers the advantage or reduced friction and the free rotation of the roller produces less wear on the chain. The axle must be sufficient in diameter to carry the load

and the cleats or guard high enough to prevent the chain jumping over.

Q.44 To what should one make fast the anchor line?

A.　The sampson post if possible. Avoid cleats and bollards, the reason being that the sampson post passes through the deck and is supported by the keel, while cleats and bollards are merely bolted to the deck. (Fig. 69(a))

Q.45 What care should be exercised when securing the anchor line?

A.　Care should be exercised that the fastening may be easily released e.g. fastening a chain with two half hitches can be difficult to release owing to the links becoming wedged into one another when tightened. It is preferable to take a couple of round turns, pass a bight of a about $\frac{1}{2}$ metre of chain under

Figure 68 – *Anchors laid in tandem*

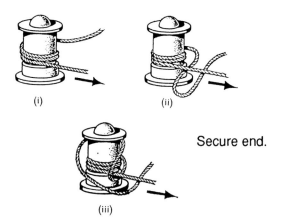

(i)

(ii)

Secure end.

(iii)

Belaying a fibre rope to a single bollard.

(a)
correct

(b)
incorrect

Figure 69 – *Methods of securing the anchor*

the standing part leading to the anchor and drop the bight over the sampson post. Repeat several times. (Fig. 69(a)) When selecting a form of connection between the vessel and the bottom, consideration must be given to its strength, its type, its resistance to wear and tear, corrosion or deterioration etc.

Chain

Chain is an excellent material for an anchor rode because its weight causes a catenary curve which absorbs shock loads and also reduces the angle of pull at the anchor.

The inconvenience of long chains lies mainly in their weight; 15 fathoms of 3/8 inch chain weighs 135 pounds compared to 41/2 pounds of equivalent nylon, ignoring the loss of weight when submerged.

Q.46 What type of chain is in service in today's fleets ?

A. Short link, stud link and high tensile.

Q.47 In the manufacture of anchor chain what provision is made for joining the length of cable?

A. An enlarged link either end to take the shackles.

Q.48 Which is greater in strength, stud link or short link chain ?

A. Stud link. The studs strengthen the links and prevent distortion.

Q.49 What is another advantage of a stud link chain?

A. The studs in the links prevent the chain from forming kinks and knots making it easier to handle.

Q.50 In what lengths are stud link chains manufactured?

A. 15 fathoms and 72 fathoms.

Q.51 What length does a shackle of chain measure.

A. 15 fathoms.

Q.52 How are shackles joined?

A. By a special joining shackle. (Fig. 71)

Q.53 How are shackles numbered ?

A. From the out-board end.

Q.54 When joining shackles of cable with lugged joining shackles, in which direction do you face the lug?

A. Inboard or towards the stern. The reason for so doing is that should the cable be surged out the lug will not foul.

Q.55 What is meant by the size of a chain cable?

A. The diameter of the iron of which each common link is made.

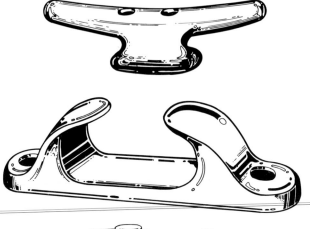

CLEAT

OPEN CHOCK OR FAIRLEAD

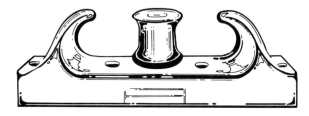

SINGLE ROLLER CHOCK OR FAIRLEAD

DOUBLE ROLLER CHOCK OR FAIRLEAD

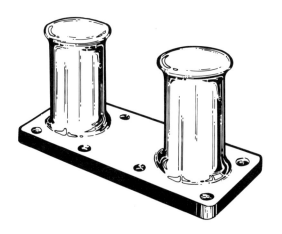

BITTS OR FAIRLEAD

Figure 70 – *Deck Fittings used in Mooring*

Q.56 A vessel is at anchor in foul weather. Two or three links of the cable at the hawse mouth are taking all the load. What action would a prudent skipper take?

A. 'Freshen the nip'. Every watch or at intervals veer a little more cable so that the same section of cable will not receive the punishment all the time.

Note: The same action would apply to anchor rope in a fairlead.

Q.57 What are some causes of cables parting?

A. (a) Cable deteriorates and becomes brittle as a result of the battering it receives when anchoring.

(b) Links are fractured by allowing cable to go with a run into lockers, or into the dock.

(c) Anchoring heavy ships with too much way on.

(d) Surging the cable when anchoring in deep water.

Q.58 Why is cable veered when approaching a deep anchorage?

A. (a) To act as a submarine sentry on approaching reef or steep-to ground.

(b) To avoid cable dropping in a heap and possibly fouling the anchor.

(c) To eliminate undue stresses and strains on all equipment.

Q.59 Describe procedure when cable is surveyed.

A. Cables are laid out in dry dock. Every bolt and pin is driven out and cleaned, pins are rubbed over with lead, bolts and shackles with warm tallow. Sockets of lugs are reamed. Every link is tapped by the blacksmith to gauge the condition of the metal. Loose studs are renewed.

Q.60 How is wear in the chain kept as even as possible?

A. In small vessels using short link chain, the chain is reversed end for end. In large vessels the first shackle is removed and rejoined onto the last inboard. No. 2 shackle then becomes joined to the anchor. No. 1 is secured to the vessel.

Q.61 How are anchor chains marked?

A. The inboard end of each shackle should be clearly marked by seizing with wire at the appropriate number of links from the joining shackle. The inboard end of the fifth shackle of cable and the outboard end of the sixth would each have the fifth link so marked. A splash of white paint on the marked links and on the joining shackles makes it easy to count the shackles as they run out. If the first few fathoms of the cable also are painted white they are readily seen at night before the anchor is in sight when being weighed.

Q.62 How is it advisable to secure heavy anchor chains?

A. It is advisable to use chain stoppers to avoid undue strain to be borne by the shaft on which the gypsy is fitted. A sudden jolt by the vessel pitching violently may bend the shaft.

Q.63 What care should be exercised in anchoring in very deep water when using chain cable?

A. Veer the cable. Should the cable be surged it may get out of control and do damage.

Q.64 Describe a 'west coast stopper'

A. A west coast stopper consists usually of a synthetic line secured in the centre to a lug on the deck. The two parts are then entwined around the warp (required to be stopped) in opposite directions and towards the load. The parts criss-cross either side of the warp until sufficient friction to perform the duty is obtained. The loose ends are then seized off with yarn or commonly tied with a clove hitch.

Note: A 'west coast stopper' is preferable to the single 'jamming' type and in cases where a heavy surge can be expected on mooring lines, two west coast stoppers, one short, one long, may be successfully used.

Q.65 What is the difference in fibre structure between material and synthetic ropes?

A. The synthetic fibres run the full length of the line whereas natural fibres do not. In most instances, natural fibres are approximately $1\frac{1}{2}$ metres in length.

3. ½ JOINING SHACKLE

WIRE

3rd SHACKLE OF CABLE
TO ANCHOR

4th SHACKLE OF CABLE
TO CABLEHOLDER

Marking of cable — Stud-link chain

Close-link chain

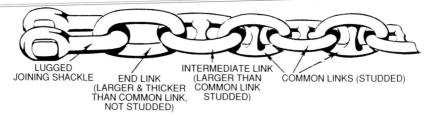

LUGGED
JOINING SHACKLE

END LINK
(LARGER & THICKER
THAN COMMON LINK,
NOT STUDDED)

INTERMEDIATE LINK
(LARGER THAN
COMMON LINK
STUDDED)

COMMON LINKS (STUDDED)

Cable with lugged joining shackle

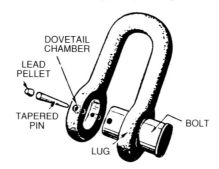

DOVETAIL
CHAMBER

LEAD
PELLET

TAPERED
PIN

BOLT

LUG

A lugged joining shackle

Senhouse slip

Devil's claw

Figure 71 – *Anchor Gear*

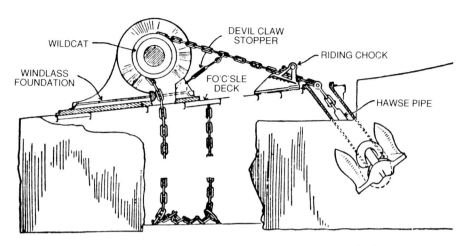

Figure 72 – *A vessel's anchor gear connected as a single unit*

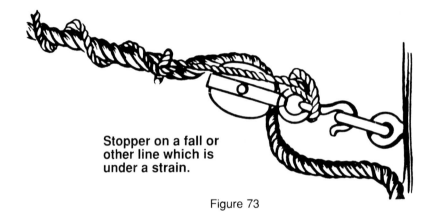

Stopper on a fall or other line which is under a strain.

Figure 73

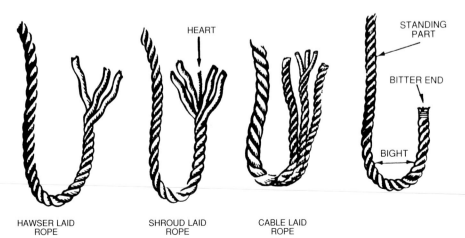

HAWSER LAID
ROPE

SHROUD LAID
ROPE

CABLE LAID
ROPE

Figure 74 – *Parts and Types of a Line*

The shorter the length of fibre the tighter must be the twist of strands. Of all the hemps, sisal has the shortest fibre.

Q.66 What precautions should be adopted when handling synthetic lines ?

A.   When synthetic lines are on the winch heads, great care should be taken not to surge them with winch heads rotating. Surging can cause fibres of the lines to heat and melt, adhering to the metal, thus causing permanent damage to the lines.

Bitts and winch heads should be kept in good condition when synthetic lines are used.

Grooves or rough surfaces should not be allowed to develop because such defects damage the lines and also cause them to grab.

Deep chocks should be kept smooth and free of rust and burrs.

Rollers should be kept free to turn.

Chafing gear or parcelling should be used as necessary.

Manila or wire should never be used on the same chocks or bitts in conjunction with synthetics.

Mooring lines should be checked frequently to spot buckling of strands – a sign of unbalance.

Lines should be checked for broken strands and frayed yarns.

If the strands are twisted open and powdered fibre is found, it is a sign of internal wear.

Q.67 What care should be exercised when coiling polyprop lines ?

A.   Polyprop lines should not be coiled in the same direction as it will unbalance the lay. If a polyprop line is used continually on the same side of the winch or windlass, in a counter clockwise direction, it will extend the lay and shorten the twist of each strand. Kinks and hocks will develop. If it is used continually in a clockwise direction, the lay is shortened and the rope becomes stiff and will kink. Alternate directions regularly, starting with clockwise turns on new lines.

Note: Never stand in the path of a line under strain – especially with synthetics.

Causes of accidents

In analysing a number of mooring line accidents in which synthetic lines were involved, it has been found that replacing manila on a 'strength for strength' basis with synthetics results in a synthetic line of too small a diameter to take a stopper properly and one which presents too small a surface to the face of a capstan head or bitt for even heaving or surging when under strain. The result is that they melt and stick and then let go all at once. It is recommended that manila mooring lines should be replaced by synthetics on a 'diameter for diameter' basis, rather than 'strength for strength'. The longer wear and the safer handling characteristics will justify the greater initial cost.

The recommended way to handle this type of line on a capstan is to hold three to four turns. This permits surge while giving enough grip for haulage. They cannot be surged or slackened with more than two turns on a pair of BITTS. See Page 168.

It will be found that if the above method is not followed and the line has numerous turns, it will stretch to its maximum and finally explode off the capstan.

Fouled Anchor

If the anchor does not break out (break ground) while being hauled vertically, the brake is set on the winch and the vessel is propelled ahead. Then if the anchor does not break out it is fouled. To clear it, the anchor chain is made fast with cable stoppers or alternatively a few turns around the sampson post and the vessel run slowly in wide circles on a taut line. When it is impossible to break free, the vessel should be run up as close as possible, a float marker that will be visible at high tide attached to the chain on the anchor, and the chain broken at the nearest shackle. This scope of the marker must be of sufficient length to reach the bottom at high tide. This will make it possible to retrieve the anchor later.

Note: It is essential to secure the anchor chain by the stoppers or to the sampson post so as to avoid undue strain being exerted on the winch. Sudden jerks or extreme tension could damage the winch in many ways. The damage most common is to bend the shaft on which the chain gypsy is fitted.

Maintenance

Regular inspection of the anchor gear should be carried out and the following items examined before each voyage.

(a) The anchor pins for wear.

(b) The anchors are well home in their hawse pipes and kept taut so they cannot move.

(c) Hawse and spurling pipes should be stopped off so no salt water can spill on to the deck or down the chain lockers.

(d) The chain is not stowed foul of mud or weed.

(e) Shackles inspected for wear and rust.

(f) Chain in weather from spurling pipe to anchor is protected against corrosion.

(g) Shackles of chain marked correctly.

(h) Brake drums and bands protected from salt water and sand so they won't grow rust blisters and pit making them less reliable.

(i) Bearing kept well greased and covered to keep out all water and sand.

(j) Hydraulic pipes and cocks in good condition and free from leaks.

(k) Shaft to be kept free from rust to facilitate ease of dismantling.

Chapter 8
METEOROLOGY

METEOROLOGY

The Bureau Of Meteorology is responsible for the issue of routine weather forecasts and for warnings of harzadous weather conditions including those that threaten shipping (within its area of responsibility).

Enquiries relating to forecasts or warnings should be directed to the duty forecaster at the Regional Forecasting Centre in any state capital city.

Q.1 Describe what is meant by the term "Fine".

A. No rain or other precipitation (such as hail, snow, etc). The use of the word "fine" is generally avoided in excessively cloudy, windy, foggy or dusty conditions.

Q.2 Describe what is meant by the term "Showers".

A. Precipitation which is often short-lived and heavy, falling from convective clouds. Showers are often characterized by their sudden ending and beginning. Meteorologists distinguish between "showers" and "rain" by considering the type of cloud from which the precipitation occurs, and hence, the physical processes responsible for its formation.

Q.3 Describe what is meant by the term "Rain".

A. Precipitation of liquid water drops greater than 0.5mm in diameter. In contrast to showers, it is steadier and normally falls from stratiform (layer) cloud.

Q.4 Describe what is meant by the term "Drizzle".

A Fairly uniform precipitation composed exclusively of very small droplets of water (less than 0.5m in diameter) very close to one another.

Q.5 Describe what is meant by the term "Atmospheric Pressure".

A. The atmospheric pressure at any point is the weight of the air which lies vertically above a unit area, centred at that point. Atmospheric pressure is now expressed in hectopascals (hPa) which is equal to 100 Newtons per square metre. In the past it was expressed in inches of mercury and millibars.

1 inch of mercury = 33.8639 millibars = 33.8639 hectopascals

1 millibar = 1 hectopascal

Water vapour is lighter than air and displaces air, therefore a column of moist air is lighter than a column of dry air of the same dimensions.

Extreme Australian region values are 1054 hPa and 904 hPa.

Q.6 Describe what is meant by the term "Isobar".

A. A line joining parts of equal atmospheric pressure. All pressures are adjusted to mean sea level for comparison.

Q.7 Describe what is meant by a "High" or "Anticyclone".

A. Region of high atmospheric pressure represented on weather maps by a closed system of isobars. Air within the high is descending in the centre and flows in an anticlockwise direction (in the Southern Hemisphere) slightly outwards across the isobars.

Q.8 Describe what is meant by the term "Ridge".

A. Elongated area of relatively high atmospheric pressure with characteristics of high pressure system. No closed isobars.

Q.9 What is meant by a "Low" or "Cyclone"?

A. Cyclone or low are the terms applied to weather systems in which the winds blow in a clockwise sense in the Southern Hemisphere.

Following this definition are the low pressure systems which migrate from west to east across the ocean south of Australia or sometimes across southern parts of the continent. This type is cold cored, that is the air inside the low through the middle atmosphere is colder than the surrounding environment. It should be noted that it is NOT the custom of the Weather Bureau to refer to these lows as "cyclones"; this term is reserved in practice for tropical cyclones.

It is known that central parts are warmer, level for level, than outer parts; this arises from the way in which a tropical cyclone is formed.

Q.10 Describe what is meant by the term "Depression".

A. An area of low pressure – low or trough. Alternative name for cyclone or low.

Q.11 Describe what is meant by the term "Tropical Cyclone".

A. A cyclone originating in tropical latitudes and whose energy comes from the heat released when ascending warm moist air condenses to form cloud and rain. Winds exceeding gale force (63 km/h) occur near the centre and may extend for several hundred kilometres.

Q.12 Describe what is meant by the term "Tropical Low".

A. Low pressure system in tropical latitudes with closed isobars but winds below gale force. Alternative name for tropical depression.

Q.13 Describe what is meant by the term "Trough".

A. An elongated area of relatively low atmospheric pressure. No closed isobars. The opposite of a ridge.

Q.14 Describe what is meant by the term "Pressure Gradient".

A. Change of pressure with distance. The greater the change with distance (i.e. the closer together isobars are) the greater the wind strength and vice versa. In situations of "weak" gradients i.e. light winds, wind direction is variable and could be opposite to direction suggested by isobars.

Q.15 Describe what is meant by the term "Fronts".

A. Border between two air masses having different characteristics of air temperature and density or moisture.

Q.16 Describe what is meant by the term "Cold Front".

A. Border where warm air is being replaced by undercutting cold air.

Q.17 Describe what is meant by the term "Warm Front".

A. Border where cold air is being replaced by overriding warm air.

Q.18 Describe what is meant by the term "Temperature Inversion".

A. A layer of warmer air overlaying cooler air. Prevents vertical air currents and may lead to increased accumulation of pollutants if near the ground.

QUEENSLAND – WEATHER FORECAST DISTRICTS

Chapter 9
THE ANEROID BAROMETER

THE ANEROID BAROMETER

For very precise barometric readings we can use a digital aneroid barometer. However, it is a very costly instrument and requires special care in handling. For general use an easier though less precise means of measurement has been devised - the ANEROID BAROMETER (aneroid, meaning without fluid).

What a Barometer Does

A barometer measures atmospheric pressure, which is the weight of a column of air above it. It is well known that air has weight, but the earth's atmosphere gets thinner with increasing height. It follows that as we ascend from the earth's surface, the weight of air will grow less, that is, the pressure will fall. Roughly for every 300 metres of ascent, atmospheric pressure decreases by 34 hectopascals in the lower atmosphere.

A barometer's main use, however, is not to measure altitude, but to measure changes in atmospheric pressure in a particular place. High and low pressure systems in the atmosphere move around the earth's surface. The movements shown on the face of a barometer attached to the bulkhead of your vessel, indicate the changes in pressure as they occur directly above you. These changes, when they are considered together with the indications of wind, temperature, moisture and cloud can be a great help in forecasting approaching weather.

How it Works

This instrument consists of a thin cylindrical metallic chamber, partially exhausted of air and hermetically sealed. It is thus susceptible to the slightest change in external pressure. The top of the chamber is connected to a pointer by an arrangement of levers and springs, and this has the effect of greatly magnifying its movements This pointer can be set at any pressure by means of a screw at the back of the instrument. Since the metal of which the aneroid chamber is made cannot be relied on to maintain its form indefinitely, the zero varies slightly. The reading of the instrument should therefore be compared frequently with that of the mercurial barometer. Before the instrument is read, the glass face should be tapped gently.

Q.1 **What is the principle of the aneroid barometer?**

A. The pressure of the atmosphere on the metal cell which is a partial vacuum moves a system of levers which activates a pointer over a graduated dial.

Q.2 **What is the average atmospheric pressure at sea level?**

A. Approximately 100 newtons per square metre, or to one millibar.

Q.3 **What is a hectopascal?**

A. A hectopascal is the standard unit of pressure. It is equivalent to 100 Newtons per square metre, or to one millibar.

Q.4 **What are the corrections required for a barometer reading before it can be compared with a standard reading?**

A. It should be corrected for index error (if any), also altitude, temperature and latitude.

Q.5 **What precautions should be taken installing an aneroid barometer?**

A. (a) Choose a position in the wheelhouse free from salt spray, direct sun and wind gusts.
(b) Choose a position free from vibration.
(c) Make certain that the air vent is not sealed off. A common fault is to paint around the barometer and seal off the metal cell from the atmosphere.

Q 6 **How is the barometer adjusted?**

A. Contact the Bureau of Meteorology or an other reliable source and adjust the reading of the aneroid barometer to their instruments. The adjustment is made with a small screw driver to a screw at the back of the instrument.

Q.7 **On the face of some barometers are printed Rain, Change, Fair. Do they mean anything?**

A. No, they are mostly decorative.

Q.8 **Would the barometer be of any use if it had not been corrected?**

A. Yes, the most important factor is movement of the pointer. It is only when

The illustration represents the mechanism of a simple type of aneroid.
The box B expands and contracts when the pressure of the atmosphere decreases and increases. The pointer is pivoted at the centre of the dial and a fulcrum rests on the side of the box at B and moves up and down with it, the light tension spring G exerting sufficient leverage to keep the fulcrum in contact with the box.
The pointer moves up and down the scale S.

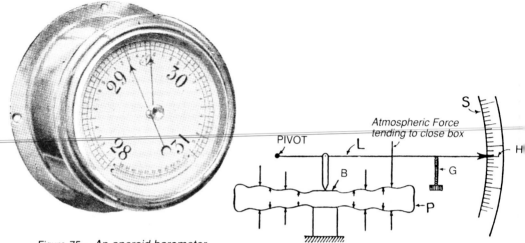

Figure 75 – *An aneroid barometer*

you wish to compare your readings with the weather reports, that it is convenient for it to have been adjusted.

Q.9 Should the pointer rise, what would this indicate?

A. That the atmospheric pressure is increasing due to an approaching high pressure system or due to diurnal pressure variations.

Q.10 Should the pointer fall, what would this indicate?

A. That the atmospheric pressure is decreasing due to an approaching low pressure system or due to diurnal pressure variations.

Q.11 Give an explanation on how you would read your Aneroid Barometer.

A. To read my Aneroid Barometer I would first tap the glass lightly but firmly to ensure that the linkage mechanism is not sticky. Barometers of the modern variety are usually marked in hectopascals or millibars but sometimes in inches. If marked in inches they would be subdivided into tenths. These divisions of tenths may again be halved, giving twentieths. This enables a

reading to be easily calculated to one hundredth of an inch if required. After a reading is made the set hand is turned by means of a knob at the centre of the glass so that it covers the reading hand. This permits the reader to know when next taking a reading whether the pressure has risen or fallen and by how much.

Q.12 Give an explanation of how the Aneroid Barometer is used in forecasting.

A. To repeat what was said at the beginning, an Aneroid Barometer is an instrument which measures air pressure. It does NOT foretell weather, so you would be well advised to put little faith in the words STORMY, RAIN, CHANGE, FAIR and DRY which appear on the face of many popular makes of barometer.

Many of you will know from the weather charts displayed on television or published in the city newspapers that highs and lows move in general from west to east, especially in the more southern latitudes. Bad weather is often associated with the lows, though

Conversion Table
Inches to Hectopascals.

INCHES	HECTOPASCALS
29.5	999.0
29.6	1002.4
29.7	1005.8
29.8	1009.1
29.9	1012.5
30.0	1015.9
30.1	1019.3
30.2	1022.7
30.3	1026.1
30.4	1029.5
30.5	1032.9

NOTE: 1 Hectopascal = 1 Millibar
1 Inch of Mercury = 33.8639 Hectopascals

moist onshore winds can cause rain in coastal areas even if the pressure is high. In other words, the actual reading of the barometer does not give unmistakable information concerning the weather to come.

Your barometer will show whether pressure is rising or falling, that is, whether a high or low pressure system is approaching, or perhaps developing in intensity.

But here, a word of caution! Owing to a daily atmosheric effect, the pressure will normally fall by about 3 hectopascals between 10.00 a.m. and 4.00 p.m. and will rise by a nearly similar amount between 10.00 p.m. and 4.00 a.m., even if weather systems are stationary. A smaller rise and fall occurs during the night and early morning. These daily ("diurnal") changes must be allowed for before you can really say whether the "glass" is rising or falling due to weather systems. The best way to avoid this difficulty is to observe changes over 24-hour periods, using your movable pointer or Set Hand, in other words, check your barometer at the same time each day.

When there is a fairly large fall, say more than 6 hectopascals in 24 hours, you can assume that a high is moving away or that a depression is approaching, or both.

Chapter 10
TROPICAL CYCLONES

TROPICAL CYCLONES

Australia's official tropical cyclone season is between November and April. The preferred months are January, February and March when there is a combination of high sea temperatures, high humidity and low level winds converging into the monsoon trough. However, sufficient occurrences have been noted during the transition months to warrant vigilance.

Although the highest incidence of tropical cyclones in the Australian region is in the Gulf of Carpentaria, the greater percentage of severe ones has been observed off the northwest coast of the continent.

Tropical cyclones form over the warm tropical oceans from which they derive their energy as clusters of thunderstorms. These may persist for many days before the circulation pattern characteristics of a tropical cyclone forms. Over land or cooler waters there is insufficient energy available to sustain them.

A mature tropical cyclone is characterized by a central low pressure system (usually between 910 and 990 hPa) called the eye. Surrounding the eye is a ring of cloud in which the maximum wind belt is embedded. Outwards from the maximum winds, the wind speed gradually decreases as the atmospheric pressure and distance from the eye increases.

Winds in the eye are light and variable and therefore a lull in the wind ferocity will occur when the eye arrives. After some time, perhaps an hour or two, possibly only minutes, the eye passes and the belt of maximum winds is back. Since the winds blow more or less circularly around the eye, the direction of these winds will be different, perhaps the very opposite to that which preceded the lull. Over the whole disturbance there is usually much low cloud and torrential rain with poor visibility.

Radar and satellite imagery indicate that the eye wall clouds are the innermost coil of a series of spiral rain band clouds. These bands can stretch over 1000 km from the cyclone periphery into the eye wall, which itself can vary in diameter from about 10 km to more than 100 km. The spiral rain bands are often associated with very strong wind squalls.

Q.1 Define the term 'path'.

A. The central calm along which the centre of the storm will probably travel.

Q.2 Define the term 'track'.

A. The track of a storm is the actual path travelled.

Q.3 Define the term 'vortex'.

A. The central calm at the heart of the storm also known as the eye of the storm.

Q.4 Define the term 'vertex'.

A. Sometimes called the cod of the track, the vertex is the most westerly point reached by the centre of the storm before it curves back.

Note: Do not confuse 'vortex' with 'vertex'.

Q.5 Define the term 'right semicircle'.

A. The right semicircle is that half of the storm which lies to the right of an observer looking along the track.

Q.6 Define the term 'left semicircle'.

A. The left semicircle is the half of the storm which lies to the left of an observer looking along the track.

Q.7 Define the term 'navigable semicircle'.

A. The navigable semicircle is that semicircle which lies to the right of the path in the Southern Hemisphere.

Q.8 Define the term 'dangerous quadrant'.

A. The advanced quadrant of that semicircle which lies on the side of the path nearest to the normal direction in which the storm recurves, so named because a vessel caught in the dangerous quadrant may be blown towards the path of the storm-centre or the path may recurve and pass over her.

Q.9 Define the term 'angle of indraft'.

A. The angle which the direction of the wind makes with an isobar.

Weather

Q.10 What is a 'gust' ?

A. A gust is a sudden increase in the force of the wind, of very short duration.

Q.11 What is a 'squall'?

A.   A squall is a sudden increase in the force of the wind of greater duration and violence than a gust. They are both caused by the meeting of air of different temperatures.

Q.12 Describe a 'nimbus cloud'.

A.   "Nimbus" means rain bearing. Nimbostratus clouds are thick, dark, stratiform (layer) clouds from which heavier intensity rain or snow is falling.

Cumulonimbus clouds are towering convective (cauliflower shaped).

Q.13 Explain 'mist' or 'fog'.

A.   Fog is the suspension of very small water droplets in the air, reducing the visibility at the Earth's surface to less than 1000 metres. Mist and fog is caused by the condensation of water vapour in the air due to cooling of the atmosphere below the point of saturation.

Q.14 What causes the 'trade winds'?

A.   They are caused by the air being impelled from areas of high pressure towards the low pressure regions at the equator, their direction is influenced by the earth's rotation which deflects the air currents to the left in the southern hemisphere.

Q.15 State Buys Ballot's Law for the southern hemisphere.

A.   Buys Ballot's Law states that in the Southern Hemisphere an observer with his face to the wind will find lower air pressure on the left hand side and higher pressure on the right hand side. This law is a corollary of the fact that winds in the Southern Hemisphere blow anticlockwise around high pressure systems and clockwise around low pressure systems.

Q.16 What are the signs of an advancing tropical storm?

A.   (a) A long heavy swell.

(b) A lurid sky effect.

(c) An unsteady or falling barometer.

(d) Heavy humid atmosphere.

(e) Radio warning broadcasts.

A long heavy swell.

A swell rolling up from the direction of the coming storm will give the first indication of a tropical cyclone. The swell may extend to a distance of over 1609 kilometres (1000 miles) from the actual storm and can usually be relied on to make itself felt 644 kilometres (400 miles) from its centre. When the storm is at a greater distance than 322 kilometres (200 miles) from a vessel, the direction of the swell is the most reliable of all indications of the direction in which the centre lies. Although the swell increases as a storm approaches, its state does not give any reliable indication of distance from the centre.

A lurid sky effect.

Cirrus clouds generally, but not always, precede a storm. In the tropics if cirrus stretches in convergent streaks or bands, and the convergent formation remains visible in a fixed direction, it is a fairly good warning, and the centre of the storm probably lies in the direction of the point of convergence. Such a formation may appear as much as 400 kilometres (250 miles) ahead of the centre. centre.

The cirrus clouds associated with a storm sometimes cause the most lurid sunsets and sunrises. A fiery copper-coloured sky is not uncommon, but any or all colours of the rainbow may be visible.

An unsteady or falling barometer.

Although the barometer cannot be relied on to give adequate warning of the approach of a storm on all occasions, it assists, when considered in conjunction with other precursory signs. On many occasions the barometer will be unsteady when a storm approaches, but the barometer is often unsteady on other occasions notably during tropical thunderstorms and summer squalls. Moreover the barometer is not always unsteady when a storm is approaching.

In ideal circumstances, and on occasions when a cyclone is going to pass reasonably close to the observer, there are usually three fairly definite phases in the fall of the barometer:

(i) a slow fall during which the diurnal variation is still apparent on the barograph trace. This usually occurs between 800 and 200 kilometres

(500 to 120 miles) from the centre of' the storm.

(ii) A distinct fall during which the diurnal variation is almost completely masked. This usually occurs between 200 and 100 kilometres (120 and 60 miles) from the centre. Throughout this phase the barometer is sometimes very unsteady.

(iii) A rapid fall. This usually occurs between 100 and 16 kilometres (60 to 10 miles) from the centre.

In the rear of the storm the barometer rises as rapidly as it fell in advance of the storm.

It is not uncommon for the barometer at the centre of the storm to stand 60 to 70 hPa lower than in the region just outside the storm field. The steepest barometric gradient normally met with is 11 hPa in 24 kilometres (15 miles).

Heavy humid atmosphere.

The weather is usually sultry and oppressive and there is a feeling that all is not well. Within 161 to 241 kilometres (100 to 150 miles) from the centre, heavy continuous rain sets in, which a little later becomes torrential.

When the centre approaches the vessel she may experience increasing winds with violent squalls, later increasing to hurricane force and mountainous seas. As the vortex passes overhead the wind drops. When it has passed the wind may suddenly blow from the opposite direction, with renewed violence, beginning with a terrific squall. This could be particularly dangerous to vessels at anchor, because they may be caught with the squall abeam. As the storm recedes from the vessel the wind moderates, the sky is much brighter and blue sky may appear through rifts in the clouds. A very violent high confused sea is experienced. Heavy continuous rain which preceded the storm again sets in, but it does not last as long, because the rain area in the rear of a storm is generally a good deal smaller than the area in front of it.

Radio warning broadcasts.

The Commonwealth Bureau of Meteorology have a series of coastal stations monitoring the weather in Queensland. They are equipped with radar for the purpose of locating and tracking tropical storms. A cyclone detected when forming allows the weather stations to give ample and accurate warnings of its movements. The frequency of the warnings is increased as the storm approaches.

Commercial radio stations have a special alarm signal which they broadcast when a cyclone threatens the area of their location.

Q.17 What is a 'storm surge'?

A.   One of the most dangerous aspects of a tropical cyclone near the coast is the storm surge. This is a raised dome of water about 60 to 80 kilometres across and typically about 2 to 5 metres higher than the normal tide level.

The reduced pressure causes seas to rise by about 10 millimetres for each hectopascal. The main cause of storm surge is wind stress on the sea surface which has about triple the effect of the pressure drop.

The amplitude of the surge is strongly influenced by geographic factors such as the shape of the sea bed and coastline, the angle of approach of the tropical cyclone to the shore and other factors such as prevailing currents. Bays and estuaries, by converging the waters as they move towards the shore, can increase the amplitude of the surge by more than 50 per cent. If an estuary is already in flood, the amplitude will be further increased. The worst possible conditions arise when a large storm surge arrives upon a spring tide.

Practical Rules for Avoiding Cyclones

If there is reason to suppose a storm is approaching, it is necessary to determine:-

(a) The direction in which the centre of the storm lies.

(b) In which semicircle the vessel is situated.

To find the bearing of the centre allowing for the uncertain incurvature of the wind-

The angle of indraft of the wind is greater on the outskirts of the stormfield than near the centre, where the wind is considered to make an eddy round a central calm. For this reason the general rule is to allow about 12 points from the direction cf the wind when the storm begins, 10 points when the barometer has fallen 10 hPa (.3 of an inch) and 8 points when it has fallen 20 hPa (.6 of an inch) or more. The barometer may stand as much as 70 hPa lower at the centre than on the outskirts of the stormfield.

Note: It must be remembered that the wind to be considered is the true wind, not the wind that is felt. It's necessary to stop the vessel to obtain the direction of the true wind as the vessel's speed produces deflection.

To find in which semicircle the vessel is situated.

No time should be lost in deciding to heave to at once. Even though the vessel may have a fair wind, this wind may be taking her right into the path of the storm. Having hove to, the seaman must then observe how the wind shifts as the storm advances.

The rule is then the same for all storms:-

   (i) If the wind shifts to the RIGHT (veers), the vessel is in the right-hand semicircle.

   (ii) If the wind shifts to the LEFT (backs), the vessel is in the left-hand semicircle.

   (iii) If the direction of the wind DOES NOT CHANGE, but increases in force as the barometer falls, the vessel is in the direct path of the centre of the advancing storm.

Since it is always advisable to be prepared for the worst, it should always be assumed until found otherwise that the vessel is in the most dangerous semicircle. She should therefore be hove to with the wind on the port bow in the southern hemisphere. The quadrant in advance of the trough line is called the dangerous quadrant. This is always that quadrant in which the wind is sweeping the vessel towards the path of the advancing storm centre. In the southern hemisphere the dangerous semicircle, and the dangerous quadrant, are to the left of the path of the storm. If the barometer is falling, the vessel is before the trough of the storm; and if it is rising, the vessel is to the rear of the trough.

It is not possible to estimate the distance of the centre of the storm from a vessel. This arises partly from uncertainty about the relation between the bearing of the centre and the direction of the wind, but mainly

because there are no means of knowing whether the storm is large or small. If the barometer falls slowly and the weather gradually gets worse, it is reasonable to suppose that the centre is distant, and conversely, with a rapidly falling barometer and increasing bad weather, the centre may be dangerously near.

The following are the most advisable courses to pursue to avoid the centre:-

   (a) If in the path of a storm, run with the wind on the port quarter in the southern hemisphere, away from and at right angles to the assumed path of the storm, until the barometer begins to rise.

   (b) If in the dangerous semicircle, (that is the left-hand semicircle in the southern hemisphere) a fishing vessel should steam to windward away from and at right angles to the assumed path of the storm. A sailing vessel should heave-to on the port tack in the southern hemisphere, because the wind will then always be drawing aft. Be careful to note the land and navigational dangers in the vicinity, because it may be possible to run into harbour, or under the lee of the land, for shelter, but in some circumstances it is better to remain at sea.

   (c) If in the navigable semicircle (that is the right-hand semicircle) run with the wind on the port quarter in the southern hemisphere, away from and at right angles to the assumed path of the storm, until the barometer begins to rise.

    It is better to proceed at full speed ahead of the storm into some recognised 'cyclone anchorage' than to be caught in narrow waters, because the visibility becomes very low due to driving rain and spray, and quite large seas are experienced as the result of surface currents set up in the sea by the gale force winds of the storm.

   (d) If in harbour or at anchor, watch carefully the shifting of the wind ascertain the direction of the centre

Determine to which side of the path of the storm the vessel is situated so that the centre passes over the vessel. It may be possible to point the vessel in the direction of the coming squall.

Q.18 With the knowledge of a cyclone approaching, what steps should be adopted for the safety of the vessel?

A. Action taken to prepare the vessel for an oncoming cyclone would be described under the following headings:-

(a) Record as accurately as possible the path of the cyclone.

Care should be taken to listen to weather bulletin broadcasts, plot the position, and any movement of the cyclone. The eye of the storm can be tracked with reasonable accuracy, from information supplied by the Weather Bureau.

(b) Prepare the vessel.

A programme to make the vessel seaworthy should be organised and carried out immediately. Listed on the programme would be:–

(i)   Batten down all hatches securely.

(ii) Close all dead lights on ports.

(iii) Close all valves on skin fittings except those essential for the servicing of the engine.

(iv) Board up all large panes of glass – if boarding up is not possible run vertical and horizontal strips of masking tape to prevent glass from flying if fractured.

(v)   Pump all bilges. Clean strainers and strum boxes.

(v)   Close any watertight doors.

(vii) Check all life preserving gear - keeping in mind accessibility.

(viii) Prepare anchors so they may be let go in an emergency.

(ix) Clear the decks, stow and secure all moveable gear below.

(x)   Lower derricks, booms or any gear that may cause excessive windage.

(xi) Keep all heavy weights as low as possible.

(xii) Make sure all freeing ports are working and are clear of obstructions.

(xiii) Ballast the vessel for best trim.

(xiv) Have extra rations – especially fresh water in convenient plastic jars readily accessible in case of having to abandon ship.

(xv) Check fuel and stores so that an estimation can be made of the vessel's endurance.

(xvi) Report position on all ship to shore radio schedules.

(c) Determine the action to be taken for the vessel's safety under the prevailing conditions.

There are many conditions as listed, that would influence the decision of the master bearing in mind the following:-

(i)   Size and speed of the vessel.

(ii) Seaworthiness and endurance of the vessel.

(iii) Proximity to dangers.

(iv) Proximity to harbours, anchorages etc.

(v)   The relative position of the vessel to the position of the path of the cyclone.

For the average trawler the safest place to be during a cyclone is in a creek, head upstream and aground, with anchors leading well ahead and well secured on the shore.

In broad terms a fall of the barometer could mean an indication of about twelve hours in advance of bad weather. In Queensland, which is in a cyclone belt, a marked fall could indicate the approach of a cyclone.

Q.19 Outline the Warning System for cyclones as provided by the Bureau of Meteorology for the Queensland coast.

A. On the first evidence of a tropical cyclone or developing tropical depression, with potential to become a tropical cyclone, poses a threat of gales to the coastal/inland community within 48 hours but not within 24 hours, a CYCLONE WATCH is issued by the Bureau of Meteorology. The message contains a brief estimate of the cyclone's location, intensity and movement and identifies the coastal areas which could become affected.

On the declaration of a CYCLONE WATCH people should listen for further announcements on the radio and be prepared to act quickly if the threat increases. The cyclone's progress is monitored continuously and updated cyclone watch messages are issued through the media every six hours.

Q.20 Outline when the Bureau of Meteorology declares a cyclone warning.

A.   The Bureau declares a CYCLONE WARNING when a cyclone or potential cyclone is expected to cause at least gale force winds in coastal areas WITHIN 24 HOURS. Cyclone warnings are issued every three hours. When a cyclone is under radar surveillance close to the coast and posing a severe danger, warnings are given at hourly intervals through the media.

Q.21 What information is broadcast with a cyclone warning.

1. It identifies the communities and coastal areas being threatened.

2. Contains the cyclone's name.

3. Gives the location and intensity including maximum wind gusts and its movements.

4. Where relevant forecasts of heavy rainfall, flooding, storm surge and abnormally high tides are included.

5. The warning also gives a forecast of the cyclone's behaviour over the next 12 hours and when appropriate the estimated time and place of landfall.

Q.22 Describe what is meant by a FLASH CYCLONE WARNING.

A.   A Flash Cyclone Warning is issued should an area not previously warned come under threat by a cyclone.

(Note) The term Flash may also be used to prefix an urgent amendment to an earlier warning. Example: Should a cyclone unexpectedly change direction.

Q.23 Does the Bureau of Meteorology give other storm warnings.

A.   Yes. The Bureau also issues STRONG WIND, GALE and STORM WARNINGS when conditions are hazardous for shipping and boating.

Q.24 Name the three Tropical Cyclone Warning Centres.

A.   Brisbane, Darwin and Perth. These are responsible for cyclone detection and warning in the eastern northern and western regions respectively of tropical Australia and adjacent oceans.

Q.25 To whom would persons seek advice if a cyclone were threatening their area.

A.   Contact your State or Territory emergency services organisation. (Note) Radio and television broadcasts of Bureau warnings are frequent and provide more up-to-date information than that in newspapers. It is recommended that a transistor radio with spare batteries is an added insurance of keeping in touch with the organisations if floods or power failure isolate your area.

Tropical Storm Strategy

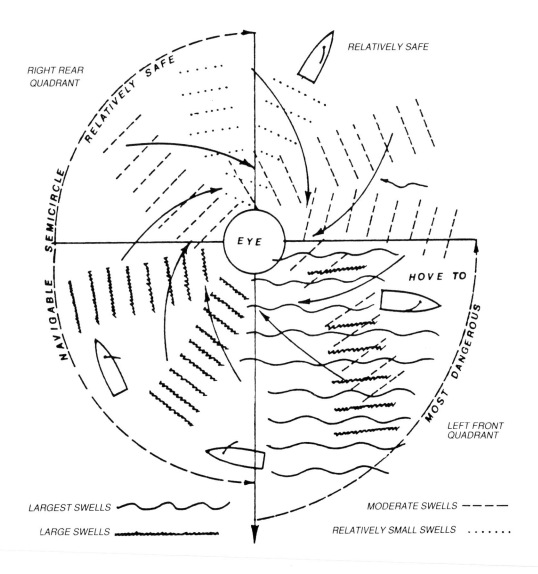

STORM'S DIRECTION OF MOVEMENT ➝

BOATS ARE SHOWN ON RECOMMENDED COURSES

RELATIVELY SAFE

RIGHT REAR
QUADRANT

RELATIVELY SAFE

NAVIGABLE SEMICIRCLE

EYE

HOVE TO

MOST DANGEROUS

LEFT FRONT
QUADRANT

LARGEST SWELLS

LARGE SWELLS

MODERATE SWELLS ― ― ―

RELATIVELY SMALL SWELLS . . . .

Figure 76

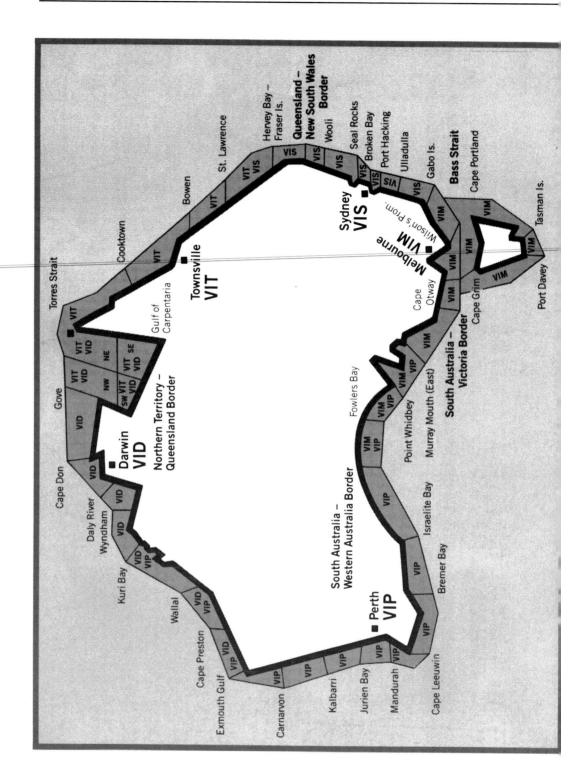

Figure 77 – *Coastal waters forecast areas*

Chapter 11

MANAGEMENT OF VESSELS
IN HEAVY WEATHER

MANAGEMENT OF VESSELS IN HEAVY WEATHER

It never makes sense to drive a vessel in a storm especially into a head sea in such a way that she sustains damage to the hull or is placed in danger of foundering. The fact that modern sea-going vessels have powerful engines means that in rough weather they not only have the means to extricate themselves from danger, but also the means to inflict great damage upon themselves. Superficial damage in heavy weather can usually be avoided without jeopardising the achievement of the vessel's task.

Knowledge of the stability of his vessel and of the various steps that can be taken to improve it, is essential to the seaman if he wishes to preserve her safety in heavy weather.

Q.1   What precautions should be taken before leaving harbour ?

A.   Before leaving harbour the vessel should be fully prepared for sea and this work must include the proper securing of everything that is moveable. Batten down hatches and secure locking bars over hatch covers. Stow all mooring lines and loose cordage, nets, floats etc. Close all port holes, deadlights, watertight doors, cover and secure all moveable gear. The preparation includes inspection of fishing gear and rigging, testing main engines, steering gear, sirens, radio, radar, compasses, and the rigging of life lines where necessary.

Q.2   What additional measures would be advisable if the weather suddenly deteriorates?

A.   Shut all outlets other than those required for engine operation.

Note: Special attention should be given to toilets installed below water line. Run strips of masking tape across large window panes to avoid flying glass should they be stove in.

Q.3   What effect has wave motion on a vessel?

A.   All ships have a natural period of roll and pitch according to their dimensions and conditions of loading.

The period of roll is the time a vessel takes to roll from one side to the other and back again.

The period of pitch is the time the stem of a vessel takes to rise from the horizontal, fall below it and return to the horizontal.

The period of encounter is the time interval between the passage of two successive wave crests past any given point in the vessel.

The movement of a vessel in roll or pitch depends on the size of the waves and the relation between the period of encounter and the vessel's period of roll or pitch. The greatest movement develops when there is synchronisation. The period of encounter depends on the wave length (which governs the wave speed), and also on the course and speed of the vessel relative to the waves. Thus the period of encounter can be varied by alteration of the vessel's course and speed.

When the period of pitch and roll is small, in comparison with the period of encounter, she will tend to ride the waves, keeping her deck parallel to their slope.

In a beam sea this will result in rapid, heavy rolling. In a head sea a small period of pitch should result in an easy motion, without much water being shipped.

When the period of roll or pitch is large in comparison with the period of encounter, she will roll or pitch independently of the waves. In a beam sea this should mean a comparatively easy motion, though waves slapping against the weather side may make her wet. In a head sea a comparatively long period of pitch may result in occasional burying of the bows and exposure of propellers and rudder.

When the period of encounter approaches synchronisation with the period of roll or pitch, the vessel's motion will be violent. In a beam sea this may result in dangerously heavy rolling, while in a head sea the savage and rapid pitching movement may cause frequent racing of propellers and undue hogging and sagging strains.

Q.4   What factors contribute to heavy rolling?

A.   Light draught.

As fuel and fresh water are consumed the load is reduced and the draught of the vessel becomes less. Due to the weight low in the vessel being reduced, the centre of gravity is raised, causing the roll to increase.

Free water.

The free movement of water from one side of the vessel to the other - whether in flooded compartments below the centre of gravity, or on deck - will increase the period and degree of roll. This effect will be most marked when the free water is high in the vessel e.g. in vessels having bulwarks or with inadequate or inefficient freeing ports. In vessels with continuous bulwarks or well decks, the correct functioning of freeing ports is essential to stability in rough weather.

Q.5 Are anti-rolling devices available for vessels?

A.   Yes. There are various designs of stabilizers. The most common is streamed from the end of the outrigger beams. Use of a steadying sail will also reduce roll.

Q.6 What is the effect of wind on the handling of a vessel?

A   Should a vessel be obliged to reduce to slow speed in a storm the pressure of the wind on her hull will have an increased effect on her handling qualities. The effect is enhanced if the vessel is lightly laden, or is of shallow draught, or has large super structures. When going very slowly or when stopped, most vessels tend to lie broadside-on to the wind, and in exceptionally strong winds it may be difficult to turn them up into the wind, though it may be possible to turn them away downwind. In a cyclone it may be impossible to turn them away downwind. In a cyclone it may also be impossible to turn certain vessels into the wind, which is one good reason why any seaman avoids such conditions with dangers to leeward.

Q.7 What precaution should be taken in a strong wind with regard to leeway?

A.   The amount of leeway a vessel makes in a gale depends on her speed, draught, freeboard and on her course in relation to the direction of the wind and sea.

It is a common mistake among inexperienced seaman to make insufficient allowance for leeway, particularly in a prolonged gale when, in addition to the wind, there will be a surface current in the sea caused by it. The amount of leeway made by a vessel in various circumstances can only be judged by experience, but it is wise to allow a liberal margin of safety when passing dangers to leeward. Many vessels have gone aground through failure to make sufficient allowances for leeway in the course steered.

Handling a Vessel in a Seaway

Q.8 What are some factors to be considered when heading into a seaway?

A.   (a) The force of impact of the waves on her bows.

(b) The pitching of the vessel and the resultant strains caused by hogging, sagging and pounding.

(c) The waves breaking on board, whether this is caused by their impact with the hull or the pitching of the vessel, or both.

The formula for the force of impact of waves is the product of the vessel's mass with the square of the combined velocity of the vessel and the waves. It will be reasoned therefore; that a small reduction of speed will considerably lessen the force of impact. The larger the area offered to the seas, the greater will be the shock of impact. Vessels with flared bows are forced to reduce speed sooner then vessels with comparatively straight-sided bows.

The trim of a vessel may have a considerable effect on her behaviour when steaming into a head sea. If she is trimmed by the head, or heavily laden forward, she will probably pitch sluggishly tending to bury her bows in the waves. Conversely, if she is trimmed too much by the stern, her bows will tend to pay off to one side or the other, and it will be difficult to keep her on her course heading into the seas. The best condition for a vessel steaming into a head sea is for her to be trimmed slightly by the stern and lightly laden forward, thus ensuring that her propellers and rudder are well immersed and that her bows are buoyant.

Pitching may be lessened by altering course so as to bring the seas on the bow, but the resulting motion with both pitch and roll may be more uncomfortable. It may cause more water to be shipped. However such action may prove essential in order to prevent the stern being continually lifted out of the water, causing the propellers to race, thus straining the underwater gear.

Q.9 What are some problems associated with steaming with the sea abeam?

A. The rolling caused by a beam sea may be so excessive that men have difficulty in keeping their feet, let alone carrying on with their work efficiently, particularly in small vessels. The best way to reduce the rolling is to alter course so as to prevent the vessel's rolling period from being synchronous with the period of encounter.

Alterations of speed are unlikely to affect the amount of rolling at all. Vessels seldom incur damage to the hull through rolling, but superficial damage caused by seas breaking on to low decks may occur. Objects may break loose if they have not been properly secured.

Q.10 What are some dangers associated with running before a sea?

A. The dangers consist of broaching-to, or being pooped. They arise in the following way:-

If the vessel's length is comparable to, and her speed practically the same as those of the waves, she may find herself running for a considerable time on the crest of a wave. The stern will be high in the water and the control by the rudder will become less effective. She now pitches on to the forward slope of the wave and the wave breaks, the entire vessel will be carried forward with the breaking water and she will start surfing. The forward motion further diminishes steering control, and a yaw either to starboard or port may develop rapidly. This yaw may be quite difficult to correct. The bows may now bury themselves deep into the trough and the stern swing round until the vessel lies broadside to the waves. This process is called broaching-to. She may now roll heavily, and if a following wave should break upon her in

such a way as to reinforce her roll to leeward, she may be heeled further over and capsize.

WIND AND SEA ————————▶

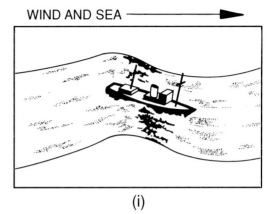

(i)

(ii)

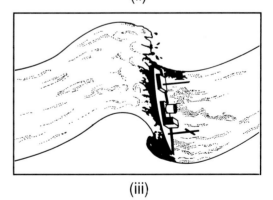

(iii)

Figure 78 – *Stages in a vessel being broached to*

If the vessel is on the forward slope of a wave that breaks upon her, the water may sweep along her upper decks from aft, causing damage. She is then said to be pooped. A vessel may be pooped without having lost steerage control, and usually when going slower than the speed of the waves.

WIND AND SEA ──────────▶

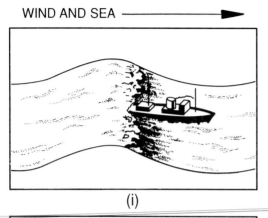

(i)

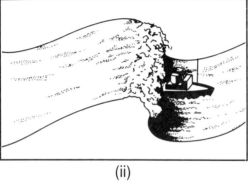

(ii)

Figure 79 — *Stages in a vessel being pooped.*

Q.11 Where is a vessel most likely to experience conditions of broaching-to or being pooped?

A.　When running before the sea, towards an estuary river mouth, or towards shallower water. The waves will become higher and steeper, increasing the danger of broaching-to, and adding to it the danger of yawing right out of the navigable channel into shoal water. Any attempt to increase speed above the wave speed will involve a period of lack of steering control as the vessel's and wave's speeds coincide, and is, in these circumstances, foolhardy.

Q.12 Does the length of the wave have any effect on broaching-to or pooping?

A.　Yes. The possibility of being broached-to or pooped decreases greatly if the length of the waves is either much greater or much smaller than that of the vessel. Steering before a heavy sea is, however, always liable to be difficult, and allowance must be made for a certain degree of inevitable yawing on either side of the intended course.

Constant supervision of the steering by the skipper will be required.

Q.13 What action would be taken to avoid broaching when running before a heavy sea?

A.　It is of paramount importance to avoid surfing and this can be done invariably by reducing the speed of the vessel to well below that of the waves. To be safe, the vessel's speed should be at least 40 per cent below wave speed. A vessel may still be pooped if a very heavy sea breaks aboard, and the steering will probably be difficult. Better control may be possible and so damage more easily avoided by steaming downwind in heavy seas than by attempting to keep head to sea.

Q.14 What methods could be adopted to reduce the vessel's speed when running before a heavy sea?

A.　Methods adopted as a means of reducing speed are:-

(a) Reduce the power output of the engine.

(b) Stream a drogue.

(c) Stream a number of mooring lines secured to the taffrail.

(d) Unshackle the otter boards and stream the warps of the trawling gear.

(e) Stream the anchor chain from over the stern.

Conditions at the time often dictate the action taken. Reducing the power output of the engine is to be avoided more especially with a single screw vessel. The reason is that it lessens the effective steering of the vessel by reducing propeller thrust on the rudder blade.

The aim of the exercise is to obtain maximum steerage and control of the stern yaw, by applying drag on each quarter with 75 per cent power. An effective drag in addition to those mentioned above is to secure two or more car tyre fenders to a doubled up mooring line and stream from each quarter.

Q.15 When running before a sea in certain conditions a rooster tail may be observed to form and gradually snowball. If left unchecked it may build up in size and speed until it eventually breaks over the stern. What action would you take on sighting this phenomenon forming?

A. Stream four or five mooring lines by securing them side by side across the taffrail. The purpose of the lines is to level the top of the rooster tail preventing the build up. Another effective method is to stream the loose end of a fishing or trawl net, the action being the same.

Turning in a Heavy Sea

There may be considerable risk in attempting to turn a vessel about in a heavy sea, and good judgment is required in selecting the most suitable moment to start the turn.

Q.16 How would you execute the manoeuvre of turning in a heavy sea?

A. If head to sea and one wishes to turn and run before it, the risk of damage will be greatest probably half-way through the turn, when the sea comes abeam. At that moment also the vessel will be most reluctant to turn. Groups of relatively low waves alternate with groups of higher ones, and therefore one should try to get the vessel round so that she is beam-on to the sea during one of the calmer periods. At the first part of the turn one must avoid gathering too much headway, because this may cause heavy pitching. Short bursts of ahead power against a fully angled rudder, possibly combined with reversals of the screw should get the vessel half-way round. From there the turn should be completed as rapidly as possible, using full power for a short time on the screw if necessary.

In a following sea, speed should be reduced as far as practicable before starting the turn. Never go so far as to gather sternway into a heavy sea, as the impact of the waves on the rudder

and propellers may damage them severely, leaving the vessel helpless. Again, if possible choose a relatively calm period to start the turn and, having got half-way round (which should not be difficult) use plenty of power and full rudder to start the vessel turning into the wind. As soon as she starts to answer her wheel, reduce the speed of the engines to the minimum judged necessary to turn her head to wind and keep her there.

Q.17 If in a tight corner with restricted sea room, or if, due to a strong wind, it was found that the vessel would not answer her helm sufficiently to bring her head short round to avoid stranding or a collision, what action could be taken?

A. Drop an anchor under foot or, should the anchor be stowed on deck, surge out the bight of the anchor chain. There is a lot to commend the latter method for use with small vessels, more especially if it is a strong wind presenting the challenge. The chain is much more easily recovered and less likely to damage either gear or vessel. Some vessels turn shorter in one direction than the other.

Heaving-to

The weather may become so violent in the open sea that the performance of the current task, whether it be a passage from one place to another, or some operation, must become subordinate to the overriding need to steer and handle the vessel in the best possible way to avoid damage and to keep her afloat. The course and speed are abandoned and the vessel is hove-to, the aim being to keep the vessel as steady as possible and to prevent seas breaking on board and damaging or flooding her, and, in the last resort, to prevent the vessel foundering through flooding or capsizing.

Q.18 What are three methods of heaving-to?

A. The three methods are:-

(a) Lying with the sea on the bow and steaming ahead at the minimum speed sufficient for steerage way.

(b) Lying with the sea on the quarter and steaming ahead at the minimum speed sufficient for steerage way.

(c) Stopping engines and allowing the ship to drift with sea anchor over bow.

Method (a)   Sea on the Bow.

The decision to adopt this method may be forced on the skipper because of lack of sea room to leeward. To keep her bows up the ship will require revolutions for a speed of anything from, say, 3 to 5 knots. She may make little headway or may even lose ground to leeward. If she has a reasonably long and high forecastle the ship may be protected to a certain extent from seas breaking over her decks. The disadvantage of the method is that the engines are being used to drive the ship against the sea, and hence to increase its power to damage her. Heavy pitching and pounding may occur, even if the revolutions are reduced to the minimum needed to keep steerage way. Vessels with wide, flared bows stand a greater risk of incurring structural damage forward.

Because of the cant to port a single-screw vessel may find it easier to keep the vessel's head up with the wind fine on the port, rather than the starboard bow. The reason is that a single-screw vessel is normally fitted with a right hand propeller. A right handed propeller will cant the bows to port.

Method (b)   Sea on the Quarter.

This method can be adopted provided there is plenty of sea room to leeward. Certain vessels may prove drier and more comfortable in this attitude, but the speed must be adjusted to avoid broaching-to or being pooped and the steering must be carefully supervised. All vessels will find that steering is more difficult downwind, and some may be quite unmanageable.

Method (c)   Drifting with Engines Stopped.

Again, if this method is adopted there must be plenty of room to leeward for the vessel to drift. Not only will the wind and breaking seas carry the vessel to leeward, but the wind will set up a surface current. The rate of drift in winds of gale force may reach 2 to 3 knots, and at cyclonic force it may even reach 5 knots.

It has been argued that if a vessel approaches near to the centre of a tropical storm, this method of heaving-to is the only logical one to adopt because, the sea being confused and not coming from any particular direction, it is impossible to place the vessel either head to sea or stern to sea. The use of the engines is likely at one moment to push the vessel into a huge wave and possibly drive her forecastle under, or at the least to cause damage, while at the next moment she may force herself down the crest of a wave approaching from astern and broach-to.

Method to Adopt:

Having considered the above remarks, the skipper knowing his own vessel and her stability and handling qualities, forecasting the future trend of the weather and considering the sea room available, must decide which is the best method to adopt in prevailing circumstances.

Emergency Action when Towing

Encountering heavy weather:

In foul weather when towing it is probably preferable to turn and run slowly before wind and sea. Heaving-to head to sea is likely to result in far heavier strains on the gear, although steering may be easier. When running with the gale it may be possible to steady the tow by streaming a drogue. Obviously one cannot run if this is likely to bring the vessels near a lee shore.

In extreme weather conditions which the gear cannot be expected to withstand, it may be preferable to slip the tow rather than to hold on until the gear parts. The disabled vessel may ride more easy when drifting, with the towing gear trailing as a sea anchor, while the towing vessel will have freedom of manoeuvre and can spread oil where it will be most effective.

Q.22 What method could be adopted to lessen the sea for a vessel being towed that was yawing badly?

A.   The towing vessel should sling the bag described in method (c) of distribution of oil, by a bow-shackle on the towing hawser, tail it with a strong messenger, and allow it to slide well down the hawser so that it will distribute the oil ahead of the towed vessel within the limits of her yaw.

If oil is used when taking a vessel in tow, the lines and hawsers should, if possible, be kept clear of the oil, otherwise they will become slippery and very difficult to handle.

General Advice on Heavy Weather at Sea

From the information given so far the reader will realise that no hard-and-fast rules can be laid down on handling a vessel in heavy weather at sea. It depends on the type of vessel, her handling qualities, the wind and sea, the room available and other circumstances. Experience shows that there are few generalisations about the behaviour of vessels in heavy seas that hold good in all similar circumstances. Perhaps it may be helpful to summarise this advice in a series of 'do's' and 'don'ts'.

Do

(a) Make sure that you are kept informed continually about expected changes of weather.

(b) Know the factors affecting the stability of your vessel and take steps to improve stability, if necessary, before encountering heavy weather.

(c) See that the vessel is made thoroughly seaworthy before leaving harbour, or before the approach of a storm.

(d) Consider the effect of the vessel's motion on the activities being carried out by members of the vessel's crew.

(e) Appreciate the signs of an approaching tropical storm and take the necessary action to avoid it.

(f) Alter course, if possible, in a beam sea to break the synchronisation of the period of the waves with that of the vessel's rolling.

Don't

(a) Drive a vessel too fast into a head sea; particularly a fast, lightly built vessel.

(b) Fail to reduce speed soon enough in a hard sea or swell through being unable to visualise the consequence, or fear of being considered too cautious.

(c) Run too fast before a following sea, particularly when the length of the vessel and that of the sea are about the same.

Heavy Weather in Harbour

Anchoring in a gale:

If it is expected that the vessel will have to ride out a strong and prolonged gale, and both anchors are used, let them go in such a way that when the vessel is riding to the cables the angle between them will be about 20°.

While this method of anchoring does make use of the maximum holding power of the two anchors, it also carries with it the danger of getting the cables crossed if the wind shifts direction considerably.

Steaming into the bight of the cables:

Having anchored as above in a gale with both anchors down and the cables fully veered and spread about 20° apart, it may happen that despite these precautions the vessel starts to drag because of the excessive strength of the wind. If the sea is reasonable, a useful expedient in such a case is to steam up to windward between the anchors until the cables are growing aft on either quarter and then to hold the vessel there with the engines going slow ahead. Further dragging is prevented and with the constricting effect of the cables it is a fairly simple matter to keep the vessel stationary and head to wind until the weather moderates. While doing so, one should take the precaution of fixing the vessel's position frequently.

Action in Emergency

In the various manoeuvres covered in this feature it has been shown how, in order to keep the vessel under the control of her skipper, rather than under the dominance of wind or current, it is necessary to plan fully in advance, to use moderate speed, to employ warps and anchors when necessary. In short, when manoeuvring in narrow waters, prevention is better than cure. If, however, the shiphandler starts to lose control there is often some emergency action that will enable him to reimpose it. If it is to be effective this action must be applied quickly and resolutely. The action usually available is the use of full rudder, the use of full power ahead or astern on the engines, or letting go an anchor.

The quick effect of a burst of power ahead on the engines with the wheel hard over must be appreciated. To start a vessel swinging in the desired direction, or to stop her swinging in the undesirable direction, even in a multiple-screw vessel this action is usually far quicker in its effect than to go astern on one side and ahead on the other, particularly in shallow water. The headway gained at first is not very great. But, of course, if full power ahead or astern is used, the shiphandler must watch the vessel like a hawk and take off the power almost before it has begun to have effect, otherwise he will soon find that the vessel is shooting ahead or astern and getting into worse difficulties than she was in before.

Finally, even when an accident appears inevitable, there is usually some action that can be taken to minimise the damage. This is one reason why every seaman should have a good knowledge of the construction of his vessel, and hence of how she can best withstand an impact. Consider the following:-

(a) If the choice lies between colliding with another vessel and running aground, it may be preferable to go aground and thus confine the damage to one vessel.

(b) The most vulnerable parts of a vessel's hull, and those where extensive damage is most difficult to repair, are the bilges, the propeller shafts with their 'A' brackets, the propellers, and the rudder. If grounding is inevitable it is therefore preferable to ground head-on than to attempt to turn and so risk ripping open the bottom of the vessel.

(c) If collision with another vessel is inevitable the damage can be minimised by striking her a glancing blow, preferably bow-to-bow, quarter-to-quarter, or bow-to-quarter. Striking the other vessel head-on amidships or turning athwart her bows and so allowing the other vessel to strike amidships must, if possible, be avoided. A vessel is very vulnerable amidships, because any serious underwater damage there will flood her largest compartments, i.e. the engine room, and when this is flooded the vessel may founder.

(d) There should be no hesitation in using anchors in an emergency to check a vessel's headway, or to turn her, or to prevent her from drifting on to a lee shore.

(e) If collision with a jetty is unavoidable, it is better to turn and strike it a glancing blow than to strike it head-on. The resulting damage will probably be above the waterline and not so extensive as that caused by a head-on collision.

Prevention is better than cure:

Unfortunately many occasions requiring drastic and rapid action are allowed to arise quite unnecessarily, through the inattention or lack of foresight of skippers. This applies particularly to crises where danger of collision or grounding materializes apparently without warning. Early action to put the vessel on a safe course, or to take the way off her, would have prevented a crisis from developing at all.

Q.23 What are some common causes of accidents at sea with reference to vessel handling?

A. (a) Failure to take the correct action because of incomplete knowledge of the Rule of the Road.

(b) Failure to keep a good lookout.

(c) Failure to take seaman like precautions in potentially dangerous circumstances such as low visibility, or when steaming without lights.

(d) Failure to check the vessel's position, course and speed frequently.

(e) Failure to look ahead and realise that, unless some action is taken now, a dangerous situation will arise in the future.

(f) Indecision and consequent delay until it is too late to save the situation.

Q.24 In a situation where there is any cause for doubt what action must the watchkeeper take?

A. If in doubt call the skipper and do so in good time, so that he can reach the bridge and take the necessary action before the situation has become dangerous.

Running into fog:

When visibility closes down to within about a mile the precautions to be taken depend on whether the vessel is alone or in company. As soon as you find the visibility is closing down, or if you sight a fog bank ahead, inform the skipper.

Q.25 What is the normal action taken when visibility is closing down or moving into a fog bank?

(a) Reduce to a moderate speed consistent with safe navigation.

(b) Operate radar if installed.

(c) Fix vessel's position noting time.

(d) Station extra lookouts.

(e) If in soundings, start sounding.

(f) If in the vicinity of land, have an anchor prepared for letting go.

(g) Keep vessel as silent as possible.

(h) Start the prescribed fog signal and see that the person who works it can time it accurately.

(i) If in any doubt about the vessel's position, alter course to a safe course, parallel to or away from the coast (or danger), or stop the vessel.

Interaction

It is now generally accepted, as a result of model tests and practical experience gained by vessels that when two vessel pass close to one another, on roughly parallel courses, forces of attraction and repulsion are set up between them. This effect is known as interaction. It is greatest in shallow water and when two vessels are moving at high speed in the same direction with little difference of speed. In the case of two vessels passing on opposite courses interaction has little effect, but in overtaking situations the course of one or both of the vessels may be affected considerably, especially when a large vessel is overtaking a smaller one.

The maximum distance between two vessels at which interaction may be noticed will vary with the size, speed and the depth of water. It may be over 300 metres in some cases. Interaction can be a factor even in deep water when fast vessels are overtaking at small distances.

Overtaking vessels should not attempt to pass too close in open waters when there is plenty of room to manoeuvre. In narrow channels it may well be dangerous to overtake another vessel which is itself moving at high speed.

Should a vessel move at an appreciable speed there is a built-up region of pressure in the water near the bow and stern and an area of decreased pressure amidships. If two vessels pass close to one another on parallel courses forces of attraction and repulsion may be set-up between them. The action on one another may be seen in Figure 80.

As the bow of Vessel "A" overtakes the stern of vessel "B" there will be a repulsive force between them making a tendency for Vessel "B" to swing her bows across the path of vessel "A" (i) As the bows of the two ships draw level the bow of vessel "B" will tend to swing outward as shown in (ii).

When the sterns of the two vessels come together there will be a repulsive force between them so that once again there will be a tendency for the bow of Vessel "B" to swing towards "A" (iii). As the stern of vessel "A" passes the bow of vessel "B" there will be a tendency for the bow of vessel "B" to be forced away from vessel "A" (iv).

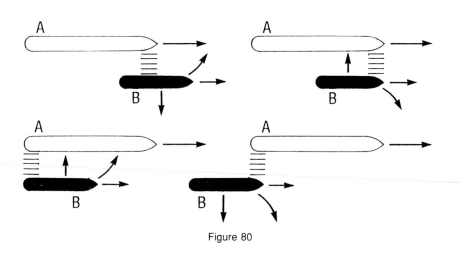

Figure 80

Chapter 12
SURVIVAL AT SEA

SURVIVAL AT SEA

Australian mariners who work inshore or in distant waters must be prepared to meet all emergencies. If their boat is wrecked on a reef, burnt out, or capsized in a cyclone - it then becomes a question of survival.

Unless there is a particularly good reason for doing so a seaman should never attempt to leave the area where his vessel has sunk or been disabled. Searching aircraft will more easily detect the disabled vessel than its rafts.

A national air and sea rescue service is available to help those in distress at sea but if a sea-going vessel goes down from land or in a remote area, it may be days or even weeks before survivors can be found and picked up.

Experience has proved that the outstanding causes of death among shipwreck victims are:-

(a) Exposure to cold.

(b) Dehydration due to insufficient fresh drinking water.

(c) Drinking sea water or urine.

The qualities which are essential to the survival of crews of boats or rafts when adrift in the open sea are a determination to survive, discipline, confidence, cheerfulness and willingness. The person in charge of the raft has the most exacting task, because, in addition to looking after his craft, he must inspire the crew with confidence both in himself and themselves and maintain strict but sympathetic discipline at all times. He should arrange for each of the crew to be given a specific duty, work out a daily routine and see that it is strictly carried out. He must also take charge of the rations and supervise their issue, and make sure that the sick and injured are looked after.

Preparation

Every precaution should be taken to ensure that survival equipment such as life craft (fully provisioned), hand-operated radio, radio beacon, radar reflector, dye-markers, flares, heliograph and smoke generators are checked out before each voyage. First aid kits and emergency packs should be complete and life-rafts should be inspected for chafing and wear.

It is recommended that sea-going vessels carry a quantity of demineralised water in convenient plastic containers for topping up their batteries. These containers should be stowed in an accessible position for transfer to the life craft in an emergency.

Quick rescue depends upon the co-operation of survivors. Logically this begins with an accurate vessel's position radioed to the Coastal Radio Station (C.R.S.) when trouble is suspected. Because searching aircraft can receive only radio beacon signals and searching vessels can receive or home-in only on ship station frequencies the C.R.S. should also be aware of the type of radio equipment in the liferaft so that operations can be planned accordingly.

If, due to radio failure or other cause, authorities are not alerted, rescue may take some time.

Q.1 What information would you transmit in a distress message?

A. The distress call shall be followed by the distress message which should state:-

Who you are (call sign of vessel or name).

Where you are (your vessel's position in latitude/longitude or bearing and distance in nautical miles from a well known geographical point - local names known only in the immediate vicinity are confusing).

What is wrong (nature of distress).

Kind of assistance required.

Number of persons aboard and condition of any injured.

Present state of seaworthiness of the boat.

Description of the boat, length, type, cabin, masts, power, colour of hull, superstructure and trim.

Listening frequency and schedule of the vessel's radio.

If another vessel in difficulties is sighted, the following information should be given:-

Your name or call sign.

Your position and the bearing and distance of the vessel in difficulties.

Nature of the emergency.

Description of the vessel in distress.

Your intentions, course and speed.

Your listening frequency and schedule.

Q.2 What is the penalty for misuse of distress signals?

A. In addition to being liable in respect of the offence, the offender is liable to pay compensation for any labour undertaken, risk incurred, or loss sustained in consequence of the signals having been supposed to be a signal of distress, as stated in the Queensland Marine Safety Act.

Q.3 What are the international code of distress signals ?

A. A gun or other explosive signal fired at intervals of about one minute.

A continuous sounding with any fog signal apparatus.

Rockets or shells, throwing red stars fired one at a time at short intervals.

The signal SOS ...---... sent in morse code.

A signal sent by radiotelephony consisting of the spoken word MAYDAY.

The international code signal of distress indicated by N. C.

A signal consisting of a square flag having above or below it a bag or anything resembling a ball.

Flames on the vessel.

A rocket parachute, or a hand flare, showing a red light.

A smoke signal giving off a volume of orange coloured smoke.

Slowly and repeatedly raising and lowering arms outstretched to each side.

The radiotelephone alarm signal consisting of two tones transmitted alternately over a period of from 30 seconds to one minute.

The automatic radio alarm signal consisting of a series of twelve dashes sent in one minute, each dash having a duration of four seconds, with an interval of one second between every two consecutive dashes.

Although not laid down as distress signals articles of clothing flown from the masthead, or an ensign flown, upside down, are generally recognised signals of distress.

On no account are any of the foregoing signals to be made except in, cases of emergency of distress.

Q.4 What is the signal sounded in an emergency ?

A. Six or more short blasts followed by a prolonged blast on the whistle or alarm signals when fitted.

Q.5 What is the abandon ship signal?

A. Morse "A" sounded three times on whistle or bells.

·— ·— ·—

Abandoning Vessel

If it becomes necessary to abandon a seagoing vessel, this must be carried out in an orderly manner, particularly with respect to launching and boarding of lifeboats and liferafts. Though seamen should always remain with their vessels as long as it is safe they should know when to abandon it. A man's chances of safely leaving a vessel and of being rescued are good if he knows what to do.

Q.6 If possible what duties should be carried out before abandoning the vessel?

A. A distress signal should be sent giving the vessel's position, the propeller stopped and if time permits watertight doors and hatches closed tightly. Before leaving the vessel, drink your fill of fresh water and gather water and extra provisions.

Q.7 If forced to leave directly into the water, what is the best method ?

A. When leaving a vessel directly into the water it is safer to jump in feet first, keeping legs together and slightly bent, rather than to dive. When wearing a lifejacket seamen should avoid jumping into the water from any great height as the impact of the jacket on the water may cause an upward jerk which can produce an injured or broken neck.

Q.8 What action should be attempted immediately by a survivor in the water from a vessel sinking close by?

A. He should swim from a sinking vessel as quickly as possible because there is a violent local suction when it founders. In addition air and wreckage from the vessel reach the surface with great force.

Q.9 On a Queensland fishing trawler what may be used as a make shift raft?

A. The sorting tray or refrigeration box on deck.

Q.10 On receipt of the abandon ship signal should clothing be discarded?

A. No. Do not discard clothing. On reaching the water swim slowly and steadily.

Q.11 Should the water surface around the vessel contain oil on fire, what would you do?

A. If it is necessary to swim through fire, jump feet first, upwind of the boat. Swim into the wind using the breast stroke and try to make breathing holes by splashing the flames away from head and arms.

Q 12 What is a hydrostatic release mechanism, and how does it operate?

A. A life-raft and its container are buoyant. If they are stowed in a rack on the open deck and secured to the deck by means of a hydrostatic release mechanism, when the life-raft is immersed its buoyancy gives an upthrust which operates the release mechanism and frees the life-raft so that it floats to the surface. If the painter has been secured to a strong point on board, as the vessel sinks it will pull on the painter and operate the raft inflation mechanism.

Q.13 Describe the procedure of launching and boarding an inflatable life-raft .

A. To launch and board an inflatable life-raft:-

(a) Check that the painter is well secured to a strong point

(b) Check that it is all clear overside. Let go lashings, take the raft to the vessel's side, and remove a portable rail if necessary.

(c) Launch the life-raft overboard in its container or valise.

(d) Pull the remainder of the painter out of the floating container or valise and tug it hard to fire the gas bottle.

(e) The life-raft will take 20 to 30 seconds to inflate.

(f) Board the liferaft from a side ladder, a rope, or from the sea. Avoid jumping onto the life-raft.

(g) Jettison all shoes and sharp objects.

(h) When everyone is aboard, cut the painter with the safety knife.

(i) In cold weather inflate the double floor.

Endeavour to remain in the vicinity with other rafts and boats. Stream the sea anchor.

Note: Should the life-raft fail to inflate or only half inflate, give the painter another hard tug.

Q.13.1 What equipment is required to be carried in an inflatable coastal life-raft?

A. The equipment and rations to be provided in an inflatable coastal life-raft are as follows:-

1. one sponge for each person included in the carrying capacity of the liferaft;

2. two paddles;

3. where the carrying capacity of a liferaft is thirteen persons or more, two bailers and two safety-knives, otherwise one bailer and one safety-knife;

4. one repair outfit capable of repairing punctures in buoyancy compartments;

5. one topping-up pump or bellows;

6. one waterproof electric torch suitable for morse-signalling together with one spare set of batteries and one spare bulb in a waterproof container;

7. one sea-anchor, permanently attached to the liferaft;

8. one litre of fresh water for each person in carrying capacity of liferaft, to be contained in watertight and rustproof receptacles;

9. one safety tin-opener;

10. two red hand held flares and one hand held orange smoke signal complying with the requirements of items 2 and 4 respectively of part B of Appendix V;

11. an approved first-aid kit;

12. one copy of the rescue signal table used by life-saving stations, marine rescue units and vessels and persons in distress;

13. 500 grams of

(i) barley sugar; or

(ii) other non-thirst provoking food, containing no protein or fat and providing at least 1500 kilojoules per 100g weight for each person included in the carrying capacity of the liferaft (being barley sugar, or other food that has been in the liferaft for a period not exceeding 2 years);

14. six sea-sickness tablets for each person included in the carrying capacity of the liferaft;

15. one fishing line and six hooks;

16. one daylight—signalling mirror;

17. a watertight container - being furnished with a water-proof match-striker as part of, or attached to the container and holding not less than 25 matches of a type that is not readily extinguishable by wind;

18 six chemiluminescent lights of an approved type;

19. retro-reflective tape of an approved type (and being not less than 50 millimetres in width) shall be fitted to the underside of the floor of a liferaft in such a way that the tape forms a cross at the centre of the floor. The length of the tapes shall be:

19.1 for a circular liferaft – not less than half the diameter of the liferaft; and

19.2 for other liferafts – not less than half the width and length respectively, of the liferaft;

20. retro-reflective tape of an approved type (each tape being not less than 300 millimetres in length and not less than 50 millimetres in width) shall be spaced around the cover,

or each of the covers, with which the liferaft is fitted in such a way that:

20.1 the distance between the centre of one tape and the centre of the tape next in line is not greater than 500 millimetres; and

20.2 the distance between the lower edge of the tape and the lower edge of the cover is not less than half the height of the cover; and

21. two retro-reflective tapes of an approved type (and being not less than 50 millimetres in width) shall be placed at the centre of the top of a liferaft cover in the form of a cross. The lengths of the tapes shall be:

21.1 for a circular liferaft - not less than half the diameter of the liferaft; and

21.2 for other liferafts - not less than half the width and length, respectively, of the liferaft.

Q.14 If a loud whistling noise is heard after a life-raft has inflated, what is the cause?

A. The life-raft has inflated to its correct pressure and the excess of gas from the bottle is escaping through the safety valves. The entrances to the life-raft should not be closed whilst the whistle is sounding.

Q.15 What action should be taken for protection against cold?

A. On boarding the life-raft clothes should be taken off and wrung out and put on again.

Q.16 What action should be taken for protection against heat?

A. In hot climates, unnecessary clothing should be discarded but the whole body should remain covered with one thin layer of material. The head and neck should always be kept covered if exposed to the sun's rays.

During the day, clothing may be soaked in sea water but garments should be dried out thoroughly before sundown. Eyes should be protected from sunlight and reflected glare by wearing sun glasses or eye shades.

To counter sunburn, which can occur even in cloudy weather, anti-sunburn cream from the first aid pack should be used. Every precaution should be taken against sunstroke and heat exhaustion.

Q.17 The life-raft is now launched and inflated. What is the next procedure to adopt?

A. Cut the painter.

Post a lookout and search for other survivors. Treat injuries, even minor ones, immediately. Instructions are given in the first aid kit and in the 'Handbook for Survivors', which is a part of the equipment of the raft.

Gather any wreckage which you think may be useful. Containers of any type are valuable. Extra clothing is of vital and immediate importance in cold weather.

Secure to other rafts if possible.

Dry out the raft, using bailers and sponges, spare wet clothing or any suitable containers. Wring out all wet clothes.

Q.18 What is the function of the buoyant rescue quoit and the buoyant line which must be carried in life-rafts ?

A. If a survivor is sighted away from the life-raft, the rescuer should place the quoit around his arm and swim out to the survivor. When he has a hold of the survivor he should raise one arm above his head when those on board the life-raft can haul the survivor and rescuer back to the life-raft.

Q.19 Describe the procedure to get an unconscious or injured person from the sea into a life-raft.

A. Turn him so that his back is towards the entrance of the life-raft. Take a firm hold of him under the armpits and push him down into the water. His natural buoyancy, plus that of his lifejacket, if worn, will assist in raising him back out of the water when he could be guided backwards into the life-raft.

Q.20 Having cleared yourself from the wreck, protected yourself from wind and weather, what are the next considerations ?

A. Stream the sea anchor, steady the motion and prevent the raft spinning. Check and prepare all signalling gear and activate the EPIRB. If there is no radio equipment or radio beacon, the heliograph or a mirror, smoke generator, flares and fluorescent dye-markers must be ready for immediate use to aid detection. A radar reflecting screen, if carried, should be slung properly to ensure good signal bounce.

Searchers depend upon the co-operation of survivors to pin-point their location. Maintain a constant lookout and use signalling devices or other means to attract attention, but do not expend these aids wastefully.

Q.21 How is a life-raft stabilised?

By use of water pockets fitted to the bottom of the raft.

Q.22 If a life-raft inflated in an inverted position, how might it be righted?

A. A person in the water should take a hold of the life-raft near the gas bottle and swim round till the life-raft faces into the wind. He should then stand on the gas bottle, facing the life-raft, take a hold of the strap which lies across the underside of the life-raft and lean backwards to bring the life-raft over after him.

Q.23 For what purpose is provision made for inflating the floor of a life-raft ?

A. It insulates the occupants from cold sea water.

Q.24 When should sea sickness tablets be issued?

A. As soon as possible after boarding the life-raft.

Q.25 How many seasick tablets may be taken?

A. Never more than 2 per day, one first thing in the morning, half midday and half a tablet in the evening.

Q.26 What effect has sea sickness on survivors ?

A. It is demoralising, causes dehydration of the body by wasting vital fluids and as a result induces thirst.

Q 27 What is a survivor's most essential need?

A. Fresh drinking water.

Q.28 When should the first ration of drinking water be issued?

A. Not for at least 24 hours after boarding the life-raft.

Q.29 Why is it that no water should be issued for at least the first 24 hours?

A. Because if water should be drunk on the first day, the kidneys will not then be conserving water fully.

Q.30 What is the minimum amount of water you would issue per day.

A. 250ml.

Q.31 What effect has the consumption of alcohol on the human body?

A. It dehydrates the liver and kidneys.

Q.32 How long can a person in good health live without food and water?

A. A person in good health can live up to 25 days without food; without water he can live only for about 10 days, and even less in the tropics. A minimum of 568ml (1 pint) a day is necessary to keep fit, but survival is possible on 57 to 142ml (2 to 8ozs) a day.

While no hard and fast rules can be laid down for the rationing of water, the following is suggested.

Based on the assumption that in most cases rescue is effected in four or five days-

1st day - No water issued, except for the injured. The body acts as a reservoir and can live off water it has stored.

2nd, 3rd and 4th days - 398ml (14ozs) per head daily, if available.

5th day onwards - 57 to 142rnl (2 to 8ozs) per head daily,depending on the climate and the water available.

Note-: The initial water ration should be adequate and not based on a meagre supply over a protracted period.

Water Conservation

Obviously the preservation of water in the body is as important as having water to drink. Sweating is a potential cause of water loss. To reduce sweating the body should be kept cool by using sea water to dampen the body and clothes and by taking advantage of breezes. Immersion in the sea is inadvisable because of the risk from sharks (and other dangerous marine creatures) and the effort required to reboard the raft or dinghy.

Sleep and rest are most important during a shortage of water and exercise must be kept to a minimum to prevent any increase in body heat which may produce sweating.

To allay thirst, and keep the mouth moist by increasing saliva, suck on a piece of cloth or a button. Smoking will encourage thirst.

For survival over a prolonged period, especially in the tropics, it will be necessary to depend on rain for drinking water. Be prepared to collect rain water from the dinghy canopy and fill all available containers.

Q.33 If it were raining what precautions are taken in collecting rain water from an inflatable raft?

A. Before collecting, wash the french chalk and encrustation of salt off the canopy to prevent contamination.

Q.34 If all available containers were full should the issue be restricted to that of the daily ration?

A No. The crew should be permitted to have their fill on any excess.

Q.35 All containers being full, what precaution should be taken on the next issue of rations?

A. Water collected should always be issued first before opening the sealed cans of the life-raft rations.

Note:When filling fresh water containers, a small space must be left for air so that the water will not become foul.

Q.36 Would you allow survivors to drink sea water?

A On no account should sea water be drunk - it contains more salt than the body can excrete. Salt is thus concentrated in the tissue and dehydration occurs more rapidly. Alcohol is also dangerous to drink. It has no thirst quenching value and in fact dehydrates intestines and kidneys. Urine is injurious also and should never be drunk.

Experience has shown that fish juice, squeezed or sucked from fish, is a poor substitute for water. It is estimated that a 9 kg fish would be required to produce 600 ml of juice. Because of the protein content of fish additional fresh water is necessary to assimilate the juice.

Q.37 Discuss how you would regulate the food intake?

A.   It is vital to realise that the amount of the water ration will determine how much food may be eaten and what it should consist of. The body requires water for the digestion of food and the elimination of waste products.

Because foods high in protein need considerably more water for metabolism than carbohydrate foods, only carbohydrate foods should be eaten when the supply of water is low. These include potatoes, fruit, malted milk tablets, boiled sweets, sweetened condensed milk and high fat toffee.

Protein foods which require large amounts of water for assimilation include meat, fish and shellfish, eggs, beans, peas, cheese and some greenleaf vegetables including seaweed.

The quantity of food and water rations must be varied in direct proportion to each other. If there is plenty of water the food ration can be increased, but as the water ration decreases the food intake must also be reduced.

Live off natural foods if water permits and save emergency rations for the real emergency when water is getting low.

A minimum daily ration of the following foods with approximately half a litre of water would be necessary for good health:-

Boiled sweets	99 g
Toffee (30% fat)	99 g
Sweetened condensed milk	99 g

Q.38 Describe some signs that could indicate the position of the craft?

A.   Natural smells can be valuable as a guide. Mariners are well famillar with the sickly smell of exposed coral reefs, fresh water from rivers, guano from sea bird colonies etc. At night in tropical waters, the breakers on the reef show a luminous glow.

Rivers, especially in the rainy season, are responsible for the muddy discoloured water along the coast.

There is a defined line of demarcation which gives a warning on approaching some coasts. The coastal waters of New Guinea are marked with flotsam such as logs, nipea palm fronds, etc. The direction of a flight of birds in the late afternoon is towards land.

Q.39 What precaution would you take against dangerous fish?

A.   Dangerous fish, such as shark, will not normally attack without provocation. Simple rules to deal with them are:-

- Embark on flotsam if available and do not let anything trail in the sea.
- Keep clothing on and maintain a good lookout.
- Do not fish if sharks are in the vicinity.
- Do not trail hands or feet over the side of the dinghy.
- Do not throw waste food or scraps overboard during the daytime.
- Remain quiet and the likelihood of attack will be reduced, move only to keep the shark or other fish in sight. If it is necessary to swim use rhythmic strokes, never thrash about.

Note: Several survivors in the water without a dinghy who are approached by dangerous fish should form a circle facing outwards and beat the water with strong regular strokes.

Q.40 What action should be taken in the case of a man overboard ?

A.   The following steps are recommended in the case of a man overboard:-

(a) Swing the stern of the boat away from the man to reduce the danger to the man overboard.

(b) Throw a lifesaving device to him as soon as possible, even if he can swim. Care should be exercised not to hit the man. A lifebouy, if handy, is the best lifesaving device to use for this purpose. It can be thrown farther and is easier for the man in the water to use.

Don't wait to get a lifebuoy if there is another lifesaving device closer at hand. Speed may be most important.

(c) Keep the man in view at all times. If there is another person in the boat he should act as lookout. If it is night, direct the best possible light on the man in the water.

(d) Manoeuvre to approach the man from downwind or into the sea (waves). The particular manoeuvre that is used in approaching the man depends upon common sense and good judgement based upon existing conditions, and availability of any other ready assistance.

(e) If there is capable assistance in the boat it might be advisable to have the assistant put on a life preserver, fitted with a line attached to the boat. He could then get into the water to assist the person in difficulties.

(f) Assist the man in boarding the boat. It is often difficult to climb into a boat from the water, and if a man is hurt or cold, he may not be capable of pulling himself in without assistance. In small boats the weight of a man suspended frorn the side might be enough to up the boat and cause it to take in water. Recommended procedure for going over the side or coming aboard a small boat would be by way of the stern or bow, depending upon the boat's size and construction. Common sense dictates that the propeller should be stopped when taking a man over the stern. In the case of an outboard boat where there is a danger of accidentally bumping the controls, the engine should be turned off. Many boats have stern ladders and these can also be valuable in the case of man overboard.

Q.41 Should it be necessary, how is mouth to mouth resuscitation applied?

A. (a) Move an injured casualty cautiously.

(b) Place the unconscious casualty on his back to be able to see his face.

(c) If there is foreign matter visible at the mouth, turn his head to the side, force his mouth open and quickly clean the mouth and throat with your fingers or a piece of cloth.

(d) Place the casualty's head in 'sniffing position'. Place the head as far back as possible so that his neck is extended. Hold his lower jaw upward so that it 'juts out' (it is most important that the jaw be held in this position).

(e) Hold the jaw in this position in one hand, approach the casualty's head from his left side.

(f) Insert the thumb of your left hand between the casualty's teeth and grasp his lower jaw at the midline.

(g) Lift the lower jaw forcefully upward so that the lower teeth are higher than the upper teeth.

(h) Hold the jaw in this position as long as the casualty is unconscious.

(i) Close the casualty's nose with your right hand.

(j) After taking a deep breath, place your mouth over the casualty's mouth, with airtight contact. Do not hold the casualty's mouth open widely, as you must take the entire mouth of the casualty inside your lips.

(k) Blow into the casualty's mouth, forcefully if adult and gently if children.

(l) While blowing, watch the casualty's chest. When the chest rises, stop blowing and quickly remove your mouth from the casualty's mouth.

(m) When the chest does not rise, improve the support of the air passageway and blow more frequently.

(n) Repeat these inflations 12 to 20 times per minute.

Q.42 If the heart is not beating and you must give external heart massage together with the mouth to mouth resuscitation, how is it done?

A. Make sure the casualty is lying flat with his back on a firm surface. Place the heel of one hand on the lower part of the breastbone, put the other hand over the first and press the breastbone firmly downwards 38mm to 51mm (11/2 to 2 inches).

Apply the weight with arms straight at all times and keep your fingers off the chest. Less pressure is required for children and the pressure of two fingers may be enough for small babies.

Compress the chest once every second for adults; the younger the casualty the faster the compressions should be. Small babies need 100 to 120 compressions a minute.

If you are alone you should give 15 compressions of the heart then two quick lung inflations and repeat. If you have assistance, you should give one lung inflation for every five chest compressions.

Note: Remember. While you are reviving the victim, send someone for help. The victim should reach hospital as soon as possible, but you must avoid interrupting resuscitation to go for help yourself.

Q.43 If you were in a life-raft at night and a lookout reported hearing the engines of an aircraft, what action would you take?

A.   Have a distress flare or rocket ready at the leeward entrance, to the life-raft and impress upon the other survivors that there is only a limited supply of pyrotechnics available, and that one must not be lit until it is established beyond any doubt that an aircraft is near at hand. When lit a flare must be held at arms length away from the life-raft.

Q.44 What is the maximum distance at which a searching aircraft may sight a life-raft on a bright sunny day?

A.   Approximately 4 nautical miles.

Q.45 How can this range be extended by those on board the life-raft?

A.   By correct use of heliograph or pyrotechnic.

Q.46 What are the maximum ranges at which distress signals can be seen at night in good visibility conditions?

A.   Rocket Parachute Signals –
                    25-35 nautical miles
      Hand Flares 5 -10 nautical miles

Note: Remember that these ranges will be reduced considerably in poor visibility conditions such as usually exist when distress signals are required to be used.

Like most man made devices there is a right way, and a wrong way to use distress signals. Read the directions carefully.

TO SAVE YOUR SIGNALS MAY SAVE YOUR LIFE.

It is obviously a waste of valuable signals to display them unless the following conditions exist:-

(a)   Parachute Signals: You have good reasons to believe that a possible rescue ship, or an aircraft, or an inhabited shore, is within the estimated visibility range of your signals.

(b)   Hand Flares: The lights of a ship or aircraft or lights on shore are visible to you.

Note: The official daylight signal is the Buoyant Orange Smoke Signal. These, however have a very limited visibility range especially in a stiff breeze. Many tests have shown that in normal daylight conditions a hand flare or a rocket parachute signal can be seen at a greater range than can an orange smoke signal. The ideal combination, therefore, is smoke and flare.

Q.47 What are 'radar reflective rocket signals' ?

A.   They are signals not widely used as yet. They eject a cloud of radar reflective material which produces a distinctive echo on a ship or aircraft radar for a period of 10 to 20 minutes and from a considerable range. They can therefore be used both by day and night when it is considered that a search for survivors is in progress.

Q.48 What are the specifications of lifebuoy smoke signals ?

A.   A smoke signal attached to a lifebuoy shall be capable of:-

      (a) Parachute Signals: You have good reasons to believe that a possible rescue ship, an aircraft, or an inhabited shore, is within the estimated visibility range of your signals.

      (b) Hand Flares: The lights of a ship or aircraft or lights on shore are visible to you.

Q.49 What are the specifications of lifebuoy buoyant lines?

A.   A life line filled to a lifebuoy shall be of a buoyant material and shall be of at least 27.5 metres (90 feet) in length.

Appendix C

Life-Saving Signals

Landing signals for the guidance of small boats with crews or persons in distress

	MANUAL SIGNALS	LIGHT SIGNALS	OTHER SIGNALS	SIGNIFICATION
Day signals	**Vertical** motion of a white flag or of the arms	or firing of a green star signal	or code letter **K** given by light or sound-signal apparatus	This is the best place to land
Night signals	**Vertical** motion of a white light or flare	or firing of a green star signal	or code letter **K** given by light or sound-signal apparatus	

A range (indication of direction) may be given by placing a steady white light or flare at a lower level and in line with the observer

	MANUAL SIGNALS	LIGHT SIGNALS	OTHER SIGNALS	SIGNIFICATION
Day signals	**Horizontal** motion of a white flag or of the arms extended horizontally	or firing of a **red** star signal	or code letter **S** given by light or sound-signal apparatus	Landing here highly dangerous
Night signals	**Horizontal** motion of a light or flare	or firing of a **red** star signal	or code letter **S** given by light or sound-signal apparatus	
Day signals	1 **Horizontal** motion of a white flag followed by 2 the placing of the white flag in the ground and 3 by the carrying of another white flag in the direction to be indicated	1 or firing of a **red** star signal vertically and 2 a **white** star signal in the direction towards the better landing place	1 or signalling the code letter **S** (...) followed by the code letter **R** (._.) if a better landing place for the craft in distress is located more to the *right* in the direction of approach 2 or signalling the code letter **S** (...) followed by the code letter **L** (._..) if a better landing place for the craft in distress is located more to the *left* in the direction of approach	Landing here highly dangerous. A more favourable location for landing is in the direction indicated
Night signals	1 **Horizontal** motion of a white light or flare 2 followed by the placing of the white light or flare on the ground and 3 the carrying of another white light or flare in the direction to be indicated	1 or firing of a **red** star signal vertically and 2 **white** star signal in the direction towards the better landing place	1 or signalling the code letter **S** (...) followed by the code letter **R** (._.) if a better landing place for the craft in distress is located more to the *right* in the direction of approach 2 or signalling the code letter **S** (...) followed by the code letter **L** (._..) if a better landing place for the craft in distress is located more to the *left* in the direction of approach	

Life-Saving Signals

Signals to be employed in connexion with the use of shore life-saving apparatus

	MANUAL SIGNALS	LIGHT SIGNALS	OTHER SIGNALS	SIGNIFICATION
Day signals	**Vertical** motion of a white flag or of the arms	or firing of a **green** star signal		**In general:** affirmative **Specifically:** rocket line is held – tail block is made fast – hawser is made fast – man is in the breeches buoy – haul away
Night signals	**Vertical** motion of a white light or flare	or firing of a **green** star signal		
Day signals	**Horizontal** motion of a white flag or of the arms extended horizontally	or firing of a **red** star signal		**In general:** negative **Specifically:** slack away – avast hauling
Night signals	**Horizontal** motion of a white light or flare	or firing of a **red** star signal		

Replies from life-saving stations or maritime rescue units to distress signals made by a ship or person

Day signals		**Orange** smoke signal	or combined *light and sound* signal (thunder-light) consisting of 3 single signals which are fed at intervals of approximately one minute	**You are seen** – **assistance will be given as soon as possible** (Repetition of such signal shall have the same meaning)
Night signals		**White** star rocket consisting of 3 single signals which are fired at intervals of approximately one minute		(Repetition of such signal shall have the same meaning)

If necessary, the day signals may be given at night or the night signals by day

Signals used by aircraft engaged on search and rescue operations to direct ships towards an aircraft, ship or person in distress

PROCEDURES PERFORMED IN SEQUENCE BY AN AIRCRAFT			SIGNIFICATION
1 Aircraft circles the surface craft at least once	**2** Aircraft crosses the surface craft course close ahead at low altitude opening and closing the throttle or changing the propeller pitch	**3** Aircraft heads in the direction in which the surface craft is to be directed	The aircraft is directing a surface craft towards an aircraft or surface craft in distress (Repetition of such signals shall have the same meaning)
	Crossing the surface craft's wake **close astern** at low altitude opening and closing the throttle or changing the propeller pitch		The assistance of the surface craft is no longer required (Repetition of such signals shall have the same meaning)

Chapter 13
STATE FIRE SERVICES

STATE FIRE SERVICES

FIRE FIGHTING

A fire onboard a vessel creates a serious threat to the lives of every person aboard. If action is taken quickly to control and extinguish the fire the threat can be minimised.

There are basic actions that can be taken in the event of fire to lessen the risk to persons aboard and the vessel.

When a fire occurs-

- an alarm should be raised as soon as a fire is discovered
- persons not involved in fighting the fire must move to a safe area
- where practical attempts should be made to extinguish the fire
- where possible the fire should be contained in the compartment of origin
- if a fire cannot be controlled the vessel should be abandoned

Factors to be considered should fire occur-

- is any person at immediate risk from the fire
- what is burning
- can the fire fuel be removed
- how can the fire area be accessed
- what equipment is available to fight the fire, what else is threatened
- what precautions can be taken to prevent spread of the fire
- how can the ship's construction be used to aid extinction or prevent spread of fire

Other factors to be considered

- are there flammable gases or liquids likely to be present
- should electric circuits be broken
- have ventilator fans to the fire area been stopped; can the fire compartment be sealed to exclude fresh air
- is there any flammable material in contact with the bulkheads or decks of the fire compartment
- should the bulkheads or decks be cooled with water spray
- is smoke giving a false impression of where the seat of the fire is situated, is the stability of the ship threatened. Should provision be made for pumping out excess water, would a change in the vessel's course assist the fire fighting operation.

When the fire is under control -

- is it expedient to open up compartments for inspection
- is it safe to ventilate the compartment to clear heat and smoke

When the fire appears to be out -

- check whether the fire is out. Make sure that materials are not burning behind linings or deep seated smoulderings
- make steps to prevent reignition
- check damage to electrical apparatus and circuits

Rules for Fighting Fire

The removal of fuel, heat or oxygen from a burning substance will extinguish a fire.

Removal of fuel

The removal of a fire's fuel may simply involve the closing off of a fuel line stop valve or a gas cylinder valve. Remote control valves and extension handles facilitate such an action, however, it may be necessary to use a water spray to drive heat and smoke away from such valves to enable a person to close the valve.

Removal of heat

The value of water as an extinguishing agent lies in its capacity to absorb large quantities of heat. If applied efficiently water will cool material to below its ignition point. Consequently, in addition to extinguishing fires, tanks and cylinders containing flammable liquids and gases that are exposed to fire may not become involved in the fire if they can be kept cool with water spray.

Removal of oxygen

The removal of oxygen from a fire zone is ordinarily a smothering or blanketing operation. For example - when foam is applied onto a burning surface it forms a blanket between that surface and the atmosphere, thereby excluding the oxygen, or when a person's clothes catch fire, by wrapping that person in a blanket the fire is smothered by excluding the oxygen. Vaporizing liquid extinguishing agents such as CO_2 or halon gas dilute the oxygen content of the atmosphere to a point below which flaming combustion can exist. A water spray excludes oxygen as well as having a cooling effect.

How to use Portable Fire Extinguishers

Read the operating instructions on the extinguisher. Approach fire from up-wind direction.

Water Type
1. Carry to fire
2. Remove locking device
3. Squeeze lever or trigger
4. Direct stream at base of fire

Foam Type
1. Carry to fire
2. Remove locking device
3. Squeeze lever or trigger
4. Direct stream to flow foam over burning surface

Dry Powder
1. Carry to fire
2. Remove locking device
3. Squeeze lever or trigger
4. Direct discharge at fire with a fanning motion
5. Beware of reignition if surface cover is interrupted.

Gas Type
1. Carry to fire
2. Remove locking device
3. Squeeze lever or trigger
4. Sweep downwards to base of fire
5. Evacuate confined spaces

Where to use Portable Fire Extinguishers

Classification of Fires

Class A   Fires in ordinary combustible materials such as wood, cloth, paper, rubber and many plastics

Class B   Fires in flammable and combustible liquids and greases

Class C   Fires in combustible gases

Class D   Fires in combustible metals

On extinguishers, (E) indicates that the extinguisher is suitable for fires which involve energized electrical equipment where the electrical non-conductivity of the chemical is of importance.

Q.1   What conditions may cause fires and or explosions on vessels?

A.
- lack of devices for prevention of accumulation of flammable fuel and combustible oils and greases in bilges.
- fuel and oil tanks and flexible pipework installed close to heated surfaces.
- inefficient ventilation of confined spaces that allow flammable and explosive gases to accumulate.
- innefficient exhaust installations to main and auxiliary machinery.
- inefficiently set up pipework for high and low pressure conducting of fuel, lubricating oil and hydraulic oil.
- selection of unsuitable material for flexible pipework for conducting flammable and combustible liquids and flammable gases.
- oil saturated timber work in machinery and other spaces.
- installation of batteries without protective covering.
- installation of electrical switchgear adjacent to battery banks.
- installation of electrical conductors where they might be subject to mechanical damage.
- faulty installation and maintenance of A/C alternators and associated equipment.
- inefficient ventilation of battery rooms and compartments for volatile gases emanating from battery cells.
- incorrect storage and misuse of flammable liquids and gases.
- incorrect installation and misuse of open element heating devices.
- overfilling of fuel tanks causing spillage.
- lack of maintenance, cleanliness and care of machinery, fuel installations, electrical installations and machinery spaces.
- careless use of naked lights and smoking material. Storage of flammable gas cylinders in enclosed spaces. (L.P.G. and acetylene cylinders should be stored on deck).

Q.2 What precautions should be taken during maintenance and repair periods on a vessel?

A. • ventilate work area to remove any flammable or explosive gases.

• check that an appropriate type of fire extinguisher is at hand and in fully charged and working condition.

• check that electrical tools, welding units etc are properly earthed.

• protect combustible materials from accidental ignition from welding sparks or oxy-acetylene cutting with a non-combustible blanket.

• check for flammable and explosive gases and combustible material in adjacent compartments that could be accidently ignited.

• whenever possible have another person observing and patrolling the adjacent area should there be an undesirable risk.

• check the immediate area on completion of work to ensure that there is no smouldering material, oily rags etc.

Q.3 How many fire extinguishers are required to be carried on a vessel?

A. Not less than two extinguishers of adequate capacity and type suitable for the risks involved, unless special approval has been granted by the Board.

Q.4 Where should fire extinguishers be installed?

A. • in proximity to but clear of the risk.

• clearly visible in the path of travel towards the exit.

Q.5 What care should be exercised when fixed vaporising liquid or dry powder extinguishing systems are installed in engine rooms and equipment spaces?

A. All persons should vacate the area before the system is operable. The discharge can be asphyxiating and visibility can be seriously impaired.

Q.6 What type of fire extinguisher should be used on fires involving electrical equipment?

A. Any fire extinguisher that has an (E) categorisation shown following the rating and classification eg 20B(E)

Other suitable extinguishers may be used for adjacent burning combustible material if the electrical circuitry has been de-energised.

Q.7 Can water be used on a fire involving flammable liquid?

A. Every fire must be assessed individually.

• A water spray could be an effective extinguishing media provided -

– the whole surface of the burning liquid can be covered by the water spray.

– the container or compartment has sufficient volume to contain the burning liquid and the water applied without further spreading the fire.

– the quantity of burning liquid may be irrelevant if the structure around the container is involved in the fire.

Q.8 What are the different values of extinguishing agents suitable for flammable liquid fires?

A. • foam is suitable where the liquid is contained in a receptacle or compartment. It will provide a blanketing effect to exclude oxygen and have a minor cooling effect on the liquid.

• dry powder is most effective in extinguishing fire on surfaces. It is ideal for fires where liquid has been spilt over a large area. Dry powder has little cooling effect and a fire can quickly reignite if the surface layer is broken before the liquid has cooled to below its ignition temperature.

• water spray is effective over large surface areas. It can have an emulsifying effect on the burning surface and has good cooling qualities.

• total flood CO_2, halon and dry chemical are effective in enclosed compartments; as they interrupt the fire cycle. It is important that compartments are not ventilated until the risk of fire has ceased.

- portable CO_2, and halon extinguishers are effective on small fires in containers, electrical switchboards, machinery etc.

Q.9 How often should fire extinguishers be inspected, tested and recharged?

A.
- every extinguisher must be recharged after use. A partially discharged extinguisher must never be replaced in its assigned location or left in service.
- before each sailing a visual inspection must be made that each extinguisher is in its assigned position and fully charged.
- 6 monthly -

  check accessibility, antitamper seal, support hook, exterior and operating instructions, external damage or corrosion, discharge nozzle, outlet hose and nozzle, contents, any pressure indicator, operating lead, actuating device without discharging.
- check internal components of water (soda acid) and foam (chemical) type contents.
- check compressed gas container of water, foam and dry powder type.

  replace in assigned location and record maintenance.
- yearly - carry out 6 monthly programme and in addition,
  - discharge water (soda-acid) and foam (chemical) type.
  - check internal components water, foam and dry powder type.
  - check internal condition of all extinguishers except water and dry powder (stored pressure), CO_2 and halon types.
- 3 yearly - carry out 6 monthly and yearly programme and in addition, check internal condition of water (stored pressure) type.
- 6 yearly - carry out 6 monthly, yearly and 3 yearly programme and in addition, discharge and hydrostatically test all extinguishers.

Q.10 If a fire started in the cabin of a vessel and a fire extinguisher- was not readily accessible what action could be taken?

A.   Smother the fire with a fire blanket or other blanket or bag. Douse the fire with buckets of water.

Q.11 What colour code is used to indicate fire hydrants?

A.   Red.

Q.12 If a fire extinguisher is coloured blue what should this indicate?

A.   It is a foam type extinguisher.

Q.13 What types of fire extinguishers should not be used on electrically energized switchgear or equipment?

A.   Water and foam types. These extinguishers are electrically conductive.

Q.14 How is a CO_2 fire extinguisher distinguished?

A.   It should be coloured red with a black band.

Q.15 How are fire buckets identified?

A.   They should be red and be marked FIRE in white lettering.

Q.16 How many buckets should be fitted with lanyards?

A.   At least two. Lanyards must have sufficient length to reach the sea from the deck.

Q.17 What are the disadvantages of using a BCF type fire extinguisher?

A.
- the fumes given off when extinguishing a fire may be toxic, care must be exercised when used in a confined space.
- halons have a detrimental effect on the environment.

Q.18 How would you know if a fire extinguisher is being properly maintained?

A.   A numeral marking stamped on a metal tag attached to the extinguisher will denote the maintenance work and servicing that has been performed i.e.

"1" denotes 6 monthly programme,

"2" denotes yearly programme,

"3" denotes 3 yearly programme,

"4" denotes 6 yearly programme,

"5" denotes serviced after use,

Q.19 What are the contents of a foam (stored pressure) type extinguisher?

A. Water, and premixed foam solution. When mixed and aerated they produce a solution of air-filled bubbles that form into a blanket of foam.

Q.20 How should fire hose be stored?

A. The hose should be flaked in a hose box or cradle commencing from the hydrant connection end and laying the hose flat backwards and forwards in flakes finishing with the nozzle laid on top of the hose.

Q.21 What would indicate that a C02 fire extinguisher required refilling?

A. The extinguisher is weighed.

- the tare weight and gross weight of the extinguisher is stamped on the cylinder,

- should a loss of contents exceed 5% by mass the extinguisher must be recharged.

Q.22 Is it permissible to use fire hoses for washing down a vessel?

A. • fire hoses are susceptible to abrasive damage and should not be used for general purpose cleaning.

- fire hoses should be tested at hydrant pressure after use and at best once in every year.

- damaged hose and couplings should be repaired and hydrant valves and pumps regularly serviced.

Q.23 What precautions should be taken where gas installations are installed in enclosed compartments?

A. Gas detector units should be provided to detect gas leaks.

Q.24 What type of fire hose should be used where foam producing installations are provided?

A. Hose should be rubber or plastic lined to reduce friction that will cause bubbles of foam to breakdown.

THE 3 STEP FIRE DRILL

Call the Fire Service first

DIAL 000

State: address,
location,
nature of the fire

What kind of fire is it?

WOOD & PAPER
Also grain, fabric, coke,
coal, sawdust

FLAMMABLE LIQUIDS
Waxes, paints, varnish, thinners, kerosene, petrol

ELECTRICAL
Motors, switchboards,
generators

GAS

Choose the right fire extinguisher

WATER
Not to be used for
electrical fires or
flammable liquids

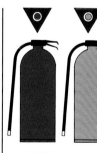

FOAM   **WET
CHEMICAL**

Not to be used
for electrical fires

**CARBON
DIOXIDE**   **POWDER**

**CARBON
DIOXIDE**

POWDER

Chapter 14

HANDLING AND CARRYING DANGEROUS CARGO

What are the requirements for the Handling and Transport of Dangerous Cargo within Queensland Ports and Waters?

CLASS 1 Explosives	**CLASS 2.1** Gases, compressed, liquefied or dissolved under pressure Flammable gases; Poisonous (toxic) gases; Non-flammable compressed gases).	**CLASS 2.2**	**CLASS 2.3**	**CLASS 3** Flammable Liquids (Low Flash Point Group; Intermediate Flash Point Group; High Flash Point Group).
CLASS 5.1 Oxidising Substances (Oxidising Agents; Organic Peroxides).	**CLASS 5.2**	**CLASS 6.1** Poisonous (Toxic) Substances, Infectious Substances.	**CLASS 6.2**	**CLASS 4.1** Flammable Substances (Flammable liquids; Substances liable to Spontaneous Combustion; Substances which in contact with water emit flammable gases).
CLASS 7 CATEGORY I Radioactive Materials	**CLASS 7 CATEGORY II** Radioactive Materials	**CLASS 7 CATEGORY III** Radioactive Materials	**CLASS 8** Corrosive Substances	**CLASS 4.2**
				CLASS 4.3
				CLASS 9 Miscellaneous Dangerous Substances.

(This class includes substances which present a danger whilst being handled and transported, and are not covered by other Classes. These substances are listed in the International Maritime Dangerous Goods Code, Volume IV.

How Is Dangerous Cargo Classified?

Dangerous Cargo has been divided internationally into a number of classes, according to the hazard they present.

- Operators are required to complete a dangerous cargo report (or it's equivalent) as stated in this section of the Small Ships Manual.

Operators Should Ensure They Are Fully Conversant With -

- the classification of dangerous cargo intended to be handled and transported.

- the need for identifying, marking, labelling, and where necessary placarding of dangerous goods.
- correct packaging, segregation and stowage procedures for dangerous goods.
- all necessary safety and fire precautions to be observed when handling dangerous cargo.
- Port Authority regulations concerning the handling and storage of dangerous cargo where the port of loading or discharge is administered by a Port Authority.

Remember!

- The handling and transport of dangerous cargo creates the need for strict adherence to recognised safety procedures. It is essential that operators of vessels fully understand the dangers associated with the type of cargo proposed to be handled and carried, and are aware of emergency procedure action to be taken in the event of an accident or escape of dangerous cargo. Safety equipment and protective clothing relative to the type of dangerous cargo must be carried on board.

- In the event of an accident involving dangerous cargo which could cause:
  - fire
  - spillage
  - leakage of toxic
  - explosions

within port areas or other places of loading or discharge, the accident must be immediately reported to the nearest Harbour Master's and Port Authority Office, Police Station or Fire Brigade in order to minimise potential danger and alert Emergency Services. It is an offence not to report an accident.

HANDLING AND CARRYING DANGEROUS CARGO

Vessel operators are responsible for damages and costs resulting from an accident involving dangerous cargo, including clean up costs and emergency services response. The occurrence of an accident or any damage caused to a package or container must be reported to:

(a) in a pilotage area – the relevant harbour master; or

(b) outside a pilotage area – the chief executive(Director-General, Queensland Transport).

Duties of person sending dangerous cargo by ship

(1) A person must not send a dangerous cargo by ship unless, before sending the cargo, the person gives the master of the ship a written notice about the cargo stating the following –

(a) the proper shipping name of the cargo;

(b) the UN number for the cargo stated in the IMDG Code;

(c) the quantity of the cargo; and

(d) if the cargo has a flash point – its flash point or flash point range.

Maximum penalty – 200 penalty units.

(2) A person must not send dangerous goods by ship unless the person –

(a) packs, secures, marks, labels, placards (for a cargo transport unit) and documents the goods as required by the IMDG Code; and

(b) gives to the master of the ship the documents required under the IMDG Code.

Duties of owner and master of ship about dangerous cargo

(1) The owner and master of a ship handling a dangerous cargo (other than dangerous goods) on the ship must, so far as is reasonably practicable, comply with the appropriate dangerous cargo code for the cargo while handling the cargo.

Maximum penalty – 200 penalty units.

(2) The owner and master of a ship handling dangerous goods on the ship must, so far as is reasonably practicable, comply with the IMDG Code.

Further information can be obtained by contacting the nearest Regional Harbour Master's Office.

One of the less welcome side effects to result in recent years from Queensland's rapidly expanding boating industry has been an acceleration in boating accidents. Sometimes boat owners and skippers quite unwittingly put themselves, their passengers and crew at risk by the incorrect handling of dangerous cargo on board.

To ensure those afloat keep out of harm's way, the Queensland Department of Transport is mounting a boating safety campaign to educate all ship owners about operating a ship.

This book is intended as an introduction to the basic safety requirements for the handling and transport of dangerous cargo within Queensland ports and waters.

Anyone intending to handle or transport dangerous cargo in these areas should be fully conversant with the contents of –

- The Transport Operations (Marine Safety) Regulation and Standards. (Available from departmental offices and the Queensland Government Printing Office, Brisbane).

- The Association of Australian Port and Marine Authority Guidelines for the Safe Transport, Handling and Storage of Dangerous Substances and Oils within Port Areas. (Available from A.A.P.M.A., G.P.O. Box 32, Sydney, NSW 2001). These guidelines are being revised to Australian Standards.

- The International Maritime Dangerous Goods Code. (Information concerning this Code can be obtained from departmental offices.)

Reporting requirements for ships loading dangerous cargo

A ship is required to report it is carrying dangerous cargo if;

- it is to arrive at, or depart from, a pilotage area or at a berth or anchorage in a pilotage area;

- it is to be removed to another berth or anchorage in the pilotage area;

- it is to transfer the cargo to another ship in the pilotage area;

- it is to load dangerous cargo while in the pilotage area; or

- it is to be operated on a local marine service.

The owner and master of a ship must report, in the approved form, the following:

- the expected arrival, departure, removal transfer or loading of the ship;
- the start of the local marine service and voyages under it; and
- any other information required on the Queensland Transport Dangerous Cargo Report.

Reports should be supplied as follows:

for an arrival – not less than 48 hours before the expected arrival;

for a departure or removal – not less than three hours before the expected departure or removal;

for a transfer – not less than 24 hours before the expected transfer;

for the loading of a ship – not less than 24 hours before loading is expected to start;

for a local marine service – for the start of the service, not less than 48 hours before the start of the service; and

for subsequent voyages, at the time (if any) the person to whom the report advising of the start of the service considers reasonable, and gives written notice at the time to the owner or master of the ship.

The chief executive may, by gazette notice, change the above mentioned times, for a particular place, if the chief executive is satisfied the change is necessary to ensure marine safety, or enable the effectiveness and efficiency of the Queensland Marine Industry to be developed.

Dangerous Cargo Reports should be submitted to the relevant Harbour Master if in a pilotage area or the chief executive if outside a pilotage area through the nearest Regional Harbour Master's Office.

The owner and master of a ship operating the ship on a local marine service must notify the chief executive within 14 days after the owner and master stops the service.

PLEASE NOTE

A dangerous cargo report may be provided in the following approved forms –

- on The Queensland Transport 'Dangerous Cargo Report'.
- in the case of the Port of Brisbane, a properly completed SIS Booking Form provided the cargo details are forwarded to the Regional Harbour Master; and
- electronic communication (other than voice) of the information which is required on the 'Dangerous Cargo Report'.

DEFINITIONS

- "dangerous cargo" means any of the following cargoes, whether packaged, carried in bulk packagings or in bulk –
  (a) crude oil and petroleum products with a flash point not more than 60 degrees Celsius;
  (b) dangerous goods;
  (c) liquefied gases mentioned in the Codes for the Construction and Equipment of Ships Carrying Liquefied Gases in Bulk issued by the IMO; and
  (d) liquid chemicals mentioned in the Codes for the Construction and Equipment of Ships Carrying Dangerous Chemicals in Bulk issued by IMO and Annex II of MARPOL.
- "dangerous goods" means the goods mentioned in the International Maritime Dangerous Goods (IMDG) Code.
- "local marine service" means a shipping service where a ship is operated on Queensland intrastate voyages to handle dangerous cargo.

OPERATORS SHOULD ENSURE THEY ARE FULLY CONVERSANT WITH:

- the classification of dangerous goods intended to be handled and transported;
- the need for identifying, marking, labelling and where necessary, placarding of dangerous goods;
- correct packaging, segregation and stowage procedures for dangerous goods;

- all necessary safety and fire precautions to be observed while handling dangerous goods; and
- Port Authority requirements in respect to movement and handling of dangerous cargo in ports.

REMEMBER!
The handling and transport of dangerous cargo creates the need for strict adherence to recognised safety procedures. It is essential that operators of vessels fully understand the dangers associated with the type of materials proposed to be handled and carried, and are aware of emergency procedure action to be taken in the event of an accident or escape of dangerous cargo from packages or containers. Operators and masters of ships are directed to the appropriate emergency procedures and material hazard sheets and the provisions of the IMDG codes.

In the event of an accident involving dangerous cargo which could cause
- fire
- leakage of poisonous vapour
- spillage
- explosions

within port areas or other places of loading or discharge, the accident must be immediately reported to the nearest Regional Harbour Master's and Port Authority office, Police Station or Fire Brigade in order to minimise potential danger and alert Emergency Services. It is an offence not to report an accident.

HANDLING AND TRANSPORT OF DANGEROUS CARGO
The handling of Dangerous Cargo in Queensland is controlled by the Transport Operations (Marine Safety) Regulation.

Q.1 Operators of vessels must be familiar with the Transport Operations (Marine Safety) Regulation. Identify four major aspects of these regulations they should be fully conversant with.

A. 1. The classification of dangerous cargo.
2. The need for identifying, marking, labelling, and where necessary placarding of dangerous cargo.
3. Correct packaging and stowage

procedures for dangerous cargo.
4. All necessary safety and fire precautions to be observed handling dangerous cargo.

Q.2 What other requirements concerning dangerous goods are vessel operators required to be familiar with?

A. Port Authority requirements.

Q.3 What are four common results of an accident involving dangerous cargo?

A. 1. Fire
2. Explosion
3. Leakage of toxic vapour.
4. Spillage of flammable, corrosive or toxic substances.

Q.4 The Master of a vessel must be familiar with emergency procedures to be followed if an accident involving dangerous cargo occurs. From whom should this information be obtained?

A. The consignor or shipper of the dangerous cargo and information contained in the IMDG code.

Q.5 In addition to being familiar with the requirements of the Transport Operations (Marine Safety) Regulation, operators of vessels intending to transport dangerous cargo should be familiar with two other publications dealing with practices and procedures for the safe handling of dangerous cargoes. What are they?

A. The International Maritime Dangerous Goods Code and the Association of Australia Port and Marine Authority Guidelines for the Safe Transport, Handling and Storage of Dangerous Substances and Oils within Port Areas.

Chapter 15

MARINE POLLUTION

MARINE POLLUTION

Laws regulating the prevention of pollution by oil of waters within the jurisdiction of Queensland are contained in the Transport Operations (Marine Pollution) Act and Regulation 1995.

It is an offence against the Act to discharge oil into any water from a ship, a place on land or from apparatus used for transferring oil to or from a ship or to or from a place on land.

Q.1 How is "ship" defined under the Transport Operations (Marine Pollution) Act and Regulation 1995?

A. "Ship" means a vessel of any type whatsoever operating in the marine environment and includes hydrofoil boats, air cushion vehicles, submersibles, floating craft and fixed or floating platforms.

Q.2 What is the meaning of "Oil"?

A. Oil means oil or oil products of any description and includes spirits produced from oil, coal tar and any mixture of oil with any matter.

Q.3 Who is held responsible for a discharge of oil from a ship or from apparatus used for transferring oil to or from a ship?

A. Both the owner and the Master.

Q.4 It is an offence for the owner and Master of a ship not to report a discharge of oil as soon as possible. To whom should the discharge be reported?

A. If the discharge occurs within the limits of a harbour, the Port or Authority or, the Harbour Master. If the discharge occurs in waters outside the limits of a harbour the nearest Harbour Master, or Queensland Boating and Fisheries Patrol Office.

Chapter 16
STABILITY

STABILITY

For any vessel that proceeds to sea stability is of prime importance. An unstable vessel runs the risk of capsizing or sinking, thus endangering the lives of those on board.

Once a vessel has been built, the only way, barring damage, that stability can be influenced, is by the placement or movement of weights or liquids on board. Here, common sense should prevail at all times.

For example in the case of a fishing vessel it can become unstable when trawl gear becomes "hooked up', or when an exceptionally big catch is made and there is insufficient room in the hold or refrigerated space to store it so excess fish are carried on deck.

Another cause of instability can be overloading the decks with gear while on passage to another port. The free movement of liquid such as water or fuel in tanks also can be a contributing factor.

Should a vessel become tender or unstable the prime objective is to lower the centre of gravity of the vessel. This can be done in a number of ways.

(a) Discharge weights from above the vessel's centre of gravity.

(b) Shift weights downwards.

(c) Press up slack tanks.

(d) Add bottom weight such as ballast.

Ballasting may be considered the most direct solution to the problem, although it is an operation that necessitates a great deal of care. An obvious prerequisite is that the vessel has sufficient reserve buoyancy to cope with the added weight. Secondly, if by chance the vessel's instability has caused an angle of loll and in addition she is fitted with bottom wing tanks, it is vitally important that the tank on the lower side is filled first so as to lower the centre of gravity. Initially this will mean an even greater angle of heel, however this is far more desirable than flopping dangerously to the other side with perhaps going too far and capsizing.

1. DEFINITION

The term 'stability' normally refers to the ability of a vessel to return to the upright position after being heeled by an external influence such as wind or wave action, or an internal influence such as a movement of cargo or an indiscriminate transfer of liquids in the ship's tanks.

This ability of a vessel to right itself when heeled is governed by the physical shape of the hull together with the superstructures, and the effectiveness of the closing devices in the hull and on the weatherdeck.

2. TERMS

Q.1 What is meant by 'ships displacement'?

A. It is the amount of water the vessel displaces when afloat. The weight of the water displaced is always equal to the weight of the vessel.

Q.2 What is meant by the term 'freeboard'?

A. It is the vertical distance from the lowest point of the main deck (usually near midships) to the waterline at which the vessel floats.

Q.3 What is meant by the term 'centre of gravity'?

A. 'G', the centre of gravity, is that point in the vessel at which the whole weight of the vessel is assumed to act vertically downwards.

Q.4 What is meant by the terms 'buoyancy' and 'centre of buoyancy'?

A. "B", the centre of buoyancy, is the centre of the underwater volume and the point through which the force due to buoyancy is assumed to act vertically upwards.

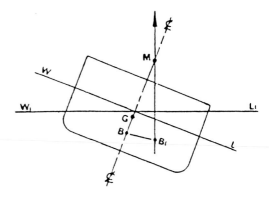

Figure 81 – *Illustrating a vessel's metacentre*

Q.5 What happens to the centre of buoyancy when a ship heels?

A. When a ship heels the change in shape of the underwater form causes B to move away from the ships centreline to a position B1.

Q.6 What is meant by the term 'a vessel's metacentre'?

A. 'M', the metacentre, is the point on the vessel's centre line which is vertically above B when the vessel heels to small angles.

Q.7 What is 'metacentric height' or 'GM'?

A. Metacentric height is the vertical distance between the metacentre (M) and the centre of gravity (G).

Q.8 Does the ship's stability depend on the 'metacentric height'?

A. Yes, to a point, certainly initial stability (i.e. stability for small angles of heel) has a direct relationship to GM. However it does not necessarily follow that a vessel with a large GM will have a big range of stability. Among other things it must have a substantial freeboard, because the stability is reduced dramatically when the deck edge becomes immersed. It is very important that this situation does not occur.

Q.9 Would you expect the centre of gravity (G) to be above or below the metacentre (M) if a vessel was stable?

A. For a vessel to be stable 'G' must be below 'M'.

Q.10 If a vessel was in a state of neutral equilibrium where would you expect 'G' to be relative to 'M'?

A. For neutral equilibrium the centre of gravity (G) and the metacentre (M) are in the same place. See fig. 82A (Page 247).

Q.11 If you suspect a vessel is becoming tender, or, has heeled to an angle of loll showing obvious instability, what is your course of action?

A. The centre of gravity of the vessel must be lowered immediately. This can be done a number of ways but the actual condition of loading at that time will indicate what should be done first.

If the vessel has ample freeboard and the bottom ballast tanks are not full then they should be pressed up remembering of course that if she **is** heeled to an angle of loll, the tanks on the lower side should be filled first.

If heavy gear etc., can be placed lower in the vessel easily, then do SO. Should the vessel be simply overloaded, whether the cargo be fish or otherwise, and there is no way of stowing it below then there is no other option than to ditch it over the side, however much such action is against one's grain.

The movement of the centre of buoyancy during heeling, from B to B1 indicates the ability of the vessel to right itself (see figure 82) or its tendency to capsize (see figure 83) depending upon the couple caused by the weight acting downwards through G and the buoyancy acting upwards through B1. The arm of the couple is the perpendicular distance between the two forces and is known as the "Righting Lever" or "GZ".

3. **ASSESSMENT**

The stability of a vessel is assessed by drawing a curve of the righting levers at varying angles of heel (see figure 84) and comparing the properties of the curve against standard values which should ensure a satisfactory degree of stability.

The standard values, known as stability criteria, are used by all Marine Authorities in Australia when checking the stability information provided by a consultant.

The criteria require that for each loading condition of the vessel the righting lever curve should have certain qualities which vary according to the type of vessel and its area of operations. Details of the requirements can be obtained from the Department's Naval Architect.

It should be noted that whilst the criteria fix minimum but not maximum values, it is advisable to avoid excessive values since these may result in acceleration or rolling forces which could be prejudicial to the safety of the vessel, the comfort of the crew, and the operation of propulsion and navigational equipment.

4. CAPSIZING INFLUENCES

Capsizing due to instability can be caused by many factors, major ones being:-

(a) Wind Forces. In normal circumstances, a vessel with a steady beam wind will roll to an angle of heel caused by that wind pressure acting on the "sail area". (The profile area above the waterline). Should the vessel be struck by a gust when already rolled leeward then the combined effect could result in the vessel capsizing.

(b) Wave Action. The calculations performed to produce the righting lever curves presume that the vessel is in perfectly calm water, but should the vessel be running before a sea whose wave speed is close to that of the vessel, then the situation may arise where the ship is supported for a relatively long period with the wave crest amidships. This can be very critical as the effect is to reduce considerably the magnitude of the righting levers and the range of stability, consequently the vessel may roll heavily and capsize.

(c) Water on the deck. The shipping of moderately large quantities of water onto the deck of a vessel can have very serious consequences. Initially the added weight of the water will increase the draught and consequently reduce the available freeboard. The centre of gravity of the vessel is raised and this will reduce the vessel's stability. If the water is constrained upon the deck by bulwarks then the lateral movement of the water can also create large upsetting moments with a further serious effect on the vessel's stability. To overcome these factors, bulwarks are required to have freeing ports in order to free the deck of water as quickly as possible.

(d) Deck Cargo. should never be carried on deck unless the stability information provides appropriate details regarding stowage of deck cargo. In the case of a fishing vessel where relatively large quantities of fish may be carried on the deck the effect is similar to having water on the deck in that the relatively high centre of gravity of the catch will reduce the vessel's stability levers. Coupled with this, the fact that wet fish will move in a fluid manner unless restrained by pound boards can produce serious transverse heeling moments.

(e) Free Surface. When a fuel or water tank is only partially filled, the fluid in the tank can move transversely as the vessel heels in a seaway. The effect of this 'free surface' is to reduce the vessel's metacentric height and consequently reduce the value of the ordinates of the righting lever curve. The reduction is a function of the area of the free surface and is quite independent of the amount of fuel or water in the tank.

(f) Fishing Gear "Hook Up". If trawl gear on one side of the vessel becomes "hooked up" a large upsetting moment is exerted on the vessel. Protection in the form of a 'weak link' or snatch block should be provided.

5. ADVICE REGARDING STABILITY

The following recommendations should be borne in mind by all persons having charge of a vessel at sea.

(a) External doors and hatches should always be kept closed in adverse weather conditions to prevent water entering the hull or superstructures.

(b) Hatch covers on the weatherdeck should be kept closed and properly secured when not being used.

(c) Deadlights fitted to sidelights should be kept in good condition, and securely closed in adverse conditions.

(d) Flaps or closing plates fitted to freeing ports should be kept in operable condition and should never be locked in the closed position.

(e) Closing devices provided for air escapes to fuel and water tanks or ventilators to below-deck spaces should be secured in adverse conditions.

(f) The number of slack (partially filled) fuel and water tanks should be kept to a minimum at all times.

(g) Any instruction regarding the filling or emptying of ballast tanks or the transfer of fuel and water whilst at sea should be carefully observed.

(h) Caution should be exercised when manoeuvring in following or quartering seas and speed should be reduced if excessive heeling or yawing occurs.

(i) Care should be taken in the composition of weights in a vessel. Cargo should only be carried on deck when the vessel has sufficient reserve stability to allow it.

(j) Fishing vessels should take care when nets are hauled in by winch. Excessive heeling moments can be caused by attempting to haul-in too large a catch or when the trawl is snagged on an underwater obstruction.

To reduce the possibility of capsizing by a sudden external force on the trawl line (should it become snagged) owners and operators are strongly recommended to employ some form of quick release gear in the line.

This would usually be in the form of a snatch block at the end of the arms or other form of "weak link" so that the trawl line of action is immediately transferred to the vessel.

(k) Quite a few vessels have a tendency to make water and extreme care should be taken to keep 'loose water' in the bilges at an absolute minimum. This is particularly pertinent when the vessel may suffer heavy weather damage resulting in water entering the main hull via hatchways, skylight etc. or even as the result of fire fighting operations.

(l) Last, but not least, if the vessel is supplied with a Stability Information Book, make yourself familiar with its contents and how to put into practice the guidance given in the explanatory notes.

Approximate Determination of GM

It is possible for the Master of a small vessel to approximate the stability condition of his vessel by using a ROLL PERIOD TEST. the roll period for the vessel can be measured, an approximate figure for Metacentric Height (GM) can be calculated The calculation involves a factor – the roll period factor – and this can be given an approximate value of 0.8 for a small conventional vessel.

Consider the formula:

$$GM = \left(\frac{0.8B}{T}\right)^2$$

Where:

B = Breadth of vessel (Beam) in metres

T = Time in seconds for a complete roll cycle (e.g. port to starboard to port)

GM = Metacentric Height in metres

Students will note:

- a larger beam gives a larger GM; and
- a longer time gives a smaller GM.

An example:

A vessel, beam 5 metres, has a roll period of 6 seconds.

$$GM = \left(\frac{0.8 \times 5}{6}\right)^2 = 0.44 \text{ metres}$$

Conclusion:

Remember that 0.8 for the roll period factor is an approximation. Record your roll period when you know your stability conditions are satisfactory. if the period of roll becomes larger or longer or the vessel becomes sluggish then find out why and correct the situation.

Remember:

When a weight (or mass) is added to a vessel G moves towards the added weight. When a weight (or mass) is removed, G moves away from the point of removal.

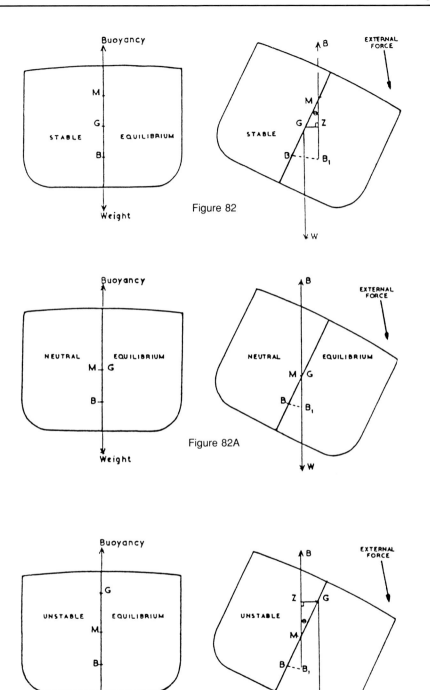

Figure 82

Figure 82A

Figure 83

The conditions necessary for a vessel to be in stable equilibrium can be summarised as:–
1. Dispalcement of the vessel must equal the upthrust due to buoyancy.
2. The forces of gravity and buoyancy must be on the same vertical line.
3. The centre of gravity must be below the metacentre

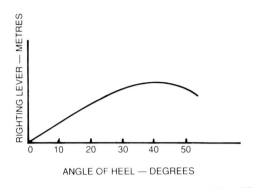

Figure 84 – *Illustrating a righting lever curve (GZ curve)*

Chapter 17
ENGINEERING

TYPICAL QUESTIONS AND ANSWERS
FOR
MARINE ENGINEER CLASS 3 AND MARINE ENGINE DRIVER
EXAMINATIONS

This Section consists of Parts I to VII. The relevant parts for various certificates are as listed hereunder:-

* Marine Engineer Class 3 (Motor) Parts I to VII

* Marine Engineer Class 3 (Steam) Parts I to VII

* Marine Engine Driver Grade I (Motor) Parts II to VII

* Marine Engine Driver Grade I (Steam) Parts II to VII

* Marine Engine Driver Grade II (Motor) Parts III to VII

* Marine Engine Driver Grade II (Steam) Parts III to VII

* Marine Engine Driver Grade III (Motor) Parts IV to VII

* Marine Engine Driver Grade III (Steam) Parts IV to VII

  Marine Engine Driver Grade III Q (Fishing) (M) Parts V and VI

  Marine Engine Driver Grade IV Q (Fishing) (M) Part VI

* Marine Engine Driver Grade IV Q (Trading) (M) Parts IV to VII

* Coxswain - Engineering Content Part IV (excluding refrigeration)

* It should be noted that these questions are typical questions only and may differ within the scope of the subject.

EXAMINATION FOR MARINE ENGINE DRIVERS AND MARINE ENGINEERS CLASS 3
(ALSO ENGINEERING CONTENT OF COXSWAINS CERTIFICATE)

Certificate	Time	Papers
(1) Coxswain (Motor Engineering)	1 hour	Engineering Knowledge
(2) M.E.D. III Q Fishing	2 hours	Engineering Knowledge
(3) M.E.D. IV Q Trading	2 hours	Practical Mathematics
	2 hours	Engineering Knowledge
(4) M.E.D. IV Q Fishing	2 hours	Engineering Knowledge
(5) M.E.D. Grade III (Motor)	1 hour	Engineering Knowledge
(6) M.E.D. Grade III (Steam)	1 hour	Engineering Knowledge
(7) M.E.D. II (Motor)	3 hours	Engineering Knowledge
(8) H.R.E.D. II Bridging Exam as M.E.D. II (Motor)	1½ hours	Engineering Knowledge
(9) H.R.E.D. I, C.E.D. II (M) and M.M.E.B. Bridging Exam as M.E.D. II (Motor)	1 hour	Engineering Knowledge
(10) M.E.D. II (Steam)	3 hours	Engineering Knowledge
(11) M.E.D. II Steam Endorsement to Motor Certificate	1 hour	Engineering Knowledge
(12) M.E.D. II Motor Endorsement to Steam Certificate	1 hour	Engineering Knowledge
(13) M.E.D. I (Motor)	3 hours	Engineering Knowledge
	3 hours	Mathematics
(14) C.E.D. I (M) and M.M.E.A. Bridging Exam as M.E.D. I (Motor)	1½ hours	Engineering Knowledge and Mathematics
(15) * M.E.D. I (Steam)	3 hours	Engineering Knowledge
	3 hours	Mathematics
(16) M.E.D. I Steam Endorsement to Motor Certificate	2 hours	E.K. with Maths Question related to Steam Heat
(17) M.E.D. I Motor Endorsement to Steam Certificate	2 hours	E.K. with Maths Question related to Diesel Engines
(18) Marine Engineer Cl. 3 (Motor)	3 hours	Engineering Knowledge
	3 hours	Mathematics
	1 hour	Electrotechnology
(19) Marine Engineer Cl. 3 (Steam)	3 hours	Engineering Knowledge
	3 hours	Mathematics
	1 hour	Electrotechnology
(20) Marine Engineer Cl. 3 Steam Endorsement to Motor Certificate	3 hours	Engineering Knowledge
(21) Marine Engineer Cl. 3 Motor Endorsement to Steam Certificate	3 hours	Engineering Knowledge

* A person requiring M.E.D. I Steam Certification (Whilst holding a C.E.D. Steam Certificate) will be required to sit for the full M.E.D. I Steam Examination. C.E.D. steam may be converted to M.E.D. II steam by oral examination.

Steam and Motor endorsements by oral examination are available for the Marine Engine Driver Grade III Certificate.

ALL CERTIFICATES ARE ALSO SUBJECT TO ORAL EXAMINATIONS

PART I

MATHEMATICS

Q.1 **The total volume of a cylinder liner is 0.58 cubic metre.**

The diameter of the piston is 760 mm and the thickness of the liner is 200 mm.

Find -

(a) **the length of stroke, neglecting clearance space; and**

(b) **the weight of the cylinder in tonnes if the mass density of the liner is 7210 kg/m³.**

A.　Volume = 　(Area 1 – Area 2) x length

　　Length = $\dfrac{\text{Volume}}{(A1-A2)}$

Length cms = $\dfrac{0.58 \times 100^3}{\dfrac{\Pi(580)^2}{(10)} - \dfrac{\Pi(380)^2}{(10)}}$

　(a)　Length of Stroke = 96.19cm

　　　$\dfrac{.58 \times 7210}{1000}$

　(b)　Weight = 4.18 tonnes

Q.2 **(a) Describe a Scalar Quantity.**

(b) Describe a Vector Quantity.

(c) A point "O" is in equilibrium with three (3) forces acting upon it. One force (A) of 5 tonnes is at 45° to another force (B) of 3 tonnes, both acting toward the point "O". What would be the other force (C) value in tonnes, and its direction in regard to the other forces (A&B)?

A.　(a) A Scalar quantity has magnitude but not direction.

　　(b) A Vector quantity has magnitude and direction.

　　(c) By scale

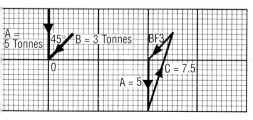

Figure 85 – *Vector Diagram*

Force "C" = 7.5 Tonnes at 152° to Force "B" and 163° to Force "A"

C relative to Force A = 180° – 17° = 163°

C relative to Force B = 180° – 28° = 152°

Q.3 **(a) Describe what is meant by Velocity Ratio.**

(b) Describe what is meant by Mechanical Advantage.

(c)

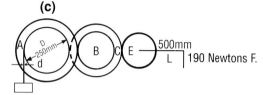

Figure 86 – *Compound Winch*

In the compound winch shown, E has 15 teeth, C has 50 teeth, B has 38 teeth and A has 120 teeth. The drum is 250 mm diameter and the rope is 25 mm diameter and handle is 500 mm long. If the force at the handle is 190 Newtons, what weight can be lifted if efficiency is 80 per cent.

A.　(a) Velocity Ratio is the speed of the fast moving end of the machine compared with the speed of the slow end =

　　　$\dfrac{\text{Distance Travelled by Force}}{\text{Distance Weight Rises}}$

　　(b) The Mechanical advantage is the actual leverage of the machine

　　　$\dfrac{\text{Weight Lifted}}{\text{Actual Force Applied}}$

V.R.= $\dfrac{L}{D+\dfrac{d}{2}} \times \dfrac{A}{B} \times \dfrac{C}{E} = \dfrac{500}{(125+12.5)} \times \dfrac{120}{38} \times \dfrac{50}{15}$

　　　= 46.78

Weight Lifted = $46.78 \times \dfrac{190 \times 0.8}{9.81}$

Weight Lifted = 724.88 Kgs

Q.4 **(a) What is torque?**

(b) A shaft transmits 500 K.W. Brake Power at 860 revolutions per minute. Find the mean twisting moment in kg. metres.

The maximum stress is not to exceed 53 MPa.

The maximum twisting moment is 1.5 x the mean.

Find the diameter of the shaft -

(i) $T = \dfrac{KWP \times 974}{n}$ (ii) $T = \dfrac{D^3 \times q}{5.1}$

N.B. MOTOR PAPER ONLY

A. (a) Torque is the turning moment applied to a twisting shaft.

(b) Mean Torque $= \dfrac{KWP \times 974}{n} = \dfrac{500 \times 974}{860}$

$= 566.28$ Kg M

Maximum Torque $= 566.28 \times 1.5$

$= 849.42$ Kg M

& Torque $= \dfrac{D^3 \times Stress\ (q)}{5.1}$

$849.92 = \dfrac{D^3}{5.1} \times \dfrac{53 \times 10^6}{9.81}$

$D^3 = \dfrac{849.42 \times 5.1 \times 9.81}{53 \times 10^6}$

$D = \sqrt[3]{0.000801} = 0.0929$ m

$= 92.9$mm

Q.5 (a) An electric heater has three resistance elements connected in parallel across a 110V supply. The resistance of each element is 20 ohms. Find the energy dissipated as heat in joules per second.

(b) Two groups of three cells each in series are arranged in parallel. The E.M.F. of each cell is 1.5 volts and the resistance in each cell is 0.5 ohms. The external circuit has a resistance of 0.75 ohm. Find the total power output.

A. (a) Current in each element

(I) $= \dfrac{110}{20} = 5.5$ Amperes

Total I - $5.5 \times 3 = 16.5$ amperes

Energy Dissipated $= 1815$ W

$= 1815$ Joules/second

(b) Total E.M.F. (E) $= 3 \times 1.5 = 4.5$ Volts.

Resistance (R) of each series Group

$= 3 \times 0.5 = 1.5$ ohms

$\dfrac{1}{R} = \dfrac{1}{1.5} + \dfrac{1}{1.5} = \dfrac{4}{3}$

Resistance of Battery $= 0.75$ ohm

Total Resistance of Circuit $= 0.75 + 0.75 = 1.5$ ohms

It $= \dfrac{E}{R} = \dfrac{4.5}{1.5} = 3$ amps

P.D. across terminals $= IR = 3 \times .75 = 2.25$ volts

Total Power (Wt) $= EI = 2.25 \times 3$

$= 6.75$ Watts

Q.6 (a) Define "Linear Expansion".

(b) A block of steel measures 450 mm x 400 mm x 125 mm. The coefficient of Linear Expansion for this material is 0.0000121 per degree celsius. Find the increase in volume when heated through 50 celsius degrees.

The 'coefficient of cubical expansion' is equal to three (3) times the 'coefficient of Linear Expansion' i.e.

Change in volume = 3 KVT

V = Volume of the block of steel

A. (a) Linear Expansion

When a body is heated or cooled all its linear measurements change slightly, provided the body is free so that there is no restriction to its change of size.

(b) Increase in Volume $= 3$ KVT

$= 3 \times 0.0000121 \times 450 \times 400 \times 125 \times 50$

$= 40837.5$ mm^3

Q.7 A mass of 6 Tonnes is moved transversely through a distance of 14 metres on a ship of 4300 tonne displacement, when the deflection of an 11 metre pendulum is found to be 120 mm.

The transverse metacentre is 7.25 metres above the keel.

Determine the height of the centre of gravity above the keel.

A. $GM = \dfrac{m \times d}{\Delta \tan \varnothing}$

$\dfrac{6 \times 14 \times 11}{4300 \times 120 \times 10^{-3}} = 1.79$ m

$KG = KM - GM$

$= 7.25 - 1.79$

$= 5.46$ M

Q.8 A ship of 5000 tonne displacement has a rectangular tank 6 metres long, and 10 metres wide. Calculate the virtual reduction in metacentric height if the tank is partly full of oil (SG 0.8)

$GG_1 = GG_2 \tan \varnothing$ and $GG_2 = \dfrac{Pi}{\Delta}$

$\Delta = \nabla$ Pi

P1 = water density

∇ = Volume of displacement

P = liquid density

i = 2nd moment of area of free surface about tank centreline.

A. P= 1000 x 0.8 Kg/m³

$i = \dfrac{1}{12} \times 6 \times 10^3$ m⁴

P1 = 1025 Kg/m³

$= \dfrac{5000}{1.025}$ M³

$GG_2 = \dfrac{1000 \times 0.8 \times 6 \times 10^3 \times 1.025}{1025 \times 5000 \times 12}$

Reduction in Metacentric Height = 0.08m

Q.9 A steel bar is 3 metres long and 25 mm diameter and its normal working tensile stress is 92.7 Newtons/mm². Find the load on the bar in tonnes, the total extension, the strain and the F.O.S. The yield stress of the material is 280 MPa and the modulus of elasticity (E) is 208656 MPa.

A.   LOAD = AREA x STRESS

Π x 12.5² x 92.7 = 4550622 Newtons

$= \dfrac{4550622}{9.81 \times 1000}$

LOAD = 4.64 Tonnes

STRAIN = STRESS ÷ YOUNGS MODULUS (E)

$\dfrac{92.7}{208656}$

STRAIN = 0.00044

EXTENSION = ORIGINAL LENGTH x STRAIN

= 3000 x 0.00044

EXTENSION = 1.3 MM

FACTOR OF SAFETY = Yield Stress (σy)

÷ Working Stress (σw)

$= \dfrac{280}{92.7}$

F.O.S. = 3.02

Q.10 A four stroke single acting diesel engine has eight cylinders. The M.E.P. being 690 kPa, cylinder diameter 200 mm, stroke 280 mm, and revolutions per minute being 1400. Find the Brake Power.

A.   I.P. = PLAN (watts)   B.P.= I.P. x 0.8

$= \dfrac{690 \times 10^3 \times 0.28 \times \Pi \times 0.1^2 \times 8 \times 1400}{120}$

$= \dfrac{566565.5}{1000} = KW = 566.6$ KW

B.P. = 566.6 x .8

Brake Power = 453.25 K.W.B.P.

N.B. Motor Paper Only

Q.11 A boiler makes 20 000 kgs of steam per day with a heat value of 9000 kilojoules per kilogram of steam. The efficiency of the boiler is 0.736. Given that the fuel has a heat value of 41 770 kilojoules per kilogram, how much fuel would the boiler consume in tonnes per day?

A. $\dfrac{20\,000 \times 9\,000}{1\,000 \times 41\,770 \times Tf} = 0.736$

Tf = Tonnes fuel

Efficiency = $\dfrac{\text{Heat for work}}{\text{Heat value of fuel}}$

Tf = $\dfrac{20\,000 \times 9\,000}{0.736 \times 1\,000 \times 41\,770}$

Tonnes of fuel consumed = 5.855

N.B. Steam Paper Only

ENGINEERING

Q.1 **Enumerate the properties required for the materials used in the construction of the following components:**

(a) Cylinder relief valve lid

(b) Cross-head guide shoe bearing
   Give a sample material for each component.

A.   (a) Resistance to high temperatures and pressure. High Alloy steel of ferritic type having a high aluminium and silicon content.

(b) Low friction and good wearing qualities. Hoyts No. 11 whitemetal or similar due to the relatively low speeds of a crosshead shoe.

Q.2 **What are the physical properties required in materials intended to be used for (a) piston rings; (b) connecting rod bolts; (c) a stern tube? Name the material considered most suitable in each case.**

A.   (a) Good wearing qualities, low friction characteristics which are found in pearlitic gray cast iron.

(b) Needs to be tough material of fine grain structure due to sharp loadings. Bolts should be tempered low alloy steel rolled bar.

(c) Stern tubes material depend on the vessel hull material and may be in mild steel, aluminium, F.R.P. or copper in the case of wooden vessels. The stern tube, being open to the sea should be as thick as practicable and requires heavier sections at each end to carry bearing and glands as necessary.

Q.3. **Describe, with the aid of a sketch, a typical fixed gas fire smothering system as fitted to the machinery space of a vessel.**

A.   The Gas smothering system indicated is manually activated. Should fire occur the products of combustion detectors activate alarms both audible and visual at the control Position (wheelhouse). The crew member responsible checks M/C space after shutting off the audible alarm. If the situation warrants use of the fixed system then the engine is stopped, all openings closed, including

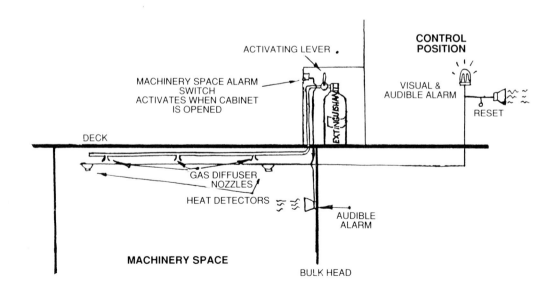

Figure 87 – *Typical fixed fire smothering system*

vents and the alarm to machinery space activated so that if any person is in the space they have time to get out. The activating valve is then opened extinguishing the fire.

Q.4 What risks are associated with opening and entering recently opened oil tanks, ballast tanks or hot crankcases? Describe how to prepare a fuel tank for internal inspection.

A. **Risks**

Recently emptied fuel tanks may be full of fuel vapour. When opening the tank a spark or other source of heat may cause an explosion depending on the vapour/air mixture. Opening crankcase doors before the engine has cooled down can also be dangerous due to fresh air entering the crankcase and mixing with the oil vapour. If a source of heat, such as an overheated bearing is present, an explosion may follow. Ballast Tanks may be devoid of oxygen due to corrosion inside the tank or poisonous gas, such as Oliphant gas, may be present.

Preparing a fuel tank for internal inspection.

A current of fresh air, if led to the bottom of the tank, will drive the gases out at the top. Since the explosive gas is heavier than air the desired results cannot be obtained if the air is admitted to the top of the tank. A tank can also be freed of explosive gas by steaming out. In either case the tank must be well drained before gas-freeing operations begin, otherwise the operation will take considerable time. Another method is to fill the tank with water.

Q.5 Write a report to a fleet manager regarding a breakdown caused by a cracked cylinder liner enumerating the repairs carried out, probable cause of the failure and recommended action to prevent a re-occurrence.

A. Report on Breakdown caused by a cracked cylinder liner – Vessel "NAME"

Introduction

1. As reported by telephone on "date" the vessels departure from "Port" was delayed from that day until "time" on the following day due to a cracked liner in No. 3 cylinder.

Breakdown

2. The breakdown occurred when the vessel was entering Port on the morning of "date". A tug was called to berth the vessel.

3. The problem became apparent when the second engineer noticed cooling water overflowing from the header tank and vapour was seen issuing from the exhaust. The engine also was running "roughly" and No. 3 cylinder relief valve lifted.

4. When the engine had cooled crankcase doors were removed and water was observed running from No. 3 cylinder.

Repairs

5. The cylinder head was removed from No. 3 cylinder following the engine cooling down and the piston rod was disconnected at the crosshead and the piston lifted using the lifting gear provided on board.

6. Whilst the engine was cooling the spare liner was prepared and new top and bottom rubber seals lightly greased and fitted. A new set of piston rings were readied for fitting, and the spare piston cleaned and prepared in case the No. 3 piston had been badly damaged.

7. The fuel valve was renewed and both inlet and exhaust valves reseated to No. 3 head.

8. As No. 3 piston had received only minor damage it was not necessary to renew the piston and after clearing and deburring the ring grooves the new rings were fitted.

9. The cylinder liner had cracked vertically near the bottom. The rings were damaged and the lower two compression rings were broken. Some minor scoring of the piston had occurred but this was remedied by honing.

10. The new cylinder liner had been prepared and after withdrawal of the cracked liner, which was easily accomplished using lifting gear provided, the mating jacket surfaces were cleaned and lightly oiled. Waterways were noted to be clear and the liner locating key was refitted to the new liner. Lube oil injection quills were checked and found to be satisfactory.

11. The new liner was then lowered and fitted to the jacket. Clearances at the top and bottom were to maker's directions. Checks were made to ensure the seals were correctly positioned and the liner drawn home. The liner was then sized for future reference.

12. The piston was then refitted. Ring butt clearances checked and adjusted. No. 3 crosshead bearing and bottom end bearings had been checked and clearances noted to be within prescribed tolerances.

13. The cylinder head was then refitted with new joints, and air was removed from fuel system.

14. Header tank was refilled and water treatment added. No leaks from the new liner were apparent.

15. The engine was then closed up and lubricating oil changed.

Trials

16. The engine was test run satisfactorily for 15 minutes and then stopped. Pressures and temperatures were taken during trials. The engine was then test run for another 30 minutes without problems.

17. Following trials, the vessel was prepared for sea, and two hours later left "port" for "port". The engine was slowly brought up to operating speed and is running smoothly and reliably with all pressures and temperatures within maker's recommended ranges.

Conclusion

Probable cause of liner failure

18. The rings were renewed at recent overhaul and may have been badly fitted and after breaking caused unacceptable pressures on the liner.

19. A spare cylinder liner and set of rings are now required, and it would be appreciated if delivery of these items can be arranged as soon as possible.

N.B. MOTOR PAPER ONLY.

Q.6 Sketch and describe the construction of a cylinder head for a diesel engine. Mention the principal defects to which cylinder heads are liable.

Describe with the aid of a timing diagram the sequence of events in this type of engine.

A.

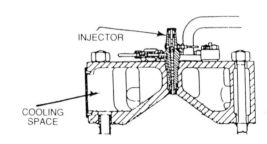

Figure 88 – *Typical 2 stroke engine cylinder head.*

The cylinder head forms the cover for the cylinder and houses the fuel injector and in some cases necessary valves for engine functioning. It is made of cast iron or steel and is attached to the block by studs and nuts. The type shown is from a 'fully ported' trunk type vertical engine.

Cylinder heads can crack due to overheating caused through coolant failure or incorrect tightening of nuts to material between piston crown and cylinder head. Cooling spaces should be kept clear. Cylinder heads with valves have problems through valve, valve seat and valve guide wear due to friction and heat.

Figure 89 – *Typical 2 stroke Cycle Timing Diagram*

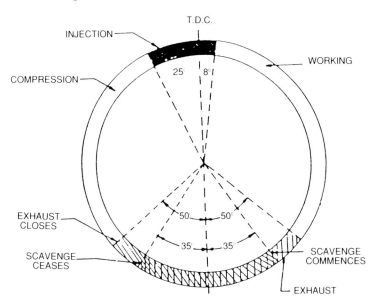

Q.7 Briefly describe the routine maintenance required to keep an auxiliary power source in a 'ready to operate' condition.

A. The auxiliary power source may be storage batteries or an auxiliary diesel generator which may be used, on occasion, when the main power source is out of commission.

The following procedure should be carried out weekly to ensure the generator is 'ready to run'.

(a) Turn over manually.

(b) Check lubricating oil level.

(c) Check fuel tank. Drain off water.

(d) Ensure engine starting arrangements are operable and in good condition, i.e. check air start receiver pressure and drain oil and water. Check and run compressor.

(e) Check cooling arrangements.

(f) Start and run auxiliary generator off load for five minutes and then on load for half an hour. Check all temperatures and pressures during run including cooling medium, oil and exhaust.

Q.8 List some causes of corrosion in boilers and methods to reduce the effects of corrosion.

A. (a) Air and carbon dioxide gas entering the boilers with the feedwater.

(b) Acids contained in the oils used for engine lubrication entering the boilers with feedwater.

(c) Sea water entering boilers due to leaky condensers. Sea water contains magnesium chloride which when dissociated (at 193°C) forms hydrochloric acid.

(d) Galvanic action caused by different materials in the boiler.

A contact feed heater installed in the feedwater system separates and liberates the air and CO_2 from the feedwater. A closed feed system, as used in conjunction with water tube boilers is advantageous in excluding air and carbon dioxide.

Efficient filters of towelling, matting or coke will prevent oils and fats entering the boilers.

To prevent seawater entering the boiler ensure that the condenser is well maintained and in good condition. If sea water has entered the boiler lime or soda should be added to the feedwater. This neutralises the acid formed by the sea water. Soda also softens hard scale.

To neutralise the effects of galvanic action zinc plates (anodes) may be fitted inside the boiler.

N.B. STEAM PAPER ONLY

Q.9 Explain how a steam engine is reversed with Stephenson's link motion.

A. When the eccentric rod is in line with the valve rod the travel of the valve is equal to two laps plus two port openings. When the link motion is in mid position, i.e., when the ahead eccentric rod and astern eccentric rod are equidistant on either side of the valve rod, the travel of the valve is equal to top lap plus top lead PLUS bottom lap plus bottom lead (two laps plus two leads).

Thus, as the link motion is being brought toward mid position the travel of the valve is being reduced.

With Stephenson's gear reduced valve travel makes all events occur earlier,

i.e. - lead, cut-off, release and closing to exhaust all occur earlier.

Hence as the gear goes over from ahead to astern the engine will slow up as the link reaches mid position then remains stationary until the astern eccentric rod and valve rod approach in line position.

N.B. STEAM PAPER ONLY

Q.10 Describe, with the aid of sketches steam turbine governor and emergency steam shut down arrangements.

A. Turbine Governor in conjunction with a Bulkhead steam stop valve.

The forced lube oil passes through the lantern plug and floating sleeve, shown on right, and keeps the latter lubricated. On the limit revolutions speed being exceeded the springs are pulled out radially by centrifugal force and the governor face valves separate and are locked open by the pawls, thus relieving the oil pressure, which has the instant effect of closing the stop valves as described elsewhere. To close the governor valves and allow the emergency stop valve to re-open, the

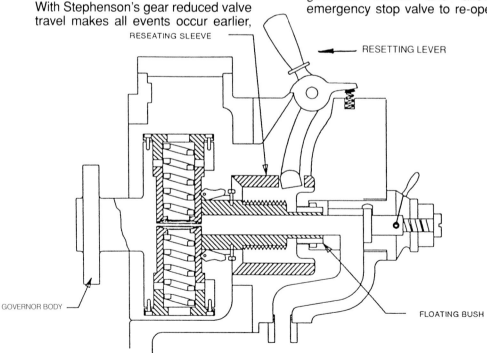

RESEATING SLEEVE

RESETTING LEVER

GOVERNOR BODY

FLOATING BUSH

Figure 90 – *Typical Turbine Governor*

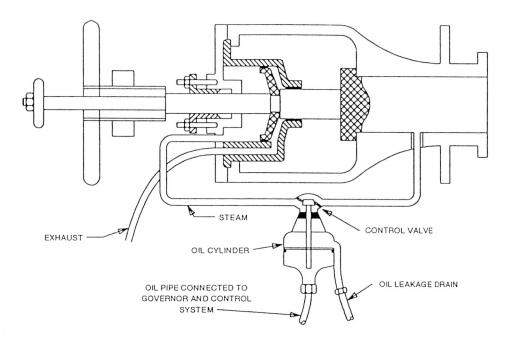

EXHAUST

STEAM

CONTROL VALVE

OIL CYLINDER

OIL PIPE CONNECTED TO
GOVERNOR AND CONTROL
SYSTEM

OIL LEAKAGE DRAIN

Figure 91 – *Bulkhead Stop Valve*

resetting lever is moved forward when the bevelled edge on the resetting sleeve comes in contact with the pawls and depresses same, which unlocks the governor valves, and the springs act to close them face to face.

The bulkhead piston operated type valve shuts when the oil pressure back of the piston drops.

This can be caused by

1. Forced lubrication pressure failure

The load on the underside of the pressure breaking relay is reduced. The piston in the oil cylinder being no longer supported the control valve is opened and in turn exhausts the pressure from the underside of the main valve piston closing down the main steam valve.

2. Governors acting due to overspeed on the turbines

When the turbines reach a predetermined speed the governor cuts out, permitting oil pressure to drop at the governor and then at the pressure breaking relay valve, the main valve then closing down as described already.

3. Turbine rotor having excessive end movement

When excessive end movement fore and aft develops in a rotor the governor bush moves thus uncovering the port in the index bush and drops oil pressure. After that the main valve closes down as before.

4. Hand emergency control lever being operated

The oil pressure from the forced lube oil supply is cut off. The main valve then closing down as before.

5. Loss of vacuum

As it is also desirable to guard against loss of vacuum a further arrangement has been developed. When the vacuum in the condenser falls below a predetermined pressure the vacuum control unit is brought into operation by the flexible disc which deflects and operates the levers which in turn open the steam control valve and exhaust the pressure from the underside of the emergency valve piston. The main valve then closing down.

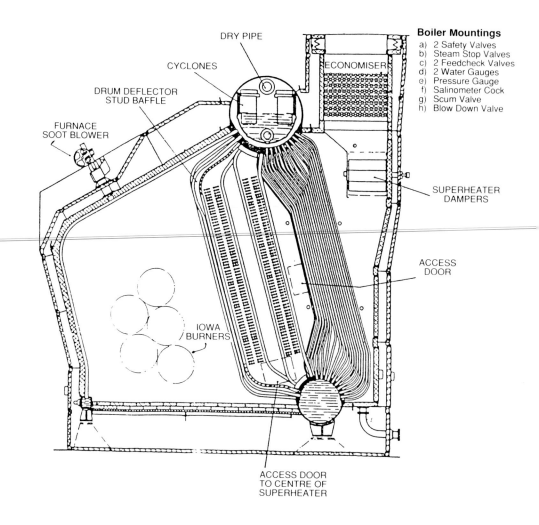

DRY PIPE

CYCLONES

DRUM DEFLECTOR
STUD BAFFLE

FURNACE
SOOT BLOWER

ECONOMISER

Boiler Mountings
a) 2 Safety Valves
b) Steam Stop Valves
c) 2 Feedcheck Valves
d) 2 Water Gauges
e) Pressure Gauge
f) Salinometer Cock
g) Scum Valve
h) Blow Down Valve

SUPERHEATER
DAMPERS

ACCESS
DOOR

IOWA
BURNERS

ACCESS DOOR
TO CENTRE OF
SUPERHEATER

Figure 92 – *Typical selectable-superheat boiler*

Q.11 Describe, with the aid of a sketch, a typical marine "water tube" main boiler. List the various boiler mountings.

A. Boiler Mountings
   a) 2 Safety Valves
   b) Steam Stop Valves
   c) 2 Feedcheck Valves
   d) 2 Water Gauges
   e) Pressure Gauge
   f) Salinometer Cock
   g) Scum Valve
   h) Blow Down Valve

This boiler offers controlled superheat over a large range. Furnace design is advantageous for utilizing heat available. The main generating surface consists of three rows of tubes before the superheater and twenty rows of smaller diameter tubes after the superheater. Sidewall tubes curve over and form the roof of the furnace. A stud tube baffle wall between the superheater and saturated sections also supports the refractory material. Steam temperature control is by two gas flow dampers which divert the gas flow. Side and back walls consist of large diameter downcomers, which help rapid circulation. The double casing space forms the air passage for air to the burner registers.

N.B. STEAM PAPER ONLY

Q.12 Describe, with the aid of a sketch, if necessary, the following terms:

(a) Tumble home

(b) Freeboard

(c) Camber

(d) Depth (moulded)

(e) Metacentric height

(f) The effect of 'slack tanks' on the stability of a vessel.

A.   (a) The inwards curvature of the hull surface above the waterline.

    (b) The vertical distance between the actual (or permissible) waterline and the upper surface of the deck at the side to which it is measured.

    (c) The transverse curvature given to decks.

(d) The vertical height amidships from the top of the bar or plate keel at the centreline to the top of the deck beam at the side.

(e) The transverse metacentric height is equal to the distance between the transverse metacentre (M) and the centre of gravity (G) and is represented by GM.

(f) Slack tanks cause free surface effect which effectively raises the centre of gravity (G) and thus reduces the metacentric height (GM). This reduces the righting lever and increases the angle of heel.

Q.13 Describe, with the aid of a sketch, a fixed Kort Nozzle, and discuss its advantages.

Increases in thrust of up to 50% are claimed using a Kort nozzle plus up to 10% speed increases for similar power. In rough seas the effects of pitching on propulsive efficiency are markedly less.

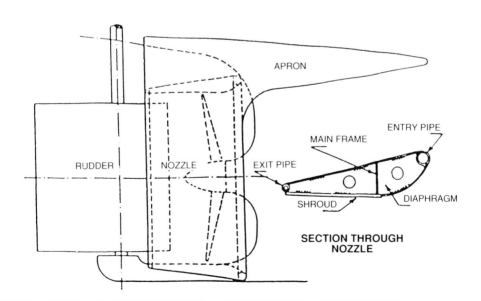

FIXED KORT NOZZLE

Figure 93 – *Fixed Kort Nozzle*

Q.14 Describe the action of a centrifugal pump suitable for bilge and ballast duties. How is the pump primed on starting and if the suction is lost while working?

A. In a centrifugal pump liquid enters the centre or eye of the impeller, and flows radially out between the vanes, its velocity being increased by the impeller rotation. A diffuser or volute is then used to convert most of the kinetic energy in the liquid into pressure.

Centrifugal pumps are not self priming and require means of removing air from the suction pipeline and filling it with liquid.

When the pump is below the water level this is easily accomplished by providing an air bleed cock, alternatively an air pumping unit can be provided.

Q.15 Describe, with the aid of a sketch, a hydraulic steering gear telemotor control arrangement.

A. This system consists of a transmitter on the bridge and receiver (motor cylinder) in the steering gear space connected to the valve operating gear. Movement of the transmitter piston displaces liquid causing the receiver to move a corresponding amount. The spring causes the telemotor to return to midship position when the wheel is let go.

Rods are connected to the crosshead at one end of the cylinder which attach to the control gear of the steering engine.

Q.16 What steps should be taken to prevent oil pollution when a vessel is in port, and at sea.

A. (a) Keep bilges clean and free from oil
(b) Regular check for oil leaks throughout the machinery and all storage areas.
(c) Repair oil leaks as soon as possible
(d) All waste oil and oily rags to be sent ashore for disposal.

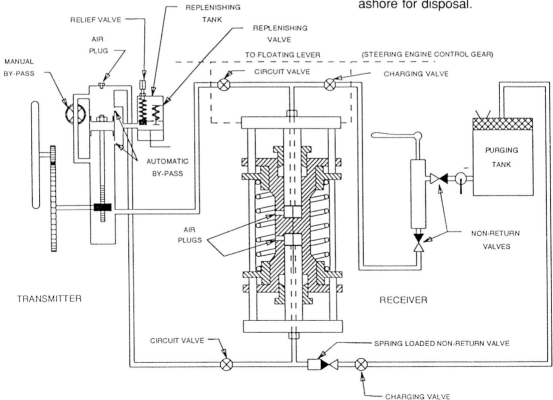

Figure 94 – *Typical Telemotor Gear*

(e) A proper watch to be kept when bunkering or transferring oil.

(f) Oil drums to be kept securely retained.

(g) Oil spills to be retained on the vessel and cleaned up as soon as possible.

(h) No oil or oily waste to be dumped over the side.

Q.17 What attention do compressed-air reservoirs require? If corrosion takes place, state where it generally occurs and how it is caused.

A. Compressed-air reservoirs should be opened up for inspection every twelve months and the various fittings overhauled every two years, or more often if required. The reservoirs should be thoroughly cleaned internally and carefully examined for corrosion which, when it occurs, generally takes place along the bottom of the reservoir, and sometimes around the main stop-valve. Corrosion is generally caused by condensation of the moisture held in suspension in the air delivered by the air-compressing machines. Another probable cause of corrosion is decomposition of the compounded oil, sometimes used to lubricate the pistons of the air compressor, by the high compression temperatures, resulting in the formation of acids which attack the internal surfaces of the air reservoirs. For this reason all traces of lubricating oil inside air reservoirs should be removed, and after the reservoirs have been wiped dry they should be coated with a good quality anti-corrosive paint suitable for this purpose.

ELECTROTECHNOLOGY

Q.1 Enumerate the major components of an alternator. Explain how alternating current is produced and how the frequency of the supply may be determined.

A. Compounded A.C. Generator with D.C. Exciter.

   a. Outer casing (yoke)
   b. Main Poles
   c. Main Armature core
   d. Commutator
   e. D.C. Winding
   f. Stationary unwound compensator core
   g. Rotating compensator core
   h. A.C. Winding
   i. Sliprings
   j. Bearings

Generation of Electromotive force is accomplished by a conductor of electricity moving across a magnetic field i.e. the armature moving across the magnetic field produced by the poles. This electricity is collected through the A.C. Windings and transmitted through the sliprings.

Current frequency is determined using a frequency meter which measures the cycles per second produced by the supply alternator.

Q.2 (a) Describe, with the aid of a sketch, a typical small ship's Extra Low Voltage (D.C.) Electrical Installation.

(b) What care and maintenance is necessary to keep the ship's batteries in good condition.

A.

a) Main switch is a linked double pole switch. Each sub circuit is controlled (switch or circuit breaker) and protected (fuse or circuit breaker).

Navigation lights are also individually switched and fused (or circuit breakers).

Other individual sub circuits are supplied with fuse or C.B. protection.

b) (i) Cells must be kept fully charged.
   (ii) Electrolyte level must be kept above the plates.
   (iii) Terminals must be kept clean and free of corrosion.
   (iv) The charge and discharge rate should not exceed the manufacturer's recommendation.
   (v) Impurities should not be allowed to enter the cells.
   (vi) Connections to the terminals should be kept clean and tight.

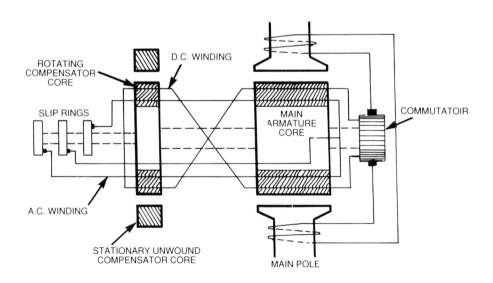

Figure 95 – *Typical Alternator (3 Phase) with exciter*

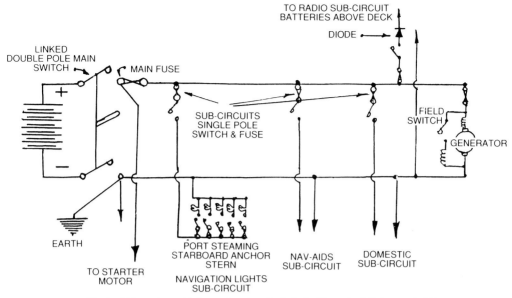

Figure 96 –*Typical Extra Low Voltage (under 32v) D.C. Electrical Schematic Diagram*

Q.3 What dangers are associated with the connection of shore power to a vessel. List the various devices which would be incorporated on board the vessel to lessen these dangers.

(a) Incorrect polarity/phase sequence

(b) Active lead to earth; Discontinuity of earth conductor

(c) Incorrect frequency/voltage

(d) Overload

Incorrect polarity. A polarity indicator/phase sequence indicator.

Active lead to earth or Discontinuity of earth conductor - Earth continuity testing and active conductor test facility.

Incorrect frequency/voltage - frequency meter, voltmeter.

Overload - Linked circuit breaker at the connection facility.

A light to indicate when shore power is connected is also provided at the main switchboard.

As well as damage being caused to electrical machinery by faults (a) and (b) the latter could also cause the hull to become live with inherent danger to human life. The former could cause, in a three phase system, motors to run in the wrong direction. Faults (c) and (d) also would cause damage to electrical machinery. For instance, should a 60 Hz supply be provided to a 50Hz system all motors will run at 20 per cent overspeed and all centrifugal loads will increase 73 percent.

Overheating of electrical components would take place with both (c) and (d).

Q.4. Describe, with the aid of a sketch, the construction and operation of a silicon diode rectifier unit.

A. Construction

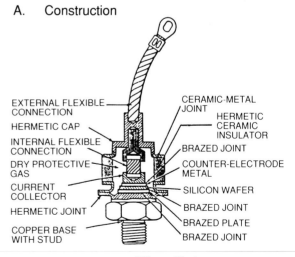

Figure 96a –*Silicon Diode*

Operation

If current operation is applied to the positive (p) side of the rectifier the current will flow readily and resistance to the current flow will be low. If the polarity is reversed, resistance to current flow will be high and only a negligible current will pass. Therefore if an A.C. voltage is applied the current will flow during one half cycle but will be blocked during the other half cycle. This is the basis of the semi conductor rectifier.

Q.5 Describe with the aid of a sketch the operation of a meter for measuring voltage or amperage.

A. Moving Coil Meter.

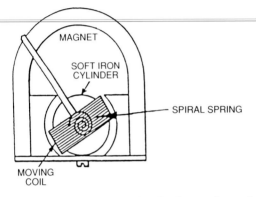

Figure 97 –*Diagramatic sketch of a moving coil meter*

The ends of the coil are brought out at each end and connected to spiral springs. These springs lead the current in and out and provide control for the meter.

When current passes through the coil this tends to produce a mechanical force which rotates the moving coil across the field of the permanent magnet, and the amplitude of the force is proportional to the current. The amount of rotation is limited by the springs.

Damping is provided by eddy currents set up in the frame carrying the coil.

This instrument is suitable for measuring D.C. values only because if current is passed the other way the coils operate (rotate) in the reverse direction.

Moving coil meters have uniform scales.

PART II

MATHEMATICS

Q.1 A safety valve is 55 mm in diameter, and the receiver pressure is 0.6 MPa. The uniform lever weighs 5 kgs. The valve and spindle weighs 2 kgs.

If the lever is 550 mm long and the valve is 65 mm from the fulcrum, find the load (W) required to hang from the end of the lever.

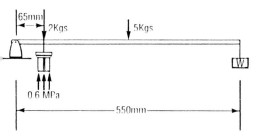

Figure 98

A. Area of valve $= \Pi r^2 = 3.142 \times 27.5^2$

$= 2376.14$ mm^2

and taking moments about 0

Clockwise moments = Anticlockwise moments

$(W \times 550) + (5 \times 275) + (2 \times 65) = (0.6 \times 2376.14 \times 65) \div 9.81$

$9266.95 = 550W + 1375 + 130$

$9266.95 = 550W + 1505$

$\dfrac{9266.95 - 1505}{550} = W = 14.11$ Kgs

Q.2. (a) Given that the electrical resistance (R) of a conductor varies directly as its length and inversely as its cross sectional area, find the resistance in a conductor which has twice the cross sectional area and three times the length of a conductor of similar material having a resistance of 9.5 ohms.

(b) In a lighting circuit the current is 2 amps and resistance is 12 ohms.

(i) Find the voltage (potential difference)

(ii) Find the power in watts.

(c) A circuit has three resistances in parallel

$r = 8\ \Omega$

$r = 16\ \Omega$

$r = ?\ \Omega$

Figure 99

Two of the three resistances values are 8 ohms. and 16 ohms, what would be the value of the third resistance if the equivalent resistance (R) is 4 ohms?

A. (a) Resistance of conductor

$= \dfrac{9.5 \times 3}{2} = 14.25$ ohms

(b) $I = \dfrac{E}{R}$

(i) $E = R \times I = 12 \times 2 = 24$ Volts

(ii) $W = I.E. = 2 \times 24 = 48$ watts

(c) $\dfrac{1}{4} = \dfrac{1}{8} + \dfrac{1}{16} + \dfrac{1}{x}$

$\dfrac{4}{16} = \dfrac{2}{16} + \dfrac{1}{16} + \dfrac{1}{x}$

$\dfrac{1}{x} = \dfrac{1}{16} = 16$ ohms

Q.3. (a) A three-phase motor operating off a 415 V system is developing 18KW at an efficiency of 87% and a power factor of 0.82. Calculate: (a) the line current if the windings are delta-connected. Given that input power in watts $= 1.73\ I_L V_L \times$ p.f.

(b) An Electrical Circuit has a diversity factor (maximum demand factor) of 0.8. If the power available is 50 K.V.A., what would be the maximum total load in K.V.A.?

A. (a) Since efficiency $= \dfrac{\text{output power in watts}}{\text{input power in watts}}$

$= \dfrac{KWBP \times 1000}{1.73 I_L V_L \times \text{p.f.}}$

$\therefore 0.87 = \dfrac{18 \times 1000}{1.73 \times I_L \times 415 \times 0.82}$

$\therefore$ line current $= I_L = 35.14A$

(b) $0.8 \times \dfrac{50}{x}$ $\quad \therefore x = \dfrac{50}{0.8} = 62.8$ K.V.A.

Q.4. A ring is made of round bar 75 mm in diameter, the inside diameter being 200 mm. Find the mass if a cubic metre of the material weighs 7750 kg.

A.   Mean Diameter = 200 + 75 = 275 mm

Mean Circumference = ΠD = 863.94 mm

Sectional area = Πr^2

= Π x 37.5^2

= 4417. 86 mm^2

Material Volume = $\dfrac{417.86 \times 863.94}{10^9}$ m^3

Mass = 3.8167 x 10^3 x 7750

= 29.58 k

Q.5 A stay is 50 mm in diameter. The ultimate tensile stress of the material is 443 MPa. Find the safe working load in tonnes if the factor of safety is 6.5.

$$\text{Safe Working Stress} = \frac{\text{U.T.S}}{\text{Factor of safety}}$$

A. Stay Diam = 50 mm   UTS = 443 MPa

F.O.S. = 6.5

Safe Working Stress = $\dfrac{\text{UTS}}{\text{FOS}}$ = $\dfrac{443}{6.5}$ = 68.15 MPa

Find Safe load in tonnes

Area = Πr^2 = 3.142 x 25^2 = 1963.75 mm^2

and $\dfrac{\text{MPA}}{.00981}$ = tonnes/m^2 = 6946.99

tonnes/mm^2 = $\dfrac{6946.99}{1000 \times 1000}$

and Safe W.L. = $\dfrac{6946.9.9}{1000 \times 1000}$ x 1963.75

S.W.L. Stay 13.64 tonnes

Q.6 Compare the strength under torsion of a solid shaft 150 mm in diameter with a shaft 120 mm in diameter. State as a percentage how much one is stronger than the other. Strength varies as the cube of the diameter.

Strength αD^3

150^3 : 120^3

3,375,000 : 1,728,000

= $\dfrac{3375000}{172800}$

= 1.95 : 1

the 150mm diameter shaft is 95% stronger than the 120mm shaft.

Q.7 A vessel travels a distance of 13 nautical miles up river against the current in 82 minutes and then returns down river for the same distance in 70 minutes.

Find:-

(a) average speed up river;

(b) average speed down river;

(c) the speed of the current; and

(d) the average speed for the round trip.

A.   Average speed up river = $\dfrac{\text{Distance}}{\text{Time}}$

= $\dfrac{13 \times 60}{82}$ = 9.51 Knots

Average speed down river = $\dfrac{13 \times 60}{70}$

= 11.14.Knots

Average speed of current = $\dfrac{11.14 - 9.51}{2}$

= 0.82 Knots

Average speed for round trip - $\dfrac{26}{\left(\dfrac{82 + 70}{60}\right)}$

= 10.26 Knots

Q.8 A ship travelling at 15 knots leaves port 12 hours before another vessel travelling at 18 knots. How far will they travel before the second overtakes the first?

Ship 1 = 15 knots   Speed x time = distance

Ship 2 = 18 knots

15 (t + 12) = 18 x t

15 t + 180 =18t

180 = 18t– 15t   180 = 3t

and t = $\dfrac{180}{3}$

= 60 Hours

Q.9 A cylindrical oil tank measures inside 1 metre diameter. When the depth of oil in the tank is 1.30 metres, what mass of oil with a density of 820 kg/m3 will it contain?

$\Pi r2$ x 1.3 x .82

= 0.84 tonnes.

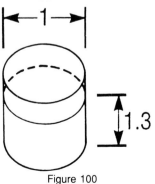

Figure 100

Q.10 If a tank is 2.1 metres long and 1.26 metres wide, what mass of oil in tonnes at a density of 902 kg/m3 would be in the tank when the sounding was 1500 mm?

A. Tank Volume = L x B x D

= 2.1 x 1.26 x 1.5 = 3.97M³

mass of oil = $\dfrac{3.97 \times 902}{1000}$

= 3.58 Tonnes

Q.11 A feed pump can pump out a tank in 12 hours and a ballast pump can pump it out in 3 hours. If both pumps are used together, how long will it take to empty the same tank?

A. Total capacities per hour =$\dfrac{1}{12} + \dfrac{1}{3} = \dfrac{5}{12}$

Total time to pump out = $\dfrac{12}{5}$ = 2.4 hours

Q.12 A vessel burns 177 grams of fuel per kW brake power per hour. The daily consumption of fuel is 1.75 tonnes.

(a) What would be the B.P. of the engine?

(b) Given that the specific gravity of the fuel = 0.82 what volume in litres would be consumed by the engine per hour?

A. (a) $\dfrac{1.75 \times 1000 \times 1000}{177 \times 24}$ = 412 B.P.

(b) $\dfrac{177 \times 412 \times 1000}{1000 \times 1000 \times .82}$ = 88.93 litres

Q.13 A vessel has a propeller with 600 mm pitch. What would be the speed of the vessel in knots if the shaft revolutions were 800 per minute and neglecting slip? The actual speed of the vessel was found to be 13.7 knots. What has been the percentage slip?

A. 1852 m = 1 n. mile

= $\dfrac{600 \times 800 \times 60}{1000 \times 1852}$ = 15.55 Knots

% slip $\dfrac{15.55 - 13.7}{15.55}$ = 12%

Q.14 A boiler makes 20,000 kg of steam per day with a heat value of 9,000 kilojoules per kilogram of steam. The efficiency of the boiler is 0.736. Given that the fuel has a heat value of 41,770 kilojoules per kilogram, how much fuel would the boiler consume in tonnes per day?

A. Efficiency = $\dfrac{\text{Heat out}}{\text{Heat in}} = \dfrac{20{,}000 \times 9000}{1000 \times 41770 \times X} = .736$

X = $\dfrac{20000 \times 9000}{.736 \times 1000 \times 41770}$

= 5.855 tonnes

N.B. STEAM PAPER ONLY

Q.15 The diameter of an I.P. cylinder of a double acting steam engine is 680 mm and the stroke is 1 metre. The I.M.E.P. is 0.55 mpa and the revolutions are 104 per minute. Find the indicated power in kilowatts.

A. I.P. = PLAN

= $550 \times 10^3 \times 1 \times \Pi \times .34^2 \times \dfrac{104}{60}$ = Watts

I.P. = 346.22 KW x 2

= 692.44 KWP

N.B. STEAM PAPER ONLY

Q.16 The four stroke single acting diesel engine has eight cylinders. The M.E.P. being 690 kPa, cylinder diameter 200 mm, stroke 280mm, and revolutions per minute being 1400. Find the Brake Power.

A. I.P. = PLAN (watts)

= $690 \times 10^3 \times 0.28 \times \Pi \times 0.1 \times 0.1 \times 8 \times \dfrac{1400}{2 \times 60}$

I.P. = $\dfrac{566565.5}{1000}$ = KW = 566.6 K.W.

B.P. = 566.6 x .8

B.P. = 453.25 KWBP

N.B. MOTOR PAPER ONLY

ENGINEERING

Q.1 Can pre-ignition of fuel occur in a diesel engine? If so, how?

A. Preignition can occur only by the fuel being injected too early relative to the crank position. This may be caused by the fuel injection valve leaking or opening too early.

NOTE- The point at which injection of fuel begins depends upon the rotational speed of the engine, it being about 15° before top dead centre in fast-running engines and 3° in slow-running engines.

N.B. MOTOR PAPER ONLY

Q.2 When fuel is injected into the cylinder of a diesel engine, does an explosion, or in other words a rapid increase in pressure, occur? If not, why?

A. An explosion does not occur because ignition of fuel is timed to begin when the piston is commencing the outward stroke and the volume of the space available for the expanding gases is consequently increasing. Moreover, the admission of fuel takes place over a comparatively long period and the rise in pressure caused by the burning fuel can be controlled.

N.B. MOTOR PAPER ONLY

Q.3 Of what material are fuel-valve rocking-lever rollers made? What part of the machining operation is very important, and why?

A. The rollers are made of case-hardened steel. The hole for the case-hardened pin must be absolutely central, otherwise the fuel injection valve may be lifted a varying amount.

N.B. MOTOR PAPER ONLY

Q.4 (a) Why is a gauze diaphragm fitted on the outlet of a fuel tank vent?

(b) What is the meaning of the following in regard to diesel fuel?

(i) closed flash point;

(ii) calorific value; and

(iii) specific gravity.

A. (a) The gauze diaphragm prevents flame entry into the vent, should expanding gases from the tank be accidentally ignited. The gauze prevents the passage of flame by dispersing the heat.

(b) (i) Closed flashpoint is a test carried out on fuel in a closed vessel to indicate the temperature at which that fuel will ignite.

(ii) Calorific value is the amount of heat given by a specified quantity of fuel.

(iii) Specific Gravity is the relative weight of fuel expressed by a ratio of given volume to the same volume of fresh water.

Q.5 Describe, with the aid of a sketch, an instrument suitable for measuring alternating current.

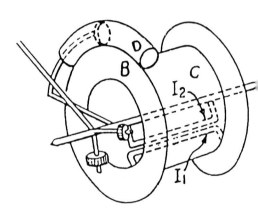

Figure 101 – *Moving Iron Meter*

A. "B" is the flange of an insulating bobbin on which is wound a coil of insulated wire "C". Inside this bobbin a strip of soft iron 1_1 is attached. Soft iron strip 1_2 is attached to the bearing mounted spindle. The pointer is attached to this spindle. When current flows through the coil (c) both iron strips become magnetized in the same direction. As they are magnetized in the same direction and as like poles repel the moveable iron moves away from the fixed iron moving the pointer with it. The greater the current, the greater the repulsion force and therefore the further the movement. A damper (D) is connected to the pointer spindle.

Q.6 Describe the role sensors play in the operation of control equipment and the extraneous effects to be considered by or on the sensor.

A. Sensors play an essential role in all systems for transmitting information to control and other remote positions. The quantities necessary to sense include counting, fluid flow, humidity, liquid levels, noise, position, pressure, salinity, smoke density, speed, strain, temperature, viscosity, torque, power, etc.

The type of sensor must take into account the relative importance of the effect of its presence on the quantity to be measured, together with the extraneous effects by or on the sensor. For example:

1. It should not affect the quantity to be measured, e.g. flow metering.

2. The effect of ambient and adjacent temperatures should be either known or be capable of elimination.

3. Speed of response in respect to rapid changes.

4. Independence from magnetic fields, humidity, barometric pressure, local heat.

5. Independence from variations of electrical supplies (e.g. frequency and voltage) or be provided with means for compensating for variations.

6. Linearity, hysteresis, repeatability and zero-point drift are also important.

Sensors may be required to initiate mechanical operation, for example, such as the high forces required to operate cargo valves in tankers and for hatch closing and opening and as most sensors cannot provide the mechanical effort required this can be provided via transducers. The electrical or pneumatic signals obtained from them can in turn operate alarms, relays or instruments. Bourdon tubes, diaphragms and floats can provide sufficient power to operate instruments directly or can act as transducers.

Q.7 Describe, with the aid of a sketch, a typical bilge pumping and fire fighting system for a vessel.

The pumping system shown includes sea water pumping arrangements.

The system includes suctions to each main space through S.D.N.R. valves and drains from the fore and aft spaces.

This system may be operated using the power pump or hand pump and may be operated from deck if necessary.

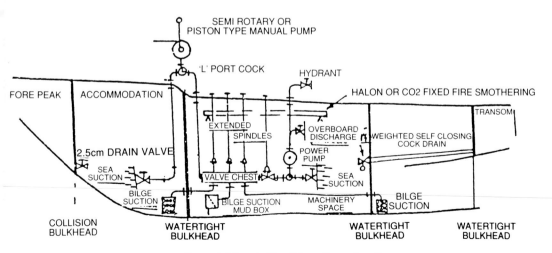

Figure 102 – *Typical Bilge & Fire Water Pumping System*

Q.8 (a) Describe what is meant by the following terms:-
(i)   free surface effect;
(ii)   righting moment; and
(iii) vessel is 'tender'.
(b) What effect does the flooding of a space have on the stability of a vessel?

A.   (a) (i) Free Surface Effect

When a tank on board a ship is not completely full of liquid, and the vessel heels the liquid moves in the same direction as the heeling. This effects the centre of gravity by moving it away from the centreline, reduces the righting lever and increases the angle of heel further.

(ii) Righting Moment

Is caused by the buoyancy of the vessel tending to right the vessel when the vessel is inclined by an external force. The centre of gravity stays in the same position but the centre of buoyancy moves - this creates a righting lever.

(iii) Vessel is 'Tender'.

A vessel is said to be tender when the metacentric height is small and causes instability in extreme cases when the metacentric height is negative.

A tender vessel is slow to right when heeled.

(b) The flooding of a space creates "free surface effect" and has an adverse effect on the stability of a vessel as explained above.

Q.9 In regard to two types of fire extinguishers, explain:-
(a) how they are used; and
(b) the type of fires they can be used on.

A.   Dry Chemical (cartridge operated or stored pressure)

(i) Pull pin and free nozzle

(ii) Point nozzle at the base of the fire and pull the trigger.

Use for the following fires -
Type A. Ordinary combustibles (wood and paper etc.)
Type B. Flammable Liquids
Type C. Flammable Gases
Type E. Electrical Fires
Foam type (stored pressure)

(i) Hold vertical.

(ii) Pull pin and free nozzle.

(iii) Direct stream to spray on flame.

Use for the following fires -
Type A. Ordinary combustibles (wood and paper etc.)
Type B. Flammable Liquids

Q.10 Describe, with a sketch if necessary, the safety and control features you would expect to find in a small vessel D.C. electrical system and indicate the type of system being described.

A.   Earthed negative pole system.

(a) Control and protection.

(i) Double pole linked main switch immediately on the load side of the batteries.

(ii) Main fuse immediately on the load side of the main switch in the positive pole only for the main switchboard power supply conductors

(iii) Sub-circuit isolating switches, single pole, and fuses on the supply side of the switches.

(iv) Navigation lights. Individually switched and fuses in the positive poles.

(v) Other individual circuits provided with fuse protection.

N.B. All control and protection may be provided by suitable circuit breakers in lieu of switches and fuses.

(b) Conductors. Would be double insulated or single insulated and run in conduit, and would be of higher current carrying capacity than the associated fuse rating.

Conductors would also be adequately supported and protected from abrasion or mechanical damage.

(c) Batteries.

Situated in a suitable tray (G.R.P.) to prevent spillage in an accessible and well vented area.

Q.11 What is meant by the term "diversity factor" in regard to an electrical circuit?

A.   Diversity Factor.

In a multi-use circuit which incorporates various power using devices it is apparent that many of them will not be in use at the same time.

The feeder cabling and protection may then be rated on an estimation of probable maximum loading. The diversity factor used is less than unity and is based on the percentage of maximum use, i.e. if only 60% of the total applicable power demand is the probable maximum loading then a diversity factor of 0.6 may be used. A diversity factor is not permitted in the final sub-circuit.

Q.12 Describe, with the aid of sketches if necessary, an alternating current shore power connection facility for a vessel.

A.   Where arrangements are made for the supply of electricity from a source on shore or elsewhere, a suitable connection box is to be installed in a position on the ship suitable for the convenient reception of flexible cables for the external source. This should contain a circuit breaker and terminals of ample size and suitable shape to facilitate a satisfactory connection. Suitable cables, permanently fixed, are to be provided by connecting the terminals to a suitable changeover switch at the main switchboard.

The circuit breaker should operate in all live conductors and be of the linked type, i.e. for 415 V 3 phase system a 4 pole linked C.B. would be required and for 240 V single phase system a 2 pole linked C.B. would be required.

An effective earth terminal is to be provided for connecting the hull to the shore earth.

The shore connection is to be provided with an indicator at the main switchboard in order to show when the cable is energized.

Means are to be provided for checking the phase sequences (for three phase alternating current) of the incoming supply in relation to the vessel's system.

In the case of single phase installation, efficient arrangements are to be provided to ensure proper connection of the shore supply to the vessel's system.

At the connection box, a notice is to be provided giving full information on the system of supply and the normal voltage and frequency of the ship's system and the procedure for carrying out the connection. The cable shall not be a permanent fixture.

The phase rotation/polarity changeover switch and indicators are to be positioned on the supply side of the ship/shore power changeover switch.

A separate test facility is to be provided adjacent to the shore power connection unit with labelled instructions. The test facility is to be used to test the shore lead for a continuous shore earth connection and to test that the earth pin in the shore power lead socket is not active.

Q.13 Describe, with the aid of a sketch, a typical steering arrangement for a vessel. What emergency steering arrangements would be fitted?

A.   Ram type hydraulic steering gear

The tiller is keyed to the rudder stock and has two arms, which are designed to convert linear movement of the rams to the rotary movement of the tiller arms and rudder stock.

This arrangement is generally used on small to large ships.

Hydraulic pressure is supplied by variable delivery pumps, with electric motor drive, running at constant speed in the same direction. Pumps may be of the Hele-Shaw radial piston type or of the axial piston V.S.G. In both, the stroke of the pump pistons can be varied and flow of oil to and from the pump can be reversed. When the operating rod of the pump is in mid position, there is no flow of oil.

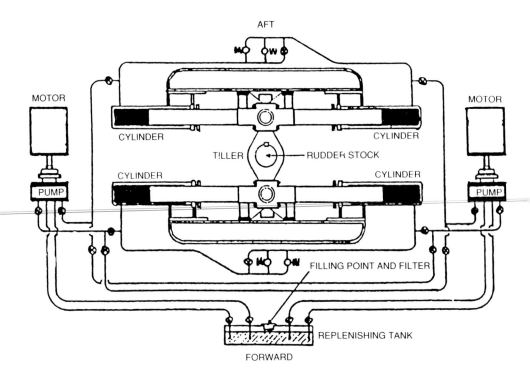

Figure 103 – *Typical Power Steering System (Pump controls not indicated)*

Control of the system is by telemotor transmitter at the centre position which hydraulically signals the receiver which controls the operating rod of the pump and operates the steering engine.

Smaller vessels may have a single hydraulic ram operating the tiller arm which is direct hydraulically connected to the wheel cylinder transmitter.

As can be seen from the sketch two (2) hydraulic pumps are provided and the system will operate on one (1). The hydraulic telemotor control may be bypassed in case of malfunction and a rod and bevel gear emergency control engaged to the operating rod as emergency steering.

In the case of smaller vessels generally an emergency tiller which attaches to the rudder stock head is provided.

Q.14 Sketch and describe a fuel pump as fitted to a diesel engine. How does it regulate the timing and quantity of fuel supplied and how is it adjusted?

A. Helix or Jerk type fuel pump. This type of pump with small variations is used in many diesel engines.

The pump consists of a cam operated, single acting plunger of fixed stroke. Helical springs are fitted to return the plunger on its down stroke and to maintain contact of follower on the cam.

No timing valves are required and fuel delivery commences at a fixed point on the up stroke when the top edge of the plunger blanks off the suction port. A helix or scroll is machined on the plunger and delivery of fuel ceases on the up stroke, when the curved surface of the helix uncovers the suction port. This allows fuel pressure above the plunger to fall to the suction pressure through a vertical slot or hole.

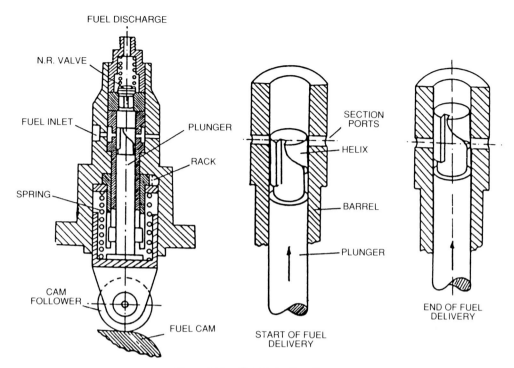

Figure 104 – *Fuel Injection Pump*

The quantity of fuel delivered is regulated by the vertical length of the helix where it is in line with the suction port. This setting may be altered by rotating the plunger.

A rack is fitted to the pump to engage with a pinion machined on the outside of a sleeve. The sleeve fits over the plunger and has slots engaging with keys. In this way the plunger may be rotated by movements of the rack.

The fuel cam is designed to raise the plunger at the rate required to build up fuel pressure and maintain this for the corresponding period to operate the fuel injector. Since the pump only discharges on its up stroke, only one flank of the cam operates the timing. The trailing flank of the cam returns the plunger to the bottom of its stroke to allow the chamber to refill.

N.B. MOTOR PAPER ONLY

Q.15 Describe, with the aid of a sketch, a typical bottom end arrangement.

A.	In the conventional design of marine type bottom end the palm end of the rod matches the bearing housing. If this type of rod is to be drawn up through the cylinder bore the limits to bearing size are obvious. The modified design shown in which the palm end is smaller than the bearing housing and is attached by separate studs, overcomes the problem to some extent.

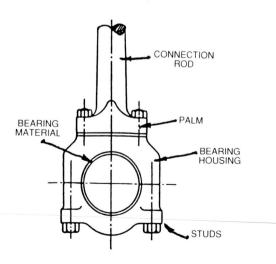

Figure 105 – *Bottom End*

Materials.

Connecting Rod = Forged Plain Carbon Steel

Bearing Housing = Plain Carbon Steel-Case

Studs (bolts) = Rolled low alloy steel bar

Bearing Material = Tin based whitemetal alloyed with cadmium or nickel.

The piston and rod may be lifted for maintenance on this arrangement without "splitting" the bottom end bearing. The palm bolts only need to be undone.

N.B. MOTOR PAPER ONLY

Q.16 Sketch and describe a type of water level indicator suitable for use on high pressure water tube boilers.

A. All boilers must have at least two independent means of indicating the water level, and in the case of high pressure water tube boilers working at values above 3400kN/m², these usually take the form of double-sided, plate glass type water level indicators, with mica protection for the glass plates. This protection is necessary as at high pressures hot distilled water erodes the glass away, and unless a sheet of mica is placed between the glass and the water, attack takes place quickly, indeed at the higher pressure ranges the glass will burst within a few hours if this protection is omitted.

Q.17 Sketch and describe a vertical smoke tube boiler suitable for auxiliary purposes.

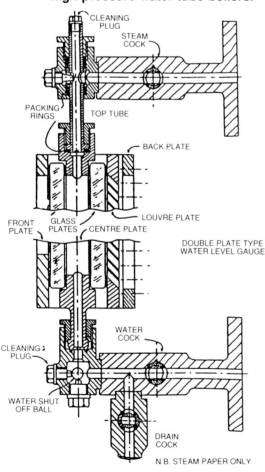

Figure 106 – *High pressure boiler water gauge glass – Diagrammatic*

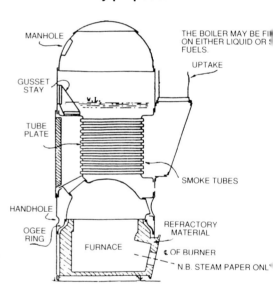

Figure 107 – *Tank Type Boiler – Diagrammatic*

A. The sketch is a typical tank boiler of vertical type suitable for producing relatively small amounts of low pressure steam for auxiliary purposes.

The fuel is burnt in a furnace having a seamless hemispherical crown attached to the boiler shell by means of an ogee ring. The products of combustion pass from this furnace into a combustion chamber lined with refractory material, and then through smoke tubes into the smoke box at the front of the boiler.

The cylindrical boiler shell with its hemispherical crown, together with the hemispherical furnace forming the bottom of the pressure space, requires no stays. However the combustion chamber top requires support, and this is provided by means of a gusset stay which transfers the stresses from the flat top of the chamber onto the boiler shell. The flat tube plates are tied together by means of stay tubes screwed into them.

The boiler may be fired on either liquid or solid fuels.

Q.18 Describe with the aid of a sketch, typical Piston Rod packing to prevent the escape of steam.

A *Duplex Packing* is designed for use with high pressures. It consists of a block packing used in conjunction with a cone packing which includes a set of white metal rings (11) placed in a vibrating cup (10), the interior of which is partly conical. The duplex follower ring (12) holds the cone rings in position, and transmits to the latter the pressure from the duplex follower springs, which are held in the ring (14) and protected by the spring cover (13). In this arrangement the inner cone packing checks the steam pressure, and the outer block packing is thus assisted, and the escape of steam absolutely prevented.

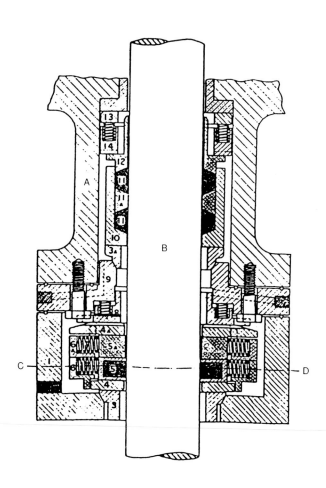

Figure 108 – *Typical Duplex Packing arrangement*

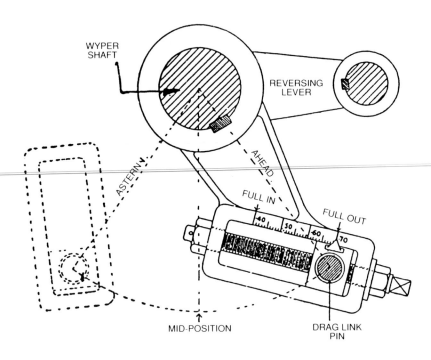

WYPER
SHAFT

REVERSING
LEVER

ASTERN

AHEAD

FULL IN

FULL OUT

40 50 60 70

MID-POSITION

DRAG LINK
PIN

Figure 109 – *Reversing Gear Bell Crank with Expansion Block*

Q.19 Briefly describe how balancing would be accomplished on a triple expansion steam engine.

A. Balancing is carried out by means of the expansion blocks (levers) which are used to vary the back pressure of the preceeding cylinder and thus at the same time varies the initial pressure on the engine whose expansion block has been adjusted.

Opening out an expansion block increases the valve travel making cut off later.

Opening out the I.P. block reduces the back pressure on the H.P. engine and opening out the L.P. block will reduce the back pressure on the I.P. engine.

Similarly shutting in an expansion block will make cut off earlier thus increasing the back pressure on the preceding cylinder.

By adjusting the expansion blocks each cylinder may be made to develop equal power without varying engine output.

"Shutting in" or "linking up" as it is often called may be done equally on all cylinders at the same time by using the reversing gear.

Q.20 Sketch and describe a rotor suitable for a modern HP turbine. Give the material used in the construction and state any test to which it is subjected.

A. In most cases modern HP turbine rotors are of the Rateau or pressure compounded design employing only a few stages for the expansion of the steam, about eight to ten, to give the

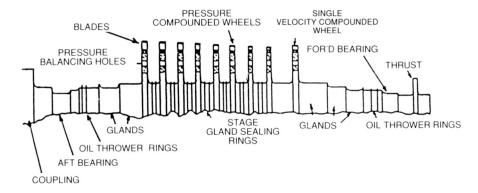

Figure 110 – *H.P. Turbine Rotor*

required heat drop. This arrangement produces a shorter rotor and provides savings in weight and overall length. Such rotors are usually solid forged steel providing a homogeneous rotor with an even grain flow, giving an even expansion, good thermal stability with less likelihood of distortion under high temperatures.

The rotor is subjected to a thermal stability test after rough machining and following final machining and the fitting of blades it is subjected to static and dynamic balancing tests.

The rotor is made of solid forged ferretic steel containing up to 0.36% carbon and with varying amounts of manganese, phosphorous sulphur, silicon, chromium, nickel molybdenum and vanadium.

N.B. STEAM PAPER ONLY

Q.21 Discuss with the aid of a sketch, a schematic diagram of a simple refrigeration system, and explain the pressure cycle.

A. The components required for a compression refrigeration system are a compressor, condenser, liquid receiver, expansion valve, and evaporator or cooling coils. The refrigerant flows from the expansion valve through the evaporator coils where it absorbs heat and becomes a gas or vapour. Then it flows to the compressor where it is compressed to the condenser pressure. In the condenser the heat is removed, and the refrigerant vapour becomes liquid and flows to the receiver. From the receiver it flows to the expansion valve

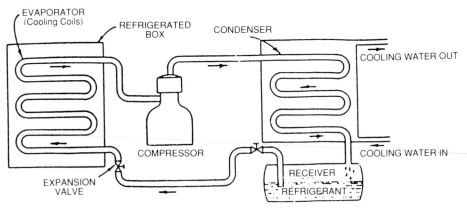

Figure 111 – *Refrigeration Gas/Liquid Circuit*

to start the circuit again. The refrigerant is under low pressure from the expansion valve through the evaporator to the compressor suction. This portion of the system is called the "low pressure side". The refrigerant is under high pressure from the compressor through the condenser, liquid receiver, and liquid line to the expansion valve. This portion of the system is called the "high pressure side'.

Q.22 Describe, with the aid of a sketch, an automatic refrigeration expansion valve.

A   The automatic expansion valve is a pressure-reducing device. It is activated by the evaporator pressure which keeps pressure of the refrigerant in the evaporator and determines the evaporator temperature. It is a diaphragm or bellows-operated valve, with the evaporator pressure acting on the lower side of the diaphragm and atmospheric pressure plus adjustable spring pressure acting on the upper side. As the compressor operates to remove the gas from the evaporator, reducing the pressure in the evaporator and under the diaphragm, the adjusting spring pressure pushes the diaphragm down. This motion is transmitted through push rods (or by the needle valve stem) to the valve needle, opening it enough to allow more refrigerant to flow to the evaporator. As more liquid enters the evaporator, the pressure increases, forcing the diaphragm upward and allowing the valve to close. A properly sized valve will pass enough liquid refrigerant to maintain constant temperature and pressure conditions.

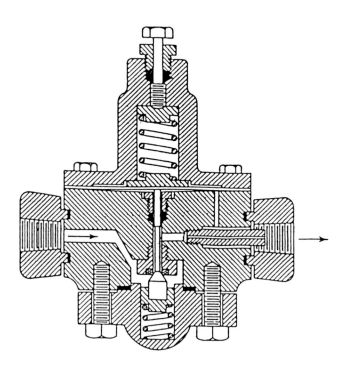

Automatic expansion valve is diaphragm-operated.

Figure 112

PART III

ENGINEERING

Q.1 What is meant by indicated thermal efficiency and brake thermal efficiency of an oil engine?

A. Indicated thermal efficiency is a measure of the heat units contained in the fuel which are transformed into work, or indicated power in the engine cylinders; while the brake thermal efficiency represents the heat units converted into work at the engine flywheel.

NOTE: Brake thermal efficiencies are most generally employed, as they indicate more truly the efficiency of an engine. If the indicated thermal efficiency is given it must also be known what accessories are driven by the engine, in order to arrive at the actual efficiency of the engine.

N.B. MOTOR PAPER ONLY

Q.2 As the flash point of fuel generally used in oil engines rarely exceeds 94°C, why is the air in the cylinders compressed to give a temperature under normal working conditions in the neighbourhood of about 6650°C?

A. Compressing the air to a temperature very much higher than the flashpoint of the fuel ensures the engine starting when the cylinders and pistons are cold, and regular ignition of the fuel when working at reduced speeds. Another reason for compressing the air to such a high temperature and pressure is to increase the compression ratio, whereby a higher thermal efficiency is obtained.

N.B. MOTOR PAPER ONLY

Q.3. What type of speed governors are generally found on –
(a) Propelling engines
(b) Auxiliary engines
and why are they used? Illustrate your answer with a sketch of an Auxiliary Engine type governor.

A (a) Variable Speed Governors (Propelling Engines) are used on propelling engines as these engines need to have speed governed through a large range depending on the speed required of the vessel. External forces such as wave action causes less or more pressure on the propellor, tending to increase speed or slow down the engine.
The governor adjusts input of fuel to the engine to counteract these forces.

(b) Constant Speed Governor (Auxiliary Engine)

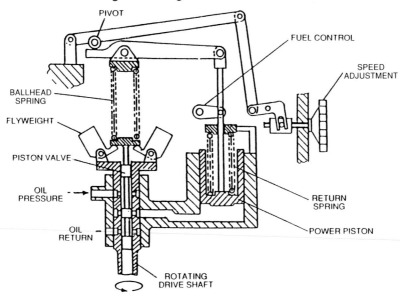

Figure 113 – *Typical Speed Governor*

Mechanical Hydraulic Governor

Is used to maintain the engine at the same speed. Used for generator prime movers to ensure voltage remains constant despite loading demands.

The governor automatically adjusts fuel pump settings to regulate power output.

This governor incorporates two systems. The mechanical ball head which detects changes in the speed of the engine due to increased loading. The hydraulic piston valve and power piston operates the fuel pump control setting to give the required change in power output.

N.B. MOTOR PAPER ONLY

Q.4 List the various fittings which should normally be found on a fuel tank.

A. (i) Spring loaded self closing drain.

(ii) Outlet valve able to be closed from outside the machinery space.

(iii) Manhole or handhole adjacent to valves.

(iv) Crossover valve to other tank in some installations.

(v) Sounding arrangements. Sounding pipe or gauging.

(vi) Filling pipe.

(vii) Vent with gauze (antiflash).

Q.5. (a) Describe how you would extinguish an oil fire in the engine room bilge of a vessel.

(b) Would water be used on an oil fire?

A. (a) An oil fire would be extinguished using foam, dry chemical, b.c.f., or CO_2 extinguishers. If this is unsuccessful the engine room should be closed including closing all vents and the fixed gas fire smothering system activated.

(b) Yes, but only with a fine spray nozzle.

Care should also be taken regarding the vessels stability which may be adversely affected with too much water in below deck space bilges.

Q.6 Describe the types of protection and control which should be fitted to a low to medium voltage (240V-415V AC) Electrical Installation on a vessel. Where, in relation to the various circuits, would protection and control be installed and what would govern the rating of these items?

A. Protection and control is provided to the main circuit and the various sub-circuits. This may be in the form of circuit breakers or switches and fuses. Final sub-circuits protection, C.B.s or fuses only, is also provided.

Protection and control is provided on the load side of each circuit as close to the supply source as possible so that no cable is unprotected.

The rating of fuses and C.B.s should always be equal or marginally less than the current carrying capacity of the associated cable.

Q.7 What safety arrangements are provided to a small vessel's sea water fire pumping and bilge pumping system.

A. (a) Arrangements in the form of an emergency manual pump and valve controls outside the space containing the main pump in case of fire or flooding in the main pump space.

(b) Non-return valves in bilge suctions or similar arrangements to prevent cross flooding from other spaces in case a valve is left open and to prevent back flooding from the sea.

(c) Strainers or mud boxes at bilge suctions to prevent blockage.

(d) All sea water pipes should be in suitable metal as should bilge pumping pipes within the machinery space.

Q.8 Describe with the aid of a sketch a typical fuel valve (injector).

A.

The general design of this fuel valve is similar for most engines and consists of a spring loaded non return needle valve operated by fuel pressure from the fuel pump.

The fuel is atomised from the nozzle for combustion following each stroke of the fuel pump.

N.B. MOTOR QUESTION ONLY

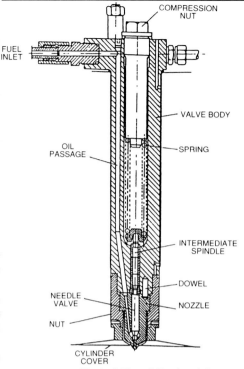

COMPRESSION NUT

FUEL INLET

VALVE BODY

OIL PASSAGE

SPRING

INTERMEDIATE SPINDLE

DOWEL

NEEDLE VALVE

NOZZLE

NUT

CYLINDER COVER

Figure 114 – *Typical Diesel Engine Injector*

Q.9 Describe with the aid of a sketch a typical diesel engine piston.

A. The piston may be manufactured from low expansion aluminium alloy castings and is attached to the connecting rods by fully floating gudgeon pins.

The type of piston shown is with three compression rings and two slotted oil control rings. The top compression ring may be chromium plated.

Cooling oil is fed into the centre of the piston via a slipper connection at the top of the connecting rod.

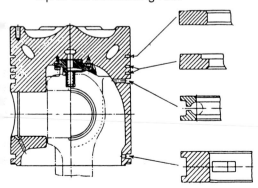

Figure 115 – *Typical Diesel Engine Piston*

Q.10 Describe, with the aid of sketches, what is meant by the terms 'open and crossed rods' relating to valve gear.

A. The terms 'open rods" and "crossed rods" are used to distinguish between the manner in which the eccentric rods are connected to the quadrant in reversible steam engines using Stephenson link gear.

Rods are said to be open if they appear open when the eccentrics are above the centre line of the shaft when the crank is on either top or bottom dead centre depending upon whether the valve is using inside or outside steam.

With outside steam the crank will be put on bottom centre and with inside steam the eccentrics will be above the centre line when the crank is on top centre.

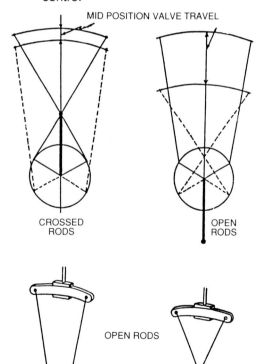

MID POSITION VALVE TRAVEL

CROSSED RODS

OPEN RODS

OPEN RODS

BOTTOM CENTRE

TOP CENTRE

N.B. STEAM PAPER ONLY

Figure 116 – *Eccentric Rod Arrangement*

Q.11 Discuss the advantages and disadvantages of the common D. slide valve, the double ported (D.P.) valve and the Piston valve.

A. In comparison with the other types, the only advantage of the common D type valve is that it could be used in small engines where the passages of a double ported (D.P.) valve are too small.

The disadvantages of the common valve are that it needs twice the travel of the D.P. valve and therefore its friction loss is greater. Unless a relief ring is fitted on the back of the valve considerable work is required to drive the unit.

For a piston valve with inside steam the load is taken off the gear by having the top diameter larger than.the bottom giving a floating action and the energy lost to friction is reduced because only the rings bear on the liner wall. Another big advantage is that high pressure steam is kept off the gland. However it is difficult to keep the rings steam tight for any length of time, and in the event of water getting into the receiver there is more likelihood of serious damage with a piston valve whereas with the D valve the water forces the valve off its face and escapes into the casing.

N.B. STEAM PAPER ONLY

Q.12 Describe with the aid of a sketch a typical boiler safety valve.

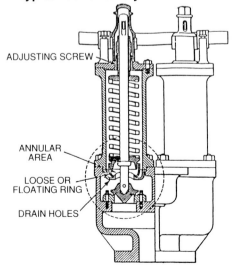

ADJUSTING SCREW

ANNULAR AREA

LOOSE OR FLOATING RING

DRAIN HOLES

Figure 117 – *Improved High Lift Safety Valve*

A. Improved high lift safety valve.

The Safety valve is a device mounted directly to boilers to prevent Overpressure.

The improved high lift type is a development of the ordinary spring loaded safety valve and due to the design additional lift is gained through pressure in the waste steam space (above annular area) acting on what is in effect a piston attached to the valve spindle.

Waste steam pressure which acts against the lift of ordinary safety valves assists the lift in the case of these high lift types.

N.B. STEAM PAPER ONLY

Q.13 Describe, with the aid of a sketch. a simple impulse (De Laval) turbine.

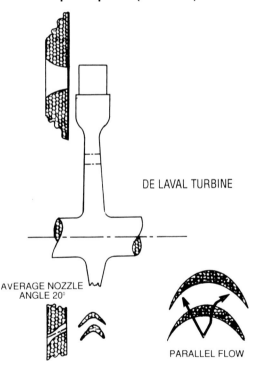

DE LAVAL TURBINE

AVERAGE NOZZLE ANGLE 20°

PARALLEL FLOW

Figure 118 – *De Laval Turbine*

A. Consists of one set of nozzles, usually four or six, and one row of turbine blading, parallel flow.

This type of turbine operates at high speed, 20,000 to 30,000 R.P.M. and is suitable for dynamos.

Blade speed = 0.5 steam velocity. Because of equal pressure on both sides of the wheel there is no relevant axial thrust.

The turbine blading is stronger and heavier than reaction blading. This allows greater steam flow and less risk of damage when starting. Turbine casing is short thus saving space.

N.B. STEAM PAPER ONLY

Q.14 Why is a pressure relief device fitted to the cylinder head, or as near to as possible, on the high pressure discharge side of a refrigeration compressor.

A. To relieve overpressure which may occur due to a blockage on the discharge side of the compressor. Overfilling the system or overheating may also cause an overpressure problem.

This problem can be especially dangerous when the compressor is vee-belt driven from the main (propulsion) engine which can provide much more power than the refrigeration unit is capable of transmitting and may result in pressure carrying equipment bursting due to overpressure.

Q.15 Details of a four stroke engine of a vessel are as follows:-

Number of cylinders - 8

Bore and stroke – 152 mm and 225 mm

R.P.M. = 2100

M.E.P. = 750 kpa

If the daily fuel consumption is 1.5 tonnes and fuel tank dimensions are 3.5 m x 2.25 m x 1.8 m depth calculate the following:

(a) The K.W.B.P. of the engine

(b) The fuel consumption for K.W.B.P. per hour in litres

(c) Assuming the fuel tank was full at the start of the voyage find the sounding rod reading in metres after 2 days 14 hours steaming.

(d) The day's steaming available at the same consumption with the remaining fuel in the tank.

N.B. I.P. = Plan (W) Fuel S.G. = 0.82

B.P.= I.P. x 0.8

A.   I.P. = PLAN (W)

(a)

$$I.P. = 750 \times 10^3 \times 0.225 \times \Pi \times .076^2 \times \frac{8}{2} \times \frac{2100}{60}$$

$$= 428{,}751.04 \text{ W}$$

I.P. = 428.751 KW

B.P.= 428.75 x .08

$$= 343 \text{ KW}$$

(B) Daily fuel consumption

$$= 1.50 \text{ tonnes} = \frac{1500}{0.82} = 1829 \text{ litres}$$

$$= \frac{1829}{343 \times 24}$$

$$= 0.22 \text{ litres/KWBP/Hr}$$

(c)   Consumption/hr $= \frac{1.5}{24} = 0.06$

Consumption for 2 days 14 hours = 3.88 tonnes

Vol. tk. = 2.25 x 3.5 x 1.8 = 14.18

and assuming S.G. = 0.82

Capacity = 11.62 tonnes

Consumption = 3.88 tons

Fuel left = 11.62 – 3.88 = 7.74 tonnes

$$\frac{7.74}{0.82} = 9.44 m^3$$

9.44 = 2.25 x 3.5 x d

d = 1.2 metres

(d) Days Steaming available $= \frac{7.74}{1.5} = 5.16$

N.B. MOTOR PAPER ONLY

Q.16 The diameter of an H.P. cylinder of a single acting steam engine is 400 mm and the stroke is 0.8 metres. The I.M.E.P. is 0.5 mpa and the revolutions are 120 per minute. Find the indicated power in kilowatts.

A.   I.P. = PLAN

$$= 500 \times 10^3 \times 0.8 \times \Pi \, 0.2^2 \times \frac{120}{60} = \text{watts}$$

$$= 100544.0 \text{ watts}$$

I.P. = 100.54 KWP

N.B. STEAM PAPER ONLY

PART IV

ENGINEERING

Q.1 **What would be the causes of low lubricating oil pressure in a diesel engine?**

A. (a) Blocked filters or suction.
   (b) Low oil level.
   (c) Oil overheating.
   (d) Oil dilution.
   (e) Oil pump worn.
   (f) Oil leaks.
   (g) Excessive bearing clearances (worn engine)

Q.2 **What is the purpose of a fuel tank drain and why is it spring loaded and self closing?**

A. This drain is fitted to allow water and sludge to be drained off as it settles out of the fuel.

The reason for the drain to be spring loaded and self closing is to prevent it being left open and fuel oil filling the bilges.

Q.3 **What are the various methods or means of extinguishing fires? What are the usual precautions taken to prevent fires occurring in a ship?**

A. (a) Oil Fires may be extinguished using hand held foam, CO_2 B.C.F./B.T.M., or dry chemical type extinguishers.

A fine spray of water may also be used.

(b) Galley fat fires may be extinguished using the extinguishers previously mentioned at (a) or a fire blanket which is carried in the galley area.

(c) Wood, paper etc. fires may be extinguished using the extinguishers previously mentioned and also water type extinguishers. A water hose may also be used for this type of fire.

(d) Machinery spaces are usually provided with fixed fire extinguishing systems. When hand held extinguishers are insufficient this fixed system is used.

(e) Electrical fires may be extinguished using hand held CO_2, B.C.F./B.T.M. or dry chemical type extinguishers.

Q.4 **Describe what action you would take in the case of an alternating current system electrical fault.**

A. (a) Isolate the faulty equipment.

(b) Call in a properly qualified electrician to repair the equipment.

Q.5 **Describe with the aid of a sketch a full bore safety valve as fitted to a steam boiler.**

N.B. STEAM PAPER ONLY

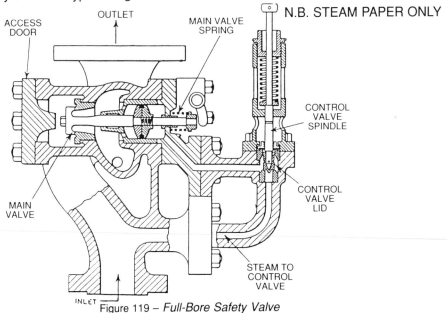

Figure 119 – *Full-Bore Safety Valve*

A. Each main valve is operated by its own control valve, and that both of these valves are in direct communication with the steam drum or superheater header on which they are mounted.

The action of the valve is as follows: Steam from the boiler exerts pressure on the underside of the control valve, which lifts at a predetermined pressure. In lifting, the top part of the control-valve lid blanks off ports leading to atmosphere and allows steam to pass through a passage leading to the piston on the main valve spindle, causing the main valve to open against the boiler pressure (the area of the piston is about twice that of the valve).

When the boiler pressure drops the control valve shuts down, and in so doing uncovers the ports above it which lead to atmosphere. This relieves the pressure from the main valve piston, and the boiler pressure then shuts the main valve. The foregoing is the action of one control valve and its main valve; there are, of course, always two or more control and main valve units per boiler.

N.B. STEAM PAPER ONLY

Q.6 How would misalignment of a steam engine piston be indicated. How would this be remedied?

A. Where alignment is correct the wear will tend to be greater athwartships due to the thrust of the connecting rod. Should the fore and aft diameter be the larger, it is almost certain misalignment exists. There is only one effective cure for fore and aft misalignment: "hang" the piston and scrape out the brasses. Packing with tin liners under the crosshead brasses usually does more harm than good.

N.B. STEAM PAPER ONLY

Q.7 Explain the reasons for warming through a steam turbine plant prior to departure and what considerations apply to warming through.

A. The object of warming through is to raise gradually the temperature of the rotors and casings to an even level so that when the turbines are started, irregular expansion or distortion,

excessive condensation, which in itself can cause distortion, with associated thermal shocks and excessive stresses are avoided.

There is a tendency for hot steam to flow to the upper parts of the turbine and the condensate to fall to the lower parts when warming through, the upper parts are therefore more likely to become hotter than the lower ones, causing the cylinder to hog. This condition can be aggravated in the LP turbine if a high vacuum and corresponding low temperature is permitted during this period. The rotors also tend to hog in similar fashion if they are not turned frequently. The greatest care should be taken to prevent the localized heating of any part of the turbine and the admission of gland steam should be kept to a very minimum to avoid local overheating of the turbine spindles, just sufficient steam being used to maintain the required vacuum. Similarly, the greatest care should be taken when using astern steam.

N.B. STEAM PAPER ONLY

Q.8 Describe with the aid of a sketch the type of water level gauges usually fitted to lower pressure type boilers.

A. For boiler pressures up to about 2050 KPa it is normal practice to use round glass tubes suitably connected to the boiler by means of cocks and pipes for indicating the working level of the water. Above 2050 KPa the glass tube is replaced by what is in effect a built-up rectangular-section box having a thick plate-glass front and back.

Tank-type boilers, coming in the lower range of pressures, are invariably fitted with round glass-tube gauges, these being connected to the boiler in one of the following ways:

(a) the gauge cocks are fitted directly to the boiler;

(b) the gauge cocks are fitted to a large-bore bent pipe, one end of which communicates with the steam space and the other with the water space;

(c) the gauge cocks are mounted on a hollow column, the ends of which

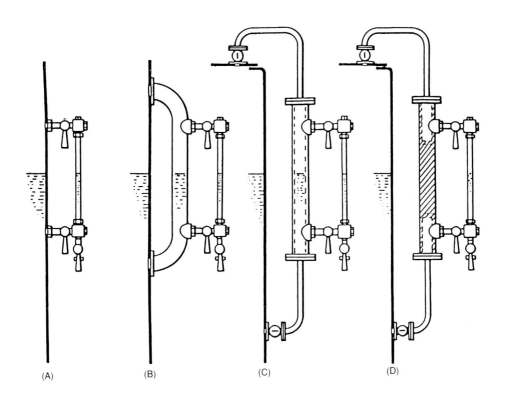

Figure 120 – *Boiler Gauge Glass Diagrams*

are connected by pipes to shut-off cocks on the top and bottom of the boiler;

(d) the gauge cocks are mounted on a column as in (c), but the centre part of the column is solid, the ends again being connected by pipes to shut-off cocks on the top and bottom of the boiler.

N.B. STEAM PAPER ONLY

2.9 If the daily fuel consumption of a vessel is 1 tonne, and the dimensions of a fuel tank are 3.5 metres x 2.75 metres x 1.8 metres depth, find the sounding rod reading in metres after 2 days steaming. Assume fuel S.G. = 0.82.

A. Volume of Tank = 3.5 x 2.25 x 1.8 = 14.18 cu.m.

Capacity = 14.18 x .82 = 11.62 tonnes

Consumption = 1 x 2 = 2 tons

Fuel left after 2 days = 11.62 – 2 = 9.62 tons.

and $\frac{9.62}{0.82}$ = 11.73 cu.m.

sounding = $\frac{11.73}{2.25 \times 3.5}$

= 1.49 m

PART V

ENGINEERING

Q.1 List and describe the various safety devices which may be found on a marine diesel engine.

A.   (a) High jacket cooling water temperature alarm.

(b) Low lubricating oil pressure alarm.

(c) Emergency stop control.

(d) Crankcase relief doors.

High jacket cooling water temperature alarm.

The function of this device is to give warning of an abnormal temperature rise; this may be caused by any, or several of the following:-

(i) Blocked sea water strainers.

(ii) Blocked heat-exchanger tubes.

(iii) Faulty thermostat.

(iv) High engine overload (bent propellor or shaft).

(v) Faulty injection equipment.

(vi) Incorrect injection timing.

(vii) Low primary coolant level (fresh water only).

Low lubricating oil pressure alarm.

This device is designed to give warning when the lubricating oil pressure falls below a predetermined level. The various causes of this condition are as follows:-

(i) High lubricating oil temperature.

(ii) Fractured lubricating oil pressure line.

(iii) Faulty oil pressure relief valve.

(iv) Low oil level.

(v) Faulty or worn bearings.

Emergency stop control.

This component can be in the form of a damper fitted to the air intake. A cable is normally led to the wheelhouse which enables stopping of the engine in emergencies when other controls fail.

Crankcase relief doors

A crankcase relief door can be fitted to one or several of the crankcase inspection covers. It is held in the closed position by a light spring; its function is to open and release any contained pressure due to oil vapour and gas

which can be generated from the effects of a hot bearing, thus avoiding the risk of a serious explosion.

Q.2 What is meant by supercharging or pressure charging in relation to diesel engines?

A.   Supercharging or pressure charging, is a system of introducing air into the engine cylinder at a pressure higher than atmospheric, thereby increasing the quantity consumed, and thus allowing for a proportionate increase in amount of fuel to be burnt to provide an increase in the power output of the engine.

Q.3 Explain the use of wire gauze diaphragms fitted to fuel oil tank vent pipes.

A.   Fuel tank vent pipes have their open ends covered with wire gauze, the object being to prevent the passage of flame which might ignite the gases and cause an explosion. It is well known that before a combustible substance will take fire, its temperature must first be raised to its point of ignition, and, if after it has been ignited the temperature is reduced in some way below this point, the flame will be extinguished. A moderate flame can be extinguished by passing a current of air over it as for instance, blowing out a candle. The reason for this is that more air than is required for combustion is supplied to the burning gas, the surplus tending to cool the flame below its point of ignition. In a similar way wire gauze, which is a good conductor of heat, prevents the passage of flame, since it looses its heat very rapidly, and the flame upon coming into contact with it is cooled below the point of ignition; consequently no flame appears on the other side of the gauze.

Q.4 What is cavitation when applied to a ship's propeller? State the main conditions necessary to avoid cavitation.

A.   A ship's propeller acts by giving the water making contact with it velocity in an astern direction. When a ship is afloat and at rest the pressure at the forward side of the propeller is due to the head of water above the propeller and when the propeller is revolving the pressure due to head is diminished an amount depending upon the speed of the propeller and other factors.

Should the pressure due to head be eliminated on particular parts of the propeller, the pressure forward of the propeller will be momentarily zero at these points, and at zero pressure the water will 'break' and cavities will be formed. Whilst cavitation mainly occurs at the forward side of the propeller 'slack water' also occurs at the after side due to centrifugal action. The main conditions necessary to avoid cavitation are:–

(a) The propeller must be well submerged.

(b) The form of the vessel's stern must be fine so as to give a clear run of water to the propeller, and maintain as high a pressure as possible on the forward side of the blade.

Q.5 To what forces are propeller shafts subjected? When is it necessary to take steps to correct alignment?

A. Propeller shafts are subject to combined twisting and bending forces which produce both tensile and compressive stresses in the material. The bending force occurs abaft the stern tube. It is inadvisable to allow the wear-down of the propeller shaft to exceed a reasonable level, otherwise the bending force will be extended inboard, and with the increased leverage resulting there is greater risk of the material becoming fatigued and eventually break.

Q.6 How might the gases in an enclosed crankcase, resulting from vaporization of the lubricating oil, be exploded when:-

(a) The engine is running; and

(b) When the engine is at rest?

A. Ignition of the gases whilst the engine is running may be brought about by an overheated piston or bearing. Ignition whilst the engine is at rest may occur if a naked light is taken into the crankcase, or if the engine has been recently stopped because of some part in the crankcase being overheated; the action of opening a crankcase door and allowing air to enter may cause an explosion, the admission of air having the effect of bringing the gaseous contents of the crankcase within the explosive range.

Q.7 Should a piston of a multiple cylinder engine become overheated and it is not possible to stop the engine because of the vessel's position, what steps should be taken to get the piston back to its normal condition?

A. If the engine cannot be stopped, the speed should be reduced as much as circumstances will allow, and the fuel should be shut off from the cylinder concerned at once. The decompression gear should then be engaged to prevent the air in the cylinder being compressed. The engine may be run in this manner for a short time, after which the supply of cooling water to the engine should be increased, if possible, to further reduce the temperature. Once temperature stabilization has been obtained, the decompression gear may be disengaged and the cylinder set working on fuel.

Q.8 What precautions are necessary to prevent accidents connected with compressed air starting systems with diesel engines?

A. (a) Correct grade of lubricating oil to be used in compressor and other parts of air system requiring lubrication.

(b) Excess lubrication to be avoided.

(c) Compressor cooler drains to be operated at regular intervals.

(d) Air reservoirs to be kept drained of moisture.

Q.9 Sketch a timing diagram showing the sequence of events in both four stroke cycle and two stroke cycle diesel engines. Approximate angles at which the various events occur are to be indicated.

A.

Figure 121 – *Typical Four Stroke Cycle Timing Diagram*

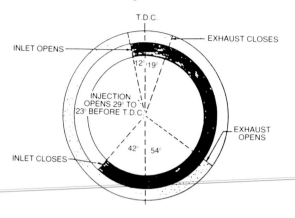

Figure 122 – *Two Stroke Cycle Timing Diagram*

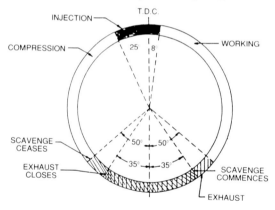

Q.10 Describe with the aid of a sketch a fuel system suitable for a fishing vessel, state precautions to be taken and care required to maintain this system in order.

A.   Refer to Schematic Sketch of a Fuel System Arrangement.

1. Fuel storage tanks should be strongly constructed, fitted with suitable baffling arrangements, dependent upon size, and be securely fastened to seatings to prevent movement in relation to the vessel's hull.

2. Fuel tank shut off valves must be provided, attached directly to the

tank outlets, and are to be fitted with means of closing operable from an accessible position outside the machinery space.

3. Tank drain valves are to be fitted below the level of fuel tank outlets. Valves used for this purpose must be of the self closing type. These drains should be operated at regular intervals, particularly following refuelling to ensure that no water or other contaminant is present in the tanks.

4. Fuel tank filling and sounding pipes are to be fitted continuous to deck level in order to prevent spillage during refuelling; and above deck are to be fitted with a sealed cap to prevent the accidental admission of water.

5. Fuel tank vent pipes are fitted to extend at least .76 m (30") above deck, and terminate in a goose neck to prevent accidental admission of water. The open ends of these pipes are fitted with anti-flash gauze wire. These pipes are to be kept clear of obstructions.

6. Primary fuel filter and moisture trap fitted before fuel lift pump, provides secondary means of ensuring no moisture reaches fuel injection equipment which could cause corrosion in those finely machined components.

7. Fuel lift pump – usually of the diaphragm type, requires maintenance in accordance with engine manufacturer's specifications. It is advisable to carry a spare kit for this pump for use in the event of a breakdown; however, it is possible that in the event of such a failure, fuel can be delivered to the suction side of the injector pumps by gravity feeding from a drum or bucket.

8. Secondary fuel filter – requires cleaning at regular intervals in accordance with manufacturer's recommendations or earlier if conditions warrant it.

9. Fuel injection pumps – require servicing as recommended by manufacturers; some injection pump units incorporate their own separate lubrication system, this should be checked at regular intervals.

10. Fuel injectors – require servicing as recommended by manufacturer.

NOTE: Servicing of items 9 and 10 should always be carried out by service workshops possessing the correct type of test equipment and trained personnel.

13. Two way cock – fitted in fuel return line, this cock should always be open to working tank to avoid overflowing tank not in use.

15. Fuel tank inspection and cleaning doors – either positioned or fitted in sufficient numbers to provide free access for cleaning and inspecting tanks.

1. Fuel Storage Tanks
2. Fuel tank shut off valves
3. Fuel tank drain cocks
4. Fuel tank filling and sounding pipes
5. Fuel tank vent pipes
6. Primary fuel filter and moisture trap
7. Fuel lift pump (engine driven)
8. Secondary fuel filter
9. Fuel injection pumps
10. Fuel injectors
11. Excess fuel return pipe
12. Injector leak off pipe
13. Two way cock
14. Fuel return pipes
15. Fuel tank inspection/cleaning doors
   Schematic Sketch of a Fuel System Arrangement

General

Care should be taken to ensure that all joints and glands in fuel systems are kept free of leaks, that all piping is secured against vibration that could cause fatigue failure, that materials used in fuel systems are impervious to heat and not likely to fail in the event of fire and precautions should be taken during refuelling operations to prevent overflows or spillage.

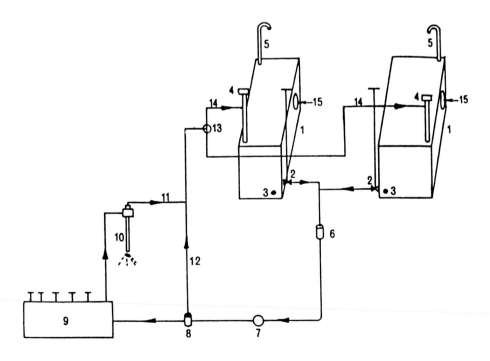

Figure 123 – *Typical Fuel Tank Installation*

Note: Should a gauge glass be fitted to determine tank contents in lieu of a sounding pipe, then such gauge glass is to be fitted with a self closing cock at the lower end, attached directly to the fuel tank.

Q.11 State as many reasons as possible for the following faults in diesel engines.

(a) Low cranking speed.

(b) Engine will not start, or difficult to start.

(c) Black smoke at exhaust.

(d) Blue/white smoke at exhaust.

(e) Vibration.

(f) Excessive vapour from crankcase breather.

(g) Poor compression.

A.   Low cranking speed -
   (i)   Battery capacity low
   (ii)   Bad electrical connection
   (iii)   Faulty starter motor
   (iv)   Incorrect grade of lubricating oil

Engine will not start, or difficult to start
   (i)   Low cranking speed
   (ii)   Fuel tank empty
   (iii)   Blocked fuel feedpipe
   (iv)   Faulty fuel lift pump
   (v)   Choked fuel filter
   (vi)   Air in fuel system
   (vii)   Faulty fuel injection pump
   (viii) Faulty injectors
   (ix)   Incorrect fuel pump timing
   (x)   Incorrect valve timing
   (xi)   Poor compression
   (xii)   Exhaust pipe restricted

Black smoke at exhaust-
   (i)   Restriction in air cleaner
   (ii)   Faulty fuel injection pump
   (iii)   Faulty injectors

   (iv)   Incorrect fuel pump timing
   (v)   Incorrect valve timing
   (vi)   Poor compression
   (vii) Incorrect grade of fuel
   (viii) Exhaust pipe restricted
   (ix)   Engine overloaded

Blue/white smoke at exhaust -
   (i)   Incorrect grade of lubricating oil
   (ii)   Broken, worn or sticking piston rings
   (iii)   Worn cylinder liners
   (iv)   Overfull air cleaner (oil bath type)

Vibration -
   (i)   Faulty fuel injectors or injection pump
   (ii)   Poor compression
   (iii)   Engine overheating
   (iv)   Sticking valves
   (v)   Piston seizure/pickup
   (vi)   Faulty engine seatings
   (vii)   Engine and shafting out of alignment
   (viii) Damaged or fouled propeller

Excessive vapour from crankcase breather-
   (i)   Worn cylinder bores
   (ii)   Broken, worn or sticking piston rings
   (iii)   Worn valve stems and guides
   (iv)   Piston seizure/pickup

Poor compression-
   (i)   Restriction in air cleaner
   (ii)   Incorrect valve timing
   (iii)   Cylinder head gasket leaking
   (iv)   Incorrect tappet adjustment
   (v)   Sticking valves
   (vi)   Worn cylinder bores
   (vii)   Pitted valves and seats
   (viii) Broken, worn or sticking piston rings
   (ix)   Incorrect piston height

PART VI

ENGINEERING

Q.1 List and describe the various safety devices which may be found on a marine diesel engine.

A. (a) High jacket cooling water temperature alarm.

(b) Low lubricating oil pressure alarm.

(c) Emergency stop control.

High Jacket cooling temperature alarm.

The function of this device is to give warning of an abnormal temperature rise; this may be caused by any, or several of the following:-

(i) Blocked sea water strainers.

(ii) Blocked heat-exchanger tubes.

(iii) Faulty thermostat.

(iv) High engine overload (bent propeller or shaft).

(v) Faulty injection equipment.

(vi) Incorrect injection timing.

(vii) Low primary coolant level (fresh water only).

Low lubricating oil pressure alarm.

This device is designed to give warning when the lubricating oil pressure falls below a predetermined level. The various causes of this condition are as follows:-

(i) High lubricating oil temperature.

(ii) Fractured lubricating oil pressure line.

(iii) Faulty oil pressure relief valve.

(iv) Low oil level.

(v) Faulty or worn bearings.

Emergency stop control.

This component can be in the form of a damper fitted to the air intake. A cable is normally led to the wheelhouse which enables stopping of the engine in emergencies when other controls fail.

Q.2 What is the most widely used and efficient system of supercharging?

A. By using the engine exhaust gases to drive a turbine which is directly coupled to a rotary air compressor or blower supplying compressed air to the engine intake. Refer to Diagrammatic Arrangement of Exhaust Gas Turbo Charger.

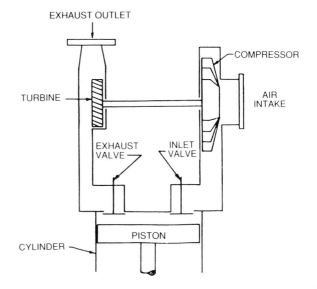

Figure 124 – *Diagrammatic Arrangement of Exhaust Gas Turbo Charging*

Q.3 Outline the procedure you would adopt in fitting a new propeller and propeller shaft.

A. Firstly, all bearings should be thoroughly cleaned, and the respective channels for the lubrication medium tested to ascertain whether the bearings are receiving a full and uninterrupted supply.

Secondly, the bearing clearance should be checked; this may be done with micrometers, or by using long feeler gauges after the shaft has been inserted.

Prior to fitting the shaft a thin smear of the lubricant should be applied to facilitate easy entry. Once the shaft has been fitted and the clearances checked the propeller may then be fitted to the shaft. The quality of fit should be checked in the workshop before despatch, although it is always wise to check for clearance above the key to be sure the propeller is fitting snugly to the taper and not riding on the key. The propeller nut can be tightened and securely locked; the nut must never be backed off to match up with an old locking position.

Q.4 Discuss the various reasons which may cause a water pump to lose suction.

A. For a pump situated below the water line and operating under the influence of a flooded suction, the following causes may apply:-

(a) Blocked suction strainer.

(b) Sheared impeller drive key.

(c) Air entering the sea suction due to rolling of the ship.

For pumps required to operate in positions above the water line, all of the above possibilities will apply, in addition to the following:-

(a) Faulty suction pipe permitting loss of vacuum.

(b) Insufficient rotational speed of pump.

Q.5 Describe a typical fuel system as fitted to a fishing vessel; and how you would go about bleeding the complete system through to the engine.

A. Fuel which is led from the tank or tanks through an outlet valve directly affixed to the tank. This valve must be capable of being closed from a position remotely external to the compartment in which the tank is situated. From the valve the fuel passes to a filter, or filters; primary and secondary filters may be fitted depending on the engine design. After leaving the filter, the fuel is free to flow to the fuel pump suction connection and hence to the injectors.

The procedure necessary to completely bleed the system is as follows:-

(a) Open the drain valve on the fuel tank and purge until any foreign matter is removed.

(b) The fuel tank outlet valve may now be opened and the fuel filter purged at the bleed screw provided.

(c) After closing the bleed screw on the filter the fuel pump can now be cleared of air in a similar manner.

(d) Once the fuel pump has been bled, the engine may be rotated with the fuel injection pipes loosened at the injector, and closed as the air is expelled.

(e) The engine can now be run.

Q.6 Describe in general terms the operation of a diesel engine governor.

A. The governor rod is connected to the fuel pump rack. When the engine speed tends to rise, the governor mechanism operates on the injection pump rack to turn the pump plungers slightly, thus shortening the effective stroke of the pumps. This has the effect of reducing the amount of fuel injected into the engine cylinders, so that the tendency of the engine to speed up is checked. If the speed falls below normal, the fuel pump rack is moved by the governor mechanism, so as to increase slightly the fuel supply to the engine cylinders.

Q.7. Describe the lubricating oil system of a high speed diesel engine.

State what attention is necessary to maintain this system in good condition.

A. Refer to Schematic Sketch of a Lubricating Oil System.

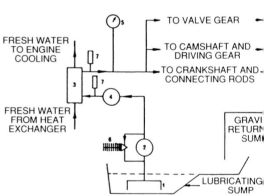

Figure 125 – *Lubricating Oil System*

1. Suction strainer located in sump
2. Lubricating oil pressure pump - gear type driven from crankshaft
3. Lub. oil cooler circulated with engine cooling water
4. Lub. oil filter
5. Lub. oil pressure gauge
6. Lub. oil pressure relief by-pass valve
7. Lub. oil thermometers

Typical Schematic Lubricating oil System

Care should be taken to ensure that engine sump is filled to the correct level with the recommended grade of oil; that the lubricating oil and filter elements are renewed or cleaned at the recommended intervals; that joints and glands in oil pipes are kept free from leaks; that no contamination of oil from water or fuel is present; that the lubricating oil cooler is cleaned at intervals to maintain oil temperature at a suitable level; that any drop in oil pressure gauge reading is noted and the cause ascertained and remedied as soon as possible; and that at least one complete spare change of the correct grade of oil is carried on board at all times.

Q.8 Describe various methods of fighting fires using fire hoses aboard small vessels.

A. (a) By use of a jet of water directed against solid combustible materials such as wood, bedding, waste materials, etc to create a cooling effect.

(b) By use of a very fine spray from a spray nozzle, directed against an oil fire. This has the effect of cooling, and where there is intense heat the steam given off has a blanket effect.

(c) Where difficulty is experienced in approaching a fire, due to intense heat, two hoses should be used to penetrate the heat barrier to reach the source of the fire. One crew member should advance with a hose having a spray nozzle which forms a protective barrier, followed by another member who attacks the fire with a jet.

(d) Where a fire breaks out in a confined space and grows in intensity, it may be restricted to that space by using hoses to cool the bulkheads and decks forming the boundary.

Note: In all cases where a liberal amount of sea water is used to fight a fire in any vessel, regardless of size, consideration must be given at all times to the effect it has on the stability of the vessel.

Q.9 What preparations should be made prior to slipping a vessel? Which items of vessel's outfitting and equipment require attention during slipping? State the attention given to such items. What precautions are taken before a vessel enters the water following a slipping?

A. (a) Prior to slipping, bilges should be pumped dry, and loose gear removed from the vessel as far as possible to facilitate inspections; provision should be made to have the necessary spare packing and seals available for such items as stern glands, rudder trunk glands and shipside valves.

(b) All shipside valves should be opened up and inspected for evidence of corrosion or electrolysis; valves lapped in as found necessary; glands repacked; securing bolts or studs replaced as necessary and valve bodies removed from skin if any evidence of deterioration in way of joints or studs is showing.

(c) Suction grids should be removed from skin where necessary, cleaned and painted with a protective coating. Internal sea strainers opened up and examined for corrosion, cleaned and painted.

(d) Sacrificial zinc anodes should be examined, cleaned off or renewed as necessary. Earthing arrangements of anodes should be bonded satisfactorily.

(e) Anchors and cables should be removed from chain locker for examination, and chain locker cleaned out, examined and painted as necessary.

(f) Propeller nut and rudder couplings should be tested for tightness and locking devices examined to ensure they are in good condition. Packing should be removed from the stern gland and the condition of the shaft examined in way of gland. Clearance in stern bearing and rudder bearings should be checked. If an oil filled stern tube is employed, the oil should be replaced after fitting new seals.

At intervals (usually determined by a survey authority) of between 3 and 5 years, the propeller shaft and rudder stock are to be withdrawn for examination.

(g) This is to be inspected for corrosion damage and failures depending on the type of hull material.

(h) Before the vessel leaves the slip all valves should be operated over the full range from open to close. Valves with flanged covers may be checked by trying a feeler gauge between valve cover and body with valve in the closed position to ensure cover is tight. A check should be made that all suction grids have been replaced and locking devices for propeller and coupling nuts replaced, and that sea strainers have been closed up. Immediately on entering water valves should be opened to ensure covers or glands are not leaking. Stern gland should be examined and adjusted as necessary.

Q.10 State the procedure you would follow in preparing your vessel's machinery before going to sea. Detail all items that would receive your attention.

A. (a) Open required sea suction and discharge valves, check for leaks from piping systems.

(b) Check level of fresh water in heat exchanger or header tank, and bleed air from cooling water system. .

(c) Check oil levels in engine crankcase and gear box.

(d) Turn engine over by hand where possible.

(e) Open shut-off valves in fuel tanks and bleed air from fuel system.

(f) Check oil level on stern tube header tank if fitted.

(g) Grease or oil various lubricating points on stern gland, shaft bearings, pumps, steering gear, main engine and auxiliaries as fitted.

(h) Inspect steering gear while operating it from hard-over to hard-over, to ensure no leaks in hydraulic systems, ensure shackles, chains, wires or sheaves in mechanical gear and tightness of tiller arm to rudder stock. Check hydraulic oil level.

(i) Check batteries to ensure full charge available, battery levels normal, and terminals tight and clean.

(j) Start engine and allow to idle, check oil pressures (as engine warms up check water temperature).

(k) Check engine remote controls operating satisfactorily.

(l) Check navigation lights and radio.

(m) On getting under way, check and adjust stern gland as necessary.

Q.11 Briefly describe the two most common types of fuel injection pumps as fitted to high speed marine diesel engines.

A. (a) Jerk Pump System - in this system, the pressure of fuel is developed by the sudden closing of a by-pass port in a (usually) constant stroke pump. The quantity of fuel injected may be controlled either by the re-opening of the by-pass at different parts of the stroke, or in a few cases by variation of plunger stroke. A separate fuel pump unit is supplied for each cylinder, these units being normally assembled as a block, with separate pipes leading from the individual fuel pump units to the spring loaded fuel injectors in the cylinders.

(b) Distributor - Type Injection Pump System - in this system, regardless of the number of cylinders, the fuel is pumped by a single element, and the fuel changes are distributed in the correct firing order and at the required timing intervals to each cylinder in turn by means of a rotary distributor, integral with the pump.

Q.12 What is the purpose of heater plugs?

A. To ensure ignition of the fuel, it is important that sufficient temperature is attained by the compressed air in the cylinder. With a cold engine, much of the heat of compression is absorbed by the cool pistons, cylinder walls and head, particularly in engines with separate or swirl combustion chambers. Electrically-operated heater plugs or torches provide this necessary heat when starting a cold engine.

Where heater plugs are used, the plug body is screwed into the cylinder head with the wire heater coil locating in a recess in the combustion chamber. The tip of the coil is more or less flush with the chamber wall to protect it as much as possible from the heat of combustion.

Q.13 What steps should be taken when-
(a) Knocking in the crankcase is heard; and
(b) When smoke is discovered issuing from openings in the crankcase; and why?

A. When knocking is heard and cannot at once be located and remedied, the speed of the engine should be reduced in order to reduce the risk of damage resulting, and provide an opportunity for locating the cause of the unusual noise. Should the engine be stopped immediately, the difficulty of locating the cause would be greatly increased, unless it results from bearing bolt nuts slackening or something that would be equally apparent. It may be of course, that the knocking is so heavy or of such a nature that it would be unwise to keep the engine running, in which case the engine should be stopped at once and an examination of the parts inside the crankcase made.

Q.14 What is the purpose of introducing lubricating oil into bearings? How does the oil act?

A. The function of lubricating oil is to separate the metallic rubbing surfaces and substitute fluid friction for metallic friction. A film of lubricating oil has a definite thickness; its thickness varies with operating conditions, such as pressure and temperature, and is very thin by ordinary standards, but it is capable of keeping apart heavily loaded metallic surfaces.

Q.15 How may an outbreak of fire occur in the engine room of a motorship?
A. The most likely causes of fire are:-
(a) Inattention to condition of bilges which should be kept clean and free of oil.
(b) Leaky joints and seams, and oil dripping on to exhaust and other hot pipes.

(c) Leaky joints on the high pressure fuel system, where the oil spray is sometimes so fine that it is almost invisible.
(d) Badly maintained electrical equipment.

Q.16 How can a tank recently emptied of fuel oil be freed of explosive gas?
A. A current of fresh air, if led to the bottom of the tank, will drive the gases out at the top. Since the explosive gas is heavier than air the desired results cannot be obtained if the air is admitted to the top of the tank. A tank can also be freed of explosive gas by steaming out. In either case the tank must be well drained before gas-freeing operations begin, otherwise the operation will take considerable time. Another method is to fill the tank with water.

Q.17 What is the usual type of fuel injector?
A. The fuel injector is a spring-controlled valve inserted into the engine cylinder head (or in the side of the cylinder of opposed-piston engines) and allows the fuel, under pressure from the injection pump, to enter the cylinder or head in the form of a fine spray or mist. The injector is held in the correct position in the cylinder head by means of an injector holder.

Q.18 What is meant by two-stage combustion in an oil engine?
A. In some types of modern oil engines it is arranged that the combustion takes place in a single chamber, which is the space between the top of the piston and the cylinder head. Another, known as the two-stage type, has an auxiliary combustion chamber which communicates with the cylinder combustion chamber by a restricted throat or air ports.

This auxiliary combustion chamber is known as the ante-chamber, and in this type of engine the fuel is injected into this ante-chamber, where it is ignited by the temperature of compression and partially consumed by the limited amount of air present.

The consequent rise of pressure forces the mixture out of the antechamber into the cylinder, where it finds the additional air necessary to complete the combustion process.

Q.19 What may be learnt from the visual appearance of the exhaust gas of a diesel engine?

A. If the exhaust gas is visible the colour should be observed. Black smoke indicates poor or insufficient combustion or engine overload, blue smoke indicates excessive cylinder lubrication, white exhaust vapour indicates an excess of moisture in the exhaust gas. It should, however, be remembered that in very cold weather condensation of water vapour in the exhaust may give a white vapour appearance, even though the exhaust gas is perfectly normal in composition. White vapour may also be caused by leaking refrigerant in the engine combustion air supply.

Q.20 What faults may be found with fuel injectors?

A. (1) Incorrect operating pressure.
(2) Distorted Spray form.
(3) Dripping injector.
(4) Injector valve not buzzing while injecting.
(5) Dirt between the injector valve and its seating.
(6) Cracked injector body.
(7) Broken injector-valve compression spring.
(8) Injector valve sticking in its guide.
(9) Compression-control spring not properly tensioned.(This is generally caused by the compression adjusting screw in the injector holder having slackened).
(10)A blued injector.
(11)Too much fuel escaping at the leak-off pipe.

Q.21 Give the four possible causes of high injector pressure and their remedies.

A. (1) Compression-spring adjusting screw shifted – adjust screw to the correct pressure.
(2) Injector valve seized up, corroded - renew injector valve and body.
(3) Injector valve seized up, dirty, sticky - clean the injector.

(4) Injector openings clogged with dir - clean the injector.

Q.22 State as many reasons as possible for a bilge pump failing to draw water from a full bilge.

A. (a) Other bilge suction valves open.
(b) Blocked suction strainer.
(c) Air leaks in suction piping.
(d) Air leaks around suction valve glands and pump gland.
(e) Pump impeller or suction valves choked with foreign matter.
(f) Pump drive failure.
(g) Pump priming device not functioning.
(h) Non-return suction valve seized in seat.
(i) Excessive clearance in pump impeller.
(j) Insufficient rotational speed of pump

Q.23 Which three single factors are necessary to create combustion? What is the greatest safeguard against fire or explosion? Where is the greatest area of fire risk in any vessel, and how can this be restricted?

A. (a) Heat
(b) A combustible material
(c) Oxygen in the form of air

The greatest safeguard against fire or explosion is cleanliness. To achieve this, engine compartment bilges should be kept free of oil and inflammable materials such as waste and rags Wooden floors, if fitted, should be kept free of oil. Pipe joints and valve glands should be kept tight. Pipes from fuel tank drains, or from engine save-alls, should preferably be led to small receptacles.

The greatest risk of fire is in the engine compartment. This can be restricted by adequately sealing the area from the rest of the vessel. Special consideration must be given when a combustible material is used as the construction medium for the vessel.

Q.24 Enumerate the various types of fire extinguishers suitable for use on

fishing vessels. Explain what class of fire for which each is suitable.

What types of extinguisher would you use if a pan of cooking fat caught alight? Would you use water, discuss reasons?

Types of extinguishers:-

(a) Foam – may be used on fuel, oil based materials, wood, trash, paper, waste.

(b) Soda Acid – wood, trash, paper, waste.

(c) CO_2 Expelled – wood, trash, paper, waste, water

(d) CO_2 – suitable for use on all types of fires and are particularly suitable for electrical fires.

(e) Dry Chemical – suitable for use on all types of fires, including electrical fires

(f) B.C.F. (B.T.M.) – as above.

Certain types of extinguishers are a statutory requirement, although other types of extinguishers over and above the requirements may be carried.

Any of the following extinguishers are suitable for cooking fat - C02, Dry Chemical and B.C.F./B.T.M.

Water should on no account be used for this type of fire. The effect of pouring water onto the pan of burning fat might well cause the fat to overflow, thus spreading the fire which was previously contained in a small area. A jet of water directed at the pan could cause the burning fat to splash out of the pan with similar results.

It has also been established that a small amount of water poured onto burning fat has no instant effect as, due to the relative specific gravity, it will sink to the bottom. However, the intense heat of the surrounding fat will very quickly convert it to steam, which will expand and flash off with an explosive effect causing considerable damage over an extensive area.

25 What is the compression ratio of a diesel engine?

When the piston of a reciprocating engine travels one complete stroke it sweeps out a volume equal to the product of its cross-sectional area and distance travelled; this is termed the 'swept volume' of the cylinder. Upon the piston reaching the end of an in-stroke it is some distance from the product of this distance and the cross-sectional area of the cylinder is referred to as the "clearance volume". The compression ratio of the engine is the sum of the "swept volume" and "clearance volume" divided by the "clearance volume".

e.g. Swept Volume   = 48cu inches
Clearance Volume = 3cu inches
Compression Ratio = $\frac{48 + 3}{3}$ = 17

Average compression ratios for a diesel engine varies between 12:1 to 19:1.

Generally speaking compression ratios are higher in small high-speed diesel engines than in large low-speed diesel engines, due to the far greater heat loss rate in the smaller cylinders, necessitating the use of higher ratio in order to achieve the necessary high temperature for ignition purposes.

Q.26 What are the basic differences between the two stroke cycle and four stroke cycle diesel engines?

A.   With the two stroke cycle of operation one working stroke occurs (in each cylinder) for every revolution of the crank shaft. With the four stroke cycle one working stroke occurs (in each cylinder) for every two revolutions of the crank shaft. In the two stroke engine, a separate air pump or blower is required to charge the cylinders with air for combustion, while in the four stroke engine the working cylinder itself performs that duty.

Q.27.How is fuel oil delivered to the cylinder of a diesel engine?

A.   By means of a fuel injection pump delivering fuel oil under pressure to the injector fitted to the cylinder. The injector needle is raised off its seat at the appropriate time by the pressure of the fuel and allows the fuel oil, in the form of a fine spray or mist, to enter the engine combustion chamber through the hole or holes in the end of the injector.

ELECTRICAL

Q.1 Name the electrolyte in each of –
(a) The lead acid battery; and
(b) The alkaline battery.

A. (a) Dilute sulphuric acid.

(b) Caustic potash.

Q.2 What first aid measures should be adopted after accidental contact between these electrolytes and the skin or eyes?

A. (a) Dilute sulphuric acid as used in lead-acid cells is not harmful to a healthy skin if it is washed off as soon as possible. A splash in the eye does, however, require immediate attention and as a first aid measure it should be swilled with water or a dilute saline solution immediately. (The saline solution recommended is one level teaspoonful of household salt to half a pint of water). The chief essentials are rapid action and large quantities of water. A drastic method is to immerse the head in a bucket of water and open and shut the affected eye under the water.

(b) The electrolyte of alkaline cells (caustic potash) should be handled with care as it is corrosive and should not be allowed to come into contact with skin or clothing, cover the affected part with boracic powder or a saturated solution of boracic powder. For the eyes, wash out thoroughly with plenty of clean water and then use immediately a solution of boracic powder - one teaspoonful to the pint. These should be available whenever electrolyte is being handled.

Q.3 Briefly describe the types of storage batteries available for use on board a vessel.

A. Practically all storage batteries used on board ship are either (a) the lead-acid type, or (b) the alkaline type.

Q.4 Briefly summarise the precautions to be taken with the installation of batteries in a vessel.

A. 1. The cells must be suitable for use on board ship and must not emit acid or alkaline spray.

2. The cells must be accessible from the top and insulators must be use underneath and at each side of the battery. The cells must be fixed s as to prevent any movement arising from the motion of the ship.

3 Ventilating fans must be such that sparking is impossible in the ever of the impeller tips touching the fan casing.

4. Acid from the cells must not damag the structure of the ship.

5. The battery compartment must b properly ventilated.

6. Rectifiers must not be located i positions where they would b subject to gases from the batteries

7. Batteries should not be installed i living quarters.

8. Appropriate control gear togethe with an ammeter and voltmeter mu be provided.

9. Where there is a separate batter compartment switches and fuse must not be installed inside th compartment. The battery cable must be protected by a fuse c circuit breaker just outside th compartment.

10. Alkaline batteries and lead-aci batteries must not be placed in th same room.

Q.5 Briefly state the care an maintenance necessary to kee batteries in good condition.

A. (i) Cells must be kept fully charged.

(ii) Electrolyte level must be kept abov the level of the plates.

(iii) Terminals must be kept clean an free from corrosion.

(iv) The charge and discharge rat should not exceed th manufacturer's recommendation.

(v) Impurities should not be allowed t enter the cells.

(vi) Connections to the terminals shou be kept clean and tight.

Q.6 Should a lead-acid battery be store or left in a discharged condition fc a period of time? Explain reasons

A. No. If left in a discharged state for an length of time the lead sulphate in th discharged plates changes to a white deposit on the surface of the plates. "Sulphating" of the plates reduces the capacity of the battery. The . white sulphate deposit is generally difficult to remove and in the case of an old battery this is impossible.

Q.7 **Explain how a number of batteries can be grouped to provide a supply of increased voltage rating?**

A. The batteries are connected in series;with this method of connection the positive terminal of one battery is connected to the negative terminal of the next and so on. Batteries of different voltages can be connected in series to provide the required voltage e.g.: two, twelve volt and one, six volt battery can be connected as shown to provide a 30 volt supply.

Beside the 30 volt supply which would be indicated on the voltmeter, a 24 volt or 18 volt supply could also be obtained. These would be as indicated on (2) and (3) respectively in Fig. 126.

Q.8 **Explain how a number of batteries can be connected to provide a supply of increased energy?**

A. The batteries should be connected in parallel. In this method of connection the batteries are connected positive terminal to positive terminal and negative terminal to negative terminal as shown in figure 127 . Note: batteries of the same voltage 'only" should be connected in this way otherwise a circulating current will flow within the closed circuit within the supply.

If three 12 volt batteries are connected as shown below, the supply voltage remains at 12 volts but the energy that can be supplied is approximately three times that which is available from one battery.

Q.9 **State why ventilation of the space containing storage batteries is so important and also state the precautions that should be adopted for the safe operation of a storage battery installation.**

A. The gases given off from any battery on charge whether of the lead-acid or alkaline type, consist of hydrogen and oxygen. If the hydrogen concentration becomes too great a spark or a naked flame can initiate an explosion. It is essential therefore that there must be proper ventilation of the battery compartment, particularly during quick charging. Furthermore every precaution

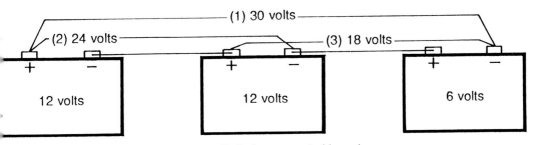

Figure 126 – *Batteries connected in series*

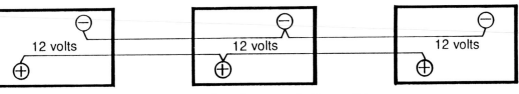

Figure 127 – *Batteries connected in parallel*

must be taken to avoid sparking taking place. All terminals should be examined from time to time to ensure that they are sound, metal jugs must not be used for topping-up purposes, and loose wires or tools must not be placed on top of the cells. Smoking must be prohibited in the battery compartment and a prominent notice displayed to this effect.

If lead-acid and alkaline batteries are both installed in the same ship it is most important that they should be mounted in separate compartments. In such cases, too, each battery should have its own topping-up jugs, hydrometers, distilled water, etc. The slightest traces of acid can cause serious damage to alkaline cells.

Q.10 In respect to a storage battery, what is "overcharging" and what effects has "overcharging" on the battery?

A. Overcharging is charging beyond the time necessary to fully charge the battery or charging conducted at an excessive rate (in amps) for the particular battery. It produces erosion and corrosion of the positive material and causes the grids to fracture reducing their ability to carry heavy currents, particularly starting currents.

Overcharging is usually accompanied by heavy gassing which will accelerate the shedding of the active material from the positive plates. Excessive deposition of active materials in the bottom of the battery container will cause a build up of silt which may bridge the plates and cause internal short circuits.

Overcharging is usually accompanied by high electrolyte temperatures resulting in rapid deterioration of the plates and separators.

Overcharging may cause buckling of the plates leading to perforation of the separators and internal short circuits.

Q.11 Briefly describe the tests performed on a storage battery to determine its condition.

A. The high rate test indicates the ability of a battery to deliver a high current for a short time without the output voltage falling too low for engine cranking requirements. The test

simulates starting a very cold engine.

Note: This test should be applied to only a well charged battery, i.e. S.G. 1,200 or higher. A poorly charged battery lacks sum to give a true indication of its condition.

The test is applied by discharging the cell or battery through a fixed resistance for about ten to fifteen seconds noting the voltage drop of the cell or battery being tested. A load or high rate tester is used to perform this test. The scale of the instrument is calibrated so that safe limits are indicated either by coloured bands or voltage figures.

If the pointer falls below the safe limit, it indicates that the cell or battery is not able to supply sufficient power or is discharged. The hydrometer should then be used to determine the state of charge, and if the cell or battery is charged, the test has then proved that the cell or battery is faulty.

Where the S.G. is below 1,200 or if in the vicinity of 1,200 and gives a 'doubtful' reading, the battery should be fully charged and retested. A stand of several days between charging and testing will help to pick out batteries with a very small "short" in a cell.

Q.12 Before removing or replacing batteries in a vessel, what precautions should be taken?

A. Switch off all lights and any other sources of power drain on the batteries, mark the battery leads and battery terminals Red + Black – use a carry strap or the handles on the battery, DO NOT lift the battery with cord or wire looped under the connecting strips. Ensure batteries are the correct voltage. Secure batteries against movement.

Q.13 When is a battery most likely to explode if a source of ignition is near it?

A. Just after it has been gassing due to a high rate of charge or discharge.

Q.14 Does a battery have an explosive gas on top of the electrolyte at all times?

A. Yes.

Q.15 Would the same precautions be

required with alkaline batteries?

A. Yes.

Q.16 What would happen in a charging system where an alternator was connected to the batteries with the incorrect polarity?

A. 1. The diodes in the alternator would be overheated and damaged.

2. Battery damage through overheating - possible subsequent internal short circuit through buckled plates.

Q.17 What is the most common cause of low charge rates from generators and alternators?

A. Slipping Drive belts.

Q.18 (i) Define the following terms: Volt, amp, ohm, watt; and

(ii) State the relationship between volts, amps, and watts.

A. (i) Volt is the unit of electrical pressure or difference in potential. It is defined as the force necessary to send a current of one ampere through a resistance of one ohm, and is symbolised with the letter 'E'.

Amp (ampere) is the unit of strength of an electric current. For engineering purposes, it is the current strength produced by unit pressure when passing through a resistance of one ohm, and is symbolised with the letter 'I'.

Ohm is the unit of resistance and is defined as the resistance set up by unit pressure forcing unit current strength through a circuit and is symbolised with the letter "R".

Watt is the unit of power and is symbolised with the letter 'W'.

(ii) Watts = Volts x amps

or

W = IE

where w = watts

I = amps

E = volts

also 1000 watts = 1 kilowatt (1kW)

746 watts = horsepower (1 HP)

Q.19 What do you understand by the

meaning of the terms Low Voltage and Extra Low Voltage?

A. Extra Low Voltage normally not exceeding 32 volts AC. 115 DC: Low Voltage exceeding 32 volts AC but not exceeding 240 volts AC.

Q.20 Is salt water a good conductor of electricity?

A. Salt water has a very low resistance, and is a very good conductor of electricity.

Q.21 What effect does the salt atmosphere have on the contacts of electrical equipment?

A. Salt has a corrosive effect on most metallic materials. When corrosion effects contacts of electrical equipment it reduces the size of the contacts causing arcing, overheating, which may be a cause of fire.

Q.22 Why is it necessary to prevent the build up of salt on the surface of electrical equipment?

A. Some form of insulation generally forms on the exterior surface of electrical equipment. If salt crystals are allowed to form they absorb moisture which becomes conductive and provides a leakage path for currents.

Q.23 What precautions should be taken when electrical components are broken and exposed contacts visible?

A. The broken component should be replaced immediately, or if this is not practical the equipment should be disconnected from the supply and labelled to prevent it being used until repaired.

Q.24 What is a fuse and describe its operation?

A. A fuse is a device for protecting a circuit against damage from an excessive current flowing in it. Its operation is by opening the circuit on the melting of a fuse element.

Q.25 If a fuse element is blown what precautions should be taken before removing the fuse wedge?

A. When a fuse element is blown the supply should be isolated by turning off the main switch, before removing the fuse wedge. When the fuse has been repaired and the wedge in position the main switch may be switched on.

Q.26 What size fuse element would you select if a fuse element was blown?

A. The fuse element should be the same current rating as the circuit it protects.

Q.27 What action would you take when, after replacing a fuse element, it blew immediately supply was switched on?

A. When a fuse element is replaced and it blows immediately it indicates (1) overloading of circuit,(2) short circuit in circuit wiring or faulty appliances connected thereto. The faulty section should be isolated or the faulty appliance disconnected. Never use a larger fuse element than the current rating of the circuit as this may cause overheating and fire.

Q.28 What precautions should be taken when hosing?

A. Keep water away from electrical equipment unless fittings and equipment are of a waterproof type.

Q.29 Should loose cans of fuel or spirit be stored in the same room as electrical equipment that may cause arcs and sparks?

A. Loose cans of fuel or spirit must not be stored in the same room as electrical equipment, unless the electrical equipment is specially designed to prevent arcs and sparks coming in contact with the atmosphere. (Flame Proof Equipment).

Q.30 What voltage would you select for a lead light to be used in wet areas or confined spaces?

A. All lead lights used in wet areas or in confined spaces should be connected to Extra Low Voltage Supply.

Q.31 To minimise risk of electric shock what precautions should be taken when using a welder?

A. 1. Always switch welding equipment "off" when not in use.
   2. Switch off before connecting or disconnecting the welding leads to the welder terminals.
   3. Ensure that welding leads are correctly connected to the 'Electrode' and 'Work' terminals and

that connections have clean contact surfaces and are securely tightened Dirty or loose connections introduce high resistance and result in overheating.

4. Ensure that in all cases, a return lead is connected between 'Work terminal of the welder and job Never use the system earth as a return path.

5. When the welder is switched 'on do not handle the electrode or the exposed metal parts of the electrode holder with bare hands. Wear an insulated glove when placing an electrode into its holder.

6. Take all possible precautions to ensure that no dangerous situations arise. Do not provide a path for electric currents e.g. through your body from the electrode to earth.

Between welding runs place the electrode holder and electrode so that electrical contact cannot be made with persons or conductive objects. Treat all parts of the welding circuit, including the return paths as alive. Inadequate body coverage, damp clothing and confined space increase the hazards.

Q.32 What precautions should be taken before welding a drum or container?

A. Do not attempt to weld any drum or container until it has been thoroughly cleaned to prevent the possibility of explosion due to flammable vapours.

Q.33 Before welding in the engine room or on the vessel what safety precautions would you take with the electrical circuits.

A. 1. Inspect power lead, plug and socket for damage, loose connections, burnt terminals etc.
   2. Make sure welder is well earthed.
   3. Disconnect batteries and alternator to avoid damage to systems.

Q.34 What precautions should be carried out when connecting a three phase extension lead to the shore supply.

A. 1. Inspect the lead together with its plug and socket.
   2. Check the lead, where a shore power lead test device is provided, to ensure that:
   a) the earth pin is not active

b) the earth is continuous

c) the neutral is continuous(where a test device is not provided an electrician is required to test the lead).

3. Ensure that lead cannot be damaged mechanically through trucks etc., running over lead vessel pinching lead against wharf etc.

4. Switch the ships power/shore power selector switch to the "off" position.

5. Connect lead & switch on shore power.

6. Verify that phase rotation is correct at the phase rotation meter and rectify by means of the phase reversing switch.

7. Switch on load gradually and check ammeter for loading.

Q.35. Should a fault occur in a medium voltage (240 V - 415 V) electrical installation what precautions must be taken?

A. 1. Isolate the fault.

2. Engage a licensed electrican to rectify the fault.

Q.36 Enumerate the types of domestic appliances that consume most power.

A. Any heating appliances such as toasters, stoves, radiators, etc

Q.37 What is the difference in the use of a circuit breaker and an earth leakage circuit breaker.

A. Circuit breaker is used to sense the amount of current to protect machinery through overload; whereas an earth leakage circuit breaker is used to sense a fault to earth and protect persons. A circuit breaker switches the power off because of overload whereas the earth leakage circuit breaker switches the power off because of an earth fault.

Q.38 Explain the difference in operation between a fuse and a circuit breaker?

A. When an excessive current flows through a fuse the element becomes heated and melts, while the circuit breaker 'trips' or opens to break the circuit.

Q.39 How is a circuit breaker re-set?

A. When a circuit breaker has "tripped" the operating handle must be moved to the "Off" position before the breaker can be reclosed.

Q.40 What precautions should be taken to avoid risk of electric shock to persons?

A. All electrical equipment should be highly insulated and installed in positions which are guarded against salt spray (unless of a weather proof type) and also guarded against mechanical damage.

Q.41 What amount of current is required to extinguish life?

A. From .013 to .02 of an amp at 240 V is sufficient for a normal person. From this it is easily seen it takes very little current to be lethal.

Q.42 If a person receives an electric shock what procedures should be adopted before removing the victim from live apparatus?

A. If a person receives an electric shock do not attempt to remove him from the energised equipment until you have disconnected the source of supply, by turning off the main switch which is situated on the switchboard or switching off the supply at the power point and removing the plug from the outlet.

Q.43 State what method of resuscitation you would use on a person who received an electric shock and is unconscious?

A. Mouth to Mouth or Mouth to Nose resuscitation should be administered in conjunction with External Cardiac Compression.

REFRIGERATION

It is recommended that operators with limited knowledge do not tamper with the systems and that competent persons be consulted. In endeavouring to save on cost it could quite often, in the end, cost much more for negligence.

Q.1 What type of oil should be used in a refrigeration compressor?

A.   A type which has:

(a) lubrication properties at low temperatures.

(b) Ability to withstand low temperatures.

(c) Is easily separated from refrigerant.

(d) Unaffected by refrigerant

(e) Non hygroscopic.

Q.2 At what levels should oils be kept in the compressor?

A.   Levels should be maintained within the centre of the sight glass or where sight glasses are not in use just below the crankshaft centre on splash feed compressors.

Q.3. What problems can stem from having to add oil frequently?

A.   Indications are, there could be a shortage of gas or blocked oil return flow.

Q.4. What gases are mostly used in small ship refrigerators?

A.   Refrigerant 12 or 502, (Freon).

Q.5. How would leaks be detected in refrigeration systems?

A.   Halogen leak detector.

Soap and water.

Electronic leak detector.

Q.6 What dangers exist with a leaky system?

A.   In small areas asphyxiation. Gas on coming in contact with heat, such as exhaust manifolds changes its character and becomes a poisonous gas.

Q.7 What are the indications of gas leaking in the engine room and passing through the combination chambers of the cylinders?

A.   On a large volume of gas the exhaust turns white.

Q.8 What problems are associated with small craft installations.

A.   Ventilation.

Q.9 How would a shortage of gas be recognised?

A.   Length of evaporation coils would not be covered with frost, it would show shortage of gas in the liquid sight glass situated in the liquid line, low head pressures.

Q.10 Enumerate some way in which moisture can enter the system.

A.   1. Moisture not fully removed from system on installation.

2. It can enter the machine during replacement of parts.

3. It can enter the system through leaks on the low side of the system

4. When adding oil to system if oil is not completely dry.

5. Leaky condensor.

Q.11 How would you eliminate moisture from the system?

A.   By fitting driers, changing regularly until the fault disappears.

Q.12 How would you tell if there is moisture in the system?

A.   By the following:

1. One of the TX valves are not freezing properly.

2. Pour a cup of hot water over the TX valve. This will cause it to immediately operate normally until the water comes around the system again. This is only a test not a cure

Q.13 How would you tell if TX valve was faulty?

A.   1. No freezing would take place if the power element had collapsed.

2. If the strainer was blocked.

Note: In the first instance a complete change of valve would be necessary whereas in the second instance cleaning would be sufficient.

Q.14 What precautions should be taken where flexible hoses are in use to aid vibration?

A. Hoses to be checked regularly to see they remain flexible and not rigid through deterioriation from heat or that wire braiding has not been effected by salt water.

Q.15 What attention should be given to the Condensers?

A. Condensers should be checked at least every three months to see that tubes are clear and clean and that zinc plugs for electrolysis are in good condition. Leaks in the condenser tubes may require re-tubing or total replacement of the condenser.

Q.16 What precautions should be taken when closing the system down?

A. Close liquid line service valves. Pump the system down until the compound gauge reaches zero. Should machine be not in operation for periods of two weeks or more the suction service valve 5 should also be closed after the compressor has been pumped down to zero and stopped.

Q.17 What are the normal operating pressures on gauges?

Note: Pressure temperature chart.

Illustration.

A. Head pressure 860 kPA per square inch, but could range from 725kPA to 965kPA

Freon 12 - Brine bins (design of equipment has an influencing effect) at designed temperature.
Back pressure can vary from 150kPA down to 68kPA.

Cold Rooms. At designed temperature back pressure can vary from 68kPA to zero.

502 Mostly cold rooms or freezer room. Head pressure 1580kPA, but could range from 1724kPA to 1380kPA. Cold Rooms Designed for - 18° celsius at temperature, back pressure 96kPA-150kPA. (suction pressure).

Q.18 What causes could be attributed to an abnormally high discharge pressure on a refrigeration compressor?

A. (a) Dirty or blocked condenser tubes.

(b) Insufficient coolant flow due to:-

(i) Faulty circulating pump; or

(ii) Choked circulating pump suction filter.

(c) Air entrapment in the refrigeration circuit due to:-

(i) Leaking compressor seals; and

(ii) Loose connection on suction side of circuit; and compressor operating at a very low suction pressure.

(d) A valve in the discharge circuit only partly open.

(e) A combination of all of the above.

Q.19 Describe the effects of air entrapment in a refrigeration system, and the procedure you would adopt in extracting this.

A. The first indication of air in the circuit is an excessively high discharge pressure and temperature. This may be removed by carrying out the following procedures:-

(a) Pump all of the refrigerant back into the condenser, then close both condenser outlet and compressor suction valves.

(b) Allow the sea water cooling to circulate the condenser until temperature stabilization is reached. The pump can then be stopped.

(c) Open the condenser purge valve and vent the air until the compressor discharge gauge reads a temperature a little in excess of the sea temperature.

The plant may now be run; should indications of air still be present, the procedure may be carried out again.

Q.20. List and describe the various safety devices fitted to a modern refrigeration plant.

A. (a) Low oil pressure cut out.

(b) Low suction pressure cut out.

(c) High discharge pressure cut out.

(d) High pressure gas relief valve.

Low oil pressure cut out

This device is connected into the lubricating oil circuit and operates to stop or disconnect the compressor, when the oil pressure falls below a predetermined level.

Low suction pressure cut out

This cut out is designed to either disconnect or unload the compressor when the suction pressure falls to a set level, possibility of liquid passing back into the compressor and causing serious damage.

High discharge cut out.

The function of this device is to stop or unload the compressor in the event of the discharge pressure rising above normal, and hence overload the machine, or lift the relief valve.

High pressure gas relief valve.

This relief valve is usually fitted to the liquid receiver and opens to release the refrigerant gas should the pressure rise to a serious level. The relief valve only lifts to release the charge when other devices have failed.

PART VII
MATHEMATICS

Q.1 In the electrical system of measurement watts = volts x amps. What would be the amperage of a 24 volt generator which is rated at 500 watts?

A. $W = E \times I$ $I = \dfrac{W}{E}$ amperes

$I = \dfrac{500}{24} = 20.83$ amperes

Q.2. A ship uses 28 litres of fuel per hour. After completing a trip of 30 days. running for 10 hours a day, what would be the cost of the fuel used if the fuel was $0.50 per litre?

A.
Total Running Time	= 30 x 10 = 300 hours
Voyage Consumption	= 300 x 28 Litres
Voyage Consumption	= 8400 Litres
Fuel Cost	= 8400 x 0.5
	= $4,200

Q.3 If an engine converts fuel to energy output at the rate of 500,650 joules every 12 seconds, what power is being delivered in kilowatts?
1 watt - 1 joule per second

A. Engine power output $= \dfrac{500,650 \text{ W}}{12}$

$= 41720.8$ W

Hence power delivered $= 41.72$ kW

Q.4 If the capacity of a water tank is 21,000 litres and its length and breadth are 4.57 m and 3.05m respectively, what would the depth be?

A. Tank volume $= \dfrac{21,000 \text{ M}^3}{1000}$

Tank area $= 4.57 \times 3.05$

Tank depth $=$

$\dfrac{\text{Volume}}{\text{Area}} = \dfrac{21000}{1000 \times 4.57 \times 3.05}$

Tank depth $= 1.506$ m Ans

Q.5 How many millimetres measured round the rim of a flywheel 1.19 m in diameter corresponds to 2 degrees?

A. Circumference Π D
Dist in mm corresponding to $2°$
$= \Pi D \times \dfrac{2}{360} = 20.771$ mm

Q.6. At noon the counter of an engine registered 624520. At 2.30 p.m. it registered 684520. What has been the revolutions turned per minute since noon, and what should the counter read at 4.00 p.m.?

A.
Watch Time	= 2.5 x 60	=	150 minutes
Revs. Turned	= 68 4520	– 62 4520	
	= 60 000 Revolutions		
R.P.M.	$= \dfrac{60\ 000}{150}$	=	400

Revolutions Turned) $= 90 \times 400 = 36\ 000$ revs.
Till 4pm   )

Projected Counter) $= 68\ 4520 + 3600$
Reading at 4pm   )

Projected Counter) $= 72\ 0520$
Reading at 4pm   )

Q.7 Find the total force on a piston 200 mm in diameter if the pressure is 2000kPa. (Area of a circle 11/14 x diameter²)

A.
Pressure	= 2000 kPa = 2 MPa
Piston area	= 0.7854 x 200² mm²
Piston area	= 31416 mm²
Force	= press. x Area.
Force	= 2 x 31416 (N) = 62832 (N)
	= 62.83 KN

Q.8 The pitch of a propeller is 991 mm and it turns 304 revolutions per minute, what will be the speed of the vessel in nautical miles per hour if slip is neglected?

1 nautical mile = 1852 metres

A. Distance Travelled Per Minute
$= 0.991 \times 304$ m
Distance Travelled Per Hour
$= 0.991 \times 304 \times 60$
Distance Travelled Per Hour
$= 18075.84$ m/hour
Speed in Nautical Miles Per Hour
$= \dfrac{8075.84}{1852}$
Speed in Nautical Miles Per Hour
$= 9.76$ knots

Q.9 The consumption of fuel is 5 tonnes per day. If the brake power of an engine is 1000 kw what will be the consumption in grammes per kw per hour?

A. Fuel Consumption Per Hour
$= \dfrac{5 \times 1000}{24}$ kg/hour
Fuel Consumption Per Hour
$= 208.3$
Consumption per kw Per Hour
$= \dfrac{208.3}{1000}$ kg/kw hr
Consumption in Grammes Per kw Per Hr
$= \dfrac{208.3 \times 1000}{1000}$
Consumption in Grammes Per kw Per Hr)
$= 208.$ grammes/kw/Hour

Chapter 18
Radio Communications

RADIOCOMMUNICATIONS

There can be no better reason for having a radio transceiver aboard your boat than that, one day, it might save your life. It provides you with the means of alerting other people to an emergency and may be the only link between rescuer and the rescued.

Some types of marine radio equipment can also provide personal communications between your boat and home or office.

However, it is important that if you do have a marine radio aboard that it is a suitable type, that you know how to operate it effectively and that you maintain it in good working order.

The Communications Operations Division of the Commonwealth Department of Transport and Communications (DOTC) is the controlling body for radio communications in Australia. Boatowners should be aware of the need to obtain the appropriate licence and personal qualification before they install or operate a marine radio.

Q.1 How many types of marine radio are there?

A. There are three recognised types-

(a) 27 MHz Marine

(b) VHF International Maritime Mobile Service

(c) MF/HF International Maritime Mobile Service

Q.2 Which type of marine radio should I have on my boat?

A. That answer must depend of your normal area of operation and the requirements of your class of survey (if applicable).

Under normal conditions, 27 MHz and VHF marine radios have a ship to shore range of no more than about 50 kilometres. If you operate further than this from a shore radio station you should fit MF/HF equipment which is capable of ranges up to several thousand kilometres.

Q.3 How can I license my marine radio

A. By simply completing a licence application form and paying the appropriate fee. This may be done 'over the counter' at any office of the Communications Operations Division of DOTC (a list of offices and telephone numbers may be found on page..... of this Manual.) Alternatively, the transaction may be carried out by post.

Q.4 Do I need to obtain a personal qualification to operate my marine radio ?

A. If you have only 27 MHz marine equipment, the answer is no. However, if you are operating either VHF marine or MF/HF marine transceivers, then under international regulations you are required to hold a basic operating qualification.

Q.5 How do I obtain this qualification?

A. The qualification is known as the Restricted Operators Certificate of Proficiency in Radiotelephony (ROCP). The certificate is issued to candidates who pass a basic operating and procedures examination conducted by DOTC.

The examination is based on the 'Handbook for Radiotelephone Ship Station Operators' which is available from any of the offices mentioned earlier. There is a small examination fee and it will take about an hour of your time.

Q.6 Do I need to attend a course of lectures in order to pass the examination?

A. No, many successful candidates have studied the Handbook at home. However, organisations such as Volunteer Coast Guard, Air Sea Rescue and some colleges of TAFE conduct brief courses leading up to the examination.

Q.7 Are there distress channels for each category of marine radio?

A. Yes, in the 27 MHz marine bands, 27.88 and 27.86 MHz (27.86 MHz being designated as a supplementary distress channel).

In the VHF marine bands, channels 16 and 67 (with channel 67 being the supplementary).

In the MF/HF marine service, 2182, 4125, 6215, 8291, 12290, and 16420 kHz.

Obviously, in order to provide the best safety network, all vessels should keep the maximum possible watch on the distress channels in use aboard.

Q.8 What is the distress signal in radio communications?

A. The distress signal is MAYDAY MAYDAY MAYDAY. It has absolute priority over all other transmissions and indicates that the station sending it is threatened by grave and imminent danger and requests immediate assistance. It must not be used at any other time, and severe penalties exist for anybody who does misuse it.

Q.9 Are there any other priority signals?

A. Yes, the urgency signal and the safety signal.

The urgency signal is PAN PAN PAN PAN PAN PAN and should be used when a distress signal is not justified but when a vessel has a very urgent message to transmit concerning the safety of the vessel or a crew member.

The safety signal SECURITE SECURITE SECURITE indicates that a station is about to broadcast an important navigational or weather warning.

Q.10 Which types of marine radio can provide me with private communications?

A. If you have 27 MHz marine equipment only, your messages will be restricted to those concerning the safety and movement of your vessel. However, if you have VHF or MF/HF marine equipment, you will have access into the Telecom phone network via coast stations operated by Telstra Maritime.

Telstra's Autodial Seaphone service enables you to direct dial any telephone number in Australia or overseas through your vessel's VHF marine radio. This service is being progressively upgraded during the 1990's to provide a continuous coverage along Australia's eastern seaboard from Melbourne to Cairns.

Q.11 When I licence my marine radio equipment, will I be told which channels are available for my use ?

A. Yes, a brochure which accompanies your licence will provide this information. Also, DOTC has available channel guide stickers which you will find helpful. Even though your radio is likely to be fitted with many channels, you may not be authorised to use all of them. Unfortunately, even the unintentional misuse of channels can have rather serious consequences - for example, unauthorised use of the VHF channels reserved for ship/tug manoeuvring operations could result in a costly accident.

Q.12 What shore facilities are provided to handle radio communications to and from boats and ships ?

A. There are two types of shore radio stations which communicate with vessels at sea. They are known as coast stations and limited coast stations.

Coast stations are operated by Telstra Maritime Services. Most of them provide a 24 hour 7 day service. They listen on VHF and MF/HF distress channels and have immediate access to rescue organisations. They also operate ship to shore and shore to ship services for paid telephone calls and telegrams. Telstra coast stations do not monitor any of the 27 MHz channels.

Limited coast stations are so-named because both their operating hours and the radiocommunication service they can provide are limited. They are operated mainly by volunteer rescue organisations such as Air Sea Rescue and Volunteer Coast Guard. Although a few of them provide a continuous service, their hours are often limited to hours of daylight at weekends and public holidays.

Limited coast stations may handle only communications concerned with the safety and movements of vessels and are not permitted to handle telegrams or telephone calls to or from vessels at sea. The majority of these stations monitor distress channels in the 27 MHz, MF/HF and VHF marine bands.

Q.13 Where can I find details of these coast and limited coast stations ?

A. Guides to the services provided by

Telstra Maritime are available from that organisation's office in Sydney, by calling Toll Free (008) 810 023 or (02) 9901 2000 or from any Telstra coast station.

Information about limited coast stations is published in the annual Queensland Tide and Boating Guide.

Alternatively, detailed information concerning both types of stations is available from any of the DOTC offices. (See list below)

Q.14 What is an EPIRB and what can it do for me?

A.   An Emergency Position Indicating Radio Beacon or EPIRB is a small, buoyant, battery-operated radio transmitter which sends a repetitive emergency signal which can be recognised by both overflying aircraft and satellites. It is an extremely valuable aid in locating vessels in distress and it is strongly recommended that every small craft making an extended coastal or offshore voyage carry one. However, an EPIRB should not be considered as an alternative to a good marine radio transceiver.

Q.15 With satellite technology involved, wouldn't the cost of an EPIRB be very high ?

A.   No, an EPIRB operating on both aircraft and satellite frequencies and effective for waters up to approximately 900 kilometres from the Australian coast would cost only about $200.

A more sophisticated model which would be detected by aircraft and satellites anywhere in the world would cost approximately $1800

DEPARTMENT OF TRANSPORT AND COMMUNICATIONS

Communications Operations Division

List of Addresses and Telephone Numbers

Headquarters

Level K3, Blue Building, Benjamin Offices, Belconnen ACT (GPO Box 594, Canberra ACT 2601)

Queensland

424 Upper Roma Street, Brisbane. Tel: (07) 3238 6322
(PO Box 555, Fortitude Valley Q. 4006)

Cnr Walker and Targo Sts., Bundaberg Tel: (071) 72 2111
(PO Box 862, Bundaberg Q. 4670)

1st Floor, 107 Lake Street, Cairns Tel: (070) 52 5560
(PO Box 1225, Cairns Q. 4870)

Cnr Victoria and Gregory Sts., Mackay Tel: (079) 57 9466
(PO Box 337, Mackay Q. 4740)

Cnr East and Fitzroy Sts., Rockhampton Tel: (079) 31 6733
(PO Box 1401, Rockhampton Q. 4700)

Commonwealth Centre, Walker St, Townsville Tel: (077) 72 9555
(PO Box 522, Townsville Q. 4810)

2 Short Street, Southport Tel: (07) 5591 1877
(PO Box 1986, Southport Q. 4215)

New South Wales

60 Miller Street, North Sydney
Tel: (02) 9922 9111
(PO Box 970, North Sydney NSW 2059)

218 Molesworth Street, Lismore
Tel: (066) 21 6393
(PO Box 34, Lismore NSW 2480)

125 Bull Street, Newcastle West
Tel: (049) 26 4199
(PO Box 5190C, Newcastle West, NSW 2302)

Cnr Burke and Marius Streets, Tamworth
Tel: (067) 66 7211
(PO Box W75, Tamworth, NSW 2340)

15 Trail Street, Wagga Wagga
Tel: (069) 211 855
(PO Box 808, Wagga Wagga, NSW 2650)

Commonwealth Offices, Burelli St, Wollongong Tel: (042) 26 0240
(PO Box 468, Wollongong East NSW 2520)

South Australia

55 Currie Street, Adelaide Tel: (08) 237 6333
(GPO Box 2248, Adelaide SA 5001)

5 Percy Street, Mount Gambier
Tel: (087) 25 6170
(PO Box 1499, Mount Gambier SA 5290)

Customs House, Horwood Street, Whyalla
Tel: (086) 45 5999
(PO Box 575, Whyalla SA 5600)

Tasmania
162 Macquarie Street, Hobart
Tel: (002) 23 2666
(PO Box 63, Sandy Bay TAS 7005)

Victoria
14 Queens Road, Melbourne
Tel: (03) 9269 9888
(PO Box 6444, St Kilda Road Central, VIC 3004)
104 Curtis Street, Ballarat VIC 3350
Tel: (053) 31 1317
56 Nunn Street, Benalla VIC 3672
Tel: (057) 62 3288
10 Mundy Street, Bendigo Tel: (054) 43 1110
(PO Box 40, Bendigo, VIC 3550)
79-81 Raymond Street, Sale VIC 3850
Tel: (051) 44 4555

Western Australia
200 Adelaide Terrace, Perth Tel: (09) 323 1717
(PO Box 6189, East Perth WA 6004)
Cnr Brand and Tonkin Sts., South Hedland
Tel: (09) 72 2333
(PO Box 2419, South Hedland WA 6722)

Australian Capital Territory
32 Lonsdale Street, Braddon ACT 2602
Tel: (062) 48 9600

Northern Territory
82 Smith Street, Darwin Tel: (089) 41 0366
(PO Box 2540, Darwin NT 8000)

Distress Procedure
TO BE USED ONLY IF YOUR VESSEL IS IN GRAVE OR IMMINENT DANGER

Transmit in the following order on 2182, 4125 or 6215.5 kHz or on VHF Ch 16 or 27.88 MHz as appropriate:

THE RADIOTELEPHONE (2 TONE) ALARM	) Alarm
SIGNAL (if fitted)	) Signal
MAYDAY MAYDAY MAYDAY	) Distress
THIS IS - name of vessel and call sign (spoken three times)	) Call
MAYDAY	)
THE NAME OR OTHER IDENTIFICATION OF	)
YOUR VESSEL	)
PARTICULARS OF YOUR POSITION IN DEGREES	)
AND MINUTES OF LATITUDE AND LONGITUDE	)
OR IN RELATION TO A WELL-KNOWN LANDMARK	) Distress
THE NATURE OF DISTRESS AND THE KIND OF	)
ASSISTANCE DESIRED	)
ANY OTHER INFORMATION TO AID RESCUERS	)
(THIS SHOULD INCLUDE THE NUMBER OF	)
PERSONS ON BOARD)	)

If no answer is received, repeat the distress call and message particularly during 'silence' periods on the other distress frequencies or any other available frequency on which help may be obtained.

NOTE: WHEN THE 'DISTRESS' CALL IS NOT FULLY JUSTIFIED THE URGENCY CALL 'PAN PAN' (spoken three times) SHOULD BE USED TO INDICATE THAT A VERY URGENT MESSAGE FOLLOWS CONCERNING THE SAFETY OF A VESSEL OR PERSON.

1. The Frequency 2182 kHz is the International Radiotelephone Distress and Calling Frequency. Ship Stations fitted for operation on 2182 kHz should keep the maximum watch practicable on this frequency at all times while the vessel is at sea.

SILENCE PERIODS •
EXCEPT for DISTRESS

All transmissions on 2182 kHz must Cease

2. ACTION WHEN A DISTRESS CALL IS HEARD

Allow a short interval to enable land stations or nearer vessels to acknowledge the call and message.

If no other acknowledgment heard, answer the call and standby to help. Relay the call to the nearest coast station or any other authority which may be able to arrange assistance.

3. PHONETIC ALPHABET

A-ALPHA	J-JULIETT	S-SIERRA
B-BRAVO	K-KILO	T-TANGO
C-CHARLIE	L-LIMA	U-UNIFORM
D-DELTA	M-MIKE	V-VICTOR
E-ECHO	N-NOVEMBER	W-WHISKEY
F-FOXTROT	O-OSCAR	X-X-RAY
G-GOLF	P-PAPA	Y-YANKEE
H-HOTEL	Q-QUEBEC	Z-ZULU
I-INDIA	R-ROMEO	

4. **RADIO EQUIPMENT**

   THE SAFETY OF LIFE AND OR YOUR VESSEL MAY DEPEND ON YOUR RADIO-KEEP IT IN GOOD WORKING ORDER.

   BE SURE THAT:

   • Batteries are kept charged.

   • The antenna is properly erected and not touching other objects.

   • Lead-in insulators are dry and free of salt deposits.

5. **CALLING AND TRAFFIC PROCEDURES**

   • Do not transmit unnecessarily.

   • Keep message brief and clear.

   • Listen before transmitting and avoid interfering with other stations.

   • Always use your call sign or the name of your vessel for identification-use of Given names or Surnames is not permitted.

   • Stop transmitting when requested to do so by a coast station.

   When sending a radiotelegram to an official Coast Station:

   (a) Write out the message before the call is made.

   (b) Speak distinctly, use the phonetic alphabet where necessary.

Chapter 19
FIRST AID

ST JOHN AMBULANCE AUSTRALIA QUEENSLAND

FIRST AID SERVICES

Among its services in Queensland St. John offers comprehensive First Aid Training and a range of quality First Aid Kits.

Courses include:

- Senior First Aid Course. This 18 hour course equips the first aider with skills to manage life threatening injury and illness and other lesser conditions.
- Advanced First Aid Course. A 15 hour course of high level first aid training.
- First Aid at Sea Course. This 35 hour course includes training to Medallion Certificate level with added modules specific to the maritime environment. The course is designed to meet the requirements laid down in Commonwealth legislation, gazetted in the Commonwealth of Australia Gazette No P 17 August 13 1984. This course is especially suited to Second Mate, Engineer Class 1, Engineer Class 2, Engineer Watchkeeper and Master Class 3 Unrestricted.

First Aid Kits include:

Coastal Marine, Marine, Family, Motorist, Industrial and many more.

For more information on St. John Courses and First Aid Kits contact St. John House on telephone (07) 3252 3450 or PO Box 64 Broadway 4006.

FIRST AID

First aid begins immediately the First Aider arrives at the scene of an accident or emergency, and continues until medical aid arrives or the casualty recovers. Medical aid is treatment by a doctor, registered nurse or ambulance officer. The First Aider should be prepared to remain and assist if needed.

First aid can:

- preserve life
- protect the unconscious
- prevent injury or illness from becoming worse
- promote recovery.

GENERAL FIRST AID PROCEDURE

When the First Aider arrives at the scene of an accident or emergency, firstly, check whether there is danger to yourself, the casualty or any other person. Only proceed if it is safe to do so.

PREVENTION

Perhaps the most important principle underlying the whole field of medicine, which includes first aid, is that of prevention. It is also probably the most neglected.

Q.1 What are the main principles of prevention?

A. The main principles of prevention are to prevent:

- the incident occurring
- complications arising from the incident
- the casualty from dying
- the casualty's conditions becoming worse
- delay in the recovery of the casualty
- your intervention being harmful.

Q.2 If a First Aider is to manage an emergency situation it is advisable to have a PLAN, one which is easily remembered and that always works. What is meant by the St. John Action Plan DRABC?

A. The St. John DRABC Action Plan is the correct sequence to be undertaken when an emergency situation has to be managed-

D = Danger   - to self; casualty; other people

R = Response - to voice and touch

A = Airway   - clear and open

B = Breathing - look, listen, feel

C = Circulation - check neck pulse

Q.3 If a life is endangered, how would this PLAN be used?

A. (i) Check if there is DANGER to the first aider, casualty and other people. Warn others to keep clear. Remove the danger or casualty - BUT - only if it is safe to do so. If not, call or radio for expert help and meanwhile keep clear.

(ii) Quickly check for a RESPONSE from the casualty to find out if he/she is conscious.

Shake firmly, but gently, Shout loudly "can you hear me?" or "open your eyes!" Command "squeeze my hand"

If the casualty does respond, check and control any serious bleeding. see page 60 Australian First Aid.

(iii) The passage from the mouth to the lungs is called the AIRWAY. The airway must be clear and kept clear and open. If not, the casualty will be unable to breathe. With the unconscious casualty:

- quickly turn the casualty onto their side
- tilt the head back as far as it will go
- turn the head slightly downwards
- open the mouth and check the mouth for foreign objects or matter. Clear away any secretions or vomitus and broken teeth.

(iv) Look, listen and feel for BREATHING. if NOT breathing:

- roll the casualty on to their back tilt the head back and support the jaw
- seal your lips over the casualty's mouth and firmly breathe into the casualty's mouth
- seal casualty's nose by pinching or block with your cheek
- inflate the lungs until the casualty's lower chest is seen to commence to rise
- remove your mouth and turn your head so that one ear is close to the casualty's mouth
- observe the chest fall and listen, or feel, for exhaling air
- give a total of five quick, full breaths within 10 seconds. Do not wait for the chest to completely fall between breaths.

(v) Check for CIRCULATION (heart beat) at the neck pulse. If NO neck pulse:

- locate the heart and commence external heart compression
- alternate external heart compressions with mouth to mouth resuscitation. A person

doing it by themselves gives 15 compressions each 15 seconds then 2 breaths, repeat this 15 compressions to 2 breaths until expert assistance has taken over.

This technique is called Cardio-Pulmonary Resuscitation or just CPR (Cardio heart, Pulmonary = lungs).

If the casualty is not breathing but DOES have a pulse:

- continue mouth to mouth resuscitation, giving one breath every four seconds. Continue this until expert assistance takes over
- check the pulse after 1 minute then every two minutes to make sure the heart is still beating It may stop anytime.

Keep resuscitation going until expert assistance takes over. Mouth to mouth resuscitation may be started in the water, however Cardio-Pulmonary Resuscitation can only be effectively carried out if the casualty is placed on a hard flat surface.

Resuscitation requires knowledge and skllls. This can only be learned effectively by attending a recognised First Aid Course.

Q.4 What is the best management of the unconscious breathing casualty?

A. An unconscious casualty is one who is breathing, but does not respond to your voice and/or touch. Irrespective of the condition of the casualty he/she must be correctly placed on their side, making sure the mouth is clear and slightly open.

Q.5 Serious bleeding

A. Serious bleeding may threaten life. Act promptly.

- expose the wound
- apply a bulky pad over the wound (e.g. a folded handkerchief or tea towel). if unavailable, apply direct pressure to the wound with your bare hand
- press firmly over the wound
- bind the pad firmly in place
- elevate and rest the injured part
- call expert assistance. If the casualty is not badly inured, it may be possible

for the casualty to be taken to medical aid.

SPECIAL NOTE:

For a shark bite, immediately control the bleeding in the water if possible. As soon as the casualty is ashore or on board, manage as a serious bleed.

Transport and handling MUST be gentle to avoid death.

Q.6 Burns and Scalds.

A. Remove danger or casualty - put out burning clothing, smother with a blanket, or similar, or use cold water. If the casualty has been scalded, quickly remove any hot clothing if not stuck to the wound.

COOL

Cool the injured area under cold but gently running water (sea or fresh) until the part has returned to normal body temperature. This usually takes about ten minutes.

COVER

Cover the injured area with a sterile or clean non-adherent dressing, e.g. a non-stick wound dressing or freshly laundered tea towel or sheet.

Do not apply any lotions, ointments or oily dressings.

Do not prick blisters. This increases the risk of infection and delays healing

- seek medical aid.

Q.7 Sunburn.

A. For adults:

- cold showers or compresses may help to relieve the pain
- rest in a cool place and give fluids to drink.

For children:

- a cold compress or bath at body temperature may help to relieve the pain (ensure the child Is not over-cooled)
- rest in cool place and give fluids to drink
- seek medical aid if the sunburn is severe enough to result in skin blistering or is very painful.

Prevention - sunburn is best prevented. It can be serious particularly for young children and infants.

Q. 8 Wounds.

A. Manage bleeding. See page 325

- clean all small wounds. Use soap and water
- make sure you do not re-start bleeding
- apply a sterile non-adherent dressing to the wound, or a clean improvised dressing
- seek medical aid, particularly if the wound is deep and dirty or may require stitches. (Puncture wounds, e.g. fish hooks, may require the casualty to have an injection to protect them against tetanus infection.)

Do not remove objects which may be impaled in the wound. Pad around the wound and seek medical aid.

Q.9 Soft Tissue Injury.

A. A blow to the soft tissues of the body or limbs will result in bleeding beneath the skin. This can be seen as swelling and bruising.

To manage soft tissue injury:

- apply a cold pack over the area and leave in place for 20 minutes.(As a rule a cold pack is applied for 20 minutes on and removed and reapplied every 2 hours for 24 hours on the first day, then every four hours for a further 24 hours the first day of injury.) If the injury is on a limb:
- firmly bandage the injured area with a wide "stretchy" type of bandage. Make sure the circulation below the bandage is not impaired, i.e. the colour of the fingers and toes is normal and warm to touch.

To improvise a cold pack - use a packet of frozen peas wrapped in thin cloth or place some crushed ice in folded towel. Gel and chemical packs may be purchased. Always have material between the skin and these cold packs.

Always seek medical aid if the bruising and/or swelling is extensive or if it involves injury to a joint, head or neck.

Q.10 Dental Injury

A. Except for the first teeth, they can almost always be replaced and saved.

1. Hold the tooth by its crown. Do not handle the root.

2. Gently rinse the tooth in milk.
3. Replace the tooth slowly but firmly into its original position in the socket.
4. Hold the tooth in place by moulding a mllk bottle top or cooking foil over the replanted tooth and adjacent teeth.
5. Advise the casualty to contact a dentist or dental emergency service immediately. If the tooth cannot be replaced in its socket, wrap it in a plastic foil or place in-milk and seek dental treatment as soon as possible.

Q.11 Head Injury.

A. The head is a bony structure in which is located the brain, eyes, ears, nose, jaws, tongue and airway. If the head is injured damage to any of these organs may occur. It is very important that any person who has had a head injury should be assessed by a doctor, particularly if they have been unconscious even if only for a short time.

Q.12 Injuries to Bones and Joints.

A. Injuries to the bones and joints can be very painful. These injuries are normally recognised by:

- pain
- swelling
- sometimes deformity
- bruising
- inability to use the limb.

It is important that these Injuries are managed immediately by:

- keeping the injured part still
- it may be necessary to steady and support the injured part
- rest the casualty, seek medical aid.

Q.13 Eye Injury.

A. Eyes are precious and delicate organs. Any eye injury must be assessed and treated by a doctor. If the eye has received a severe blow or is bleeding:

- rest the casualty on their back keeping the head still
- the casualty is best transported to medical aid by the Ambulance Service
- a light covering over both eyes will rest the muscles of the injured eye.

Do not attempt any othe management.

To remove a speck of dust

- moisten the corner of a clear handkerchief with cold water
- sit the casualty in a good light and gently lift off the speck of dirt.

CHEMICALS IN THE EYE

Any chemical in the eye may be very painfu and may injure the eye. Remove immediately by:

- gently pouring tap water or sea water over the injured eye for at least 20 minutes (the casualty may be able to cup a hand under the eye and run water into the hand and over the eyeball).

Do not attempt to remove out of place contact lenses. Leave this to the doctor

Q.14 Acute Chest Pain.

A. Not all chest pain is a heart attack, but it is better to manage ALL cases as though they were!

The need for emergency care in al cases of chest pain is paramount.

The most common causes of chest pain are:

- Heart. .... Angina, heart attack
- Lungs .... Pleurisy
- Digestive tract. ... Acute indigestion
- Skeletal .... Severe muscle strain

Q.15 Heart Pain.

A. Most heart pain is central behind the breast bone and may also be felt between the shoulder blades into the neck and jaw and into the left arm.

It is often described as vice-like or crushing.

The following may be noted:

- sweating
- shortness of breath
- pale

MANAGEMENT OF HEART PAIN

- DRABC. See page 325.
- lie casualty in a comfortable position

- loosen clothing
- if the casualty has tablets for angina give them one
- seek medical aid urgently

- if there is no pulse start cardio pulmonary (heart/lung) resuscitation immediately. See page 326.

Q.16 Preventing Heart Conditions.

A. Disease of the arteries of the heart (the coronary arteries) is very common in Western Society and the more important risk factors are:
- high blood pressure
- smoking
- a strong family history
- obesity
- diet high in cholesterol (fats) and salt
- stress.

Q.17 Heat Cramps and Exhaustion.

A. These occur when the normal heat regulating mechanism of the body is unable to cope with the environment. Excessive sweating and loss of body salts may lead to dehydration and muscle cramps.

These are painful muscle cramps together with a feeling of nausea, dizziness and weakness. There may be vomiting. The muscles may show twitching and the skin may feel moist.

Management of Heat Cramps

- remove to a cool place
- lie the casualty down
- give fluids carefully (sip) - a good preparation is 1 tablespoon of sugar and half a teaspoon of salt in 1 litre of water
- apply cold compresses to the muscles, do not massage cramped muscles.

HEAT EXHAUSTION

This is a more serious problem and tends to affect the young and elderly where the temperature regulating mechanism may not function properly.

The casualty is hot and exhausted, often with a headache and nausea. There may be giddiness and thirst, muscle weakness and cramps.

The skin feels clammy and is pale and cool to touch. There may be rapid breathing and a fast pulse.

Management

- as for heat cramps.

Q.18 Heat Stroke.

A. This is a more serious condition. The skin is always dry and hot to touch, there may be irritability and mental confusion leading to seizures (fits).

If unconscious, correctly place on their side.

If conscious, manage as for heat exhaustion.

Call for Medical Help Immediately – Heat Stroke is a Medical Emergency.

Preventative Advice

- avoid strong direct sunlight
- wear protective loose clothing and a wide brimmed hat
- avoid heavy physical tasks when the weather is hot and particularly if it is hot AND humid
- avoid alcohol but drink water freely.

Q.19 Fainting.

A. Fainting is normally a state of the body when the blood pressure drops too low and reduces the blood flow to the brain.

Most simple faints are overcome almost immediately when the casualty falls down.

The casualty may begin to yawn, feel giddy, notice a blurring of vision, become sweaty and feel weak before fainting.

There is a temporary loss of consciousness. After falling, recovery is total but the casualty may look very pale.

If a person faints while sitting up make sure they are placed in a lying position as quickly as possible and elevate the legs.

Check the airway, loosen clothing and check for any injury. If recovery is NOT total within a few minutes, suspect other causes than a simple faint (e.g. head injury or stroke), call for medical help and correctly place casualty on their side.

Q.20 Snakes (Land/Sea).

A. Snakes are normally NOT aggressive.

In order to prevent snake bites:
- leave ALL snakes alone

- wear protective clothing in snake infested country (shoes, jeans, long walk socks, etc.)
- don't put hands in hollow logs, always keep eyes open for snakes when walking in the bush.

Take seriously any information or complaint that a person, particularly a child, has been bitten.

Symptoms vary but include: headache, nausea, double vision, pains in the chest and faintness.

There may be two puncture marks 1 cm apart with redness, swelling and.bruising.

The casualty may vomit and there can be difficulty with breathing.

Management of Snake Bite

- DRABC. See page 325
- total rest, reassure the casualty
- if on a limb apply a firm pressure bandage to the whole limb commencing over the bitten area
- immobilise the limb, e.g. splint along the limb, seek medical aid urgently
- if breathing or breathing and heart beat (circulatlon) fails carry out resuscitation as necessary.

N.B. (Bites on other parts of the body are difficult to manage, however one method is for the first aider to apply pressure with hands until medical aid is available.

With Snake Bite NEVER:

- cut the bitten area
- wash the area
- suck the wound
- use a constrictive bandage.

Sea snake bites should be managed similar to land snakes.

Q.21 Jellyfish.

A. Jellyfish are found in all Australian ocean waters. The more dangerous species (the large box jellyfish) are normally found in tropical waters, north of the Tropic of Capricorn.

MAJOR JELLYFISH STINGS

Extensive stinging, particularly from the box jellyflsh, may affect the breathing and heart beat of the casualty within a few minutes.

If rescuing a casualty from the water, take care not to be stung yourself.

The casualty will complain of intense pain.

There will be dark red lines like whip marks and a 'frosted ladder" pattern is characteristic.

Management of major jellyfish stings

If necessary resuscitate the casualty.

DO NOT RUB the stung area.

If vinegar is available:

- flood the stung area with household vinegar for at least 30 seconds
- if on a limb, apply a flrm pressure bandage to the whole limb commencing over the stung area after vinegar has been applied.

If vinegar is not available do not use a substitute; instead:

- gently pick off any adherent tentacles with tweezers or gloved hand (not with bare fingers) and then apply firm pressure bandages over the complete limb.

This is a poor alternative for the vinegar method but may be all that is possible.

- continually monitor breathing and heart beat (circulation), and, if necessary, start the appropriate resuscitation technique
- seek medical aid urgently.

OTHER JELLYFISH STINGS
Management

DRABC Reassure the casualty. If any tentacles remain gently pick off or wash off with water, apply cold packs or crushed ice to stung area.

The casualty will complain of:

- backache
- pain In the chest and abdomen nausea
- pain in the area stung.

The normal signs are:

- vomiting
- a lack of coordination in the limbs
- breathing difficulty, coming on 10 to 40 minutes after stinging
- visual evidence of stinging, for example, weals, whip marks, localised area of goose pimples.

Q.22 Coral Grazes/Cuts.

A. If any part of the body comes in contact with soft coral - manage as a minor jellyfish sting.

Cuts from hard coral require special attention.

- Wash thoroughly with water (sea or fresh) and scrub out all foreign material if possible.
- Apply a cold pack (if possible) for at least 20 minutes and elevate the affected part.
- Apply a sterile, non-stick dressing and bandage firmly and keep elevated to prevent swelling.
- Seek medical aid.

Q.23 Salt Water Boils and Sores.

A. These conditions may occur when the skin is saturated with salt water for a considerable period of time, e.g. sitting in a wet raft.

Do not squeeze boils or sores, but cover with a suitable antiseptic cream, cover and leave to heal.

Q.24 Fumes and Gases.

A.
- Make sure the rescuer does not become the next casualty.
- Protective equipment should be used by the rescuer.
- The rescue must be carried out with extreme care, preferably by a person trained in rescue procedures.
- Get the casualty into the fresh air, check breathing and heart beat, resuscitation may be necessary.
- If unconscious but breathing, correctly place casualty on their side.
- Remove contaminated clothing.
- Wash contaminated skin thoroughly.
- Seek medical aid.

Q.25 Frostbite.

A. This is damage to and death of skin and deeper structures caused by freezing. The areas usually affected are:

- ears
- nose
- cheeks, chin
- fingers and toes.

Factors in the development of frostbite:

- exposure to very low temperature (-40°C to -100°C), or lower
- time of exposure; the first signs of frostbite usually appear after 6-18 hours exposure; in extreme conditions, the time required may be as little as 30 minutes
- if skin is exposed, a higher wind velocity will cause earlier onset of the condition
- onset is also hastened by wet clothing, e.g. wet socks and gloves which have become frozen.

Three grades of severity are recognized:

- Frostnip - the earliest phase, completely reversible with no resultant skin damage.
- Superficial frostbite - only the skin is involved but permanent damage and scarring results.
- Deep frostbite - deeper structures are frozen and permanently damaged with considerable tissue loss. Amputation may be required.

Symptoms and signs

Frostnip:
- Whitening of the skin with loss of feeling. Completely reversible with no resultant damage if the area is rapidly warmed.

Frostbite:
- A small painless white spot is the earliest sign. If recognised at this stage and managed effectively, further, more extensive damage, may be prevented.
- As freezing of the tissues continues, the white area enlarges and may change in colour to yellowish-white.
- Frostbitten areas feel numb and are insensitive to touch and painful stimuli. They are firm or hard to the touch.
- With thawing, blisters may form and pain may be intense.

Management

This is the same for frostnip and both superficial and deep frostbite.

Immediate:
- Protect from wind and cold; seek shelter and warmth,
- Warm the affected area with body heat (e.g. by placing the hand under the arm or by cupping the hand over the nose or ears).
- Remove any contrictions which may impede blood flow to fingers or toes.
- Protect the affected area from friction or Injury.

As soon as possible:
- Rapidly warm the affected areas by immersing them in water at 40°C - 42°C for 20 minutes. This temperature has been found by experiment to be critical In reducing and minimising permanent skin and tissue damage. The temperature of the water must be measured with a thermometer.
- Cover any blisters with a dry (preferably non-adherent) dressing and bandage lightly.

- Keep the affected area level neither elevated nor depressed.
- Seek medical attention.

DO NOT:
- rub the affected area
- apply radiant heat, e.g. from a fire or electric radiator
- give alcohol.

Q.26 How should a First Aider manage SHOCK?

A. Shock is a state of circulatory collapse associated with depression of vital body processes, e.g. function of brain or kidneys. It is a condition in which the heart and blood vessels fail to provide sufficient blood circulation to ALL parts of the body. A First Aider manages shock by managing the actual condition of the casualty, i.e. by restoring breathing and heart beat; stopping a bleed; supporting a broken bone; maintaining body heat and reassuring the casualty.

SCALE F – MEDICINES AND MEDICAL STORES
TO BE CARRIED IN MEDICAL/FIRST AID LOCKER

Articles to be carried	Quantity	Quantity In pack
Bandages open wove, 50 mm x 5 m	1	3
Elastic adhesive dressings - assorted sizes	12	2
Crepe bandage 75 MM x 1 m approx	1	1
Sterilized absorbent cotton wool	100g	2
Zinc oxide, self adhesive bandage 25 mm x 1 m	1	3
Iodine, weak solution 2.5 percent	25ml	1
Amethocaine (Tetrocaine) 0.5 percent Eye drops in vials holding one application - sterile	20	1
Cough Linctus	100ml	2
Cetrimide Cream 0.5 percent In tube	50 g	2
Non-adhesive dressing pads Novalind or equivalent 80 mm x 80 mm	25	1
Triangular bandages		2
Splints (2 arm) (1 leg)		
Safety pins - assorted sizes on card	12	1
Lancet		1
Scissors		1 pair
Splinter forceps		1 pair
Medicine measures - plastic metric		3
Clinical thermometer		2
Copy of first-aid leaflet of instructions		

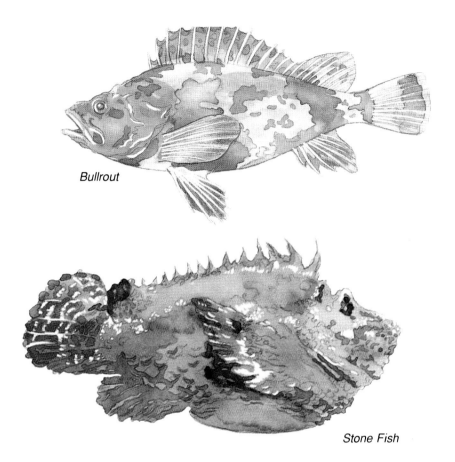

Bullrout

Stone Fish

Stone Fish

Stone Fish are found in tropical inlets, rocky beaches, coral reefs and brackish estuaries.

Prevention

- investigate before picking up 'funny looking rocks'
- take care when walking on rocks at the seaside. Always wear shoes
- do not put your hands or feet in rock crevices
- wear suitable footwear when wading in deep water or on mud flats.

Symptoms and signs

- immediate intense pain at the site of the puncture
- spread of pain along the limb
- sometimes, the presence of the stinging spine in the wound
- swelling
- stung area may be grey or blue

- the casualty may be irrational
- sometimes sweating and shock.

Management

- DRABC
- seek medical aid urgently
- while waiting, place the affected part in hot fluids, e.g. water or hot drinks, for at least 20 minutes, being careful not to scald the casualty
- remove any foreign body that comes away easily
- reassure the casualty
- observe breathing, and be prepared to supplement the casualty's breathing with EAR if necessary.

Bullrout

Bullrout are fresh water relatives of Stone Fish. Information on first aid is the same as for Stone Fish.

When you approach the scene of an accident or emergency, follow the DRABC Action Plan:

DANGER
RESPONSE
AIRWAY
BREATHING
CIRCULATION

Check for DANGER

–to you
–to others
–to the casualty

• make sure that no one else gets hurt. You will not be able to help if you are also a casualty.
• only proceed if it is safe to do so.

Check RESPONSE

–is the casualty conscious?

• gently shake the casualty and ask: 'Can you hear me?', 'What is your name?'

• if the casualty is **conscious**, check for and manage bleeding and other injuries
• if the casualty is **unconscious**, he/she should be turned on the side.

Turning an unconscious casualty on the side to clear and open the airway

1 Kneel beside the casualty.
2 Place the casualty's farther arm at a right angle to the body.
3 Place the nearer arm across the chest.
4 Bend the nearer knee up.
5 Roll the casualty away from you. Support the casualty in this position until airway and breathing have been checked.

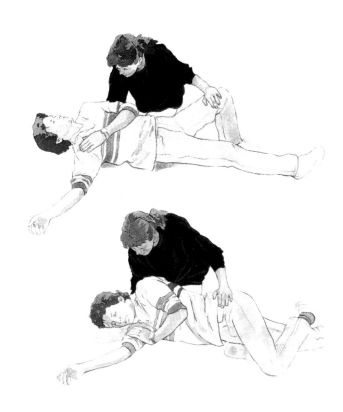

Clear and open the AIRWAY

Clearing the airway

1 With the casualty supported on the side, tilt the head backwards and slightly down.

2 Open the mouth and clear any foreign objects. Only remove dentures if loose or broken.

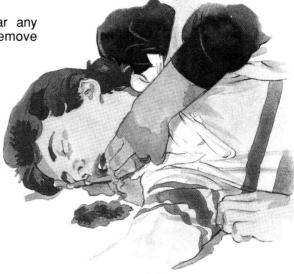

Opening the airway

1 Place one hand high on the casualty's forehead.

2 Support the chin with the other hand.

3 Gently tilt the head backwards.

4 Lift the jaw forward and open the casualty's mouth slightly.

Check for BREATHING

–look for the chest rising and falling

–listen for the sound of breathing

–feel with your cheek

- if the casualty is **breathing**, ensure that he/she is in a stable side position. Check for and manage bleeding and other injuries
- if the casualty is **not breathing**, turn onto the back and commence EAR (expired air resuscitation), giving 5 full breaths in 10 seconds.

Placing an unconscious casualty in a stable side position

1 Adjust the upper knee so that the thigh is at a right angle to the hip

2 Place the upper arm across the elbow of the lower arm.

EAR (mouth to mouth resuscitation)

1 Kneel beside the casualty.

2 Keep the casualty's head tilted back.

3 Pinch the casualty's nostrils with your fingers or seal with your cheek.

4 Lift the jaw forward with your other hand.

5 Take a deep breath and open your mouth wide.

6 Place your mouth firmly over the casualty's mouth making an airtight seal.

EAR (mouth to mouth resuscitation)

7 Breathe into the casualty's mouth.

8 Remove your mouth and turn your head to observe the chest fall and to listen or feel for exhaled air.

9 If the chest does not rise and fall, check head tilt position first, then check for and clear foreign objects in the airway.

10 Give 5 full breaths in 10 seconds, then check the carotid (neck) pulse, for 5 seconds, if pulse is present, continue EAR at the rate of 15 breaths per minute.

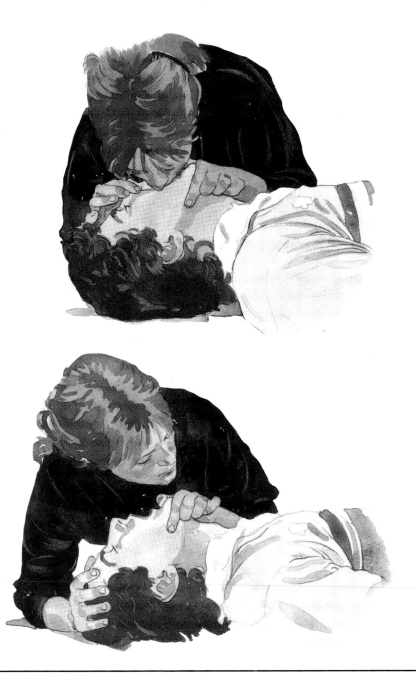

Check for CIRCULATION

- feel the pulse at the neck (carotid pulse)
- if pulse is present, continue EAR at the rate of 15 breaths per minute. Check breathing and the pulse after 1 minute, then after every 2 minutes
- if pulse is not present, commence CPR (cardio-pulmonary resuscitation)

- check breathing and the pulse after 1 minute, then after every 2 minutes. If the pulse returns, continue EAR. If breathing returns, turn the casualty to a stable side position. Check for and manage shock, bleeding and other injuries
- seek medical aid.

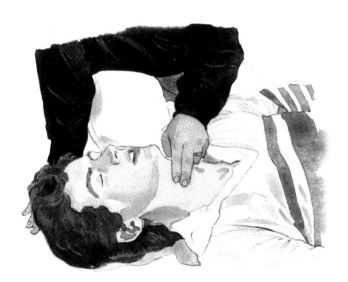

To feel for the pulse

1 Place the ends of your fingers in the groove behind the Adam's apple, on either side of the neck, but not on both sides at the same time.

2 Do not use your thumb or finger tips.
3 The pulse can also be felt at the wrist (radial pulse).

CPR for adults—one first aider

1 After finding that there is no pulse, kneel beside the casualty with one knee level with the casualty's chest and the other level with the head.

2 Your hands must be positioned correctly:

- locate the lower end of the breastbone by running your fingers along the lowest rib on each side from the outside inwards

- locate the upper end of the breastbone by placing a finger in the groove between the collarbones

- extend the thumbs of each hand equal distances to meet in the middle

- keep the thumb of the one hand in position and place the heel of the lower hand below it on the lower half of the breastbone

3 Your fingers should be relaxed, pointing across the chest, and slightly raised.

4 Place your other hand securely on top of the first. Lock the top thumb around the lower wrist, or interlock the fingers.

5 Exert pressure through the heel of your lower hand. Your shoulders should be above the breastbone

and your compressing arm should be straight. Pivoting from the hips, perform the compressions rhythmically with equal time for compression and relaxation.

6 The breastbone should be depressed about 5 centimetres. Release the pressure.

7 Give 15 compressions in 10 - 12 seconds. Then give two breaths in 3 - 5 seconds. Continue at 4 cycles per minute.

b

SUMMARY

DANGER to self, others and the casualty

RESPONSE (shake and shout) ————————→ Yes —→ manage bleeding and
other injuries

No ——— turn casualty on side

AIRWAY– clear and open

BREATHING ————————————————→ Yes —→ stable side position
manage shock, control
bleeding and other
injuries

No —→ turn casualty on back
start EAR
5 full breaths in 10 seconds

CIRCULATION   check pulse ————————→ Yes —→ continue EAR 15
breaths/minute check
pulse and breathing
after 1 minute then
every 2 minutes

No —→ commence CPR
60 compressions, 8 breaths/minute
check pulse and breathing after
1 minute then every 2 minutes

Successful CPR

If a casualty is not breathing and has no pulse, you should try to give cardiopulmonary resuscitation. However, even if performed expertly, you may not be successful in saving the casualty's life. Success depends on the cause of the injury or illness, how quickly you are able to respond, and how quickly expert medical aid arrives. Call medical aid as soon as possible.

What next?

After managing life – threatening problems, turn the casualty to a stable side position. Remember that you must call medical aid as soon as possible. You should then undertake an orderly assessment of the casualty, looking for any bleeding, then other injuries such as burns and fractures. Note any tenderness, swelling, wounds or deformity.

Examine the casualty in the following order:

- head and neck
- chest (including shoulders)
- abdomen (including hip bone)
- upper limbs
- lower limbs
- back

Chapter 20
USEFUL INFORMATION

USEFUL INFORMATION

SURVEY STANDARDS

1. The basic standards for commercial and fishing ship construction, stability, machinery, electrics, equipment and vessel operations is the Uniform Shipping Laws Code. This document also calls up classification society rules as equivalent. Standards Association of Australia codes as well as International Maritime Organisation codes are also called up as minimum standards.

2. The Transport Operations (Marine Safety) Regulations 1994 and its subordinate standards calls up the Uniform Shipping Laws Code. This document is used in all Australian States and the Northern Territory.

RELATED DOCUMENTS AVAILABLE THROUGH THE DEPARTMENT OF TRANSPORT

3. Transport Operations (Marine Safety) Act 1994

4. Transport Operations (Marine Safety) Regulations 1995 and Standards

N.B. Further standards are being developed.

5. Various other pamphlets on ship survey related matters are also available on request.

OTHER RELEVANT ACTS AND REGULATIONS

6. Gas Act and related regulations.

7. Inspection of Machinery Act.

8. Workplace Health and Safety Act.

9. Commonwealth of Australia Marine Orders.

10. The Transport Operations (Marine Pollution) Act 1995.

11. The Transport Operations (Marine Pollution) Regulations 1995.

GAS INSTALLATIONS

12. Gas installations are to be installed to the requirements of the Gas Examiner, Department of Mines and Energy.

13. On completion of the installation of gas equipment by a certificated gas fitter, it is required that a Gas Examiner's Certificate is forwarded with the ship registration application.

COMPRESSED AIR

14. Fixed air compressing installations should comply with Australian Standard AS 2030 where applicable or other relevant standards.

15. Portable equipment shall be inspected and maintained to Australian Standards requirements in AS 2030, AS 2704 and AS 2705.

CLASS LISTING UNIFORM CODE

Under the Uniform Code for the purposes of classification, the numbers indicate the ships use whilst the suffix indicates the area of operation.

Passenger Ships (for ships carrying in excess of 12 passengers)

Class 1B – Queensland Coastal Waters – 200 nautical miles seaward.

Class 1C – Within fifty (50) nautical miles of the coast or within the Great Barrier Reef Region or the Torres Strait Zone.

Class 1D – Partially Smooth Water Limits as prescribed in Schedule 8 of the Transport Operations (Marine Safety) Regulations 1995.

Class 1E – Smooth Water Limits as prescribed in Schedule 9 of the Transport Operations (Marine Safety) Regulations 1995.

Non Passenger Ships – (Not more than 12 passengers plus crew)

Class 2 – As above

Lighters of 15 metres in length and over (dumb barges) generally enter this Class also, although some ships qualify as Class 1.

Fishing Ships

Class 3B – Queensland Coastal Waters – 200 nautical miles seaward.

Class 3C – Within fifty (50) nautical miles of the coast or within the Great Barrier Reef Region or the Torres Strait Zone.

Class 3D – Partially Smooth Waters (Bay Fishing etc.)

Fishing ships under 10 metres in length are not required to be registered with Queensland Transport.

Vessels in Class 'A' category are not surveyed by the States. These ships have unlimited operational areas including interstate and international and they are surveyed and manned under A.M.S.A. (Australian Maritime Safety Authority).

Commercial Hire Ships
– (Class 1F)

'C' Class – The operational area for C Class ships is defined in Section 79 of the Transport Operations (Marine Safety) Regulations.

'D' Class – Partially smooth water limits as prescribed in Schedule 8 of the Transport Operations (Marine Safety) Regulations.

'E' Class – Smooth water limits as prescribed in Schedule 9 of the Transport Operations (Marine Safety) Regulations.

These classes of ships cover auxiliary sailers, motor ships and house boats which are hired out to tourists on a drive yourself basis.

Further standards are being developed for these operations.

Chapter 21

HINTS FOR SEAMEN

HINTS FOR SEAMEN

The following measures should be considered as preliminary guidance on matters influencing safety of fishing vessels generally, and specifically as related to stability.

(a) All doorways and other openings through which water can enter into the hull or deckhouses, forecastle, etc, should be suitably closed in adverse weather conditions and accordingly all appliances for this purpose should be maintained on board and in good condition.

(b) Hatchcovers and flush deck scuttles should be kept properly secured when not in use during fishing.

(c) All probable deadlights should be maintained in good condition and securely closed in bad weather.

(d) All fishing gear and other large weights should be properly stowed and placed as low as possible.

(e) Particular care should be taken when the pull from fishing gear might have a bad effect on stability, e.g. when nets are hauled by power-block or the trawl catches obstructions on the sea bed.

(f) Gear for releasing deck load in fishing vessels carrying catch on deck, (e.g. prawns) should be kept in good working condition for use when necessary.

(g) Freeing ports provided with closing appliances should always be capable of functioning and are not to be locked, especially, in bad weather.

(h) When the main deck is prepared for the carriage of deck load there should be slots of suitable size to allow easy flow of water to freeing ports to prevent trapping of water.

(i) Fish should never be carried in bulk without proper installation of the portable divisions in the holds.

(j) The number of partially filled tanks should be kept to a minimum at any one time.

(k) Any instructions should be observed regarding the filling of water ballast tanks. It should be remembered that slack tanks can be dangerous.

(l) Any closing devices provided for vent pipes to fuel tanks should be secured in bad weather.

(m) Reliance should not be placed on automatic or fixed steering. It is dangerous in foul weather as it prevents speedy manoeuvring.

(n) Be alert to all the dangers of following or quartering seas. If excessive heeling or yawing occurs, reduce speed as a first precaution.

(o) In all conditions of loading, necessary care should be taken to maintain a seaworthy freeboard.

Don'ts for Seamen

Never smoke on deck, on barges, or on the pier when fuel oil is being loaded or discharged.

Never smoke in the vicinity of open hatches or in cargo holds.

While cargo lighters are alongside, do not throw lighted matches, cigarettes, etc, over the side or out of portholes.

Never go up and down ladders with both hands full.

Never work in the hot sun without protecting the head.

Never walk on the side where cargo is being worked.

Never walk under heel blocks of winches.

Never walk on carelessly piled hatch boards.

Never walk through unlighted 'tween deck spaces.

Never walk on weather side of decks in heavy sea.

Never walk on wet or oily decks with rubber soles or heels.

Never stand in the bight of an anchor cable or line.

Never work aloft without a safety belt and line.

Never use goggles to protect forehead instead of eyes.

Never enter a gas filled hold without a life line. Some gas masks have a ring at the back of the harness for a life line; use a French bowline if the type you have does not.

Suggestions for Seamen

Chains should never be used with links knotted or kinked.

They should never be shortened by wiring, tying or bolting two links together.

When lowering or topping booms, always take the topping lift fall to the niggerhead with at least four turns.

Topping lift wires should always be properly secured on cleats to prevent them from jumping off.

All wire splices should be parcelled and served to prevent hand injury.

When splicing wire, the marlinespike point should always be away from the body.

Chain stoppers should always be used for wire topping lifts.

Snatch blocks should be used only when other blocks cannot be used.

All hooks should be carefully moused. When possible, shackles should be substituted.

When rigging a bos'n's chair on a stay with a shackle, never allow the shackle pin to ride on the stay - it might unscrew.

Tarpaulins should never be placed over an open hatch, or over one where some of the covers or strongbacks are not in place.

Compartments which have been closed for a long time, especially tanks or double bottoms, should not be entered until tested and found to be gas free and to contain oxygen. When entering such a compartment, another person should be present.

When painting, or handling paint in a compartment, it should be well ventilated.

During a period of fumigation, no one should remain on board. When fumigation is completed, no one should go on board until all compartments have been thoroughly ventilated.

A safety belt should be put on before going over the side or aloft and should not be removed until the return on deck.

Staging should be bolted together, not nailed, and should have supports at least every 2 metres (7 feet).

All staging lines should be securely attached to strong supports, never to rails or stanchions.

When working aloft, all tools should be secured by lanyards to prevent dropping.

Loose tools should never be left on gratings or other places from which they might fall.

Q.1 On small vessels or vessels where the engine room is unmanned, what device should be installed in the vessel's bilge?

A. An alarm so that it sounds when the bilge water rises to a determined level.

Q.2 Which end of a new coil of rope should be taken out first ?

A. The bottom inside end.

Q.3 What is the meaning of the term 'flemish coil'?

A. Coiling a rope flat on the deck so that each coil lies close to, and outside the next coil, the end of the rope being in the centre.

Q.4 What is the meaning of the term 'flake'?

A. Arranging a hawser in layers so that it will run clear.

Q.5 What is a handy billy?

A. A small tackle for general use.

Q.6 How do we measure the mechanical advantage of a tackle?

A. By the number of parts in the moving block.

Q.7 Where are snatch blocks used?

A. Where it is not convenient, or too slow, to reeve a rope through a leading block.

Q.8 What is the meaning of the term 'stopper'?

A. A short length of rope used to hold a rope while it is being belayed.

Q.9 What is the meaning of the term 'springs' ?

A. Hawsers led forward from the bow or quarter.

Back springs are hawsers led aft from forward.

Ship Tonnage

Q.10 What does 'loaded' or 'light' displacement mean ?

A. The weight of water displaced by a ship when loaded or light.

Q.11 What does 'deadweight tonnage' mean?

A. It is the maximum weight of cargo, fuel, stores, and passengers a ship is capable of carrying when loaded to its maximum draught.

Q.12 What does 'gross register tonnage' mean ?

A.   This is tonnage of measurement, not of weight, and is the ship's total cubic contents expressed in tons per 100 cubic feet. Temporary structures, specific spaces above decks, and water ballast tanks are exempted. Due to variation of spaces exempted, this measurement is not the same in all countries.

Q.13 What does 'net register tonnage' mean?

A.   This is also tonnage of measurement and refers to the spaces available for cargo. The cubic contents of spaces occupied by machinery, stores, quarters, and accommodations are deducted from the gross register tonnage when assessing the net register tonnage.

HYPOTHERMIA

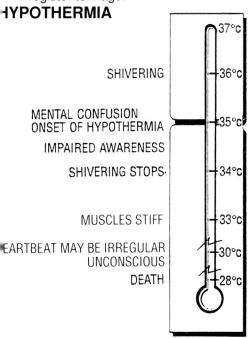

SHIVERING — 36°C

MENTAL CONFUSION
ONSET OF HYPOTHERMIA — 35°C

IMPAIRED AWARENESS

SHIVERING STOPS· — 34°C

MUSCLES STIFF — 33°C

HEARTBEAT MAY BE IRREGULAR — 30°C
UNCONSCIOUS

DEATH — 28°C

37°C

The normal body temperature is 37°C. Hypothermia (sometimes called exposure) is the name given to the condition of people with a temperature below 35°C. The cause of hypothermia is an excessive heat loss due to inadequate protection from wet, cold and windy conditions. Exhaustion and hunger will also contribute.

Children and thin individuals will lose body temperature more rapidly than normal adults.

Recognition

Immersion in cold water may result in irregularity of heart beat and even cardiac arrest.

Overbreathing is very common initially. The immersed person feels cold and as body temperature drops symptoms change.

By the time a person's temperature has dropped below 35°C it will be difficult for him to make sensible decisions to help him, survive and difficult to make any purposeful muscle movements such as swimming or holding on to an overturned craft. Often the casualty does not realise his own plight. (Refer to diagram over page).

Management

The conscious casualty must be rewarmed by whatever means available. The following procedures should be followed:

- remove the casualty from the water
- shelter from wind and rain immediately
- create a sheltered dry and warm place
- put the casualty into dry clothes between blankets, space blankets or sleeping bag
- cover all the casualty's body except for the face
- huddle together for warmth, so body temperature can rise gradually,
- if the casualty is conscious give him warm sweet drinks
- a bath at 42°C is helpful but not usually available.
- when conditions permit seek medical aid.

do not

- apply excessive external heat such as fire, electric blankets and hot water bottles
- massage arms and legs
- give alcohol
- move the casualty unnecessarily.

The unconscious casualty must be correctly placed on their side, and observe their airway, breathing and circulation.

In addition to covering with blankets and space blankets, extra warmth can be applied by:

- a companion in a sleeping bag
- warm water bottle wrapped in towels and applied to the armpits and groin.

The hypothermic casualty must always be handled very gently and re-warmed slowly.

The greatest areas of heat loss are those where there is least covering of muscle or fat, i.e. the head, sides of chest, groin and extremities of arms and legs.

The means by which body heat loss can be minimised are

a. wear a life jacket or some other means of personal flotation device which enables you to remain still;

c. assume a position which minimises exposure to the areas of greatest heat loss, sides of chest, groin etc. and try to keep, your head and neck out of the water. This is known as H.E.L.P. (Heat Escape Lessening Posture). If others are in the water with you, huddle closely with them making as much bodily contact as possible. The degree of effectiveness of the "huddle" technique depends upon how much chest contact can be maintained. This again may depend on the type of lifejacket being worn.

Figure 128 - *Critical heat loss areas*

b. it is not advisable to swim unless the shore is within close reach, e.g., under a mile. Swimming accelerates heat loss due to the increase in blood circulation;

Figure 130 – *HUDDLE technique*

A popular misconception is that alcohol helps you to keep warm in an exposure situation. This is not so. Tests have shown that the cooling rate is increased by about 20% when under the influence, due to a reduction in automatic responses, i.e., less shivering (the body's attempt to counteract large heat loss) and more blood flow to the surface areas. One would die happier but sooner.

Useful advice:

Wear a lifejacket.

Have safety lines rigged and wear a harness whenever possible.

Let someone know if you go on deck.

Be alert on deck, watch for coils of rope and deck hamper.

Keep your hands out of your pockets - free to grab for a rail if you fall.

If possible work on deck in pairs.

Figure 129 – *HELP technique*

Try to be selective in the type of clothing you wear, woollen garments with a waterproof outer layer will greatly increase your chances of survival should you go over the side.

If you do find yourself in the water, keep a positive attitude about your survival and rescue — this will improve your chances of living through action which will decrease your cooling rate.

The two maps below give an indication of a person's survival time in the water, summer and winter, off the Australian coast.

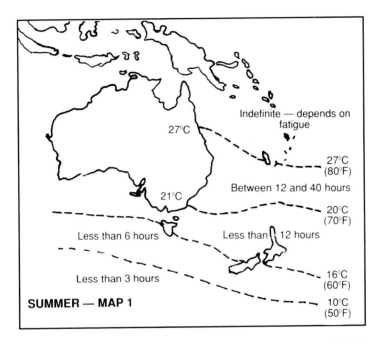

SUMMER — MAP 1

Indefinite — depends on fatigue

27°C

27°C (80°F)

Between 12 and 40 hours

21°C

20°C (70°F)

Less than 6 hours   Less than 12 hours

16°C (60°F)

Less than 3 hours

10°C (50°F)

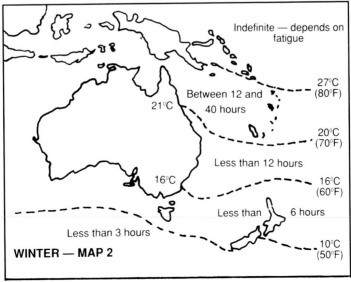

WINTER — MAP 2

Indefinite — depends on fatigue

27°C (80°F)

Between 12 and 40 hours

21°C

20°C (70°F)

Less than 12 hours

16°C

16°C (60°F)

Less than 6 hours

Less than 3 hours

10°C (50°F)

Chapter 22
"I.A.L.A." MARINE BUOYAGE SYSTEM "A"

BUOYS AND BUOYAGE
THE MEANINGS AND PLACEMENT OF BUOYS

USE OF BUOYS

Just as cautionary traffic signs on highways and roads guide drivers of motor cars, buoys and beacons are signs warning the mariner of potential danger.

Buoys are moored in deep water and beacons are driven into the sea bed or stand on concrete footings in shallow water.

Buoys are moored to the sea bed, and rest on the bottom at an anchor or, in the case of a heavy large buoy, a set of anchors, which may consist of concrete blocks or actual steel anchors. The buoy is attached to the anchor system by chain. A swivel is fitted in the chain leading from the buoy on the surface to the anchor block on the sea bed, in order to prevent this chain from twisting.

It is not wise to use buoys to fix a vessel's position, as the buoy may have dragged its mooring, broken free, or be recently, temporarily or permanently relocated by the port authority.

Lights on buoys, and marks operate either on electricity (battery) or acetylene gas. The light is actuated automatically by fading light.

It is unseamanlike to anchor near a buoy, as the vessel's anchor may foul its mooring and the vessel may also obscure the buoy from the view of another vessel.

If it is noted that a buoy is out of position, adrift, damaged, or unlit if charted as lit, the fact should be reported to the harbour authorities or to the Department of Transport.

Buoyage

When passing a buoy, the direction and rate of tidal flow can be ascertained by looking at the flow of water past the buoy. If there is no apparent flow it must be "stand of tide" (slack water) and if the buoy is not a floating buoy, whether it is high or low tide, can be ascertained by noting the water mark on the buoy.

Buoys and their moorings are inspected regularly and serviced by the authority responsible for their upkeep and maintenance.

I.A.L.A. MARITIME BUOYAGE SYSTEM

Under the auspices of the International Association of Light House Authorities (I.A.L.A.) many countries throughout the world have agreed to the implementation of what has become known as the I.A.L.A. System.

This system is simple, logical and has the great advantage of getting rid of any confusion between the different types of navigational markers.

The system of buoyage provides five types of marks which may be used in any combination:

All RED markers are PORT HAND and all GREEN marks are STARBOARD HAND when proceeding into harbour or up-stream.

If there is any doubt as to which this direction should be applied, an arrow symbol on the chart will make it clear.

The direction of flow of the Flood stream is no longer the criterion of direction.

These marks may be of any shape or of any type - beacons, buoys, spar buoys etc., and if they have a light it will be GREEN for starboard hand and RED for port hand.

Any rhythm may be used - flashing, group flashing, occulting or isophase but these colours will not be used for any other purpose.

CARDINAL MARKS

These marks indicate the direction of the clear water. For example, A means that the safe water is to the North and is known as a CLEAR WATER NORTH marker.

COLOURS. Cardinal marks will always be combinations of BLACK and YELLOW, the relative positions of the black and yellow horizontal stripes indicating which of the cardinal points of the compass is referred to.

It is probably easier to learn the top-marks first, even though they are secondary to the colours.

NORTH   The two triangles point upwards - that is, to the NORTH as in a compass rose.

SOUTH   The triangles point down = SOUTH.

WEST   The 'point to point triangles form the letter W (for WEST) standing on its side.

EAST   By elimination, must be EAST.

Now, looking at Figure 23 again, we see that the Apexes - the upper points of the triangles - point to the BLACK band in the colour combination.

NORTH   The black band is uppermost where the triangles are pointing.

SOUTH   The triangles point downwards to a black band at the bottom.

EAST   The triangles point away from the centre to place black bands at the top and bottom.

WEST   The triangles point towards the centre to indicate a central black band.

NOTE that COLOUR is the all-important factor for navigation marks, with Top Marks being a secondary (and optional) extra.

ISOLATED DANGER MARKS

Use of Marker. Apart from such obvious uses as indicators of isolated rocks and reefs, this marker may be used to indicate the location of wrecks of limited horizontal extent that are a danger to navigation.

Unlike all other types of navigation marks, this is one you steer to clear by a good, safe margin.

Colour. Black and red horizontal stripes. Topmark, if any, two vertically placed black spheres.

Light. Always a white, group flashing (2), a characteristic which, once again, is not used for any other type of channel marker, so any group flashing (2) light (other than a major lighthouse) can be safely regarded as marking some isolated danger.

SPECIAL MARKS

Colour - Always yellow.

Topmark (if any) - Yellow cross

Light - Always yellow and may be any rhythm.

Use of special markers - Special markers are not navigational marks in the generally accepted sense.

They are used to indicate such things as dredge spoil grounds, quarantine anchorages, special mooring buoys, etc.

They may also be used to mark a 'channel within a channel' - for example, the deepest part of a safe navigation area where exceptionally deep draught vessels may require special indicators. In such case they would probably be conical or can shaped to indicate the starboard and port sides of that special channel respectively.

Summarising the preceeding section remember -

COLOUR is paramount in determining the meaning of the marker.

TOPMARKS

    are optional and secondary to the day-time colour. This colour is always shown on the chart below the beacon or buoy symbol. E.g., B Y means black over yellow and would indicate a clear water North marker. Y B, on the other hand, is yellow on black and would, of course, be a clear water South mark.

LIGHTS Do not take it for granted that marks will be lit. Where this is so it will be indicated by the usual magenta 'flash' and the characteristic of the light.

ISOLATED DANGER MARKS

Topmark
(This is a very important feature by day and is fitted wherever practicable)

Light, when fitted, is **white,** Group-flashing (2)

 Fl(2)
*Gp Fl(2)

Shape: pillar or spar

SAFE WATER MARKS

Topmark
(if the buoy is not spherical, this is a very important feature by day and is fitted wherever practicable)

Shape: spherical or pillar or spar

Light, when fitted, is **white** Isophase, or Occulting, or Long-flashing every 10 seconds, or Morse A.

Iso
Oc *Occ.
L Fl.10s
Mo (A)

SPECIAL MARKS

Topmark
(if fitted)

Light, when fitted, is **yellow,** and may have any rhythm not used for white lights

Examples

 Fl.Y
Fl(4)Y
*Gp Fl(4)Y

Shape: various

Topmark
(if fitted)

If these shapes are used they will indicate the side on which the buoys should be passed

*These abbreviations are obsolescent

NOTE

These diagrams are schematic and indicate the approved shapes, colouring and topmarks of buoys in the IALA System. Particularly in the case of pillar buoys, the diagrams are not intended to convey the detailed configuration, exact colour disposition and topmark size of the buoys in use; these features will vary somewhat, depending on the individual design of the buoys in use.

CARDINAL MARKS

Topmarks are always fitted (when practicable)

Buoy shapes are pillar or spar

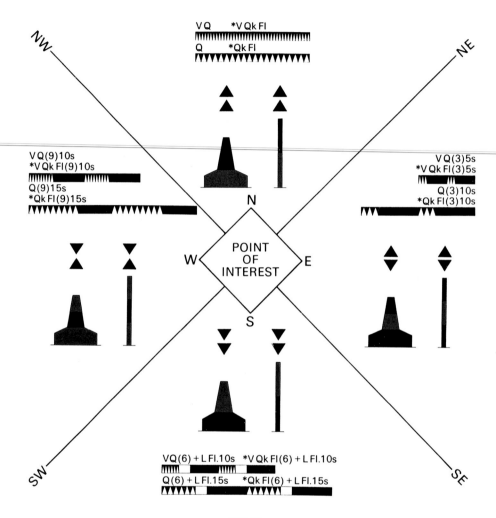

NOTES

* These abbreviations are obsolescent

Mariners are warned that certain types of buoy lighting equipment in current use on South and West Cardinal light-buoys have proved to be liable to exhibit occasionally one too many or one too few short flashes.

These diagrams are schematic and indicate the approved shapes, colouring and topmarks of buoys in the IALA System. Particularly in the case of pillar buoys, the diagrams are not intended to convey the detailed configuration; exact colour disposition and topmark size of buoys in use; these features will vary somewhat depending on the individual design of the buoys in use.

Lights, when fitted, are **white** Very Quick Lights
or Quick Lights; a South mark also has a Long
Flash immediately following the quick flashes.

LATERAL MARKS

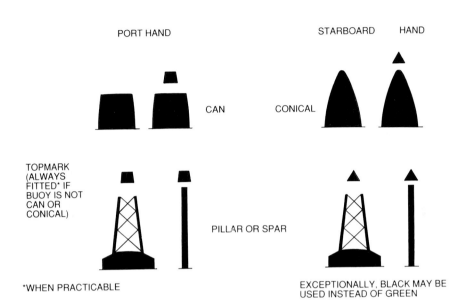

PORT HAND

STARBOARD HAND

CAN CONICAL

TOPMARK
(ALWAYS
FITTED* IF
BUOY IS NOT
CAN OR
CONICAL)

PILLAR OR SPAR

*WHEN PRACTICABLE

EXCEPTIONALLY, BLACK MAY BE
USED INSTEAD OF GREEN

LIGHTS, WHEN FITTED, MAY HAVE ANY RHYTHM

EXAMPLES
Quick Flashing
Flashing
Long Flashing
Group Flashing

I.A.L.A. MARITIME BUOYAGE SYSTEM 'A'

DISTRESS SIGNALS

Merchant Ship Search and Rescue Manual

"I.A.L.A." QUESTIONS AND ANSWERS OF THE MARITIME BUOYAGE SYSTEM "A"

The mariner when approaching the coast must determine his position on the chart and note the direction of the MAIN STREAM OF FLOOD TIDE.

The term Starboard Hand denotes that side which would be on the RIGHT HAND of the mariner either going with the main stream of flood, entering a harbour river, or estuary from seaward; the term Port Hand denotes the LEFT HAND of the mariner under the same circumstances.

Q.1 How are buoys named ?

A   Conical,Can or Spherical according to their shape above water.

Q.2 What reliance would you place on the position of a buoy?

A.   Undue reliance should not be placed on buoys and flotation beacons being in their charted positions.It is advised to regard them as simple aids to navigation and not infallible marks, particularly when located in exposed positions.

Q.3 How are buoys marked on charts ?

A.   On Admiralty charts they are not shown in colour. A red buoy is recognised by the letter 'R' placed against it. A green buoy is marked with the letter 'G'. The position of the buoys is indicated by the circle at the base of the symbol.

Q.4 How are buoys numbered?

A.   Buoys are numbered from seaward. Buoys on the port hand are even numbers and those on the starboard hand odd numbers.

Q.5 What is the colour of a starboard hand buoy?

A.   Green (can be black).

Q.6 What is the colour of a port hand buoy?

A.   Red.

Q.7 How would you pass a green buoy?

A.   Keep the buoy on the vessel's starboard side when approaching a port and on the vessel's port side when leaving.

Q.8 How would you pass a red buoy?

A.   Keep the buoy on the vessel's port side when approaching a port and on the starboard side when leaving.

Q.9 What are the night marks for buoys in Queensland ports?

A.   Red buoys are fired with red lights and green buoys with green lights.

Unlit buoys usually carry night reflector strips - red on red buoys, white on black, and green on green.

Beacons

Q.10 How may leading beacons in Queensland ports be recognised?

A   Leading beacons vary in shape. Some are triangular in shape, the front beacon having its apex upwards and the rear beacon inverted.

Others are rectangular in shape. Many new beacons carry no topmark and can be distinguished by fixed white day lights. Most major leading beacons now carry these distinctive lights.

Q.11 What are the night marks for beacons in Queensland ports?

A.   Red beacons are fitted with red lights and green beacons with green lights.

Unlit beacons usually carry night reflector strips – Red on Red Beacons, White or Green on Green Beacons.

Q.12 With a small vessel, how close would you pass off navigation marks in Queensland ports?

A.   Pass 5 to 7 metres (15 to 20 feet) off where possible.

Q.13 What precaution would be taken on approaching a channel junction?

Reduce speed until absolutely sure of the vessel's position in relation to the channel.

Q.14 Is it permitted to secure vessels to navigation marks in time of trouble?

A   No. It is illegal at any time and the offence is liable to prosecution.

Q.15 What precautions must be taken when anchoring in rivers or harbours?

A.   Do not anchor in the fairway or near pipelines or submarine cables. Look for signboards if near the foreshore or for the symbol on the chart. Damage to underwater facilities incurs heavy penalties.

Buoys and Beacons

Metric and Fathoms Charts				
41	⊡ W	White	59	↑ Y ⚓ ⌐ †⌐ †⌐	Perches, Withies, Stakes
42	⚑ B ▪ B	Black	(Lg)	⚐	Spar or pole on submerged rock (with topmark)
43	⌐ R ▦ R	Red	61	⚴ † ○ Cairn	Cairn
44	⌐ Y ⌐ Y	Yellow, amber	62	□ W Mk ▪ R Mk	Painted mark (with colour)
45	⚑ G ▦ G	Green	63	○ ○	Landmark (larger symbol if conspicuous)
47	⌐ Gy	Grey	64	Refl	Optical reflector (with colour, if known) (see note)
48	▦ Bu	Blue	(M13)	⌇ † Ra. Refl.	Radar reflector (not generally charted on IALA System marks)
48a	⌐ Or ⌐ Or	Orange	66	⌐ †⌐	Tanker mooring of superbuoy size, SPM (buoy)
51	(see L8)	Floating beacon	67	⌐ †⌐	Lanby (large automatic navigational buoy)
52	♦ BY ♦ R ♦ BRB ♦ R (minor beacon) etc. ♦ W ♦ B ♦ R ♦ BW etc.	Beacon (with topmarks and colours)	67a	⌐ ODAS	Data collecting buoy (Ocean Data-Acquisition System) of superbuoy size
53	♦ ○Bn ○Bn G	Beacon in general (see note)	(Ld)	⌐ SPM	Single Point Mooring structure, standing or pivoted on the sea bed
54	⌂ R ▪ R ⌂ BY ⌂ BRB etc. † ⚴Bn Tower † ⚴Bn Tr etc.	Beacon Tower (with and without topmarks)	(Le)	⌐ BP 21-10-FA † ⌐	Offshore platform (with designation)
	♦ Y ♦ I ♦ X ○ □ ▪ ▲ △ × (for application see L9 and L70)	IALA System beacon topmark	(Lf)	⌐ Fla	Offshore platform with flare
57	▽ ◆ † ⊤ ⊕ ↑ ♦ ⚬ etc.	Other types of beacon topmark	70	IALA Maritime Buoyage System (explanatory notes and diagrams)	See next page
58	⚬ Y ⚬Bn ○Bn	Telegraph or telephone cable (landing) beacon			

Position of a light float, buoy or beacon is the centre of the base, and is indicated by the symbols in L1.

Names, Numbers or Letters identifying light floats, buoys or beacons may be shown on the chart, eg: ♦ Humber No3   ⌐ ODAS "451"   ⌐ C R   ♦ No1   ○ Shingles Bn

Beacon in general symbol is used on smaller scale charts, or where the beacon has no topmark, or where the shape of the beacon or its topmark are unknown.

Elevations of tops of beacons above MHWS or MHHW are shown in parentheses next to the symbol, eg: ♦(5)   ○Bn(5)

Lighted Beacons are indicated by a magenta flare and sometimes by a light star (see K5 and L70). Where no topmark is charted, the abbreviation "Bn" is used, adjacent to the light star. On smaller scale charts where navigation within recognition range of the daymark is unlikely, lighted beacons are charted solely as lights.

Optical Reflectors are charted only on outer approach and fairway buoys.

Superbuoys are very large buoys, eg. a Lanby is a navigational aid mounted on a circular hull of about 12m diameter. Tanker mooring (66) and ODAS (67a) buoys, of similar size, are shown by variations of the superbuoy symbol: ⌐ Elevation and range may be included in the description of the light.

IALA Buoyage System, Region A and Region B devised by the International Association of Lighthouse Authorities is summarised on the following page (L70). For a full description of the System see NP735.

† This symbol and/or abbreviation is obsolescent

L Buoys and Beacons

Metric and Fathoms Charts		
1	Position of buoy or beacon	
2	Light buoy	(Lb) ... etc. ... etc. — Light buoy with topmark
3	Bell buoy (see note, Section N)	10 — Barrel buoy, Tun buoy
3a	Gong buoy	12 ... etc. — Light float
4	Whistle buoy (see note, Section N)	20 G G G G — Wreck buoy (not used in IALA system)
5	Can buoy, Cylindrical buoy	21 Y — Cable — Telegraph-cable buoy
6	Conical buoy, Ogival buoy, Nun buoy	22 — Mooring buoy
7	Spherical buoy	22a 22b — Mooring buoy with telegraphic or telephonic communications
8	Spar buoy, Floating beacon	(Lc) ① ② — Trot (Ground tackle and berth numbers in black on fathoms charts. Double-fluked anchors obsolescent)
8a	Pillar buoy	24a Y DZ — Practice area (Danger Zone) buoy
8b	Spindle buoy	26 — Compass — Compass adjustment buoy
(La)	High focal plane buoy (see L67)	29 Priv — Private aid to navigation
	Buoy with IALA system topmark (see L70) North cardinal	30 Y (Apr–Oct) — Seasonal buoyage (The example shows a yellow spherical buoy in use during the months April to October inclusively)
	South cardinal	
	East cardinal	31 BY BRB RGR / BW RW BR BW — Horizontal bands (the colour sequence is from top to bottom)
	West cardinal	
	Isolated danger	
	Safe water	32 RW RW / RW BR BW BW — Vertical stripes
	Port-hand REGION A REGION B	
	Starboard-hand REGION A REGION B	33 BR BW RW BW — Chequered
	Special purpose	
9	Buoys with other types of topmark	

† This symbol is obsolescent

Buoys and Beacons

IALA Maritime Buoyage System

This page is also published separately as chartlet 5044

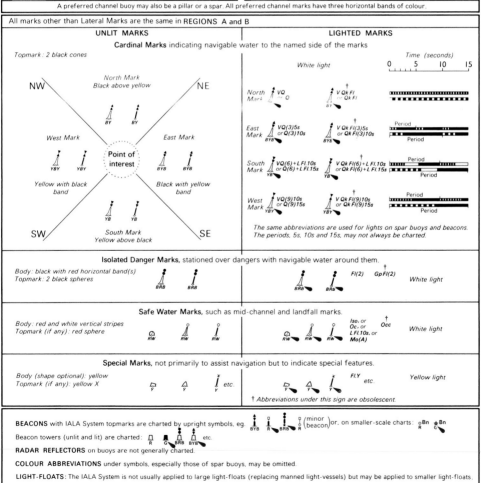

Lateral Marks (used in conjunction with a conventional direction of buoyage) are generally for well-defined channels. There are two international Buoyage Regions—A and B—where Lateral marks differ:

Port-hand Marks are red with cylindrical topmarks (if any). Lights are red and have any rhythm except Fl(2+1)R

REGION A

Preferred channel to Starboard Fl(2+1)R, if lit

Symbol showing direction of buoyage where not obvious

Preferred channel to Port Fl(2+1)G, if lit

Starboard-hand Marks are green with conical topmarks (if any). Lights are green and have any rhythm except Fl(2+1)G

Port-hand Marks are green with cylindrical topmarks (if any). Lights are green and have any rhythm except Fl(2+1)G

REGION B

Preferred channel to Starboard Fl(2+1)G, if lit

Preferred channel to Port Fl(2+1)R, if lit

Starboard-hand Marks are red with conical topmarks (if any). Lights are red and have any rhythm except Fl(2+1)R

A preferred channel buoy may also be a pillar or a spar. All preferred channel marks have three horizontal bands of colour.

All marks other than Lateral Marks are the same in REGIONS A and B

UNLIT MARKS | LIGHTED MARKS

Cardinal Marks indicating navigable water to the named side of the marks

Topmark: 2 black cones

White light

Time (seconds)
0 5 10 15

North Mark
Black above yellow

North Mark — VQ or Q — V Qk Fl or Qk Fl

East Mark — VQ(3)5s or Q(3)10s — V Qk Fl(3)5s or Qk Fl(3)10s

West Mark
Yellow with black band

East Mark
Black with yellow band

South Mark — VQ(6)+L Fl.10s or Q(6)+L Fl.15s — V Qk Fl(6)+L Fl.10s or Qk Fl(6)+L Fl.15s

Point of interest

West Mark — VQ(9)10s or Q(9)15s — V Qk Fl(9)10s or Qk Fl(9)15s

South Mark
Yellow above black

The same abbreviations are used for lights on spar buoys and beacons. The periods, 5s, 10s and 15s, may not always be charted.

Isolated Danger Marks, stationed over dangers with navigable water around them.

Body: black with red horizontal band(s)
Topmark: 2 black spheres

Fl(2) Gp Fl(2)

White light

Safe Water Marks, such as mid-channel and landfall marks.

Body: red and white vertical stripes
Topmark (if any): red sphere

Iso. or Oc. or L Fl.10s, or Mo(A) — Occ

White light

Special Marks, not primarily to assist navigation but to indicate special features.

Body (shape optional): yellow
Topmark (if any): yellow X

Fl.Y etc.

Yellow light

† Abbreviations under this sign are obsolescent.

APPENDICES

APPENDIX A

DECLINATIONS

Lat.	1°		2°		3°		4°		5°		6°		7°		8°		9°		10°		11°		12°	
1°	1°	0'	2°	0'	3°	0'	4°	0'	5°	0'	6°	0'	7°	0'	8°	0'	9°	0'	10°	0'	11°	0'	12°	0'
2	1	0	2	0	3	0	4	0	5	0	6	0	7	0	8	0	9	0	10	0	11	0	12	0
3	1	0	2	0	3	0	4	0	5	0	6	0	7	1	8	1	9	1	10	1	11	1	12	1
4	1	0	2	0	3	0	4	1	5	1	6	1	7	1	8	1	9	1	10	1	11	2	12	2
5	1	0	2	0	3	1	4	1	5	1	6	1	7	2	8	2	9	2	10	2	11	3	12	3
6	1	0	2	1	3	1	4	1	5	2	6	2	7	2	8	3	9	3	10	3	11	4	12	4
7	1	0	2	1	3	1	4	2	5	2	6	3	7	3	8	4	9	4	10	5	11	5	12	5
8	1	1	2	1	3	2	4	2	5	3	6	4	7	4	8	5	9	5	10	6	11	7	12	7
9	1	1	2	1	3	2	4	3	5	4	6	5	7	5	8	6	9	7	10	8	11	8	12	9
10	1	1	2	2	3	3	4	4	5	5	6	6	7	7	8	7	9	8	10	9	11	10	12	11
11	1	1	2	2	3	3	4	4	5	6	6	7	7	8	8	9	9	10	10	11	11	13	12	14
12	1	1	2	3	3	4	4	5	5	7	6	8	7	9	8	11	9	12	10	14	11	15	12	16
13	1	2	2	3	3	5	4	6	5	8	6	10	7	11	8	13	9	14	10	16	11	18	12	19
14	1	2	2	4	3	6	4	7	5	9	6	11	7	13	8	15	9	17	10	19	11	20	12	22
15	1	2	2	4	3	6	4	8	5	11	6	13	7	15	8	17	9	19	10	21	11	24	12	26
16	1	2	2	5	3	7	4	10	5	12	6	15	7	17	8	19	9	22	10	24	11	27	12	29
17	1	3	2	5	3	8	4	11	5	14	6	17	7	19	8	22	9	25	10	28	11	31	12	33
18	1	3	2	6	3	9	4	12	5	15	6	19	7	22	8	25	9	28	10	31	11	34	12	38
19	1	3	2	7	3	10	4	14	5	17	6	21	7	24	8	28	9	31	10	35	11	39	12	42
20	1	4	2	8	3	12	4	15	5	19	6	23	7	27	8	31	9	35	10	39	11	43	12	47
21	1	4	2	9	3	13	4	17	5	21	6	26	7	30	8	34	9	39	10	43	11	48	12	52
22	1	5	2	9	3	14	4	19	5	24	6	28	7	33	8	38	9	43	10	48	11	53	12	57
23	1	5	2	10	3	16	4	21	5	26	6	31	7	36	8	42	9	47	10	52	11	58	13	3
24	1	6	2	11	3	17	4	23	5	28	6	34	7	40	8	46	9	52	10	57	12	3	13	9
25	1	6	2	12	3	19	4	25	5	31	6	37	7	44	8	50	9	56	11	3	12	9	13	16
26	1	7	2	14	3	20	4	27	5	34	6	41	7	48	8	54	10	1	11	8	12	15	13	22
27	1	7	2	15	3	22	4	29	5	37	6	44	7	52	8	59	10	7	11	14	12	22	13	30
28	1	8	2	16	3	24	4	32	5	40	6	48	7	56	9	4	10	12	11	21	12	29	13	37
29	1	9	2	17	3	26	4	34	5	43	6	52	8	1	9	9	10	18	11	27	12	36	13	45
30	1	9	2	19	3	28	4	37	5	47	6	56	8	5	9	15	10	24	11	34	12	44	13	53
31	1	10	2	20	3	30	4	40	5	50	7	0	8	10	9	21	10	31	11	41	12	52	14	2
32	1	11	2	22	3	32	4	43	5	54	7	5	8	16	9	27	10	38	11	49	13	0	14	11
33	1	12	2	23	3	35	4	46	5	58	7	10	8	21	9	33	10	45	11	57	13	9	14	21
34	1	12	2	25	3	37	4	50	6	2	7	15	8	27	9	40	10	53	12	5	13	18	14	31
35	1	13	2	27	3	40	4	53	6	6	7	20	8	33	9	47	11	1	12	14	13	28	14	42
36	1	14	2	28	3	43	4	57	6	11	7	25	8	40	9	54	11	9	12	24	13	39	14	54
37	1	15	2	30	3	45	5	1	6	16	7	31	8	47	10	2	11	18	12	33	13	49	15	5
38	1	16	2	32	3	48	5	5	6	21	7	37	8	54	10	10	11	27	12	44	14	1	15	18
39	1	17	2	34	3	52	5	9	6	26	7	44	9	1	10	19	11	37	12	55	14	13	15	31
40	1	18	2	37	3	55	5	13	6	32	7	51	9	9	10	28	11	47	13	6	14	25	15	45
41	1	20	2	39	3	59	5	18	6	38	7	58	9	18	10	38	11	58	13	18	14	39	15	59
42	1	21	2	42	4	2	5	23	6	44	8	5	9	26	10	48	12	9	13	31	14	53	16	15
43	1	22	2	44	4	6	5	28	6	51	8	13	9	36	10	58	12	21	13	44	15	7	16	31
44	1	23	2	47	4	10	5	34	6	58	8	21	9	45	11	9	12	34	13	58	15	23	16	48
45	1	25	2	50	4	15	5	40	7	5	8	30	9	55	11	21	12	47	14	13	15	39	17	6
46	1	26	2	53	4	19	5	46	7	12	8	39	10	6	11	33	13	1	14	29	15	57	17	25
47	1	28	2	56	4	24	5	52	7	21	8	49	10	18	11	46	13	16	14	45	16	15	17	45
48	1	30	2	59	4	29	5	59	7	29	8	59	10	30	12	0	13	31	15	2	16	34	18	6
49	1	31	3	3	4	35	6	6	7	38	9	10	10	42	12	15	13	48	15	21	16	54	18	29
50	1	33	3	7	4	40	6	14	7	48	9	22	10	56	12	30	14	5	15	40	17	16	18	52
51	1	35	3	11	4	46	6	22	7	58	9	34	11	10	12	47	14	24	16	1	17	39	19	17
52	1	37	3	15	4	53	6	30	8	8	9	47	11	25	13	4	14	43	16	23	18	3	19	44
53	1	40	3	19	4	59	6	39	8	20	10	0	11	41	13	22	15	4	16	46	18	29	20	13
54	1	42	3	24	5	7	6	49	8	32	10	15	11	58	13	42	15	26	17	11	18	57	20	43
55	1	45	3	29	5	14	6	59	8	44	10	30	12	16	14	3	15	50	17	37	19	26	21	15
56	1	47	3	35	5	22	7	10	8	58	10	46	12	35	14	25	16	15	18	5	19	57	21	50
57	1	50	3	40	5	31	7	22	9	13	11	4	12	56	14	48	16	42	18	36	20	30	22	26
58	1	53	3	47	5	40	7	34	9	28	11	23	13	18	15	14	17	10	19	8	21	6	23	6
59	1	57	3	53	5	50	7	47	9	45	11	43	13	41	15	41	17	41	19	42	21	45	23	49
60	2	0	4	0	6	0	8	1	10	2	12	4	14	6	16	10	18	14	20	19	22	26	24	34
61	2	4	4	8	6	12	8	16	10	21	12	27	14	34	16	41	18	49	20	59	23	11	25	24
62	2	8	4	16	6	24	8	33	10	42	12	52	15	3	17	15	19	28	21	42	23	59	26	17
63	2	12	4	25	6	37	8	50	11	4	13	19	15	34	17	51	20	9	22	29	24	51	27	15
64	2	17	4	34	6	51	9	9	11	28	13	48	16	8	18	31	20	54	23	20	25	48	28	19
65	2	22	4	44	7	7	9	30	11	54	14	19	16	46	19	14	21	44	24	16	26	50	29	28
66	2	28	4	55	7	24	9	53	12	22	14	54	17	26	20	1	22	37	25	16	27	59	30	45

AMPLITUDES

APPENDIX A

DECLINATIONS

Lat.	13°	14°	15°	16°	17°	18°	19°	20°	21°	22°	23°	23° 28'
0	13° 0'	14° 0'	15° 0'	16° 0'	17° 0'	18° 0'	19° 0'	20° 0'	21° 0'	22° 0'	23° 0'	23°28'
1	13 0	14 1	15 1	16 1	17 1	18 1	19 1	20 1	21 1	22 1	23 1	23 29
2	13 1	14 1	15 1	16 1	17 1	18 2	19 2	20 2	21 2	22 2	23 2	23 30
3	13 2	14 2	15 2	16 2	17 3	18 3	19 3	20 3	21 3	22 3	23 4	23 32
4	13 2	14 3	15 4	16 4	17 4	18 4	19 5	20 5	21 5	22 5	23 6	23 34
5	13 4	14 5	15 5	16 5	17 6	18 6	19 7	20 7	21 7	22 8	23 8	23 36
6	13 6	14 6	15 7	16 7	17 8	18 8	19 9	20 9	21 10	22 10	23 11	23 39
7	13 8	14 8	15 9	16 10	17 10	18 11	19 12	20 12	21 13	22 14	23 14	23 43
8	13 10	14 11	15 11	16 12	17 13	18 14	19 15	20 16	21 16	22 17	23 18	23 47
9	13 12	14 13	15 14	16 15	17 16	18 17	19 18	20 19	21 20	22 21	23 23	23 51
10	13 15	14 16	15 17	16 18	17 20	18 21	19 22	20 24	21 25	22 26	23 27	23 56
11	13 18	14 19	15 21	16 22	17 24	18 25	19 26	20 28	21 30	22 31	23 33	24 1
12	13 21	14 23	15 24	16 26	17 28	18 29	19 31	20 33	21 35	22 37	23 38	24 7
13	13 24	14 26	15 28	16 30	17 32	18 34	19 36	20 38	21 40	22 43	23 45	24 14
14	13 28	14 30	15 33	16 35	17 37	18 39	19 42	20 44	21 47	22 49	23 52	24 21
15	13 32	14 35	15 37	16 40	17 42	18 45	19 48	20 51	21 53	22 56	23 59	24 28
16	13 36	14 39	15 42	16 45	17 48	18 51	19 54	20 57	22 1	23 4	24 7	24 36
17	13 41	14 44	15 47	16 51	17 54	18 58	20 1	21 5	22 8	23 12	24 15	24 45
18	13 46	14 49	15 53	16 57	18 1	19 5	20 8	21 12	22 16	23 20	24 25	24 54
19	13 51	14 55	15 59	17 3	18 8	19 12	20 16	21 21	22 25	23 30	24 34	25 4
20	13 57	15 1	16 6	17 10	18 15	19 20	20 25	21 29	22 34	23 39	24 45	25 15
21	14 2	15 7	16 13	17 18	18 23	19 28	20 33	21 39	22 44	23 50	24 55	25 26
22	14 9	15 14	16 20	17 25	18 31	19 37	20 43	21 49	22 55	24 1	25 7	25 38
23	14 15	15 21	16 27	17 34	18 40	19 46	20 53	21 59	23 6	24 13	25 19	25 51
24	14 22	15 29	16 36	17 42	18 49	19 56	21 3	22 10	23 18	24 25	25 32	26 4
25	14 30	15 37	16 44	17 52	18 59	20 7	21 14	22 22	23 30	24 38	25 46	26 18
26	14 37	15 45	16 53	18 1	19 9	20 18	21 26	22 34	23 43	24 52	26 1	26 33
27	14 46	15 54	17 3	18 11	19 20	20 29	21 38	22 47	23 57	25 6	26 16	26 48
28	14 54	16 3	17 13	18 22	19 32	20 41	21 51	23 1	24 11	25 22	26 32	27 5
29	15 3	16 13	17 23	18 34	19 44	20 54	22 5	23 16	24 27	25 38	26 49	27 23
30	15 13	16 24	17 34	18 45	19 57	21 8	22 19	23 31	24 43	25 55	27 7	27 41
31	15 23	16 34	17 46	18 58	20 10	21 22	22 35	23 47	25 0	26 13	27 26	28 0
32	15 34	16 46	17 59	19 11	20 24	21 37	22 51	24 4	25 18	26 32	27 46	28 21
33	15 45	16 58	18 11	19 25	20 39	21 53	23 7	24 22	25 37	26 52	28 7	28 42
34	15 56	17 11	18 25	19 40	20 55	22 10	23 25	24 41	25 57	27 13	28 29	29 5
35	16 9	17 24	18 39	19 55	21 11	22 27	23 44	25 1	26 18	27 35	28 53	29 29
36	16 22	17 38	18 55	20 11	21 28	22 46	24 3	25 21	26 40	27 58	29 17	29 55
37	16 35	17 53	19 10	20 28	21 47	23 5	24 24	25 43	27 3	28 23	29 44	30 21
38	16 50	18 8	19 27	20 46	22 6	23 26	24 46	26 7	27 28	28 49	30 11	30 49
39	17 5	18 25	19 45	21 5	22 26	23 47	25 9	26 31	27 54	29 17	30 40	31 19
40	17 20	18 42	20 3	21 25	22 48	24 10	25 33	26 57	28 21	29 46	31 11	31 51
41	17 37	19 0	20 23	21 46	23 10	24 34	25 59	27 24	28 50	30 16	31 43	32 24
42	17 55	19 19	20 44	22 8	23 34	25 00	26 26	27 53	29 20	30 49	32 18	32 59
43	18 13	19 39	21 5	22 32	23 59	25 26	26 55	28 23	29 53	31 23	32 54	33 37
44	18 33	20 0	21 28	22 57	24 25	25 55	27 25	28 56	30 27	31 59	33 33	34 16
45	18 54	20 23	21 53	23 23	24 53	26 25	27 57	29 30	31 3	32 38	34 14	34 59
46	19 16	20 47	22 18	23 50	25 23	26 57	28 31	30 6	31 42	33 19	34 57	35 43
47	19 39	21 12	22 45	24 20	25 55	27 30	29 7	30 44	32 23	34 3	35 44	36 31
48	20 3	21 38	23 14	24 51	26 28	28 6	29 45	31 25	33 7	34 49	36 33	37 22
49	20 29	22 7	23 45	25 24	27 3	28 44	30 26	32 9	33 53	35 39	37 26	38 17
50	20 57	22 36	24 17	25 29	27 41	29 25	31 9	32 55	34 43	36 32	38 23	39 15
51	21 26	23 8	24 52	26 36	28 21	30 8	31 56	33 45	35 36	37 29	39 24	40 18
52	21 57	28 42	25 28	27 16	29 4	30 54	32 45	34 38	36 33	38 30	40 29	41 26
53	22 30	24 18	26 7	27 58	29 50	31 43	33 38	35 35	37 34	39 36	41 40	42 39
54	23 5	24 57	26 49	28 43	30 39	32 36	34 35	363=36	38 40	40 47	42 56	43 58
55	23 43	25 38	27 34	29 32	31 31	33 33	35 36	37 42	39 51	42 4	44 20	45 24
56	24 24	26 22	28 22	30 24	32 28	34 34	36 43	38 54	41 9	43 27	45 50	46 59
57	25 7	27 10	29 14	31 21	33 29	35 40	37 54	40 12	42 33	44 59	47 30	48 43
58	25 54	28 1	30 10	32 21	34 35	36 52	39 12	41 37	44 6	46 40	49 21	50 38
59	26 44	28 56	31 10	33 27	35 47	38 10	40 38	43 10	45 47	48 31	51 24	52 47
60	27 39	29 56	32 16	34 39	37 5	39 36	42 11	44 52	47 40	5036	53 42	55 13
61	28 38	31 1	33 27	35 57	38 31	41 10	43 54	46 46	49 46	52 56	56 20	58 1
62	29 42	32 12	34 45	37 23	40 5	42 54	45 49	48 53	52 8	55 36	59 23	61 18
63	30 52	33 30	36 11	38 58	41 50	44 49	47 58	51 17	54 50	58 43	68 2	65 17
64	32 10	34 55	37 46	40 43	43 46	46 59	50 23	54 2	57 59	62 25	67 36	70 26
65	33 35	36 30	39 31	42 40	45 57	49 27	53 10	57 14	61 46	67 4	73 52	78 15

AMPLITUDES

KNOTS USED TO SECURE AN END TO A SPAR

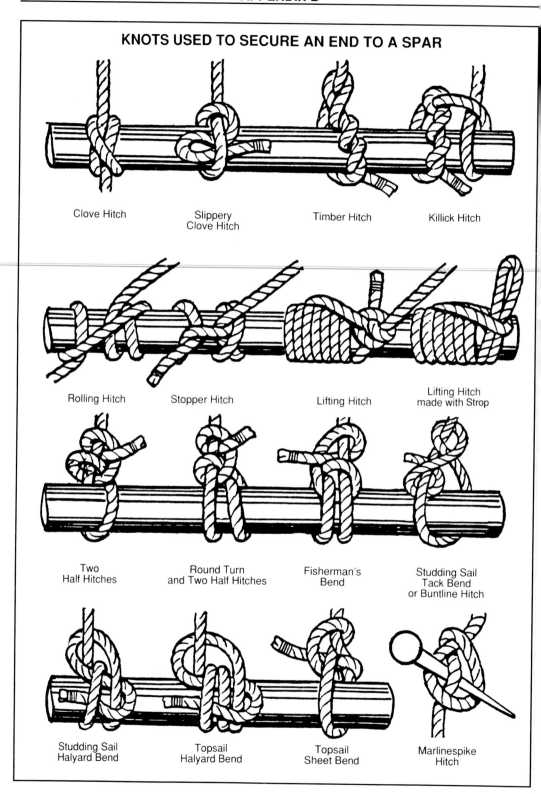

Clove Hitch

Slippery
Clove Hitch

Timber Hitch

Killick Hitch

Rolling Hitch

Stopper Hitch

Lifting Hitch

Lifting Hitch
made with Strop

Two
Half Hitches

Round Turn
and Two Half Hitches

Fisherman's
Bend

Studding Sail
Tack Bend
or Buntline Hitch

Studding Sail
Halyard Bend

Topsail
Halyard Bend

Topsail
Sheet Bend

Marlinespike
Hitch

KNOTS USED TO FORM ONE OR MORE LOOPS

Bowline

Running Bowline

Bowline
on a Bight

French Bowline

Spanish Bowline

Fisherman's Eye

Crabber's Eye

Overhand Knot

Midshipman's
Hitch

Jug Sling
or Hackamore

Tomfool's Knot

Jury Masthead

KNOTS USED TO SHORTEN ROPE

Sheepshank

Knotted Sheepshank

Toggled Sheepshank

Sheepshank with Reef

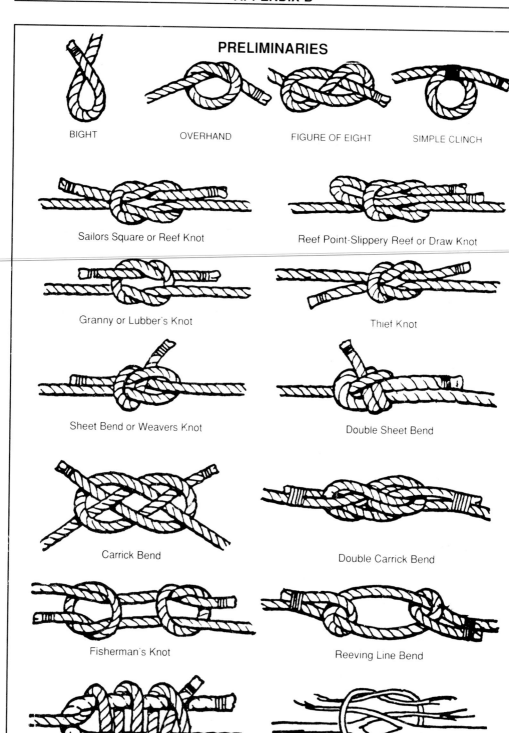

PRELIMINARIES

BIGHT

OVERHAND

FIGURE OF EIGHT

SIMPLE CLINCH

Sailors Square or Reef Knot

Reef Point-Slippery Reef or Draw Knot

Granny or Lubber's Knot

Thief Knot

Sheet Bend or Weavers Knot

Double Sheet Bend

Carrick Bend

Double Carrick Bend

Fisherman's Knot

Reeving Line Bend

Heaving Line Bend

Rope Yarn, or Marine Knot

KNOTS USED TO SECURE AN END TO A RING OR HOOK

Lark's Head

Double
Lark's Head

Catspaw
Started

Catspaw
on Hook

Blackwall Hitch

Double Blackwall Hitch

Bill Hitch

Mousing A Hook

SEIZINGS

Round Seizing

Racking Seizing

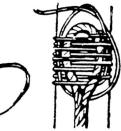

Rose Lashing

Spanish Windlass

WHIPPINGS

Started

Finished

Plain Whipping

Started

Finished

Palm and Needle Whipping

Feet	Fms.	Metres
1		0.305
1.5	1/4	0.457
2		0.610
3	1/2	0.914
4		1.219
4.5	3/4	1.372
5		1.524
6	1	1.829
7		2.134
8		2.438
9	1 1/2	2.743
10		3.048
11		3.353
12	2	3.658
13		3.962
14		4.267
15	2 1/2	4.572
16		4.877
17		5.182
18	3	5.486
19		5.791
20		6.096
21	3 1/2	6.401
22		6.706
23		7.010
24	4	7.315
25		7.620
26		7.925
27	4 1/2	8.230
28		8.534
29		8.839
30	5	9.144
31		9.449
32		9.754
33	5 1/2	10.058
34		10.363
35		10.668
36	6	10.973
37		11.278
38		11.582
39	6 1/2	11.887
40		12.192
41		12.497
42	7	12.802
43		13.106
44		13.411
45	7 1/2	13.716
46		14.021
47		14.326
48	8	14.630
49		14.935
50		15.240

Feet	Fms.	Metres
51	8 1/2	15.545
52		15.850
53		16.154
54	9	16.459
55		16.764
56		17.069
57	9 1/2	17.324
58		17.678
59		17.983
60	10	18.288
61		18.593
62		18.898
63	10 1/2	19.202
64		19.507
65		19.812
66	11	20.117
67		20.422
68		20.726
69	11 1/2	21.031
70		21.336
71		21.641
72	12	21.946
73		22.250
74		22.555
75	12 1/2	22.860
76		23.165
77		23.470
78	13	23.774
79		24.079
80		24.384
81	13 1/2	24.689
82		24.994
83		25.298
84	14	25.603
85		25.908
86		26.213
87	14 1/2	26.518
88		26.822
89		27.127
90	15	27.432
91		27.737
92		28.042
93	15 1/2	28.346
94		28.651
95		28.956
96	16	29.261
97		29.566
98		29.870
99	16 1/2	30.175
100		30.480

Feet	Fms.	Metres
102	17	31.090
108	18	32.918
114	19	34.747
120	20	36.576
126	21	38.405
132	22	40.234
138	23	42.062
144	24	43.891
150	25	45.720
156	26	47.549
162	27	49.378
168	28	51.206
174	29	53.035
180	30	54.864
186	31	56.693
192	32	58.522
198	33	60.350
204	34	62.179
210	35	64.008
216	36	65.837
222	37	67.666
228	38	69.494
234	39	71.323
240	40	73.152
246	41	74.981
252	42	76.810
258	43	78.638
264	44	80.467
270	45	82.296
276	46	84.125
282	47	85.954
288	48	87.782
294	49	89.611
300	50	91.440
306	51	93.269
312	52	95.098
318	53	96.926
324	54	98.755
330	55	100.584
336	56	102.413
342	57	104.242
348	58	106.070
354	59	107.899
360	60	109.728
366	61	111.557
372	62	113.386
378	63	115.214
384	64	117.043
390	65	118.872
396	66	120.701
402	67	122.530
408	68	124.358
414	69	126.187
420	70	128.016

Feet	Fms.	Metres
426	71	129.845
432	72	131.674
438	73	133.502
444	74	135.331
450	75	137.160
456	76	138.989
462	77	140.818
468	78	142.646
474	79	144.475
480	80	146.304
486	81	148.133
492	82	149.962
498	83	151.790
504	84	153.619
510	85	155.448
516	86	157.277
522	87	159.106
528	88	160.934
534	89	162.763
540	90	164.592
546	91	166.421
552	92	168.250
558	93	170.078
564	94	171.907
570	95	173.736
576	96	175.565
582	97	177.394
588	98	179.222
594	99	181.051
600	100	182.880

Feet	Metres
700	213.360
800	243.840
900	274.320
1000	304.800

Fms.	Metres
200	365.760
300	548.640
400	731.520
500	914.400
600	1097.280
700	1280.160
800	1463.040
900	1645.920
1000	1828.800

Inches	Ft.	Metres	Inches	Ft.	Metres
1	0.083	0.025	7	0.583	0.178
2	0.167	0.051	8	0.667	0.203
3	0.250	0.076	9	0.750	0.229
4	0.333	0.102	10	0.833	0.254
5	0.417	0.127	11	0.917	0.279
6	0.500	0.152	12	1.000	0.305

Factors

1 Inch = 0.0254 metres
1 Foot = 0.3048 metres
1 Fathom = 1.8288 metres or 6 feet

Table for Converting Feet and Fathoms to Metres

APPENDIX C

Metres	Feet	Fms.	Metres	Feet	Fms.	Metres	Feet	Fms.
1	3.281	0.547	51	167.323	27.887	200	656.17	109.36
2	6.562	1.094	52	170.604	28.434	300	984.25	164.04
3	9.843	1.640	53	173.885	28.981	400	1312.34	218.72
4	13.123	2.187	54	177.165	29.528	500	1640.42	273.40
5	16.404	2.734	55	180.446	30.074			
6	19.685	3.281	56	183.727	30.621	600	1968.50	328.08
7	22.966	3.828	57	187.008	31.168	700	2296.59	382.76
8	26.247	4.374	58	190.289	31.715	800	2624.67	437.45
9	29.528	4.921	59	193.570	32.262	900	2952.76	492.13
10	32.808	5.468	60	196.850	32.808			
11	36.089	6.015	61	200.131	33.355	1000	3280.84	546.81
12	39.370	6.562	62	203.412	33.902	2000	6561.68	1093.61
13	42.651	7.108	63	206.693	34.449	3000	9842.52	1640.42
14	45.932	7.655	64	209.974	34.996	4000	13123.36	2187.23
15	49.213	8.202	65	213.255	35.542	5000	16404.20	2734.03
16	52.493	8.749	66	216.535	36.089	6000	19685.04	3280.84
17	55.774	9.296	67	219.816	36.636	7000	22965.88	3827.65
18	59.055	9.843	68	223.097	37.183	8000	26246.72	4374.45
19	62.336	10.389	69	226.378	37.730	9000	29527.56	4921.26
20	65.617	10.936	70	229.659	38.276	10000	32808.40	5468.07
21	68.898	11.483	71	232.940	38.823			
22	72.178	12.030	72	236.220	39.370	Metres		Inches
23	75.459	12.577	73	239.501	39.917	0.10		3.937
24	78.740	13.123	74	242.782	40.464	0.20		7.874
25	82.021	13.670	75	246.063	41.010	0.30		11.811
						0.40		15.748
26	85.302	14.217	76	249.344	41.557	0.50		19.685
27	88.583	14.764	77	252.625	42.104	0.60		23.622
28	91.864	15.311	78	255.906	42.651	0.70		27.559
29	95.144	15.857	79	259.186	43.198	0.80		31.496
30	98.425	16.404	80	262.467	43.745	0.90		35.433
						1.00		39.370
31	101.706	16.951	81	265.748	44.291			
32	104.987	17.498	82	269.029	44.838			
33	108.268	18.045	83	272.310	45.385			
34	111.549	18.591	84	275.591	45.932			
35	114.829	19.138	85	278.871	46.479			
36	118.110	19.685	86	282.152	47.025			
37	121.391	20.232	87	285.433	47.572			
38	124.672	20.779	88	288.714	48.119			
39	127.953	21.325	89	291.995	48.666			
40	131.234	21.872	90	295.276	49.213			
41	134.514	22.419	91	298.556	49.759			
42	137.795	22.966	92	301.837	50.306			
43	141.076	23.513	93	305.118	50.853			
44	144.357	24.059	94	308.399	51.400			
45	147.638	24.606	95	311.680	51.947			
46	150.919	25.153	96	314.961	52.493			
47	154.199	25.700	97	318.241	53.040			
48	157.480	26.247	98	321.522	53.587			
49	160.761	26.794	99	324.803	54.134			
50	164.042	27.340	100	328.084	54.681			

Factors:– 1 metre = 3.280839895 feet or 39.370078740 inches
= 0.546806649 fathoms

Table for Converting Metres to Feet and Fathoms

S.I. - BRITISH UNITS

S.I. recommended and recognised Units	Conversion Factors	
	British Units to S.I.	S.I. Units to British
LENGTH		
millimetre (mm)	1 in = 25.4 mm*	1 mm = 0.039 370 in
centimetre (cm)	1 ft = 0.3048 m*	1 m = 3.280 83 ft
metre (m)	1 yd = 0.9144 m*	1 m = 1.093 61 yd
kilometre (km)	1 fathom = 1.8288 m*	1 m = 0.546 807 fathom
International nautical mile	1 mile = 1.609 34 km	1 km = 0.621 371 mile
(n mile) = 1,852.0 m	1 n mile (British) = 1.000 64 n mile (Inter.)	1 n mile (Inter.) = 0.999 36 n mile (British)
AREA		
square millimetres (mm²)	1 in² = 645.16 mm²*	1 mm² = 0.001 550 in²
square centimetre (cm²)	1 ft² = 0.092 903 m²	1 m² = 10.7639 ft²
square metre (m²)	1 yd² = 0.836 127 m²	1 m² = 1.195 99 yd²
square kilometre (km²)	1 acre = 4046.86 m²	
hectare (ha) = 10000 m²	1 acre = 0.404 686 ha	1 ha = 2.471 05 acre
VOLUME		
cubic millimetre (mm³)	1 in³ = 16387.1 mm³	1 mm³ = 0.000 061 0237 in³
cubic centimetre (cm³)	1 ft³ = 0.028 3168 m³	1 m³ = 35.3147 ft³
cubic metre (m³)	1 yd³ = 0.764 555 m³	1 m³ = 1.307 95 yd³
litre (l) = 0.001 m³	1 pint = 0.000 568 261 m³	
	1 gal = 0.004 546 09 m³	1 m³ = 219.969 gal
	1 pint = 0.568 261 l	1 l = 1.759 75 pint
	1 gal = 4.546 09 l	1 l = 0.219 969 gal
	1 Freight ton (40 ft³) = 1.1327 m³	
MASS		
gramme (g)	1 oz (avdp) = 28.3495 g	1 g = 0.035 274 oz (avdp)
kilogramme (kg)	1 lb = 0.453 592 37 kg*	1 kg = 2.204 62 lb
tonne (t) = 1000 kg	1 cwt = 50.8023 kg	1 t (tonne) = 0.984 207 ton
	1 ton = 1016.05 kg	1 t (tonne) = 2204.62 lb
	1 ton = 1.016 05 t (tonne)	
DENSITY		
kilogramme/cubic metre (kg/m³)	1 lb/ft³ = 16.0185 kg/m³	1 kg/m³ = 0.062 428 lb/ft³
gramme/cubic centimetre (g/cm³)	1 lb/in³ = 27.6799 g/cm³	1 g/cm³ = 0.036 127 lb/in³
tonne/cubic metre (t/m³)	1 ton/yd³ = 1.328 94 t/m³	1 t/m³ = 0.752 479 ton/yd³
FORCE		
newton (N)	1 tonf = 9.964 02 kN	1 kN = 0.100 361 tonf
kilonewton (kN)	1 lbf = 4.448 22 N	1 N = 0.224 809 lbf
meganewton (MN)	1 poundal = 0.138 255 N	1 N = 7.233 01 poundal
VELOCITY		
metre/second (m/s)	1 in/s = 25.4 mm/s*	1 mm/s = 0.039 3701 in/s
kilometre/second (km/s)	1 ft/min = 5.08 mm/s	1 mm/s = 0.196 85 ft/min
knot International =	1 ft/s = 0.3048 m/s*	1 m/s = 3.280 84 ft/s
1,852.0 m/h	1 mph = 0.447 040 m/s	1 m/s = 2.236 94 mph
	1 mph = 1.609 34 km/h	1 km/h = 0.621 371 mph
	1 knot (British) = 1.000 64 knot (Inter.)	1 knot (Inter.) = 0.999 36 knot (British)
VOLUME FLOW RATE		
cubic metres/second (m³/s)	1 ft³/s = 0.028 3168 m³/s	1 m³/s = 35.3147 ft³/s
cubic metres/hour (m³/h)	1 gal/h = 0.004 546 09 m³/h	1 m³/h = 219.969 gal/h
litres/hour (l/h)	1 gal/h = 4.546 09 l/h	1 l/h = 0.219 969 gal/h
litres/second (l/s)	1 gal/min = 0.272 765 m³/h	1 m³/h = 3.666 16 gal/min
	1 gal/min = 0.075 768 2 l/s	1 l/s = 13.1981 gal/min
ENERGY		
joule (J)	1 kWh = 3.6 MJ*	1 MJ = 0.277 778 kWh
kilojoule (kJ)	1 ftlbf = 1.355 82 J	1 J = 0.737 562 ftlbf
megajoule (MJ)	1 ftpdl = 0.042 1401 J	1 J = 23.7304 ftpdl
	1 therm = 105.506 MJ	1 MJ = 0.009 478 13 therm
	1 Btu = 1.055 06 kJ	1 kJ = 0.947 813 Btu
POWER		
watt (W)	1 hp = 745.700 W	1 W = 0.001 341 02 hp
kilowatt (kW)	1 ftlbf/s = 1.355 82 W	1 W = 0.737 561 ftlbf/s
megawatt (MW)		

* *Indicates a conversion factor which is exact.*

S.I. UNITS - PREFIXES

The prefixes for forming multiples and sub-multiples of S.I. units are:

Prefix name	Prefix symbol	Factor by which the unit is multiplied
tera	T	10^{12} = 1 000 000 000 000
giga	G	10^{9} = 1 000 000 000
mega	M	10^{6} = 1 000 000
kilo	k	10^{3} = 1 000
hecto	h	10^{2} = 100
deca	da	10^{1} = 10
deci	d	10^{-1} = 0.1
centi	c	10^{-2} = 0.01
milli	m	10^{-3} = 0.001
micro	μ	10^{-6} = 0.000 001
nano	n	10^{-9} = 0.000 000 001
pico	p	10^{-12} = 0.000 000 000 001
femto	f	10^{-15} = 0.000 000 000 000 001
atto	a	10^{-18} = 0.000 000 000 000 000 001

For example:

megawatt (MW)	=	1 000 000 watts
kilogramme (kg)	=	1 000 grammes
millivolt (mV)	=	0.001 volt
microsecond (μs)	=	0.000 001 second
picofarad (pF)	=	0.000 000 000 001 farad

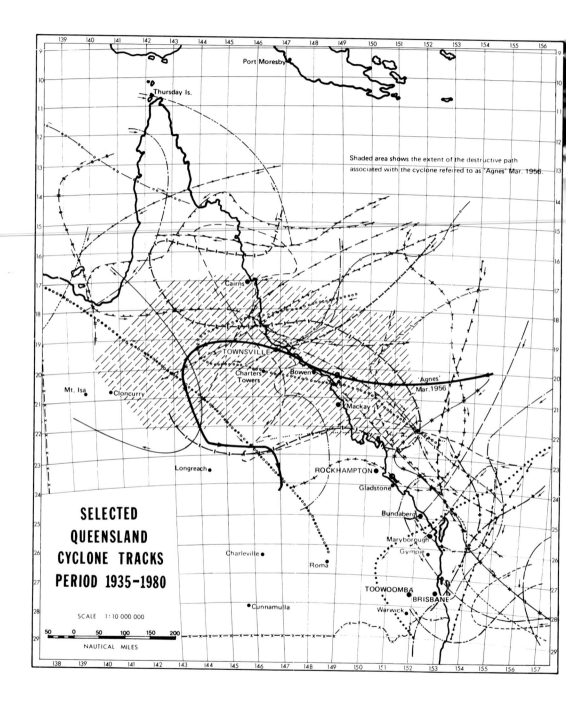

SELECTED QUEENSLAND CYCLONE TRACKS PERIOD 1935–1980

SCALE 1:10 000 000

NAUTICAL MILES

Shaded area shows the extent of the destructive path associated with the cyclone referred to as 'Agnes' Mar. 1956.

True Course to Compass Course Conversion

This conversion is necessary after plotting a TRUE COURSE on the Chart and a COMPASS COURSE to steer is required.

Example: (Using Deviation Card No. 5 from page 110.

It is required to convert a True Course of 240° to a Compass Course.

True Course (T)	=	240°	
Variation (V)	=	9° E	(from Chart)
Magnetic Course (M)	=	231°	(from above calculated)
Deviation (D)	=	5° E	(Card for 231°)
Compass Course (C)	=	226°	(from above calculated)

Further correction:

Deviation (D)	=	8° E	(from Card for 226°)
Compass Course (C)	=	223°	

Examples:

Using the Deviation Card on Practice Chart AUS 5169A, convert the True Courses of 065° and 305° to Compass Courses.

(Answers: 079¹/₂° and 312°)